Stick It Up Your Punter!

Peter Chippindale and Chris Horrie are
national newspaper, magazine, and television
journalists. They have written three books
together, including **Disaster: The Rise and
Fall of** *News on Sunday*.

'This is the funniest book of the year, perhaps of the
decade . . . a revenge tragedy with the cast of the
Carry On films' – *The Times*

'The *Sun* is the rottweiler of British journalism . . .
as this book most entertainingly explains. A
splendidly racy account' – *The Economist*

'A story which social and political historians of the
20th century will not find easy to ignore . . . the
Sun has become the purveyor of a kind of dark
vaudeville' – *London Review of Books*

'A classic of the newspaper genre' – Alan
Rusbridger, *The Listener*

By the same authors

Disaster: The Rise and Fall of News on Sunday

PETER CHIPPINDALE
and CHRIS HORRIE

STICK IT UP YOUR
PUNTER!

The rise and fall
of the *Sun*

Mandarin

A Mandarin Paperback
STICK IT UP YOUR PUNTER!

First published in Great Britain 1990
by William Heinemann Limited
This edition published 1992
by Mandarin Paperbacks
an imprint of Reed Consumer Books Limited
Michelin House, 81 Fulham Road, London SW3 6RB
and Auckland, Melbourne, Singapore and Toronto

Reprinted 1992 (twice), 1993

Copyright © Peter Chippindale and Chris Horrie 1990
The Authors have asserted their moral rights

A CIP catalogue record for this title
is available from the British Library
ISBN 0 7493 0961 X

Printed and bound in Great Britain
by Cox & Wyman Ltd, Reading, Berks

Contents

for Boot

Acknowledgements

During our research for this book we sought to interview the
three editors of the *Sun*. The first, Sir Larry Lamb (editor
1969–72 and 1975–81), was the only person who demanded
to be paid to speak to us. He charged £350 for an interview.
The second, Bernard Shrimsley (1972–75), agreed to be
interviewed at length for nothing. Kelvin MacKenzie, who
has edited the paper since 1981, was elusive. After we had
talked to Jane Reed, Director of Corporate Relations at News
International, she first told us MacKenzie had agreed to an
interview, at her suggestion, but then informed us he had
changed his mind and refused 'because of the other people
you have been speaking to'.

Obviously we owe our main thanks to other *Sun* and ex-
Sun employees. All those currently employed there would
only talk on a non-attributable basis, as we were told they
were committing a sacking offence by doing so. The same
basis was demanded by many ex-employees on the grounds
that they were still working for Murdoch publications in
either a staff or freelance capacity. However, some were
happy to be attributable, and we would therefore like to thank
Roger Bamber, Ian Blunt, John Breen, John Brown, Eric
'Scoop' Butler, Roger Carroll, Sheila Copsey, Peter Court,
Henry Douglas, David Graves, Roslyn Grose, Tony Hall,
Bruce Kemble, Nick Lloyd, Damien McCrystal, Frank

Nicklin, Kevin O'Sullivan, Peter Stephens, Walter Terry and Roger Wood.

Others outside the paper who agreed to be interviewed, sometimes at great length, or who helped us in some way, included: Dr Mark Abrams, Mary Jane Bailey, Bob Borzello, Sean Brierley, Maggie Brown, Dick Clements, Max Clifford, Pat Collins, the Devon Donkey Sanctuary, Frank Dunkley, Simon Ferrari, Monica Foot, Nigel Fountain, Tim Gopsill, Dave Gordon, Mike Hellicar, Georgina Henry, Nick Higham, Linda Joyce, Sean Langam, Michael Leapman, Rod Liddle, Fiona Macbeth, Tim McGough, Bronwen Maddox, Linda Melvern, Bart Milner, Chris Mullin, Mike Poole, Jane Reed, Alan Rusbridger, Ian Scott, Graham Smith, Ray Snoddy, John Sweeney, Delwyn Swingewood, Peter Tatchell, Mike Taylor, Jane Thynne, Martin Tompkinson, Roger Watkins, Auberon Waugh, Paul Woolwich and Tony Worthington. In Liverpool: Alf Green, Billy Butler, Wally Scott, Barry Devonside, Harry Chase and Paula Skidmore of the Edge Hill College of Further Education.

We would also like to thank our agent, Mark Lucas, and our editor, Tom Weldon, for their support and guidance.

Final thanks go to Sally and Clare for their patience.

Preface

This book does not pretend to be a definitive history of the *Sun*. For those interested the 'exclusive inside story' has already been written by *Sun* feature writer Roslyn Grose, entitled *The Sun-sation* (Angus and Robertson, 1989).

In the course of writing this book we met a large number of people connected with the paper in one way or another. We found the *Sun* to be an extraordinarily emotive subject. Many of the people we saw were defensive, others angry and bitter, and most had extremely mixed feelings. We were aware that many also had personal axes to grind, and therefore we take full responsibility for the version of events which appears in these pages.

One of the principal complaints made by the *Sun* is that a large number of the people who criticise it have little or no direct knowledge of the paper. It was mainly because of this that we wrote this book. We feel it is wrong for critics ignorantly to write the paper off as rubbish churned out for morons. Rather, it should be recognised as a sophisticated and extremely high-quality product, carefully tailored for its market by one of the world's most successful entrepreneurs, and with a strong philosophy behind it.

Neither do we think it correct for *Sun* readers to excuse the paper as they do on the grounds that it is merely entertainment. The *Sun* is a newspaper covering real events and we believe it cannot fail to influence the thinking and actions of anyone reading it regularly. As the *Sun* has consistently sold over 3.5 million copies a day for the past fifteen years, and boasts three readers per copy, this amounts to a large section of the British population.

It is a well-worn cliché that a society gets the papers it deserves. We trust this book sheds some light on that old observation.

Peter Chippindale and Chris Horrie
Hackney, north London and north Cornwall
July 1990

PART
ONE

Chapter 1

Screws of the News

Fleet Street was a hard place. And calling Rupert Murdoch's new paper, the *Sun*, 'Rupert's shit-sheet' was a hard remark. Even harder was the popular wisdom that it would last no longer than six months. But, as they propped up the bars in their various watering-holes, the hacks told each other there was a good reason for their prediction. It was impossible to take this man Murdoch seriously. When he had first arrived in Fleet Street the gossip had cast him as a wealthy Australian sheep-farmer, who just dabbled in newspapers as a hobby.

Now that he'd been around for a year or so and owned the *News of the World* the sheep-farmer myth had subsided. But he was still a long way from being a Fleet Street baron. The *News of the Screws* had always been an oddity – not a proper newspaper, and not run as one. Before this brash young Aussie had bought it it had been a fiefdom of the wealthy Carr family. Now, it appeared, it was in equally eccentric hands. It was obvious this bolt from the colonial blue, who was only thirty-eight, knew a bit about business, but he obviously knew nothing about Britain and its newspapers. Why else would he have saddled himself with the misconceived old *Sun*, which had always lost millions? It had become such an embarrassment to its former owners they'd even considered giving it away.

But there was an answer, the hacks told each other as they emptied their glasses for another round. This Aussie, Murdoch, had been sold a pup. It was obvious he had more money than sense. All according to plan he would soon be bust and sent packing back to Australia.

At the more informed level of City analysts and newspaper boardrooms the sheep-farmer myth never really ran. They knew Murdoch was the owner of a string of profitable Australian tabloid newspapers. He had apparently done well after inheriting a paper in Adelaide from his father and there was patronising admiration for his success in his backwater down-under, where, it was said, journalistic standards were much lower. The *News of the World* apparently suited his vulgarity and at the business level he was being taken more seriously, with considerable disquiet over the ruthlessness he had shown in acquiring the paper.

Murdoch, eager to expand from the limited horizons of Australia, knew more about Britain than many supposed. He had been educated at Oxford University, worked for a spell on the *Daily Express* and kept his feelers out in Britain for some time. He had been invited to London by Sir William Carr in October 1968. Carr was desperate. A family feud had put the paper up for grabs and he was now trying to fend off a takeover bid by Robert Maxwell, the pushy Labour MP who was expanding fast in the publishing business. Carr's family had owned the paper since 1891 and he was determined not to lose control, least of all to a 'foreigner' like Maxwell. The *News of the World*, he now wrote in a celebrated front-page article, was 'as English as roast beef and Yorkshire pudding'. Maxwell, on the other hand, had been born in Czechoslovakia. His original name, the paper stated, was Jan Ludwig Hoch.

The article was published on the day Murdoch arrived in London for a crisis meeting. He read it with great interest, seeing how it publicly underlined Carr's absolute determination to prevent Maxwell getting the paper. Until that point he had not decided how deeply he wanted to get involved. Now he saw his chance.

Murdoch arrived at Carr's house early in the morning, which was necessary as Sir William was a drunkard and customarily unfit to do business after 10.30 a.m. He proved to be an unlikely white

4

knight. Dispensing with the normal pleasantries, he went straight for the kill, telling Sir William and his banker, Harry Sporborg, that before anything else could be discussed he had to be given full executive control of the paper and the company which published it. Sir William spluttered and mumbled he could not do that – some way had to be found to keep control within his family.

Murdoch listened patiently for a moment, then butted in: 'Gentlemen, either you concede to my wishes or I catch the next 'plane home. I've come at my own expense. It has cost you nothing. I'll cut my losses and go home if we can't agree right now.'

Sir William was speechless. After a moment Murdoch nodded 'G'day,' got up and began walking towards the door. Sporborg jumped to his feet and pleaded to be allowed five minutes in which he could discuss Murdoch's suggestion with Sir William. Agreeing, Murdoch asked if he could wait in a room with a telephone.

While Carr deliberated with his banker Murdoch called the Australian Prime Minister John Gorton to check that he could take several million Australian dollars out of Australia at short notice. Only now was he seriously beginning to put his own bid together.

Murdoch finished the call and went back into the dining room. Sir William, his head hung low, looked absolutely shattered. Sporborg did the talking. Murdoch was given the job of chief executive, and in return he asked Sir William to stay on in the figurehead position of chairman. If Murdoch could now see off the bid from Maxwell, the paper would be his.

The tactic Murdoch used was to increase the capital value of the *News of the World* by merging it with some of his Australian assets. Murdoch ended up with 40 per cent of the shares in the new company, which was valued at £42 million – £12 million more than Maxwell's original offer. The showdown between the two came at a shareholders' meeting in January 1969. Maxwell made a fiery speech, praising himself and promising the great things he could do for the paper, and patronising Murdoch as a colonial upstart who knew little about the British market.

Murdoch just smiled through Maxwell's performance. When his time came to speak he was cool and to the point. He simply promised to bring the *News of the World* back into profit within two years. The meeting voted decisively to reject Maxwell. Six months later, after further increasing his shareholding in the company, Murdoch forced out Carr by asking him to resign both as chairman and from the board. Carr, by now a broken man, consented. Immediately afterwards he became seriously ill and was an invalid until his death in 1977.

As chief executive of the *News of the World* Murdoch emerged into the world of Fleet Street as an unostentatious figure. He wore a crumpled suit, drove an ordinary Fiat, and unlike the distant Carr plunged into every aspect of the business, working long hours in the *News of the World* offices at 30 Bouverie Street, off Fleet Street. He worked from a desk commandeered from a secretary, sneering at Sir William's priceless antique furniture.

Murdoch soon began meddling with the editorial content of the paper. He insisted that the editor, Stafford Somerfield, pay £21,000 for a rehashed version of Christine Keeler's memoirs of the Profumo affair, by now six years old. The reopening of old wounds caused by the serialisation led to his being castigated for dredging up a matter still extremely sensitive in London society. Profumo was rehabilitating himself after resigning from the government by working for a charity helping drug addicts and ex-offenders in the East End and Murdoch was invited to explain himself on a London Weekend Television chat show hosted by David Frost. Ignoring warnings that Frost would be gunning for him, he grabbed the chance to get what he saw as some free publicity.

In front of a partisan studio audience Frost ripped into him, accusing him of attempting to destroy the reformed Profumo. 'There is a man doing a fantastic job of work and you are threatening that work by this story,' he accused. Uncomfortably, Murdoch defended himself by saying: 'This easy glib talk that the *News of the World* is a dirty newspaper is downright libel and it is not true and I resist it completely.' But Frost had him all round.

Spotting that the only person in the audience applauding was Murdoch's PR consultant he sneered: 'Your PR man's going mad again. You must give him a rise.' (The PR man had advised Murdoch: 'Just go on. Be yourself. They'll love you.')

Murdoch was badly shaken by the show. He complained bitterly that a film insert from Cardinal Heenan, the leader of Britain's Catholics, had been added without his being told and Frost had lured him into the trap with the promise of a 'pally chat'. The débâcle added to his image as a rough Australian, unconversant with the subtleties of the British sense of fair play, and led to him and his wife Anna being excluded from large sections of London society. Turning round his disingenuous defence that he did not publish a 'dirty' newspaper, *Private Eye* instantly labelled him the 'Dirty Digger'.

Murdoch's main concern was that the affair would damage his plans to expand his British newspaper holdings. The massive presses in Bouverie Street, which churned out more than five million copies of the *News of the World* every Saturday evening, were nearly as ancient as Sir William's antiques. But they were also hopelessly underemployed, standing idle on the other six nights of the week. Murdoch began searching for a daily to make them earn their keep. His chance came in April 1969 when the International Publishing Corporation (IPC), the owners of the *Daily Mirror*, announced they were to get rid of their loss-making *Sun*.

In its way the broadsheet *Sun* was as much a British institution as Sir William Carr's 'roast beef and Yorkshire pudding' *News of the World*. The paper was all that remained of the old *Daily Herald*, the socialist newspaper tied to the Trades Union Congress which, in the 1930s, had been the country's biggest-selling daily. After years of decline the *Herald* had been acquired by IPC as an offshoot to its purchase of a string of profitable magazines from Odhams Press in 1961. As part of the deal IPC had made a commitment to the trade union movement to keep the paper going for seven years. It had an official commitment to support the Labour movement but at the same time was not allowed to compete with IPC's existing *Daily Mirror* for the traditional working-class readers.

When losses continued to mount, IPC decided to relaunch the *Herald* as the *Sun* in 1964. The decision was based on market research from the advertising industry, which claimed to have identified a new generation of young, educated left-wingers called the 'pacesetters'. The new *Sun*, launched with the slogan 'born of the age we live in', was only one of many products reflecting the illusions of the 1960s peddled by Harold Wilson's 'white heat of technology' revolution and was even more of an ignominious failure than the *Daily Herald* had been. Starting with the old *Herald*'s circulation of 1.5 million, by the spring of 1969 it had slumped to only 850,000. By then IPC's combined losses on the two papers totalled £12.7 million and the period of commitment to publish given to the trade union movement had ended.

Robert Maxwell, still fuming after losing the *News of the World* to Murdoch, approached the IPC chairman, Hugh Cudlipp, and offered to take the paper off his hands for nothing. He said he would prevent it closing, transfer ownership to a non-profit making trust and preserve the editorial commitment to the Labour Party. The paper would be kept as a broadsheet, and published on a small scale that would not compete with the *Daily Mirror*. But there would have to be redundancies, especially among the printers.

The print unions immediately announced their hostility to the Maxwell offer and throughout the summer threatened action against the *Mirror* if IPC handed over the *Sun* to him. Again Murdoch saw his chance. In many ways it was a re-run of the *News of the World* crisis but this time it was the unions, rather than the Carr family, which were determined to block Maxwell. Murdoch saw that if he got them on his side he would have a free hand in negotiating for the paper. He flew to Rome, met Richard Briginshaw, the boss of NATSOPA (the printers' union), who was on holiday there, and promised fewer redundancies if he got the paper rather than Maxwell.

On 2 September Murdoch's plan came to fruition. Maxwell

withdrew his bid after Cudlipp rejected his cost-cutting plan under pressure from the unions. Instead he quickly reached agreement with Murdoch at a bargain price of £800,000, payable in instalments. Formal Board of Trade approval followed on 20 October. Commenting on the deal in a speech four years later in 1973 Murdoch said: 'I am constantly amazed at the ease with which I entered British newspapers.' Maxwell, beaten for the second time in twelve months, issued a statement blaming the print unions for rejecting his offer.

Having bought the paper, the first thing Murdoch needed was an editor. He asked around the industry, gathered suggestions and compiled a shortlist. Top of the list and recommended by all the people he asked was Larry Lamb, the northern editor of the *Daily Mail* in Manchester, who had moved recently from the *Daily Mirror*, where he had risen to chief sub-editor. Murdoch called Lamb and asked him to have dinner with him in London. Sensing that his dream of becoming a Fleet Street editor might be about to come true, Lamb caught the first train south.

At this point Lamb's career was delicately poised. He had already had a long, hard climb from his start in life in the pit village of Fitzwilliam in the West Riding of Yorkshire, also the home of Geoffrey Boycott. He had been born there in 1929 as Albert Lamb, the son of a colliery blacksmith and NUM official who had never recovered his health after being gassed at the Somme in the First World War. Albert was brought up in a strongly socialist household where the old *Daily Herald* was required reading. But his schooling had coincided with the war and when he left Rastrick Grammar School at the age of sixteen he was forced by restricted access to higher education into a brain-numbing clerical job in the Town Hall at nearby Brighouse. Lamb always maintained afterwards that it was the poor quality of his schooling that prevented him going on to a better education at university. Nevertheless his background meant that, like Murdoch, he was firmly outside the British establishment and he openly admitted to carrying 'a substantial chip on my shoulder'.

As a reluctant clerk Lamb livened up the tedium of Town Hall

9

life by throwing himself into trade union activities as a self-proclaimed 'bolshie'. He was known as 'Red Larry' and his great hero was Nye Bevan, the brilliant Welsh orator who was the darling of Labour's left. Like many poorly educated but intelligent working-class men of his generation he then used the Labour movement as a route to better things, becoming union branch secretary and editor of a trade union magazine, where he was able to indulge his natural talent for words.

At the age of twenty-four, and married with one child, Lamb took the big step of belatedly moving into journalism as a career, working in quick succession for the *Brighouse Echo*, the *Shields Gazette*, the *Newcastle Journal*, the *Evening Standard* in London and the *Daily Mail*. At the *Mail* Lamb was a sub-editor or 'sub', one of the people whose job is to chop up and rewrite the reporters' copy to the required length before writing the headlines and captions. It was then that the incident for which he was best known took place. He bent down to get a cigarette from his bottom drawer and in doing so he impaled his forehead on his sub's spike –the pointed metal rod used as an instant filing system for discarded copy. The spike was sawn off in the office and he was taken to hospital, where the tip was removed without further injury. After that spikes were withdrawn at the *Mail* and replaced by copy-baskets.

In 1958, when he had been in journalism for five years and was twenty-nine, Lamb got his big break by landing a job as a sub on the *Daily Mirror*. The Labour-supporting *Mirror*, then in its heyday with a daily sale of over five million copies, suited his trade union background and he proved able, bright and very ambitious. Quickly, and with enormous pride, he graduated to the coveted post of chief sub, which put him on the 'backbench' in charge of producing the news pages every night. The job was highly skilled, required a cool head and the ability to lead, and on many nights effectively made him the editor of the paper.

But Lamb had decided that his further progress to the editor's chair he coveted was blocked by the logjam of talented people at the *Mirror*, which was anyhow hopelessly overstaffed. Instead he switched to become northern editor of the *Mail*, hoping the move would provide a stepping stone back to a higher position in Fleet Street editorship. Now, he hoped, Murdoch was going to give him his chance.

The two men rendezvoused discreetly at Rules restaurant in Maiden Lane. Over three bottles of Pouilly Fumé and lobster (Murdoch had two portions) they discussed how the *Sun*, now freed from IPC's restrictions, could compete against Lamb's old paper, the *Mirror*. The two men agreed immediately on the main point. The *Mirror* had grown old along with the wartime generation of newspaper readers who had taken its sales to five million. It needed younger readers, but it had badly misjudged the younger generation and left a huge gap in the market. The blame was laid on the paper's 'mission to educate', which had led to it being said that Hugh Cudlipp would have made a good teacher for the Workers' Education Association. For Lamb, the *Mirror's* heavyweight three times a week 'Mirrorscope' insert, a sort of tabloid *Guardian* containing in-depth material about science and the arts, summed up everything that was wrong with the paper.

Like the old *Sun*, Mirrorscope was a pet Cudlipp project, a journalist's version of what a newspaper should be. It was patronising and it irritated the readers. It was as though they were being told: 'This is the important bit – the rest, the things you are actually interested in, is rubbish.'

Mirrorscope was a 'pull-out' all right, Lamb informed Murdoch – it was pulled out and thrown away. The top decks of London buses were ankle-deep in copies. Newspapers had to be designed for the gratification of readers, not journalists, he went on in his faint Yorkshire accent. The only reliable measure of a newspaper's quality was not the opinion of journalists and critics, but the number of people who bought it.

Murdoch had found Pommie journalists a stuck-up bunch, but here at last was one who talked sense. Sales, and the bottom line, were what interested him. He enthusiastically joined in the rubbishing of the contemporary *Mirror*. Together they started thrashing out a new *Sun* to capture the spirit of the *Mirror* when it

11

had really been in its glory years in the 1950s – strident, campaigning, working class, young, entertaining, politically aware, cheeky, radical, anti-establishment, fun, breezy and, most of all, hugely profitable.

As they drained their third bottle of wine the two men agreed on another point. It was a mistake to treat TV as a rival medium, and therefore ignore it, as was conventional Fleet Street wisdom. Murdoch already owned Channel 9 in Adelaide, a second small TV company in Wollongong, New South Wales, and had ambitions to expand his holdings in the large Sydney TV stations. To both him and his Australian rivals it was second nature to promote newspapers on television.

By now telly had graduated from being the black and white 'goggle-box', despised by the middle classes, to a universal medium. TV news and current affairs programmes could beat the papers every time for immediacy and emotional impact. In July that year it had proved the ultimate power of live news broadcasts by the coverage of the American astronauts landing on the moon. Many pundits now saw the growing power of TV as inevitably causing the decline of newspapers, especially when the new attraction of colour became more widespread, and there were even wild predictions that they would die out completely.

At the top end of the newspaper market the 'Unpopulars', as Lamb called papers like *The Times*, the *Telegraph* and the *Guardian*, had fought back by providing long, detailed background to the news headlines. As the influence of TV had spread in the 1960s they spattered their pages with 'in-depth' titles like 'Focus', 'Close-up', 'Insight' and the old *Sun's* own 'Probe', flagging wall-to-wall coverage which would take hours to read out on TV. At the other end of the spectrum the *Mirror* and the *Sketch*, the *Mail's* downmarket stablemate, were trying to pretend that TV did not exist and giving it far less coverage than the huge role it played in their readers' lives warranted. The *Sun*, Lamb and Murdoch both agreed, would cover TV in great depth.

Finding themselves in agreement on the big strategic points the two men moved on to the nitty-gritty of producing the paper.

Lamb was impressed by Murdoch's detailed grasp of every aspect of the business from staffing levels and machinery to marketing and selling advertising space. The discussion went on for hours, ending up in Bouverie Street where they had a couple of whiskies in the office as the building trembled to the *News of the World* presses thundering away in the basement.

Murdoch finally dropped Lamb at his hotel at 2 a.m. Minutes later the phone in his room rang. It was Murdoch, offering him the editorship. Lamb accepted on the spot. The next morning he went round to Murdoch's house in Sussex Square. The new editor, getting his first inkling of what life would be like under his dynamic chairman, ventured to Murdoch's wife, Anna: 'He doesn't waste much time, does he?'

'No,' she replied, smiling. 'Not much.'

After Lamb's terms and conditions had been agreed in five minutes flat, Murdoch scribbled them out on a piece of scrap paper and gave them to him. It was the only formal contract he was ever to get. But, Murdoch had warned him, it was going to be a real push. Back on the train to Manchester Albert Lamb, an editor at last, immediately started planning the paper he had always wanted to produce.

Chapter 2

The Great Knicker Adventure

Larry Lamb soon found that his new proprietor was a man who
expected hard work, and as he plunged into a hectic life
commuting between Manchester and London, he also found
Murdoch as down to earth in his personal life as he was in
business. One of the things Lamb had enjoyed about his climb up
the ladder was the opportunity to go to good restaurants and drink
fine wines, but Murdoch was much more interested in just
grabbing a quick bite as they planned the new paper in more
detail. To Lamb's horror he sometimes took him across the road
from Bouverie Street to the Golden Egg, where he ordered egg
and chips, forcing Lamb to follow suit. The new editor cowered in
dread that he might be seen in such humble surroundings by his
former colleagues on the *Mirror*.

Lamb's first job was to assemble his team of senior journalists.
Ideally he needed people who had already reached executive level
on national newspapers, but none were prepared to leave the
security of their existing jobs for the murky and uncharted waters
of the 'shit-sheet'. With the Frost episode still in everyone's
minds, it was already assumed that the Dirty Digger was going to
produce a smutty daily version of the *News of the World*. A series
of interviews at the Waldorf Hotel produced a string of good
people, but it was soon realised their only interest was in
increasing their currency with their present employers. The only
top-level recruit from the rival *Mirror* was Brian McConnell,
brought in as news editor.

14

Instead Lamb had to trawl the provinces. He told Murdoch he wanted Bernard Shrimsley, editor of the *Liverpool Post*, as his deputy editor and general understudy. Murdoch agreed, adding with a smile that Shrimsley had been the next name on his shortlist for the editor's job. Shrimsley had been a senior *Mirror* executive who, after he had been caught in the promotional logjam like Lamb, had moved sideways to become editor of the *Liverpool Post*, one of the most respected provincial papers in the country. Ever afterwards Lamb was to wonder if their positions would have been reversed if Murdoch had seen Shrimsley first.

One of the reasons for Shrimsley's failure to get to the top at the *Mirror* had been his politics. He was not exactly a committed Tory, but with his middle-class values and attitudes he had never been a socialist, and this, he knew, meant he could never rise to edit the paper. His approach to journalism was more intellectual than Lamb's emotional attitude. His natural home was mid-market newspapers such as the *Mail* or the *Express*, where he was to return many years later. While at the *Mirror* he had demonstrated his approach by being involved in the setting up of Mirrorscope and even claimed to have invented the name. Murdoch, whatever he and Lamb thought about Mirrorscope, was still happy to approve the appointment. He saw the two men complementing each other ideally.

Shrimsley brought with him from the *Liverpool Post* the equally literary Henry Russell Douglas to write editorials, known as leading articles or 'leaders' in Fleet Street jargon. Two more members of the original team were also brought down from the north. Shortly after the launch Peter Stephens, the austere, unspectacular editor of the *Newcastle Journal*, was offered the job of assistant editor. The lugubrious Stephens was already in his forties and jumped at the chance, reckoning it was his last chance to get to Fleet Street. He in turn was balanced by Nick Lloyd, a bright graduate in his twenties recruited from the *Sunday Times*, where he had been deputy news editor. Lloyd, who held left-wing views and supported CND, was made a features executive.

Having got his senior team Lamb turned to the next obvious source for more rank-and-file recruits – the demoralised staff of the old *Sun*. Legally the old paper had no connection with the new one, but since all 260 of the hacks would be on the streets when the paper closed down on 15 November, they were all invited to apply for work on the new paper.

The rough and ready interviewing process consisted of grading them as A, B, C or D. At the end of the process 80 per cent had scored D. Nonetheless, in desperation seventy-five were hired. Some were keen hacks who actually wanted the new paper to work, and others were cynics hoping to pick up a second redundancy cheque to add to the one they were collecting from IPC. Stirred into the mix were deadheads who knew they would never get a job elsewhere. As a last resort Lamb trawled the Fleet Street pubs for virtual alcoholics who until then had been regarded as unemployable. They were given a simple offer – they could have a wage on strict condition they mended their ways.

On paper the team Lamb finally put together seemed distinctly second rate, and with only 100 hacks the new *Sun* was ludicrously lightly staffed compared to papers like the *Express* and the *Mirror*, which had more than 400. Lamb knew he would just have to bridge the gap by making them work harder, and started by getting rid of specialist correspondents. The old *Sun* had been lumbered with twenty-seven of them, including an air correspondent whose sole job was to cover the dying totem of the British aircraft industry. Lamb thought specialists on newspapers were mostly dilettantes anyway, under-employed and equipped with expensive perks like private secretaries. Worst of all, they became members of their respective clubs, which actually encouraged them not to dirty their patch by writing embarrassing stories. If a story was big enough, Lamb held, it could be covered by a general reporter. The alternative argument, that specialists had in-depth knowledge of their subject, did not interest him.

Murdoch's original plan had been to keep the old *Sun* limping along, making limited losses, through the winter. Late November, when it was already coming up to Christmas, was obviously a bad time for a launch. But when he saw the books he found the paper was haemorrhaging money and crucially no advertising had been sold for editions after 15 November. He called Lamb, Shrimsley and Douglas for a crisis meeting in Bouverie Street.

Murdoch had put pressure on Lamb's proprietor at the *Mail*, Lord Rothermere, and got him released in October. Now he made it clear he wanted the new *Sun* launched on the first weekday of his ownership, 17 November. This, he explained, would not only ensure continuous publication but switch the paper to his new formula immediately. Lamb said it couldn't be done. Murdoch taunted by asking him: 'If you did it, would it be any worse than the *Daily Sketch*?'

Murdoch's ploy worked. Lamb was stung by the idea that he could ever produce anything as rubbishy as the *Mail*'s down-market sister and replied proudly: 'Certainly not!', thumping the table to emphasise his point.

'Right,' said Murdoch, 'that's decided.' The *Sun*, as a tabloid, would start production in Bouverie Street on Monday, 17 November.

In the sudden rush, staff problems were now compounded by the lack of facilities at the building. The plucky 100 Lamb had scraped together were crammed into the space on the third floor next to the composing room where rows of hot-metal Linotype machines, resembling huge Heath Robinson typewriters, belched lead fumes as they produced type for the *News of the World*.

The machines, designed and in some cases, the hacks swore, built in the last century, were so old that much of the main body type was worn out. The much-used 'a's and 'e's blurred into solid lumps and the shoulders on capital 'T's were worn off – like a battered old typewriter. But Lamb didn't mind. It was all part of the rough, immediate look which was part of the design magic of the tabloids. (Later when new-technology photocomposition replaced the old hot-metal Linotype machines on newspapers, editors thought it looked too clean. Designers were brought in to make it look messy again.)

Lamb and Shrimsley wanted a bright and aggressive look for the paper, which they would get from using a new typeface for headlines. The choice, favoured by Bernard Shrimsley, was called Tempo and manufactured by a company in Chicago. Because Lamb forgot to order it, it arrived only forty-eight hours before launch. Even then there were so few letters for the main headline size that they only had three of the crucial 'e's. Headlines about the Bee Gees were out for the moment.

The design of the paper was to be based on the *Mirror* with tabloid pages bristling with irresistible hooks for the eye – graphics, montaged photos and variable ('bastard') column widths, WOB (white on black) and WOT (white on tone) headlines, underscores and overscores, rag-outs, starbursts, barkers and screamers. But few of the sub-editors recruited from the old broadsheet *Sun* had any idea how actually to produce pages like these and there was no time to learn.

There was just as much trouble with the writers and hacks from the old *Sun*. Most of them, too, started work only days before the launch and were soon churning out screeds of the writing they had been used to for their former paper. This was ideal for filling up acres of broadsheet space, but worse than useless on the bitty, tabloid *Sun*. There were no dummy editions to practise on, and everything they wrote was needed for the first edition. Lamb was reduced to chopping the articles roughly into bits himself, trying to retain the sense of what they said.

Even more basic facilities were missing right up to the week of launch. Realising that the hacks had nowhere to sit as they began to arrive days before launch Murdoch sent one of the production staff out to buy a hundred desks and chairs, with the order ringing in his ears that they must be small ones. Even then they ended up jammed together.

There was more trouble with the key element of the telephone switchboard, which in those more leisurely days had to be ordered months in advance. Eventually some discreet words in the ear of John Stonehouse, then Postmaster General, did the trick and the paper jumped the queue. But even at launch the exchange was not working properly. Reporters queued in the office to use the phones that were working, while those filing their copy from outside were forced to hang on for hours.

Problems in the basement press hall were just as severe. The ancient Bouverie Street presses were set up to print the broadsheet *News of the World*. The printers had at first told Murdoch it was impossible to convert them for a tabloid. 'Nonsense,' Murdoch replied. 'All you need is the crushers' (the bars which added on to fold the papers to the required size). Asking someone to hold his jacket, he vaulted on top of one of the presses and prised open a grubby wooden box. Inside, still in their oiled wrappings, were the vital pieces of equipment.

But there was one major production problem that defied any fixing. The *Sun*'s rivals had all grown up in the days when it was the norm to have a large staff in the north, where the papers were printed, as well as in London. Replica pages were sent up from London and combined with inside 'slip' pages with more localised content, allowing strongly regionalised editions to go on to the presses late in the evening. The *News of the World* had been able to operate by only printing in London as it was a Sunday which contained little of the previous day's news. But now Murdoch was producing a daily he would have to start printing long before his rivals to catch the trains to the north. After all the timetables had been scrutinised, first-edition time was fixed at 8.15 p.m. creating problems all the way down the line. The inside pages had to be made up long before first-edition time, and the news reporters were faced with deadlines hours before their rivals, and in some cases before the event they were covering was over. Late news and, crucially, the evening football results, would be missing in the north.

The problem of the early print forced Lamb to concentrate on filling the pages with feature material – timeless background articles, subjects of general interest that were vaguely 'in the news', 'round-ups', consumer affairs, free offers and competitions. The latest news was still as high a priority as it could be as the *Sun* was, after all, a newspaper, but neither it nor the sports reports could be the main selling point. But this made sense for the paper anyway. With its tiny editorial staff and the limited financial resources provided by Murdoch, Lamb was in no position to cover the news in depth and detail even if he had wanted to. Instead, bright, chatty features could be quickly bashed together by competent writers, and yards of 'serialisation' material – copyrighted extracts from books – could be obtained simply by writing a small cheque.

On Saturday 15 November the fast-deserting readers of the old broadsheet *Sun* were informed of what was coming their way as Lamb and Murdoch juggled these multiple problems. A banner headline urged them to 'REACH FOR THE NEW SUN' over a leader promising:

> YOUR SUN will be different on Monday. Very different.
> But the most important thing to remember is that the new SUN will be the paper that CARES. The paper that cares – passionately – about truth, and beauty and justice.
> The paper that cares about people. About the kind of world we live in. And about the kind of world we would like our children to live in.

That evening in Bouverie Street the *News of the World* ran through its normal print and on the Sunday the decks were cleared for the launch. The day was a nightmare of bodges and cock-ups and frayed tempers as everybody struggled in the unfamiliar surroundings. Finally the print union NATSOPA aroused Murdoch's ire by insisting that Anna had to become an honorary member before she could ceremonially press the button to set the presses rolling. When that had been sorted out, and she pressed the button, nothing happened.

The electrical fault was one of hundreds of little problems that bedevilled the production process and meant that the paper eventually limped off the presses three hours late. As a result many of the old *Sun* readers were unable to assess the level of its successor's passionate caring for the simple reason that they never saw it. More remote areas were not reached at all, and in northern cities like Leeds and Manchester the paper only reached news-agents' counters at 10 a.m., long after most potential readers had gone to work.

Technically the paper itself was awful – crude, sloppily presented and spattered with spelling mistakes, badly cropped pictures and headlines which didn't fit. In all there were forty-eight amateurish tabloid pages, and from a professional point of view it was rubbish. The only thing that had really worked was the paper's red masthead, known in the trade as the colour seal. Hobson Bates, the paper's advertising agents, had put forward a series of hopelessly fussy and complicated designs which Lamb had rejected. Instead he had sketched out the one that was eventually used on the back of an envelope one night when he was on the train going back to Manchester. (Years later, when the copyright of the colour seal came up in a court case against the *Mirror*, it was discovered Lamb still owned it. He generously sold it to his old masters for £1.)

The planned celebration party at Bouverie Street was a grim occasion, enlivened only by a senior print official being sick in a waste-paper basket and another being apprehended trying to leave with a full bottle of Johnnie Walker under his coat. At 4 a.m., when Murdoch eventually drove Lamb home in the Rolls which had now replaced the Fiat, his editor was in black despair. Anna suggested to her husband, only half-joking, that they would be better off driving straight to Heathrow and going home to Australia. Over at the *Mirror*, where a spoiling party was being held, there was derision from IPC chairman Hugh Cudlipp. 'We've got nothing to worry about,' he told the gathering as he inspected the grubby effort. The editor of the *Mirror*, Lee Howard, was not so confident.

Rough though it was, Murdoch and Lamb had pulled off a considerable achievement by just getting ink to cling loosely to the forty-eight pages. And at a glance the front pages of the issue of 17 November 1969, compared with the changes which have convulsed other papers over the same period, looked remarkably similar to the edition of 17 November 1989, by which time the typeface and the layout had been copied by tabloids throughout the world. The main difference was in the price – a tenth of 1989's at five old pence compared to 22 new pence.

The front page showed Lamb's eagerness to steal as much from the *Mirror* as possible. The slogan 'Forward with the People', recently dropped by the *Mirror*, was picked up and jammed under the colour seal next to the price and date. Lamb hired the son of Cassandra, the great *Mirror* columnist of the 1940s and 1950s, to write a column called 'Son of Cassandra'. Andy Capp, the *Mirror*'s best-known cartoon and a national institution, was reincarnated as the more up-to-date 'Wack', who had the same fag hanging from his lip, but sported a Ringo Starr hairstyle instead of a cloth cap. The *Mirror* sci-fi strip Garth was ripped off with Scarth, a female version complete with tits, and the title 'Liveliest Letters' was coined to trump the *Mirror*'s 'Live Letters'.

The front-page splash was headlined 'HORSE DOPE SENSATION' (using all the crucial 'e's) – a good exclusive story based on the first trainer to confess to doping his horses. It immediately stirred up the sort of controversy the paper was looking for with an attempt – which failed – to get the *Sun*'s racing correspondent banned from the Turf. The front-page picture featured Lady Leonora Grosvenor, Prince Charles's latest consort, pointing to the Royals obsession that was to become one of the paper's staples. But as far as the critics were concerned more important than all this was the contents box run down the righthand side of the front page. 'Inside your 48 page *Sun*', the blurb read, 'BEAUTIFUL WOMEN – SUN EXCLUSIVE' and 'THE LOVE MACHINE – SUN EXCLUSIVE'.

'Mr Murdoch has not invented sex,' *The Times* (which was then owned by Lord Thomson) informed its readers as it reviewed the first issue, 'but he does show a remarkable enthusiasm for its benefits to circulation, such as a tired old Fleet Street has not seen in recent years.' At the other end of the political spectrum the *Morning Star* described the new paper as 'more like a paraffin lamp in a brothel than a sun', handing down the official Communist Party line that the paper was 'a brash millionaire's opinion of what the working class ought to want'.

From day one the *Sun* had chosen sex as the battleground for the coming circulation war with its rivals, the subject Lamb and Murdoch had both identified as one of the rival *Daily Mirror's* weakest points. The *Mirror* naturally covered stories with sex interest but overall its approach was old-fashioned, coy and suggestive in a 'nudge-nudge, wink-wink' kind of way. The *Sun* might never wean the *Mirror's* older and more staid readers, but by being more upfront and pushing a seamy version of the 'sexual revolution' which had swept the country in the late 1960s, it could certainly capture the interest of the rising young generation. The first issue showed the gusto with which the subject was being tackled.

The main feature was a bought-in serialisation of a book called *The Love Machine* by Jacqueline Susann, the author of *The Valley of the Dolls*. *The Love Machine*, described as 'the world's best-selling novel of 1969', was regarded as very risqué, coming as it did only a few years after a barrister had enquired of a jury whether members would allow their servants to read *Lady Chatterley's Lover*. The serialisation also broke with an accepted Fleet Street maxim that fiction did not sell papers.

The serialisation was splattered in steaming, but ultimately mild detail across the centre spread. More sex interest was provided by 'Beautiful Women', flagged as the start of 'a remarkable series of interviews with some of the most beautiful women of our time'; a feature on the Rolling Stones hinted at orgies and showed Mick Jagger with a scantily clad 'groupie'; the fashion slot was suitably illustrated for a feature headed 'UNDIES FOR UNDRESSING'. The news pages chimed in on the theme with a story describing a man as a 'walking lust automat' and, just in case readers had still not got the message, there was the promise of a series about adultery starting the next day with issue two.

Page 3 was dominated by a picture of a pretty girl – a nameless 'Swedish charmer' allegedly studying to become a computer-systems analyst. She was wearing a loose-fitting shirt. The worthy, Labour-supporting readers of the old *Sun* had to wait until the next day for the breaking of new ground with the exposure of a pair of nipples. These belonged to model Uschi Obermeier and were printed on the centre spread. Putting the two points of the equation together to produce the Page Three girl was to take another year.

Girly pictures were a standard element of the tabloid package at that time, and were usually erected on the back of spurious fashion features, contrived PR events or flammed-up non-stories. But the *Sun* had boldly dispensed with these limp excuses. The new fashion photographer, Beverley Goodway, who had been hired from the sports desk of *The Times*, was therefore free to pick the best-looking models and pose them however he wanted. In the first year of publication various celebs were added in to be shown scantily dressed, including model Julie Ege, Anthea ('give us a twirl') Redfern of Bruce Forsyth's *Generation Game* and Britt Ekland.

The regular topless Page Three feature started on the paper's first anniversary in November 1970, with model Stephanie Rahn posed in her 'birthday suit' sitting sideways on the grass. Although the picture was in the wholesome naturist genre of *Health and Efficiency* magazine, rather than more seedy porno sytle, the caption anticipated the ensuing storm of publicity. 'From time to time some self-appointed critic stamps his tiny foot and declares that the *Sun* is obsessed with sex,' it read. 'It is not the *Sun*, but the critics, who are obsessed. The *Sun*, like most of its readers, likes pretty girls.'

Lamb and Shrimsley had no hard and fast policy for the type of Page Three pictures the paper required. If there was any doubt the women features writers were consulted and given a right to veto any they thought might cause offence to women readers. Goodway groped his way towards a style by providing a large selection for Lamb and the picture desk to choose from.

From the desk the pictures would go to be retouched in the photographic department with scribbled instructions to 'remove mole' or 'make jawline firmer', with Shrimsley adding on one memorable occasion 'make nipples less fantastic'. The models slowly evolved from girl-next-door types towards the visual clichés of the soft-porn industry. Suspenders and black stockings were added; girls were posed under the shower or glistening with body oil; all the tricks of the trade were employed such as making nipples erect by applying cold damp towels, with the stand-by of sticky tape on backs to tighten loose skin and lift insufficiently thrusting breasts.

Since the girls were purely visual objects, captions became a prime opportunity for stringing together the sort of puns which had always characterised the tabloid industry and the *Sun* was now raising to new heights. The tone was breezy – 'Cherry Gilham has gone a long way since becoming a model. She flies all over the world for assignments. And Cherry, from Essex, certainly lands some plum jobs!' And had a plum pair as well, as the paper knew the readers would be thinking.

The job of writing Page Three captions eventually settled on Patsy Chapman, an ambitious young hack recruited from a teenage girl's magazine, where she had specialised in knitting patterns. Chapman caused a severe shock for a furious delegation of feminists who arrived at Bouverie Street demanding to see the male chauvinist pig responsible. Instead '5' 2", eyes of blue' Chapman appeared to tell them it was all harmless fun. As a working girl, she could also inform them she had been recruited through an ad which had asked for women journalists only, and had got Lamb in trouble for sexual discrimination.

Sex soon crept on to the menu of every part of the paper, with the sports pages enlivened by 'artist's impressions' of female tennis stars in the nude, and crime reports which often led with the sex lives of either the villain or the victim. 'THE VIRGIN KILLER WHO LOVED POISON' headed a murder report which neatly worked in the subject by beginning: 'He was the man with no need for women . . . he had never experienced sex,' disregarding the fact that the convicted murderer's sex life had not been an issue in his trial.

The sex obsession, combined with the early deadlines, gave new currency to what rivals had previously regarded as only a small part of the news agenda. On the front page of the third issue a WOB headline screamed: 'MEN ARE BETTER LOVERS IN THE MORNING – OFFICIAL'.

The direct-marketing department kept the theme going with sexy offers like 'THE GREAT KNICKER ADVENTURE', which invited readers to apply for a pair of knickers scented with a drop of Chanel No. 5 and stuck in a tin. When Murdoch began good-naturedly grumbling that the paper was full of nothing but knickers, attention was switched to more homely offers like a competition prize of a year's supply of tights and nappies, designed for the target audience of young couples the paper was desperate to lure away from the *Mirror*.

The fact that sex sold newspapers like any other product was nothing new. But the timing of the new *Sun* enabled this basic marketing to be given spurious respectability by riding the crest of the post-1960s 'permissive society'. Lamb always believed that women readers were a crucial target audience and, although the new sexually liberated approach had been taken up by several women's magazines, so far the only paper to take it on board had been the *Guardian*. The overlapping agenda was demonstrated in the *Sun*'s first issue when the *Guardian* bought a page advertisement to boast that its women's page dealt 'frankly with topics that otherwise get wrapped up in cosy euphemisms' – indicating its open discussion of matters such as orgasms, homosexuality, masturbation and menstruation.

Murdoch did however draw the line at one of these. In the first few days Nick Lloyd produced a feature on what it was like to be homosexual. 'Do you really think our readers are interested in poofters?' The question was phrased in standard Murdoch style to inform him that they were not. The feature was spiked.

Joyce Hopkirk, the women's editor, who went on to edit the magazine *Cosmopolitan*, contributed what were considered the best and most daring ideas for explicit sexual coverage. Her strong team of young female feature writers, mainly recruited from women's magazines, were organised under the banner 'Pacesetters', one of the few editorial titles retained from the old *Sun*. Lamb took them seriously and, unlike many other national editors, did not regard feature writers as an inferior journalistic species to news reporters. The women in turn found the *Sun* a much more liberated place to work than the Unpopulars. Women writers usually found these much more sexist, with an attitude somewhere between a gentleman's club and a public school. Lamb allowed his women to work shifts, which fitted in with looking after young children, and no one in the office felt inhibited.

The Pacesetters visually indicated their liberation by sticking up pictures of male nudes, mostly culled from German naturist magazines, on what was known as the 'Willie Wall'. Lamb and Shrimsley were often amazed by the frank talk that bounced around the desks and by women hacks who marched in to slump into their chairs announcing: 'Fuck me! I'm knackered!' just like their male counterparts. But for the paper the language had to be toned down, and there was a constant hunt for a suitable euphemism for the rude word 'come', when describing an orgasm. The early solution, 'moment of fulfilment', was finally replaced after experiments by 'going for gold'.

Pacesetters set to work with gusto to churn out features like 'the Geography of Love' – where were the best lovers in Britain to be found?; 'Do Men Still Want to Marry a Virgin?'; 'Love 30 – women of thirty talking about the facts of living and loving in middle years'; 'The First Night of Love' – with riveting details of the first time; 'Are You Getting Your Share?'; 'The Way into a Woman's Bed'; 'How to Be a Cool Lover'; 'How to Pick a Mate'. One of the more interesting, 'Casanova Girls', featured an interview with a Swedish woman of twenty-one who claimed to have had 789 lovers since her first bedding at the tender age of twelve. Prince Philip, Mary Whitehouse, Lord Hailsham and Brigid Brophy were all quoted on what they thought about the subject.

A principal part of the mixture, known in the office as 'corn and porn', was serialising books, with huge emphasis on 'how to do it' manuals. The high point was reached by *The Sensuous Woman*, written by an American called Jane Garrity. The book was sold as a step-by-step guide on how to 'get, please, and keep your man'. One of the hacks who worked on it summarised it more crudely as a guide on 'how to give the old man a blow job'. The book was so explicit that the first copies ordered by Lamb from New York were impounded by Customs at Heathrow. Lamb promptly ordered a second consignment, which slipped through the net the same day. The Customs authorities were still pondering their initial seizure when Lamb sent them page proofs of the *Sun* serialisation and the resulting massive row produced satisfyingly huge publicity for the paper.

The *Sun* hyped *The Sensuous Woman* further with an announcement to its readers: 'There are sections of this book which are not suitable for publication in a family newspaper. These sections will not appear in the *Sun*. But it's the book that every woman will want to read. It's the book that could save your marriage.' The *Guardian*, disgusted, described the book as a 'lurid sex manual' and accused the paper of having 'bowdlerised' it.

The Sensuous Woman was always referred to in the office as the 'definitive corker', the standard against which all other serialisations were measured, and the like of which was daily yearned for. The paper followed up with the weaker *The Sensuous Couple* containing a 'Love Charter' which advised: 'Always make love naked. Always make love with the light on.' Although it was dismissed in some quarters as patronising as well as prurient, such basic information was eagerly sought after by the paper's target readers. The sexual revolution which they had all heard about was still to a large extent practised by a mainly middle-class and student minority. The paper's own 1971 survey of sex and marriage revealed England to be still in a chaste state, with 90 per cent of women and 25 per cent of men claiming to have been virgins when they married.

Although the features were by their very nature more leisurely than the news, they were still often slung together by the hackettes at what was considered breakneck speed. An idea suggested in the morning could be in the next day and much of the material was assembled by rehashing old cuttings, quickie interviews or rewriting articles from magazines.

Germaine Greer, the Australian feminist author of *The Female Eunuch*, slammed the paper for 'subverting the morals and the quality of the working class in a most cynical fashion'. But as the writers saw it they were providing good, clean 'how to do it' sexual coverage, with a high premium on fun, miles away from the smutty, court-case-based filth dished up weekly by their fellow *News of the World* hacks in Bouverie Street. They believed they were showing their predominantly working-class audience, especially the women, how to enjoy themselves. The slogan was 'make it breezy, not sleazy'. But, wearily repairing across the road to the pub for a reviver after a long day, both writers and subs would share the same bleak joke. The *Sun* was the only place they'd been where you got so much sex at work it put you off it for life. But compensation for all the exhausting work came in the form of gratifying leaps forward in the sales of the paper which began to put a real buzz into the office. From the first few months of publication it was clear the sex formula was definitely working and picking up readers.

When Murdoch had been negotiating to buy the *Sun* from IPC he had played a little joke on Hugh Cudlipp. After being parked in an anteroom he had noticed a chart on the wall, tracking the sales graphs of the *Sun* and *Mirror* with pieces of string. With an evil glint in his eye Murdoch reversed them, thereby reversing the market positions of the two papers. And with sales already having risen from the old *Sun*'s death rattle figure of 650,000 to 1.5 million in the first hundred days, everything about the paper indicated that one day that symbolic gesture might be turned into reality. Already Cudlipp was being asked awkward questions about why he had sold Murdoch what was rapidly becoming such a serious rival.

Chapter 3

Larry Has a Little Lamb

Rupert Murdoch has always been a 'hands-on' proprietor, involving himself in every aspect of the business, shaping his papers down to the last detail and even appearing on editorial floors to read proofs and sub pages.

Before and during launch Murdoch dominated the *Sun*, and at the end of the first week the journalists' trade paper, *UK Press Gazette*, reported how he had rolled his sleeves up and pitched in to help. 'It's bloody chaotic,' he chirped, 'but we're getting a paper out.' During launch week Lamb even found himself working next to him on the composing room 'stone', the table where the final metal versions of pages were assembled. 'I'll tell you one thing this paper's got that no other paper's got – the two highest-paid stone subs in history,' Lamb joked. Murdoch grinned back. The relative pay between them was not discussed.

But within four weeks of launch Murdoch had to disappear to Australia to field events back in the home branch of his fledgling empire. Not that KRM, as Lamb began calling him, was absent from his editor's life. Merely being on the other side of the world was no bar to his coming on the phone at all hours of the day and night. As Lamb struggled to cope with a thousand different problems every minute of his sixteen-hour days, or simply tried to grab some much needed sleep, the phone would ring yet again. He soon realised there was nothing personal in this, it was just that KRM was simply not interested enough to think what else his editor might be doing.

Communication was aided by KRM obtaining one of the first of the new international telephone credit cards, which he used in order to come on the line from any spot where he had a few spare moments. He would bark down the phone, then break the connection when he had to dash off again. Then, anything from minutes to hours later, the phone in Bouverie Street would ring again and KRM would restart the conversation from the point he had left it as if there had not been a break.

Lamb put a clock on the office wall telling him the time in different cities so he could check KRM's movements and avoid ringing him when he was sleeping, but KRM's body clock had already been destroyed by his constant intercontinental travel and since he habitually took only three hours sleep, whether it was day or night made little difference.

Murdoch wanted to get back to London to be the main architect of the *Sun*, as he had been of all his papers so far, but he was prevented by a serious threat to the life of his wife Anna when Mrs Muriel McKay, the wife of his deputy chairman, Alick McKay, was kidnapped and murdered. The kidnappers made it clear in their ransom demands that Anna had been the real target, and the police instructed the Murdoch family to stay in Australia until the kidnappers were behind bars. They were not apprehended until September 1970, almost a year after the launch, which meant that Murdoch was missing during the crucial period when the difficulties were being sorted out and the paper began to settle down and gell.

The result was Lamb playing a much larger role than usual for a Murdoch editor and he was later very proud of the fact that when Murdoch was asked about the paper, he would say: 'It's not my paper. It's Larry's.'

The first problem Lamb had tackled was the inability to get the evening sports reports into the early editions of the paper caused by printing in London. Frank Nicklin, the experienced sports editor hired from the old *Sun*, had promised the readers 'sport with four rows of teeth' in the first issue. He filled the cavities in the paper's results service with series like 'Where are they now?', tracking down famous footballers of yesteryear, coupled with regular columns by sports personalities like George Best, the glamorous but increasingly boozy Manchester United star, and Brian Clough, who promised to give football 'a big shout'. Once again the critics were confounded. The lack of a proper results service proved to be no great handicap and some readers actually seemed to like muddles in regionalised pages which meant that they would receive localised coverage from a different part of the country by mistake. As Lamb had correctly realised, the readers could get the headlines and results from the television and then look in their *Sun* for entertaining gossip about the teams.

With features so dominant in the paper Murdoch now imported the key to the whole sales package – the aggressive television advertising he had mentioned to Lamb at the first dinner at Rules. He had used this successfully in Australia to smash the opposition in the steamy and cut-throat afternoon tabloid market in Sydney, where his paper – ironically called the *Daily Mirror* – slugged it out with the *Sun* in a reverse of the British title fight which was now under way.

To introduce the technique to Britain Murdoch brought in Graham King, a tall, wiry Australian, to take charge of the Promotions Department. King was an articulate man who had written a thoughtful book about the nineteenth-century writer Emile Zola and had a deep and abiding interest in antiques and historic places. Murdoch ran him through his normal courtship routine of a tour of the Cotswolds in his Rolls-Royce but King did not need any convincing. He was already a confirmed Anglophile and itching to get his hands on this new challenge in Pommie-land. The resulting slam-bang commercials he produced were brash, gaudy and roughly thrown together under a 'composite' or 'magazine concept' formula which, like the paper itself, bristled with hooks. Ten or twelve separate items would be jammed into sixty frantic seconds, puffing sexy features, serialisations and a constant flow of free offers.

Dominant images showed bright young readers and semi-naked girls leaping about delirious with delight, spattered with key words like 'LOVE!' 'MONEY!' and, above all, 'WIN!' flashing in and out of view. Prizes were generally cheap and cheerful – a night out with a Page Three girl, a trip to New York, 'Be your own TV critic, WIN a colour TV!', 'WIN a fabulous, sexy mink-lined bikini!'

This visual assault on the viewer's senses was synchronised by the voice of a then unknown actor, Christopher Timothy, recruited from the Old Vic. Timothy was later to become well known to *Sun* readers as the Yorkshire vet in the TV series *All Creatures Great and Small*. For the ads his National Health glasses were snatched off his face, he was put into a suit and handed a microphone. Timothy let rip at an extraordinary 180 words a minute in a machine-gun delivery which always climaxed in the breathless pay-off line 'ONLY IN THE SUN!' On a Pseuds Corner intellectual level the ads seemed to owe much to the 1960s avant-garde 'blizzard of images' school of Situationist art. But features executive Nick Lloyd, who devised endless silly competitions to fuel them, summarised them more simply as 'naff – not just ordinary naff, but spectacular naff'.

The ads were run over the weekend, with a massive budget behind them, to push up Monday's sale and hook readers in for the whole week by an endless stream of series, serialisations and 'theme weeks'. Lamb ran Romance Week, Pony Week, Dog Week, Bicycle Week, Naval Week, Ooh! La! La! Week, Fishing Week – anything to keep the punters buying the paper for the next five days. The content was planned, often weeks in advance, at regular 'think-ins' held in comfortable country hotels. Here Lamb, Shrimsley, Hopkirk and other execs like sports editor Frank Nicklin would combine high living and letting off steam with brainstorming sessions garnering material for the features, free offers, competitions and other gimmicks. The team once crashed into a hotel to find a horrified Esther Rantzen, attempting to have a quiet weekend away with her husband Desmond Wilcox, breastfeeding in the corner of a room.

Lamb would come away from the sessions with a thick document full of ideas. He and King would then pick the most televisual and present them to Murdoch for a decision on whether

33

to invest in a new burst of TV advertising. In common with the sales drive dominating every aspect of the paper the ads were then used to gain additional free publicity by continuously needling the Independent Television Companies Association (ITCA), which vetted all ads before transmission. When ITCA demanded that a reference to the River Piddle (which actually exists) be cut from an ad for Fishing Week the news was splashed all over the paper, while sexual double-entendres like Pussy Week were deliberately put up as crude jibes, designed to get the paper talked about and cast the authorities as spoilsports and censors.

But the paper did finally overstep the mark with an ad for serialisation of a novel called *Rabid*, which Lamb tastefully retitled *The Day of the Mad Dogs* for the readers. *Sun* ads were made, usually in twenty-four hours, with the comparatively new technique of video only days before they were broadcast. The *Mirror* had rejected TV advertising because its selling point was news, which could not be advertised in advance as it had not yet happened. But the *Sun* used actors and sets to create mock-ups showing what their 'news' was going to be – as in 'The Huntresses', when TV viewers were treated to a scene of a randy housewife in a crimplene dressing-gown dragging a grinning male caller up to the bedroom in the middle of the day. The Mad Dogs dramatisation showed horrific scenes of a couple being attacked in their living room by their pets. There were close-ups of foaming mouths and blood-spattered bodies, screaming babies, the dogs being shot and a final scene showing a moaning victim expiring in hospital. The ad received a record number of complaints and was pulled at 11 p.m. on its first night, provoking huge delight at the *Sun*. On the Monday the paper 'walked off the newsstands', as Lamb put it. In line with the Murdoch 'magazine concept' sale strategy, readers then stayed with the paper all week to soak up the gory details, by which time, according to plan, they were hooked.

Murdoch backed up the editorial and TV advertising attack on the *Mirror* by deploying the ruthless approach to business for which he was by now famous. The ads were tied into bursts of activity in the circulation department. From the start Murdoch gave the newspaper distributors and newsagents a higher percentage of the cover price than any other paper. This ensured that newsagents made more money by selling a copy of the *Sun* than selling a copy of the *Mirror* and naturally got them behind the paper.

Among the managements of rival Fleet Street papers Murdoch soon became hated for tactics such as these. For years there had been an unwritten agreement that newspapers should present a united front to the distribution trade. If they started competing by means of discounts offered to distributors instead of editorial content the Street could easily be engulfed in a price-cutting war. It would be dog eat dog and everyone would suffer. Murdoch was dangerously close to the line.

In 1971 the *Sun* took its first scalp in the circulation war with the closure of the down-market *Daily Sketch*, which had slumped from a circulation of 871,000 when the *Sun* was launched in November 1969 to only 764,000 when it was closed in March. Its owner, Lord Rothermere, merged the *Sketch* with his other paper, the *Daily Mail*, which went tabloid at the same time. The new merged *Mail*, describing itself as a 'compact' to get away from the down-market connotations of the word tabloid, reconciled itself to losing most old *Sketch* readers. Almost all of them went straight over to the *Sun*, which Lamb cheekily described as 'The compact with impact'. The influx of *Sketch* readers took the *Sun's* circulation to over two million for the first time and created a two-horse race in the pop-newspaper market between the *Sun* and *Mirror*. And Lamb now had the main target of overtaking the *Mirror's* circulation, still over four million, firmly within his sights.

Many people in the Street had at first found it hard to take seriously the astonishing rise in sales of the *Sun*. Circulation reps announcing that they had just put on another 100,000 would be laughed at by rivals, who plainly did not believe them. There was also the old-fashioned view that the huge sex content in what purported to be a family newspaper put off as many potential readers as it attracted. The *Mirror* management, led by Hugh

Cudlipp, found it inconceivable that a paper like this could be doing so well.

Lee Howard, editor of the *Mirror* at the time of the *Sun*'s launch, had disagreed, but he found it impossible to raise the alarm – predicting the *Sun* would work was an unpopular line to push within the company which had just sold it off as a dead loss. In 1970, partly due to his heretical viewpoint, Howard had been replaced as *Mirror* editor by Michael Christiansen, who roundly attacked the *Sun* as rubbish.

Lamb was particularly angered by an attack Christiansen made on Murdoch in a speech given shortly after he had become editor. 'From the popular newspapers' point of view I think that Murdoch's arrival in Fleet Street was the worst thing that could have happened,' Christiansen said. 'The clock of journalistic standards has been put back ten to fifteen years, and it now seems that what has happened on my paper is that one's major consideration every week is whether you should have a picture that shows off pubic hair.'

Lamb was outraged. Pubic hair had been scrupulously excluded from Page Three and other nude pictures as one of the guidelines to ensure things were kept 'wholesome'. The printers, known at the paper as the 'Inkies', once played a practical joke by scratching some in on a girlie picture, which was then printed, causing Lamb and Shrimsley to turn white. But there was a thunderous silence from the readers, who did not seem at all perturbed.

Lamb found the charge that his paper was just sex and lightweight pap for the morons hard to take. He fumed at critics, saying that if they would only look at it properly they would see how his news policy worked. Heavy news was on the lefthand pages of 2, 4 and 6, while the righthanders of 3, 5 and 7 carried more cheerful material. Lamb insisted that all the important news stories in the *Daily Telegraph*, the most comprehensive of the Unpopulars, were also in the *Sun* most days. It was just that the *Sun*'s versions were shorter and therefore, he claimed, sharper. He was making no apologies for that.

Writer Tom Baistow, intellectually monitoring the paper for the erudite columns of the left-wing *New Statesman,* took Lamb's advice, measured column inches and confirmed that the *Sun's* proportion of lightweight material was no greater than the *Mirror's.* But he still complained that the *Sun* zeroed in on the 'bizarre, sexy and unpleasant,' while the *Mirror* followed the 'quaint and coy' approach typified by cute 'kitten in a wineglass' pictures and 'funny old world' stories such as 'MAN FIRED FROM CANNON HITS OWN WIFE'.

The tension between Lamb and his critics came to a head in 1971 with the two sets of annual journalistic awards. The first was presented by IPC, which could hardly be expected to give Lamb or the paper anything. Its Journalist of the Year was Alastair Hetherington, the editor of the *Guardian,* a paper which had also been prospering in the new liberated climate.

Granada TV's *What the Papers Say* did, however, give the *Sun* the ultimate accolade of making it Newspaper of the Year. But the ceremony at the Savoy was a grim affair as far as Lamb was concerned. The presenter, Brian Inglis, went to great lengths to emphasise that the panel had been split and a 'special award' was therefore being given to the other main contender, the *Financial Times.* Lamb, mortified by this calculated exercise in damning with faint praise, nearly walked out and regretted afterwards he had not done so. To demonstrate his disgust, instead of putting the award on the front page as he did the continuous sales milestones, he buried it in two short paragraphs at the bottom of page 4.

He thought it was typical of the critics, who represented only the 'prattling classes', to misunderstand the *Sun.* The readers loved the paper but for Lamb it was more than just a sales exercise. While Murdoch tended to ignore the critics completely as long as sales were going well, Lamb took a lot of the criticism personally and lost no opportunity to defend his reputation and that of the paper.

The difference between the two men came out at one industry lunch he was attending with Joan, his wife, and Murdoch. Lamb went into a cold fury when a speaker trotted out the familar tits-

and-bums jibe. Murdoch, puzzled at his strength of feeling, turned to Joan and asked: 'What's eating Larry?' 'Look, Rupert,' she replied, 'I know it's your newspaper. But to you it's only a newspaper. To Larry it's a baby.'

Of the pundits, only the *Financial Times*'s Sheila Black wrote anything which was to Lamb's liking. Black was the wife of Lee Howard, the *Mirror* editor who had taken the *Sun* seriously, and she backed him up by pointing out that the paper had a 'soaraway, crest-of-the-wave feeling' which was filling a gap in the market. As sales increased, Lamb pinched the phrase and the 'Soaraway *Sun*' became an abiding Fleet Street cliché.

Lamb competed ferociously with the *Mirror*, shamelessly stealing its best features, stories and ideas. The 1972 saga of the 'grapefruit sex wives' was typical. The *Mirror* ran a story from Rome headlined: 'GRAPEFRUIT SEX CODE – WIVES SELL THEMSELVES IN SUPERMARKETS'. The report said local housewives advertised that they were looking for sex by lining up grapefruits on the front of their supermarket trollies. The next day the *Sun* trumped the story with something closer to home. Under the headline 'THE BRIGHTNESS OMO WIVES WANT' the paper revealed that a similar code was in operation, not in exotic and far-away Rome, but in homely Swindon, Wiltshire. 'The love-hungry wife displays a packet of Omo in her window or shopping basket,' the paper explained to readers; 'the letters are a code meaning Old Man Out'.

Page Three had proved a crucial element in giving the *Sun* a younger, more sexy look than its rival but the *Mirror* held out until 1975 before printing its first bare nipple. The paper dipped its toe in the water with 'holiday girl Jilly Johnson', whose naked breasts were shown in tasteful profile. The picture was printed as much to test the response from fellow executives in the *Mirror*'s Holborn tower block as the readers. The internal outrage was led by Marge Proops, the *Mirror*'s famous agony aunt, but a couple of weeks later the experiment was repeated amid great trepidation in the form of 'The Raw Material' – a series supposedly about photography. After this nudes became a regular, but not daily, feature of the *Mirror*.

The crossing of this fleshy Rubicon failed to ease the pressure from the *Sun*, which was now achieving a daily sale of 3.5 million – only half a million behind the *Mirror*. As Proops and others feared, the *Mirror*'s nipples lost it some readers while they were not raunchy enough compared to the *Sun* to attract readers looking for something a little stronger. The paper quickly found itself in a game of strip poker it could not win.

While youth-appeal and sex were Lamb's main weapons in the war with the *Mirror*, he did not forget the older readers. For them he had successfully re-created the anti-establishment feel of the *Mirror* in the 1940s and 1950s. The approach came from the wartime spirit, when the *Mirror* had been the paper of the 'other ranks' and devoted a lot of energy to helping out with the many problems and petty injustices inflicted on soldiers and their families. Naturally the paper had patriotically supported the war effort, but at the same time it cheekily castigated the 'top brass' for their blimpish and old-fashioned establishment attitudes.

The *Sun* now captured this feel and transferred it to society as a whole. Above all it encouraged the readers – defined from issue one as the 'folks' – to identify with it. Lamb had a rule that all letters must be answered within forty-eight hours – even if only with a holding acknowledgement until the point or request for help was dealt with. And the paper did provide a lot of genuine help, even if it was only referring people on to the appropriate authority, or printing begging letters from people judged to have suffered genuinely bad luck which often raised a lot of money.

As the *Mirror* had become more establishment-minded, the *Sun*'s 'folks' were the new other ranks. The new targets were the officer class of pompous do-gooders, planners, bureaucrats and snobs and prudes who made life a misery for the fun-loving folks. Lamb's own favourite target was local government, the tedium and petty-mindedness of which he had experienced first hand in his days as a town-hall clerk in Yorkshire.

An early example was the story of the 'Silly Burghers of Sowerby Bridge'. The saga began when the Conservative council in the Yorkshire mill town removed the new tabloid *Sun* from the reading room in the public library, ostensibly because its new shape would not fit readily into the rods that held copies in place and prevented them being removed. But the real reason was soon revealed by the seventy-eight-year-old chairman of the Library Committee, Councillor Cecil Grenshaw, who had decided the paper had too much sex in it. As Stanley Robinson, the librarian, explained: 'I showed the committee six sample copies and they agreed with me that it is not the sort of paper they want. It is rubbish.'

The *Sun* fought back. Shrimsley dreamed up the 'silly burghers' jibe, backed up by an indignant leader. There was a graphic indication of the new priorities when the paper's star columnist, John Akass, was pulled out of Berlin, where he was waiting to interview Rudolf Hess in Spandau prison, for the more important job of slagging off the silly burghers. 'We should have been thrown out of better places than this,' Akass began, summarising the town as 'a glum pimple on the face of the Pennines'. His column was illustrated by a cheerful picture of five local lasses in mini-skirts.

The paper offered to pay for new library rods and provide free copies. The features department weighed in with a competition with a first prize of a free weekend in Sowerby Bridge. Second prize was a whole week. The winner, from Lichfield, Staffordshire, played the game by demanding a cash alternative. By coincidence she had been born in the town and, having got out, saw no reason to return. The silly burghers saga was flogged for sixteen months until Labour took control in the 1971 council elections, and the *Sun* went back on the shelves.

Like the rows with ITCA over its TV ads the *Sun* had moved on from reporting the news to making it. The silly burghers was what Lamb called a 'talking story' – it got the folks talking about the paper and on his side. Another opportunity to go into battle on the side of the folks came with the publication of the Longford Report on Pornography, produced by Lord Longford, a comical figure already marked down as a *Sun* target because of his campaign on behalf of the classic hate figure of Myra Hindley. Longford's summary of the *Sun* was caustic. He said the Press Council, the body set up by the newspaper industry to adjudicate on complaints about newspapers by the public, had 'not prevented the *Sun* and the *News of the World* from thriving on the uninhibited presentation of Mr Rupert Murdoch's particular Antipodean blend of erotica'.

Shrimsley's genius for pithy put-downs came into play and he instantly renamed Longford 'Lord Wrongford'. The day after the report was published Lamb printed a picture of a naked woman upside down and promised an 'Antipodean Erotica kit' for the next issue. As usual, when the puff went in, nobody had any idea what it would be, and the hastily cobbled-together package the next morning showed a naked lady in black sheets on a four-poster bed.

The bed was the prize, along with all the accoutrements of a typical *Sun* offer – a musk candle, champagne, oysters, a sunbed, a stereo with bedside controls, a two-month supply of vitamin pills and, of course, much, much more. Lamb's argument was that the discussion of sexual matters had become publicly acceptable, and the paper therefore had a positive duty to report it – but with taste and a sense of proportion. The *Sun* was saucy, even naughty, but it was all good clean fun. The sex material was informative and amusing and, unlike porn, was not designed to induce the 'the leer and the snigger'.

Apart from 'talking stories' Lamb's other major innovation on the news side of the paper was what became known as 'earthquake journalism'. If there was a really big story, like an IRA bomb outrage or a natural disaster, he would call the execs into his office any time up to half an hour before the first edition was due on the presses and announce: 'Clear the centrespread, clear pages 1, 2, 3, 4 and 5 – we can fill them all.' The execs, yet to receive a line of copy from the hacks, would twitch and ask, 'What with?' A frenzy of activity would follow as every available photograph, eye-witness report and expert opinion was grabbed and jammed into the paper.

Normally Bernard Shrimsley did much of the day-to-day editing of the paper, making hundreds of corrections and suggestions for improvement on the first proofs, leaving Lamb free to plan future coverage and deal with KRM. Most days his only 'hands-on' involvement would be to draw a plan for the front page using a thick black pencil. But on earthquake days he would be on the newsroom floor in person, supervising the whole frantic operation. The critics complained that newspapers were supposed to analyse the news and present what was important – not simply grab everything which was available. But the hacks on other papers were impressed.

The 'shit sheet' and 'six-month wonder' jibes were quietly dropped and admiration grew for the way the paper was surging ahead and breaking new ground. Word went round the pubs that the *Sun* was a kind of frontier country where you could break all the rules. The evidence could be seen every afternoon in the George, next to the Law Courts at the Strand end of the Street, where the *Sun's* complement of Aussie casuals from the Murdoch network got stuck into the then unknown delicacy of freezing cold Foster's lager. Unused to British ways, one had caused consternation when, told to do the routine police calls, instead of calling the Scotland Yard press office he picked up the phone and dialled 999.

Cartoonist Paul Rigby, one of the Aussie imports, livened up the proceedings by wearing a bowler hat made of kangaroo skin as the ultimate symbol of Anglo-Australian co-operation. The Aussie banter reminded the hacks of Barry MacKenzie, *Private Eye's* cartoon stereotype of Australian manhood, with phrases like 'point Percy at the porcelain', which signalled a visit to the George's urinals.

The horrible conditions in the rackety old Bouverie Street building only added to the air of adventure about the enterprise. At the beginning of the 1970s all newspaper premises were filthy places much more akin to factories and their position as one of the few industries left in the heart of London. But 30 Bouverie Street was much worse than most. The narrow side street off Fleet Street was clogged up every morning by articulated lorries queuing round the block to deliver the huge paper rolls for the print. They

42

were then craned into the building, looking like giant toilet rolls as they swung from chains and were lowered into the press hall in the basement. In the evening the street would be jammed again with vans taking the printed copies off the loading chutes to rush them to the main-line stations.

Inside, the building was cramped, dingy and smelly. The corridors and stairways were cluttered with leaky vats of acid and various other chemicals used in the process department to make plates for the presses. The ceilings were a tangle of ducting carrying electrical and drainage systems which had haphazardly evolved over the decades, defying any logical system of safety or planning. On one occasion an acid drain split overnight and the *News of the World* hacks arrived in the morning to find the typewriters on their desks reduced to smouldering and partly dissolved lumps of metal.

Facilities were rudimentary. The toilets were foul and swarmed with bluebottles in the summer. The canteen was filthy and infested with rats, giving the hacks another excuse to get out of the office into the Fleet Street pubs, where they could tap into the grapevine of what was happening on the other papers. Favourite was the bar on the top floor of the Tipperary pub – known as the 'Top of the Tip'.

But the squalor did make Bouverie Street an exciting and unpretentious place to work, with the day always dominated by the subconscious anticipation of press time, when there would be a deep rumble from the basement as the presses began to roll. The rumbling would build up momentum as the presses ran faster and faster until it settled down to a steady deep hum that vibrated through the building and made liquid in a glass tremble. And each turn of the rollers clicked up a tiny increase in the fortune steadily being amassed by Rupert Murdoch.

In the Top of the Tip, *Sun* subs boasted to their peers on rival papers about the *carte blanche* they were given to indulge in wildly punning text and headlines. To talented subs stuck in overstaffed rivals, the *Sun* looked increasingly inviting and fun. As ex-*Mirror* men, Lamb and Shrimsley, who took over as editor in 1972 when

Lamb was elevated to become the editorial director of both the *Sun* and the *News of the World*, knew exactly who to go for. They were beginning to find they could take their pick of frustrated Mirrormen and recruited the *Mirror*'s best three subs and other key hacks including the *Mirror*'s showbiz writer.

The news effort had also been considerably strengthened by the closure of the *Daily Sketch* and merger with the *Mail* which provided another source of recruits in the form of displaced hacks. Most important was Ken Donlan, who replaced Brian McConnell as news editor. Donlan was a godsend to Lamb and Shrimsley, the ideal man to meet Murdoch's demand that amid the sex and lightweight material there should be a solid news-reporting team. Lamb had known Donlan at the *Mail* and, since his own forte was not news reporting (Lamb had never been a reporter above local-newspaper level and had never learned shorthand) he felt confident in handing a lot of the news operation over to him.

Donlan was a small, round man with a quiet and unimposing manner which masked a ferocious temper. He was a severe disciplinarian who drove the reporters hard, insisting on basics like smart appearance. The hacks noticed that when he was angry he turned deeper and deeper shades of red.

As a devout Roman Catholic he viewed the Pacesetters' 'Willie Wall' with horror and even tried, with limited success, to make female hacks wear longer skirts and cover up exposed cleavage. All the reporters, male or female, were told they had to dress conservatively so they could be sent to events like funerals without having to change. His catchphrase was 'old boy'. Once a male reporter turned up in a sports jacket of which he was very proud. Donlan sidled up to him and whispered: 'I see you are not expecting to be sent to interview anyone of importance today. Let's go back to wearing a suit tomorrow, shall we, old boy?' The reporter took the point.

Now that Lamb was free to pick and choose staff he demanded total dedication in the war against the *Mirror*. He divided staff in his mind as either for him or against him – and being for him meant putting in as much work, dedication and enthusiasm to the enterprise as he and Shrimsley did. For many of the junior people he was a terrifying figure as he stalked stiffly about the office in his suit. They would keep their heads well down as he was going past, and found him rather like an authoritarian headmaster. Although he did not mean to, he often ruled by fear and the corridor to his office was known as 'The Giant's Causeway'.

Lamb could be ruthless if he felt an employee was slacking – like the time he sacked one of the duty lawyers for doing his own work in company time. Neither, in tune with his gritty northern background, did he suffer fools gladly, and he soon lost patience with employees who he felt were not pulling their weight. Some of the hacks who had joined reluctantly from the old *Sun* were paid off. Lamb regarded some of them as dope-smoking lefties and was glad to see the back of them, especially when they paraded about the newsroom kissing their £1,000 redundancy cheques and shouting, 'Freedom! Freedom, man!'

But hacks who were keen could join in the informal ideas sessions about the way the paper was going. After the first edition had gone to press Lamb would dispense whisky and hold court behind the huge desk in his private office. Murdoch disapproved strongly of these sessions on company premises, but Lamb would defend them by pointing out that everyone there was effectively working in their spare time.

If Murdoch was in London he would sometimes join in the discussions, contributing various wooden-headed editorial suggestions which Lamb constantly hoped would be quietly forgotten. The two men clashed often, particularly over the editorial, of which Lamb was so proud. Murdoch would compare the *Sun* and the *Mirror* page by page every day wherever he was in the world. If he was in London the exercise would take place in his Bouverie Street office. He would lay the papers next to each other and flick through the pages, complaining if he thought the *Mirror* had done better on any particular story. 'Why did you print this dreadful rubbish?' he would ask Lamb as he leafed through the pages. 'What's all this crap about poofters?' he would enquire when there was a fleeting reference to homosexuality.

Lamb began to tire of the relentless criticism. When he answered back too forcefully Murdoch would denounce him as a 'prickly Pommy bastard' and treat Lamb to his favourite anti-Pom joke: 'Y'know why the sun never set on the British Empire? God didn't trust the Poms after dark.' The joke was funny the first time, but Lamb ground his teeth as it was endlessly repeated.

And although Murdoch expected his every word to be listened to he did not always show the same interest in what Lamb and the others at the paper had to say. He would sit in meetings firing out questions into space and moving on to the next one before people had a chance to reply fully. He would leave meetings without explanation. Sometimes he would return after using the telephone, but other times, having lost interest in the topics under discussion, he would be gone for good and the meeting would terminate in disarray.

Lamb even pulled in help from the heavens as he struggled to appease KRM. Like many gamblers Murdoch is superstitious. Lamb used to lean on the paper's astrologer to doctor the Pisces entry to assure his chairman constantly that he would have a good day, and urge him to be full of goodwill and to cast his bread upon the waters. (During the war MI6 used a similar tactic by nobbling Hitler's personal astrologer to advise him against invading Britain.)

And Lamb had an unanswerable reply to all KRM's criticism. Under his editorship sales had continuously increased every year. In March 1978 the *Sun*, selling 3.8 million copies, overtook the *Mirror* and in June, helped by a series commemorating the death of Elvis Presley, regular daily sales went over four million. Despite this a curious air of anti-climax had engulfed the paper. When the *Sun* had passed two million in 1971 there had been a tremendous party at Murdoch's house in Epping Forest. All the editorial executives and many of the hacks had been invited and the evening had reached a riotous climax when Frank Nicklin threw Murdoch in the swimming pool. When the paper overtook the *Mirror* celebrations were much more muted. The subs, treated to a case of brown ale, were so unimpressed by the company's stinginess they dumped it outside Lamb's office in protest.

The edge had gone off life in the office and the hacks began to complain that Lamb had become stuffy and pompous. 'My door is always open,' he told them. 'I only keep it closed because I've got air conditioning.'

But as the *Sun*'s political stance switched from Labour to Tory, the hacks began to worry not that the door was closed, but who was behind it.

Chapter 4

The C2s See to It

From the beginning Rupert Murdoch was deeply aware that the *Sun* was in an extremely powerful position politically. As a newspaper for the working classes it was automatically expected to put its weight behind Labour – especially as it had evolved from the old *Daily Herald*. But instead of whole-heartedly backing him, Murdoch deliberately dangled the bait of the paper's support in front of the Prime Minister, Labour Party leader Harold Wilson.

As far as the readers were concerned it was a different matter. The newspaper epigram that was circulated about all the papers correctly identified that party politics was the last thing most of its readers were interested in. The joke, which began,

'*The Times* is read by the people who run the country; the *Mail* by the wives of the people who think they run the country,' ended, 'and the *Sun* by the people who don't care who runs the country as long as she's got big tits'.

Lamb was deeply resentful of critics of the first issues who sneered that the paper did not stand for anything. At the end of the first week in a '*Sun* Says' leader he fired back: 'The *Sun* has no party politics. It tries to judge political issues as they arise on their merits . . . The *Sun* is a radical newspaper. That is to say it believes in change for the better. But not in change for change's sake. . . . Above all, the *Sun* is on the side of the people . . . We are not going to bow to the Establishment in any of its privileged enclaves. Ever.' The paper committed itself on only two issues. It

48

was against hanging and corporal punishment and in favour of Britain's entry into the EEC.

The 'radical' stance also placed the *Sun* in a strong position to attack another aspect of the *Mirror's* soft underbelly – its entrenched support for Labour. And it put it squarely in line with the way thinking was changing in the political parties. Until the late 1960s it was thought that both political parties had solid and enthusiastic blocks of voters which, at election time, cancelled each other out. Victory at the polls, it was thought, depended on winning a tiny group of middle-of-the-road 'floating voters'. But research carried out privately by the Conservatives after their defeat in the 1966 election showed the electorate to be far more volatile than previously thought. Large numbers of voters were found to be 'weak' supporters of the major parties, with no strong ideological commitment. Instead they voted unenthusiastically and negatively for the party they saw as the lesser of two evils.

The Conservative historian Lord Blake, on the back of this research, defined these 'weak' voters as 'fairly young, slightly inclined to Labour, largely belonging to the skilled working class, primarily concerned with problems of housing, coloured immigration and the economy (prices and costs) rather than the condition of old-age pensioners. Only one in six was bothered about international affairs.' They were not highly educated, watched ITV rather than BBC, and either did not read a newspaper every day or were dissatisfied *Mirror* readers. In marketing-speak, which was beginning to invade politics, they were known as social group C2.

Although they did not know it, the C2s had been marked down as the new key to political power in Britain. They were discovered to be overwhelmingly concentrated in about eighty constituencies, many of which were marginal. The classic examples were southern or midlands light-engineering towns like Banbury, Stevenage and Swindon. It was quickly realised that a small shift among the C2s could deliver a parliamentary majority to the party they favoured, even if that party was lagging well behind in the national opinion polls. The *Sun's* 'radical' political stance, with its two fingers to the establishment and politicians of all parties, had enormous appeal for them.

Harold Wilson had weighed in from the start by writing a piece specially for the first issue and, between the launch and the general election seven months later, came to lunch at Bouverie Street three or four times and met Murdoch. Relations between the two men were described as cordial. Murdoch was not interested in becoming a newspaper baron like Cecil King, the owner of the *Mirror*, or using his papers as the archetypal Lord Beaverbrook had done with the *Express* and *Sunday Express* as an extension of a political party. He had had plenty of experience in Australia of using politicans to further his own interests rather than theirs.

Murdoch and Wilson, both consummate opportunists, under-stood each other perfectly. The Prime Minister had influence over both the print unions and the machinery of the Monopolies and Mergers Commission, which could prove useful to Murdoch, who gave him the endorsement he was seeking when the election was held in June 1970. The *Sun* told its readers that Wilson had a better team and that Labour cared more about ordinary people, social justice, equality of opportunity and quality of living – just like their caring paper.

Against expectations, Wilson lost. The Tories got a million more votes than Labour, mainly because of a shift among the C2s. The next day the *Sun* was unabashed. 'And Now, Ted, Take Charge,' it advised. 'Well done, Ted Heath. The British love to see an outsider come surging up to pass the favourite.' There had to be a villain somewhere, which was duly fingered. 'The election has been a rebuff to the opinion polls. That's good for democracy anyway,' the paper concluded brightly.

Heath had been elected on the same sort of 'free-market' economic platform to be offered at the end of the decade by Margaret Thatcher. But, unlike her, he began to reverse his policies as soon as unemployment started rising, and was then blown badly off course by the 1973–4 OPEC oil crisis. When inflation started roaring the power of the unions increased as workers pressed for pay increases and Heath's lame confrontations with them culminated in the disastrous three-day week. Murdoch, unimpressed, parted company with him.

But Murdoch had also fallen out with Wilson over another matter. When the Opposition leader complained that all the Fleet Street papers were conducting a 'personalised political vendetta' against him, Murdoch took it as a personal affront. He fired back at Wilson: 'A newspaper is not a private indulgence; it is not run as a personal hobby. If it were it would certainly fail . . . Mr Wilson is suggesting there is some sort of back-room or board-room process of news management. Well, coming from one of the great practitioners of news management, this really is rather rich.'

By now the C2s were as heartily sick of British politics as Murdoch, and their negative voting pattern was even more firmly established. The *Sun* caught their mood by resolutely refusing to back either of the parties in the February 1974 election, describing the choice as between 'The Devil and the Deep-Blue Sea'. Wilson won without an overall majority and held another election to try to consolidate his position in October. The *Sun* told its readers: 'WE'RE SICK OF THE TED AND HAROLD SHOW! May the Best Man Win – And Heaven Help Us If They Don't!' Labour won again, but with an overall majority of only three seats.

Wilson's fragile position in Parliament made him more dependent on press support than ever and he tried to mend fences with the *Sun* by inviting Lamb to Downing Street, where the editor approved highly of the excellent burgundy. In contrast Wilson stayed true to his 'man of the people' image by drinking Federation Bitter, the beer brewed for working men's clubs which Labour MPs were noisily lobbying to have installed in the House of Commons bar.

But Murdoch's distrust of Wilson was becoming stronger. He was particularly worried by the Prime Minister's inability to control the trade unions, now immensely strengthened by continuing inflation. Wilson had further strengthened union power with the 'social contract', under which the unions agreed to moderate their pay demands in return for higher levels of spending on public services. As a result strikes were beginning to build up and politics was dominated by a series of grubby haggles over pay policy.

Fleet Street itself was in dire economic straits. Inflation and the plummeting value of sterling more than doubled newsprint prices between 1970 and 1975. But the most serious problem was the power of the print union 'chapels', as the individual branches of print unions like the NGA, SOGAT, SLADE and NATSOPA were called. The power of the chapels was based on the very nature of newspapers, the most perishable of all commodities. As Lamb kept reminding execs at editorial conferences, the *Sun* could have the best stories in the world, but they would be useless if the paper was printed late and missed the trains because of union action.

The whip hand had been handed to the chapels principally by Beaverbrook in the 1950s, when he recklessly agreed year after year to special payments to churn out more copies of the *Express*. These were all consolidated, and by the 1970s the chapels, acting in concert to exploit each management in turn, had reduced the Street to virtual chaos.

The chapels had secured wages for the printers much higher than those of most journalists. They had also won outrageously high manning levels and the right to control the recruitment of printing staff, leading to what were known in the trade as 'old Spanish customs'. In many cases the unnecessary workers did not actually exist. Instead members of the same basic workforce signed on twice for the same job, using false names to get a second wage packet. On occasions the workers were so drunk at the end of the shift that they could not collect their second wage as they had forgotten the false name they had used. Others solved the problem by arrogantly using obvious frauds like 'Mickey Mouse' and 'Lester Piggott'.

On top of this nightmare Lamb was plunged into a different series of problems by endless demarcation disputes, many of which were caused by his radical approach to the design of the paper. The Bouverie Street print workers had learned their trade on the broadsheet *News of the World,* and were accustomed to rows of straight up and down type. Bloody-minded to begin with, they were also baffled by Lamb's bitty approach to layout and some even assumed at first that the editor did not know what he was doing. The compositors, who assembled the pages, would patiently explain: 'The type goes here, you see, Mr Lamb, and the pictures go there. That's the way a craftsman does the job.'

In exasperation the editor turned increasingly to the paper's graphic art department, staffed by younger and more flexible art-school-trained designers. Most of the art department's staff had previously worked on magazines or in advertising and they were much better than traditional compositors at producing the sort of graphics-splattered, magazine-like pages Lamb wanted. But under union demarcation rules the art department was allowed only to produce graphics and process photographs for the paper. These would then be turned into zinc blocks and handed over to the compositors who would slot them into place along with the type on the page.

Lamb and his designer Vic Giles hit upon the ruse of treating whole pages as graphics, allowing the art department to produce them as one big zinc block ready to go to press without any further work. But when this happened the compositors furiously complained that he was taking work away from them, and their NGA chapel threatened industrial action. A compromise was reached: the art department would first produce a whole page as one block. Then it would chop it up into pieces. The NGA compositors would then clamp the pieces back together again to produce the final page. On one occasion, the art department, getting fed up, cut up a page block into 500 pieces, one for each word of the feature, as an acid comment on what was happening. But the NGA comps were delighted because extra hands then had to be hired to put it all back together again, and they even tried to make it standard practice.

Sometimes in the scramble to meet deadlines Lamb would be too late to order the blocks to be cut up. The NGA chapel would then black all art department work for a day. Lamb would fill the gaps where the blacked graphics or photos should have appeared with craven apologies which always blamed the art department and their SLADE union chapel, rather than the more powerful NGA. As a result SLADE got a terrible reputation for always being on strike and readers bombarded the paper with SLADE hate mail, including Christmas cards wishing them a miserable holiday and telling them to 'fuck off back to Moscow'.

Lamb badly upset the NGA only once, when he left SLADE off one of his apologies, merely saying 'production workers' were to blame for the gap in the paper. The same message also revealed their wages – 'normal service has been interrupted by *Sun* production workers, some of whom', he added (ignoring the terrible secret that many drew multiple pay packets), 'earn more than £160 a week.' When John Breen, Deputy Father of the NGA composing room Chapel on the *News of the World*, saw the first copies off the press he went berserk.

Breen, a wiry, aggressive-looking Cockney, gathered chapel officials from the various departments and led a delegation into Lamb's office. 'That's right out of fucking order that is,' he shouted, stabbing the offending message with his finger. 'Printing our fucking wages on the front page of your shitty newspaper.' Lamb silently edged to a position of safety behind his giant desk. Breen leaned forward and snarled: 'If you don't pull that out I'll pull your fucking head off.'

Lamb drew himself up and announced pompously: 'I shall do no such thing. I shall uphold freedom on this paper, and the editor's right to edit.'

The other union officials sat quietly on Lamb's white three-piece suite, covering it with ink and oil stains. Lamb eyed the damage with horror – these people were not called the Inkies for nothing. The others were less upset than Breen and kept saying, 'Right, John, I think we've made our point,' and getting up to go.

'Siddown!' Breen snarled at them and continued hammering at Lamb. In the end he had to be pulled out of the office. The unions agreed that the damage had already been done and resumed normal work on that shift. But Lamb never repeated the trick.

Lamb's revenge came in the limited form of making ferocious speeches at newspaper-industry conferences, which echoed Murdoch's concern about the effect of union action on his profits. Lamb railed against the power of the chapels and the supposed extreme left-wing conspiracy to infiltrate newspapers. This lined him up with a powerful lobby on the right wing of the Conservative Party determined to tackle trade union power. The Tory right-wingers, intellectually led by Keith Joseph, were now blaming Ted Heath as well as Wilson for caving in to the unions and agreeing to 'consensus' politics, and in 1975 the right-wing lobby managed to get rid of Heath, replacing him with Margaret Thatcher and a new platform of curbing union power and 'rolling back' socialism.

With Mrs Thatcher's arrival the Ted and Harold Show which the *Sun* complained of was over. Now there was an alternative leader whom Murdoch decided was worthy of the *Sun's* whole-hearted support. As Conservative leader Mrs Thatcher could depend on the support of the *Mail* and *Express* in the mass market. But both papers were in effect preaching to the converted. The *Daily Mail* with its 1.5 million circulation did sterling work smoothing the feathers of loyal Tory footsoldiers after the damaging internal struggle to get rid of Heath. The *Daily Express* was still the main gun in the Tory media arsenal, but it had an ageing readership and circulation was down to three million, a fall of almost a million since 1970. Mrs Thatcher and her advisers knew they needed the *Sun's* young C2 audience if they were going to win the next general election.

In her previous incarnation as Education Secretary in the Heath Cabinet Mrs Thatcher had been a *Sun* target – a stuffy figure ranking alongside the silly burghers of Sowerby Bridge and Lord 'Wrongford' Longford. In 1970 the *Sun* had given her the famous tag 'Maggie Thatcher – Milk Snatcher' after she withdrew free school milk (Shrimsley later claimed, half seriously, that Mrs Thatcher won the 1979 election with the support of grateful first-time voters she had saved from the socialist tyranny of having state-subsidised milk pumped into them).

55

At the time Mrs Thatcher had feared she would never live down the 'Milk Snatcher' tag and that it might end her political career. She became immensely depressed about it and complained bitterly about the *Sun* to her husband Denis. 'Why don't you chuck it all in?' Denis had sympathised when the family were together for Christmas. 'You don't have to put up with this. Why go on?' His wife was in tears as she fixed the *Sun* and its cruel, left-wing editor 'Red Larry' Lamb in her mind. She looked up with the now familiar steely glare and rasped: 'I'll see them in hell first. I will never be driven anywhere against my will.'

Five years later Mrs Thatcher's attitude towards the filthy *Sun* had changed remarkably. All was sweetness and light as she and her 'boys', as key advisers like Geoffrey Howe and Nicholas Ridley were known at the *Sun*, began to drop in on Lamb's alcohol-smoothed 'chewing the fat' sessions after the first edition had gone away in the early evening. 'Maggie' would begin by accepting a glass of Lamb's whisky – an unaccustomed tipple which the hacks noted made her eyes water slightly and caused her to flush bright pink. As the meeting warmed up she would slump into an armchair, cross her legs demurely and gently flex her ankle, allowing her shoe to dangle from the tip of her toe. Lamb assumed a commanding but relaxed position, informally resting his backside on his desk.

When the hacks asked questions Mrs Thatcher would answer inconclusively, or descend into deep and puzzled thought aided by more shoe-dangling. Finally she would turn her eyes upwards towards Lamb and in a quiet, concerned voice ask: 'What do *you* think, Larry?' Lamb would puff up with pride and begin pompously expounding his thoughts on the country's problems. As he droned on Mrs Thatcher would nod steadily, mustering as much rapt attention as the whisky would allow. 'You know, that's marvellous,' she would say finally. 'If only I had people like you who really know how to communicate. Absolutely marvellous.'

Lamb would swell up again, and dish out more whisky with a flourish. Mrs Thatcher's courtship was so effective that Lamb finally decided she had become his 'tool' for bringing about a

Sun-led political sea-change in the country. Shrimsley, although a firm supporter, was far less gushing in his praise for her. But his moderating influence on the more emotional Lamb was reduced in 1975 when he moved to the floor below the *Sun* in Bouverie Street to become editor of the *News of the World*.

The steady switch to backing the Tories was unpopular with many of the hacks, the majority of whom were Labour supporters. But like others in Fleet Street they had resigned themselves to supporting the prejudices of their proprietors. There was even pride in the professionalism involved in setting personal opinions to one side and adding the required bias by writing that a by-election winner had either 'scraped in by a whisker' or 'romped home', depending on their party.

Roger Carroll, the Labour-supporting political editor, left the paper to work for the party and was replaced by Walter Terry, a hard-faced Tory hack recruited from the *Daily Express*. Murdoch further strengthened Tory input by 'suggesting' that Lamb should hire leader-writer Ronnie Spark to add an uncompromising Thatcherite line to 'The *Sun* Says' opinion slot. Spark had studied history at Oxford, where he had known Murdoch, and then worked for the *Sunday Express*, where he became a protégé of the paper's cantankerous editor John Junor, the leading practitioner of Tory political abuse. Spark was grateful to get the job as he had just been sacked for fiddling his expenses.

Murdoch always insisted that the *Sun* maintain a strong political and industrial reporting team to counter Lamb's natural inclination to make the paper lightweight. If Murdoch was in London Lamb would call Terry into the office and say: 'Look, can you do some serious political features? I've got to have something to show KRM, otherwise he'll think it's all just froth. Do a big interview with a politician – I'll give it a lot of space.'

Terry was delighted to help. The political scene was full of drama, with plenty to write about. Wilson had retired as Labour leader in 1976 to be replaced by James Callaghan. The avuncular Farmer Jim inherited a government in deep trouble. His majority was so small sick Labour MPs had to be brought into the House of

Commons in wheelchairs to vote. In March 1977 Callaghan signed the Lib-Lab pact with Liberal leader David Steel in order to avoid a general election, but the arrangement was so unstable that the government's fall was predicted almost daily. Terry became the star of the morning news conferences – brisk affairs chaired by Lamb which planned the day's edition – repeatedly predicting that the government would not survive the day's vote in Parliament, and dramatically telling Lamb to be ready for a special edition marking the announcement of a general election.

The high drama in politics was matched by growing industrial problems. The original 'social contract' deal with the unions was now in tatters as the government could not afford the higher public spending it had promised in return for wage restraint. A new wave of strikes hit the country, elevating the importance of the industrial relations staff on the paper.

Until now the job of reporting strikes had been the primary responsibility of Keith Mason, the industrial editor Lamb had recruited from the old *Sun*. But now he was to be retired to be replaced by John Kay, a general reporter who had been working on the industrial staff. Kay was an ex-minor public schoolboy from St Peter's School York who was very keen and always seemed to be very much on top of things. But his manner was all a front.

Kay's main strength was as a writer. His party piece in the Top of the Tip was picking up one of the Unpopulars and effortlessly reading out its lead story in *Sun*-ese as he mentally rewrote it on the spot. But he was much less confident about going out 'on the road' to interview people. He was sent to the 1977 TUC Congress at Blackpool in September for Mason to smooth the changeover by introducing him to top-level contacts including Callaghan and Len Murray, the TUC General Secretary. But, suddenly gripped by the responsibility of the job, Kay essentially had a nervous breakdown and locked himself in his hotel room. At the end of the conference he emerged and was taken home to try to pull himself together.

He arrived back distraught and told his Japanese wife, Harue, whom he had married a year before, that he could not do the job.

The pressure was too much for him. Neither could he resign, as that would mean his progress up the journalistic ladder would be over. He was going to kill himself, he announced. His wife was equally upset, as her family had disowned her when she married a Westerner and she would be left alone in the world.

Kay, by this time temporarily deranged, saw the depth of her problem and decided that it would be better if she died with him. He killed her by drowning her in the bath and then attempted suicide himself by cutting his wrists, putting his head in the gas oven, hanging himself and finally jumping out of the window. His fall was broken by some plastic dustbins. He then staggered to his car and drove away, cannoning off cars parked at the kerbside and finally going head-on into a bridge. He was found by the police naked and covered in blood.

Kay's father blamed the *Sun* for the tragedy, and Lamb was sympathetic, agreeing it had been a mistake to place him under so much stress. When Kay was remanded in custody, charged with murder, the *Sun* hired John Mathew, one of the best QCs in the country, to defend him when the case came up at St Albans Crown Court in December.

Lamb sent a letter to the court that said the newspaper would take Kay back whenever he was fit enough and it was allowed. Kay, 33, pleaded not guilty to murder but guilty to manslaughter on the grounds of diminished responsibility; this was accepted by the court. He was sentenced to be admitted for treatment at Friern Barnet psychiatric hospital in north London.

The *Sun* continued to look after Kay's interests and he received regular visits from many members of staff. Lamb fulfilled his promise by taking him back on condition that he be confined to the office. The uxoricide officially became a taboo subject.

The *Sun's* industrial coverage carried on without Kay and each fresh report of a strike was another nail in the coffin of the Labour government. The growing industrial crisis culminated in a rash of public sector strikes in the winter of 1978. Rubbish piled up in the streets and, in some places, NUPE grave-diggers refused to bury the dead. TV was full of scenes of militant pickets huddled around braziers. With due apologies to Shakespeare, Lamb hit the political bullseye for Mrs Thatcher by christening the crisis 'THE WINTER OF DISCONTENT'. When Callaghan returned from a summit meeting on the sunny tropical island of Guadeloupe Lamb scored again by inventing the quote 'CRISIS? WHAT CRISIS?' and putting it in Callaghan's mouth, claiming poetic licence.

After the failure of Callaghan's desperate effort to hang on in the hope of better news, he was forced to dissolve Parliament in March. The Tory machine, anticipating Callaghan's fall, had already geared up for the election and was certain of the *Sun*'s support. Lamb was befriended by Gordon Reece and Tim Bell, the key Tory media advisers retheming Mrs Thatcher for her premiership. Reece was in charge of her TV image, which he 'softened' by coaching away the harsh middle-class edge in her voice and giving her a new hairstyle. Bell, then chairman of Saatchi and Saatchi, ran her advertising campaign. At regular meetings Lamb was given the freedom to expound at length on the merits of himself and the paper at communicating with the readers, and about how he and KRM understood both the 'folks' thesis and the importance of television. Bell and Reece would nod sagely.

Lamb also became a regular visitor to Mrs Thatcher's house in Flood Street, Chelsea, where the election strategy was planned, to explain the workings of the minds of the common people. Mrs Thatcher was deeply grateful for headlines like 'WINTER OF DISCONTENT' and 'CRISIS? WHAT CRISIS?' and Lamb provided more help by writing speeches or parts of speeches for her. In return Mrs Thatcher gave the *Sun* the inside track on the Tory campaign, carefully briefing the paper on who was being planned to emerge as star performers.

Both Lamb and Murdoch saw the central point that the 1979 election was not about parties, but about personalities, in line with the growing influence of TV. The Tory manifesto and Mrs Thatcher's speeches were tailored to the three C2 preoccupations of housing, living costs and immigration, including the sensational offer of selling off council houses cheap.

On polling day Lamb weighed in with his biggest single contribution – an extraordinary 1,700-word leader. The hacks hooted with laughter at this, because for years he had been sounding off about his own genius for putting things briefly. Huge jokes followed in the Top of the Tip about the readers' lips wearing out as they struggled through the dozens of paragraphs.

Lamb had composed the leader by asking senior colleagues to put their views in writing, and then welding them together with the help of Ronnie Spark. Strapped 'A message to Labour supporters' the headline read: 'VOTE TORY THIS TIME. IT'S THE ONLY WAY TO STOP THE ROT'. Then it turned to fill the whole of page 2 with a wall of type, making it by far the longest piece of political writing the paper had ever run, and far longer – as KRM pointed out acidly – than any leader to come out of Fleet Street on that day.

> This is D-day,' 'D for decision. The first day of the rest of our lives. The *Sun* today wishes particularly to address itself to traditional supporters of the Labour Party. . . .
>
> The *Sun* is not a Tory newspaper. . . . The *Sun* is above all a RADICAL newspaper. And we believe that this time the only radical proposals being put to you are being put by Maggie Thatcher and her Tory team. . . .
>
> The choice you have to make today is quite simply the choice between freedom and shackles.
>
> FREEDOM to run your life as YOU want to run it. Or to be shackled by the bureaucrats and political bully boys. . . .
>
> FREEDOM to work, with or without a union card – or to be shackled to a dole queue in a declining economy. . . .
>
> FREEDOM to spend your money or save it – or to be shackled to an endless cash crisis because the taxman has sliced away your money before you've ever seen it. . . .
>
> FREEDOM to live life YOUR way.'

Labour was castigated:

> 'The party has become the refuge of militants, Marxist bullies, and class war warriors . . . it has all but destroyed the spirit of Britain. . . . That is the heaviest charge to lay against this Government. That it has contrived to destroy Britain's belief in itself.'

61

But Mrs Thatcher was cast in the role of national saviour:

> We believe that under new leadership, the will to make Britain proud again can be revived. That is what matters. THE WILL. . . .
> With Jim (What crisis?) Callaghan we looked into the abyss. With Margaret Thatcher there is a chance for us to look again to the skies. . . .
> The *Sun* says: Vote Tory. Stop the Rot. There may not be another chance.

Thatcher won the election with 43.9 per cent of the vote against 36.9 per cent for Labour, giving her a comfortable parliamentary majority of fifty-seven. The C2 strategy had worked. The 9 per cent swing among the C2s was almost double the national average of 5.1 per cent, and delivered a string of marginal seats in the south, midlands and north west. Most of the fifty-one seats gained were on the original Tory target list of eighty C2-dominated constituencies. The biggest scalp was Shirley Williams, a Labour Cabinet minister, unseated by the mass desertion of C2 working-class voters in Hertford.

The contribution made by newspapers to the outcome in general elections is notoriously hard to judge. But Mrs Thatcher was personally very grateful to the *Sun*. She sent Lamb what he described as a 'charming' letter, thanking him for his help and telling him she would strive to be worthy of his support, and the support of *Sun* readers. Shortly afterwards the hacks arrived at Bouverie Street to find the filthy corridors and lifts bedecked with blue bunting, rosettes, union jacks and portraits of the new Prime Minister put up to mark her attendance at a *Sun* victory celebration.

It was not long before Lamb got a more personal reward, along with Ronnie Spark's old editor John Junor at the *Sunday Express*. Both were knighted in the 1980 New Year's honours list. Victor Matthews, the new owner of the *Express*, was ennobled at the same time. *Daily Mail* editor David English had to wait until

1982 for his knighthood: a suitable period had to elapse before the fiasco of the *Mail's* British Leyland slush fund story in 1977 could be forgotten.

After the investiture Lamb insisted on being called 'Sir Larry' in the office, attracting a mixture of hilarity and resentment from the hacks. KRM was not impressed. He loathed the whole honours system on principle as the pinnacle of the patronage afflicting class-ridden British society. The fact that a knighthood had been given to such an inept businessman as William Carr, from whom he had bought the *News of the World*, was enough to put him off the institution for life.

More importantly Murdoch did not want the editor of the most important newspaper in his growing Empire to entertain delusions of grandeur and lose his anti-establishment edge. Perhaps, he thought, it was time he found another 'outsider' like himself – a younger and more energetic man, not interested in joining the club and prepared to break the established rules, just as Lamb had once done.

PART
TWO

Chapter 5

<u>A Star Is Born</u>

In 1980 Murdoch was back in England with a vengeance, moving to expand the British end of the Empire by buying *The Times* and the *Sunday Times*. The two papers had been put up for sale by a disillusioned Lord Thomson, who had lost his battle with the print unions to introduce new technology after a stoppage which had kept both papers off the streets for nearly a year. The prospect of the self-styled Top People's Paper falling into the hands of the 'Dirty Digger' caused consternation. Bitter controversy broke out over the government's failure to refer the purchase to the Monopolies and Mergers Commission because of hotly disputed figures purporting to prove that both papers were loss-makers. But Murdoch got what was seen as his reward for political support when the government put on a three-line whip in the Commons and decisively defeated the motion for referral.

The purchase dramatically changed Larry Lamb's position in News International, the company controlling the British operation of Murdoch's Empire. As well as being editor of the *Sun* Lamb was also editorial director of the company, but he knew this control would not now extend to the two new papers. Lamb believed he was capable of it, but the 'tits and bums' label he had acquired at the *Sun* ruled it out in practical terms.

Instead Murdoch gave *The Times*'s editorship to another archetypal Yorkshireman, Harry Evans, previously editor of the more populist *Sunday Times*. Evans, another 'prickly Pommie', had attracted guru-scale admiration from quality hacks for the

Sunday Times's campaigning and investigative journalism through its Insight team and exposure of scandals like thalidomide. It was obvious News International would not be big enough to accommodate both personalities without clashes, even if they were accidental.

The crunch came when the new American President, Ronald Reagan, was shot on 31 March 1981. It was the kind of story which Lamb, with his mastery of 'earthquake journalism', revelled in. Within three minutes of the news dropping he had ordered one feature on the history of Presidential assassinations and a second on Reagan's health record. A few minutes later the NGA comps were breaking up the old front page and assembling the new one he had just sketched out – 'REAGAN SHOT' in letters six inches high. The page was running within an hour, the whole paper had been revised within two, and by the final edition more than six pages were being run on the story.

The next day Murdoch called Lamb from New York. 'I know you were the best of the tabloids,' he told him. 'Harry told me.' Lamb kept quiet, but inside he was boiling with resentment. As Lamb put it, 'Those who had toiled in the Murdoch vineyard through the heat and burden of the day' bitterly resented what they saw as this patronising attitude. He and the other senior executives at the *Sun* were having to stand by while Murdoch took his editorial advice from Evans and other people on *The Times*, which, as they saw it, had been as big a failure as the *Sun* had been a success.

The new anger was piled on top of increasing bitterness at the *Sun* that Murdoch was using the paper's hard-won profits to subsidise *The Times*'s continuing losses, cutting budgets and switching his attention and resources to his new baby. The hacks at the *Sun* shared Lamb's resentment, and naturally sympathised with his complaints. But at the same time many thought he had lost his edge. His insistence that he now be addressed as 'Sir Larry', and the longer and longer hours spent in his office with the door shut, stoked a feeling among them that he was becoming aloof and pompous. Matters were not helped by Lamb falling out of a tree while gardening at his Oxfordshire mansion making his back trouble worse and obliging him to hold himself stiffly. The stiff back gave an additional regal air to his increasingly rare progressions through the newsroom.

The paper had been once round the wheel, and the initial impact had been lost. Page Three was in a time warp; the light-hearted cheeky sex formula was jaded and had been overtaken by the women's magazines like *Cosmopolitan* which had been launched under the editorship of Lamb's first women's editor, Joyce Hopkirk. The *Mirror* had stabilised, folding in the doings of TV stars as news and using TV advertising which bettered the *Sun* commercials, which now looked old and hackneyed.

On the national scene things were looking grim for Lamb's great hero Mrs Thatcher. She had signalled her refusal to bend to the growing storm with her defiant 'lady's not for turning' speech at the party conference the previous October. But her government, led by the monetarist policies of Sir Keith Joseph, was daily growing more unpopular as unemployment passed 2.5 million and redundancies ran at 4,000 a month. As a Labour-supporting paper the change on the political scene was working in the *Mirror's* favour and it had gratefully passed across the mantle of backing an unpopular government to the *Sun*.

But Murdoch was more worried about the appearance on the national newspaper scene of a new rival for the *Sun*: the *Daily Star*, a Labour-supporting paper launched in Manchester three years previously which, after expanding steadily on a regional basis, had just gone national. The launch of the *Star* in 1978 had caused the first year-on-year decline in the *Sun's* circulation since Murdoch had bought the paper and Lamb had failed to win back the lost readers.

The *Star* was the creation of Victor Matthews, an unlikely newspaper baron who had fought his way up from his Islington working-class origins through the building trade to become Nigel Broackes's strong-arm man at Trafalgar House, which had bought Express Newspapers in 1977.

Matthews had soon found the Fleet Street print unions a tougher nut to crack than UCATT and the National Union of

Seamen, which he had dealt with through the company owner-ship of the *QE2*. The London chapels had called his bluff when he threatened to move the whole *Express* operation to Manchester, underlining the fact that newspapers could not be sent away like his ships for cheaper work to be done elsewhere. Instead, in company with his smooth managing director, Jocelyn Stevens, Matthews had decided to soak up the group's spare printing and editorial capacity by starting the *Star* in the north. The decision had also marked the end of the *Express*'s delusion that it was a mass-circulation popular paper, leaving it to concentrate on its mid-market battle with the *Mail*.

Like the *Sun*, the *Star* had been thrashed out over a long working lunch. Derek Jameson, the original 'Sid Yobbo' of *Private Eye*, had been installed as editorial director of both the *Express* and the new paper. Jameson had been quoted in the Unpopulars saying that the new paper would consist of 'tits, bums, QPR and roll your own fags'. Claiming to have been misreported, he then told the new *Star* hacks in a memo: 'No newspaper in history lost sales by projecting beautiful birds. Sex sells – that goes for pictures and words. So the *Star* will have its daily quota. Bigger and better than anyone else.' The result had been 'Starbirds', the first tabloid pin-ups in full colour (though somewhat poxy), and instantly adjudged more sleazy and raunchy than Page Three.

Australian Lloyd Turner had been recruited from the *Express* backbench as editor, and the paper had been launched just twelve weeks after the original idea, attracting an injunction from the *Morning Star* for passing off its title. There had been much guffawing in the Street when the judge dismissed the attempt, saying only 'a moron in a hurry' would confuse the two papers. Popular wisdom held that this was precisely who the *Star* was aiming at. Its target market consisted of young male C2, D and Es.

The *Star*'s regional launch in 1978 aped the *Sun* formula by using saturation TV advertising, and crucially undercut the *Sun*'s 7p cover price by selling at 6p. Murdoch was alarmed that the *Star* could do to the *Sun* what the *Sun* had once done to the *Mirror*. And he was irritated by Lamb's dismissal of the threat, made in the same sort of terms as those used by the *Mirror* to write off the infant *Sun*. The *Star*, Lamb had said, was 'a cynical marketing exercise', and not 'a living, breathing newspaper' like the one he had created. (Jocelyn Stevens fired back that the new paper was not a 'cynical' marketing exercise, but a 'calculated' one.)

Both the *Mirror* and the *Sun* had both lost readers to the new paper, but the *Sun* was being harder hit. Circulation was down from the peak of over four million in 1978 to 3.6 million in 1981, when the *Star* went national. The gap between the *Sun* and the *Mirror* was closing as both lost readers. The joke among the hacks was that the *Mirror* would soon 'undertake' them.

Murdoch, who did not find it at all funny, moved to reorganise the *Sun* to see off the threat. He began the offensive with the simplest and boldest initiative of all, by cutting the *Sun*'s cover price by 2p to match the *Star* at 10p – a move described in the Unpopulars as 'a bombshell'. He then held the new low price for ten weeks, putting on 100,000 readers in the first month, and in addition authorised a TV ad campaign on a scale not seen since the early days.

Lamb believed the *Star* was selling well on the back of its new newspaper 'bingo' competition and was in favour of the *Sun* countering with its own version of the game. But he thought the price-cut was a panic measure and wrote to Murdoch setting out a long list of complaints – including the fact that Murdoch had moved his private office from Bouverie Street to *The Times* building half a mile away in Grays Inn Road. Murdoch curtly replied by suggesting that Lamb was tired and should take a six months' sabbatical.

Lamb, knowing full well what 'sabbatical' meant, said he would think about it over the weekend, but the next day an impatient KRM rang and said: 'I must have your decision. I have schedules to keep.' Lamb agreed to take the sabbatical, and his departure from Bouverie Street was as down-beat as the sour launch-night party. He simply called a few hacks into his office, announced that he was going, and shared a bottle of champagne before kissing the women members of his prized Pacesetters team goodbye, one by one.

Harry Evans did not last much longer at *The Times*. He brought in some of his favourite journalists from the *Sunday Times*, sharpened up the headlines, improved the layout and introduced the Information Service on the back page. But the rifts between his new people and the old *Times* staff led to serious problems, and, thirteen months after his appointment, on 9 March 1982 Murdoch asked for his resignation, telling him: 'The paper's in chaos and the senior staff are in turmoil.'

Evans went to America and chronicled his experiences in his book, *Good Times, Bad Times*, in which he defended his editorship and described how Murdoch had tried to bend the paper politically. One anecdote told of Murdoch gouging his ballpoint through a story by reporter Lucy Hodges which summarised evidence to the Scarman inquiry into the 1981 riots. 'Why do you use these Commies?' he asked. Evans replied that Hodges was a good reporter and it was absurd to call her a Communist.

Evans was replaced by his deputy, Charles Douglas-Home, nephew of the former Prime Minister and a caricature of an English country gentleman, who wore old shirts and jackets in the office and loved fox-hunting. In his book Evans revealed how during the height of the row over his succession Douglas-Home rang him and shouted: 'You little fucker, I'll come over there and wring your neck. You've told people Larry Lamb will be the next editor if you go, you bastard you.' Douglas-Home took the job despite Evans's assertion that he had told him in the earlier stages of the fracas over the sale of the papers: 'I would never work for that monster Murdoch.'

As Murdoch's skullduggery fuelled the Fleet Street rumour machine, bets were taken in the pubs on who would emerge as the new editor of the *Sun*. The clear favourite was Nick Lloyd, the youngest member of Lamb's original executive team, who was currently deputy editor of the *Sunday Mirror*. Shortly after the *Sun*'s launch Murdoch had picked Lloyd out as a high-flier, giving him experience as assistant editor of both the *Sun* and the *News of the World*. But a year previously, frustrated at Murdoch's failure to offer him full editorship, he had moved sideways to the Mirror Group and was biding his time. Murdoch called Lloyd at his office and asked to see him. Lloyd put down the phone. 'This is it!' he thought, and rushed round to Murdoch's office at *The Times*, wondering whether he would be offered the editorship of the *Sun* or the *News of the World*, which had fallen vacant at the same time.

Instead he got a shock. Murdoch told him the new editor of the *News of the World* was to be Barry Askew. 'Barry Who?' Lloyd asked in astonishment. Murdoch explained that Askew, nicknamed the Beast, was the award-winning editor of the Lancashire *Evening Post*. He was virtually unknown on the Street but, Murdoch said, he had just the sort of gritty northern approach he wanted.

Then Murdoch delivered his second surprise. He was going to give the editorship of the *Sun* to Kelvin MacKenzie, whom Lloyd only knew from his time on the *Sun* as a raucous sub working his way up through the ranks. Lloyd was dumbfounded and asked mournfully: 'Why did you ask to see me then?'

Murdoch smiled. 'I want you back, Nick. You've got a great contribution to make. I want you to be Kelvin's deputy. You'd make a great team. You could be the Lamb and Shrimsley of your generation.' But Lloyd was having none of it. 'You know I want to be an editor,' he said, 'I'm ready for it. I couldn't take the deputy's job – it would be a step backwards for me.'

Murdoch acknowledged that choosing MacKenzie was a gamble and said that Lloyd could still end up as editor of either the *Sun* or the *News of the World* if things didn't work out. Lloyd was finding the conversation odd, with long silences during which the two men just looked at each other. Murdoch offered him more money to take the job, but Lloyd still turned him down. The two men agreed to differ and parted without acrimony.

Murdoch's choice of MacKenzie as editor was a surprise not just to Lloyd, but to everyone on the Street, and particularly to the hacks on the *Sun*. It shouldn't have been. In 1973 Murdoch had defined his ideal editor in a speech to a newspaper industry conference. It was not a matter of paper qualifications or the correct progress through the pecking order: 'A newspaper editor either has it or he hasn't. A good editor has to train himself. He can't be manufactured,' Murdoch had said, adding: 'and he has to work like blazes.'

MacKenzie fitted that description precisely. As many people surveying his Empire have pointed out, Murdoch does not always choose the best editor, but he chooses the right one. And in MacKenzie he had picked out the right man to take the *Sun* formula further down the line by reshaping it with a harder edge for the emerging decade.

Kelvin Calder MacKenzie had been born in October 1946, the eldest of three sons of journalist parents. His father Ian had just emerged from the war with his attitude to life toughened up by a period in a Japanese prisoner-of-war camp, which also left him with a slight limp. He and his wife Mary were now working hard to consolidate their position of middle-class respectability.

The family had settled in Camberwell, south London, in a high-rent London County Council flat on a neat estate, known as 'posh', in a nice area of what was otherwise a rough, crime-ridden district. The flat was a comfortable alternative to owning their own house, which was rarer in those days even for the reasonably well off. It did not carry the cachet of being working class, and put them way above the more unfortunate families forced to inhabit the surrounding slums which had survived the blitz or the low-quality high-rise council blocks which steadily replaced them.

The three MacKenzie brothers, Kelvin, Craig and Drew, noisily competed with each other for the attention of their workaholic parents who were both on the local weekly *South London Observer*, where Ian was news editor and Mary was chief reporter. Ian MacKenzie was a strict, austere figure, with horn-rimmed glasses and prematurely greying hair, who looked and acted the tough newspaper man. Mary, in contrast, both spoke and dressed like a fashion model, and was renowned for her extraordinary beauty. She had a gentler nature than her husband, which she put to good use in charming stories out of the tough south London coppers.

74

The couple supplemented their salaries by selling stories to the London evening papers, being paid by the line, which put a premium on long and lurid crime stories which were plentiful enough in their part of town and neighbouring docklands. Their dedication to the task soon earned them the soubriquet of 'The Lineage Kings of South London'. Invited round to dinner one Sunday, one of Kelvin's friends found Mary in the kitchen, while Ian typed away at his lineage on the dining-room table.

They were both Tories, though Mary was the more committed, and later became press officer to Sir Horace Cutler, the Conservative leader of the pre-Livingstone GLC when it was said that hacks would turn up at press conferences just to gaze upon her. The MacKenzie philosophy was hard work, enterprise and making your way in the world and they practised what they preached by leaving the council flat and moving to a large, comfortable house in leafy Dulwich.

Kelvin was sent to nearby Alleyn's School, now a minor public school but at the time a direct-grant grammar. He was in Spurgeon's House, which had pink as its house colour, and always said afterwards that he hated it, though he was remembered as an unremarkable boy, with his younger brothers making more impact. He left after taking seven O-levels and passing only English literature. On his own admittance he had read only the crammer. Another attempt a year later at Brixton College was even less successful. This time he failed them all.

At the age of seventeen Kelvin started work as a district reporter on the *South-East London Mercury*, attending day release to learn shorthand and newspaper law. But mostly he learned on the job, backed up by coaching from his parents, who taught him that journalism was a matter of determination, confidence and knowing the tricks of a 'good operator' who was always able to 'deliver' on stories, no matter how thin the information. From the beginning of his newspaper career he exhibited the enormous self-confidence that was to be his main asset in life. In his first week he announced to Pat Collins, a fellow reporter: 'Apart from you and a couple of others, everyone else here is a wanker.'

In contrast to the world of Alleyn's, and the plodding route it provided into one of the proper professions, MacKenzie had found his *métier* in journalism with its emphasis on superficial summary rather than exhaustive knowledge and understanding. As Murdoch fully understood, what was needed above all was energy, determination and an elusive 'knack', which could not be taught. Either you had it, or you didn't. And MacKenzie had an abundance of knack. Underneath the razor-sharp wit was an incisive and intelligent mind, quick to exploit the weaknesses in others and with a hard edge of cruelty which gave no quarter. Many saw him as the ultimate playground bully, on his own, but always surrounded by eager acolytes willing to hold his jacket while he mentally worked over some weaker unfortunate.

Despite this MacKenzie was popular with most of the other juniors because of his endless fund of witty put-downs of their superiors. But at the same time his arrogant bragging and boasting and his loud manner made some of them doubt their own abilities. His seniors, at first regarding him as a loudmouth braggart who thought he knew it all, found they could not fault his performance on the job and were constantly reduced to weakly telling him off for cheeking his betters.

He was a hopeless drinker, who his friends said went under to a sniff of the barmaid's apron, and there was an apocryphal story that he was sick over his editor's shoes at a Christmas party. But although he was sociable he did not dissipate his time in the pub, and neither did he bend his craft to the sole object of making money by turning it into more of a business as his father had done. With his comfortable background and his parents' whole-hearted support he was happy just to get on with the job in a determined and workmanlike fashion.

The young MacKenzie soon left the dull grind of local papers and took the fast track to Fleet Street by joining Ferrari's news agency in nearby Deptford. The agency was one of the dozens round the country which send, or 'file' in the jargon, direct to the nationals and are constantly scrutinised for rising young talent. Ferrari's was regarded as one of the best in London and one of

MacKenzie's fellow reporters at the time was Richard Stott, later to become his deadly rival as editor of the *Mirror*. MacKenzie's main work was covering Greenwich court and the south-east London crime scene, running high on the big story of the Richardson gang then being hyped as the south London successors to the Krays.

MacKenzie was regarded as a good operator, who was obviously hugely at home in the anarchic world he was covering. He also took naturally to putting on 'spin' – a process also known on the Street as 'getting an angle' by which comparatively dull events were spiced up into something interesting. But he then made the fundamental switch in journalism from reporting to the more usual route to the top: joining the editing side. By now he was married to Jacqui, née Holland, a fellow local newspaper reporter who had been brought up on a council estate in Bermondsey. The couple went out of London to Birmingham, where MacKenzie mastered the arts of sub-editing, layout and headline-writing. He discovered he had an instinctive flair, not just for words in writing snappy headlines and cross-heads, but also for the visual side of the job.

He returned to London to go straight into Fleet Street as a sub on the *Daily Express*, which, with his background, was in many ways his natural home in journalism. But, instead of settling, he was attracted by the more exciting end further down the class system represented by the buzzing 'frontier country' of the *Sun*, which he joined as a sub in 1973 when the paper was really roaring. His old mates on the *Mercury* and at Ferrari's were surprised to find him in an 'inside job', as reporters sniffily called office-bound work. They had always known he was going places, but had expected him to end up as a pushy foot-in-the-door reporter, probably on the *Express*, or possibly on the *Mirror* – though they knew he had nothing but contempt for the socialist values that paper represented.

As a downtable sub MacKenzie was expected to be very respectful of his older colleagues, particularly the all-powerful backbench of the chief sub-editor and the night editor – the powerhouse of the paper which put the pages together after the material had been gathered by the reporters and the day newsdesk. But MacKenzie was a technical perfectionist, completely unforgiving of anyone he regarded as falling beneath his own standards – which was just about everyone.

Not only was he loud and noisy throughout his shift, but more than once he impertinently offered his unwanted opinion as he left by going up to the backbench and pronouncing: 'Fucking crap paper tonight.' His superiors, sitting open-mouthed, challenged him on occasion. But each time they did, as he flicked through the paper underscoring his opinion with detailed and accurate criticism of page after page, they had to agree, just as they had had to agree on the *Mercury*. He might be a loudmouth, but he was not wrong. It was a crap paper that night.

Many did not take kindly to his abrasive manner and he began to be pointed out in the office as something of a phenomenon. Physically he was unremarkable – a stocky man, a shade under average height, powerful looking but not athletic, although he kept himself in trim by regular games of squash. He had light-brown, lank hair and, except for his beaky nose, an ordinary-looking face, habitually locked into a cheeky-chappie smirk.

Unlike Larry Lamb, from the beginning MacKenzie was a social diver rather than a social climber, playing to the gallery of the rougher end and absorbing the code of the cocky, macho soccer fan personified by Millwall, the club he purported to support. MacKenzie was a million miles away from the violent hooligan element amongst the fans, but he enthusiastically embraced the two fingers to society, 'I don't give a fuck' mentality. What mattered was number one, and according to the south London and Millwall code he absorbed as he went his journalistic rounds life was a matter of grabbing what you wanted in series of 'scams', designed to beat authority, and providing the glib and clever answer. It was all later summed up in the Millwall anthem, sung to the tune of Rod Stewart's song 'Sailing': 'We are Millwall. No one likes us. We don't care.'

Now in Fleet Street MacKenzie hammered up his accent in

78

rasping south ('sarff') London, and it seemed he was incapable of opening his mouth ('marff') without emitting a stream of foul abuse, the favourites being 'fark', 'farkin 'ell', 'bollocks' and, above all, 'c***'.

The news hacks soon got to know him from the times they reeled back into the office in mid-evening from the Top of the Tip to call a cab, or make the normal excuses to wives or girlfriends (or both). A wild-eyed monstrous character would rise up from the subs' table waving their copy and shouting in his yobbish voice: ''Ere, you! Did you write this fucking stuff? It's all crap! It's absolute bollocks!' The reporters, naturally spurning the subs as a lower form of life, would hurl back equally vigorous abuse before crashing out again.

It was obvious that with this high profile MacKenzie would soon come to Murdoch's attention and he was picked out to go as managing editor to the *New York Post,* the tabloid Murdoch had acquired and been accused of sensationalising with headlines like 'HEADLESS BODY FOUND IN TOPLESS BAR'. Compared to the British tabloids most of its contents were mild. In the cordial farewell Lamb organised in the office between editions there was huge merriment at how he was going to rough up the Yanks.

MacKenzie loved the electric atmosphere of New York and thrived on the diet of mayhem and murder, soon becoming loathed by the natives as another of the 'brash Brits' being imported to change the face of American journalism. His rudeness horrified the *Post*'s journalists, used to being treated with the reverence due to their status as 'writers', and appalled by his tactic of stripping them of their all-important bylines if they fucked up a story. Murdoch, who was spending a lot of time in New York, was amused and liked his style. He had already recognised him as a fellow outsider and marked his card for yet higher things.

Although MacKenzie was thriving, Jacqui was worried about their three young children, an eldest girl and two boys, whom she did not want to grow up as Americans and demanded they return to Britain. MacKenzie was torn, being one of those 'devoted' family men who spend little time at home but at the same time take their duties as a father seriously. Murdoch entreated with him to stay but MacKenzie bowed, with some reluctance, to his wife. The family returned to make their home near Dartford, a north Kent suburb to which successful south Londoners aspire.

Back at the *Sun* Lamb could only give him the job of deputy night editor, where, riding high on New York and even more full of himself than when he left, he was soon once more the talk of the office. MacKenzie was always a great chair-tipper, teetering backwards almost to the point of no return. But on one occasion when a hot piece of news dropped his arms windmilled so much he overdid it. As he sprawled in a tangled heap he was still shrieking with excitement. 'Fucking hell!' he shouted. 'This is it! Splash! Black border!' 'Come on, Kelvin,' the hacks shouted back as they clustered round the writhing figure on the ground. 'It's a good story – but not that good.' MacKenzie glared back in astonishment: 'Whaddya mean, "Not that good"? You said the Queen's dead.' 'No, no, Kelvin,' the hacks chorused back. 'It's not the Queen. It's Steve McQueen!'

MacKenzie was just getting back into his stride when in February 1981, after he had been back only a few months, he was lured to the *Express* by the promise of a full night editor's job. The move nearly finished him with Murdoch, who did not appreciate this treachery and sent him a stinging letter of the 'never darken my door again' variety.

Express hacks still shake their heads with wonder as they recall his short reign on the back bench. At the time the *Express*, despite Victor Matthews' efforts, was known as the 'Living Dead' – a journalistic zombie plodding on to the newsstands every morning to rendezvous with its increasingly doddery readership. MacKenzie barrelled in determined to inject some fresh life with his combination of a prodigious workrate and non-stop stream of quick-fire abuse. Several big stories broke while he was there, including the shooting of the Pope. On these nights he would roar round the office shouting, 'Ferret up your trouser leg!', meaning he wanted to see all the subs leaping about as they changed the pages at maximum speed. He would set a whirlwind example himself as he made a string of split-second decisions in a blur of activity. Then he might shout, 'Reverse ferret!', and the pages would have to be changed all over again.

In April 1981 Murdoch, having forgiven MacKenzie, made him editor of the *Sun*. But the *Express*, eager to make life as difficult as possible for Murdoch, insisted he worked the full term of his contract. For a few weeks MacKenzie was therefore in the extraordinary position of both night-editing the *Express* and editing the *Sun*, dashing between the two papers, and providing the driving force for both.

The double life was made possible by Peter Stephens being appointed caretaker editor to see to the nuts and bolts of the *Sun* operation, while MacKenzie put in the drive and flair. He would go into Bouverie Street to plan the *Sun* in the morning and early afternoon, before rushing across the Street to pick up his night job at the *Express*. After getting that under way he would go back to the *Sun* to supervise the first edition going on press at 7 p.m. Then he would hurtle off back to the *Express*, with its much later first-edition time of 10 p.m., crying in imitation of Flash Gordon as he rushed out of the door: 'I've only got four hours to save the *Daily Express*!'

Back in the 'Black Lubyanka', as *Private Eye* had dubbed the *Express* in joint tribute to its 1930s glass frontage and the similarity of its internal politics to the KGB's notorious torture centre, he would immerse himself in final page proofs. The first copies of the *Sun* would then be brought across, ink still wet on their pages. He would look through them virtually keeping an open phone line to the *Sun*, denouncing the paper as rubbish, and cursing the subs for not following his orders to the letter.

Grabbing the phone he would shout instructions like: 'Page 7 is absolute fucking crap. Throw it in the bin and start again.' Sometimes there would be pandemonium round him as the *Express* subs, thinking the abusive orders were directed at them, scuttled off to make the changes. 'Not you, you useless c***s!' MacKenzie would then explode, 'I'm talking to the other load of useless c***s on the other fucking paper!'

But whatever they thought of his manner, the *Express* hacks were hugely impressed by his technical skill, and his ability to lay out crisp, clean pages which they saw as objects of real beauty. Many of the subs at the *Sun*, during his brief tenure as deputy night editor, had already come to regard him as some sort of technical genius, not just for his ability, but for the speed and decisiveness with which he worked.

The lawyers at the *Express* were not so impressed. MacKenzie vented his frustration at not being allowed to leave the paper by winding them up, expressing genuine hate as he slagged them off as 'c***s' and 'fuckpigs' in the middle of the newsroom. He did not blame his boss, the *Express*'s editor Arthur Firth, a tall man of remarkable physical appearance who was nicknamed 'Lurch' due to his resemblance to the character in the comedy horror series *The Addams Family*. But MacKenzie constantly wound him up, once booming at him in the middle of the editorial floor in mock imitation of a court official: 'Arthur Percy Firth, you are hereby accused of impersonating an editor, taking this once great newspaper and reducing it to a daily pile of crap. How do you plead?' Firth just laughed. 'I'm prepared to ride the tiger,' he would say when asked about MacKenzie's mounting insubordination. He liked the way the man had put some life back into the paper. Anyway keeping him away from the *Sun* was revenge enough.

MacKenzie's contempt for the *Express* was genuine. 'Crap' was the word he constantly used to describe anything that did not fit in with his concept of how things ought to be. It was a paper for the despised middle classes with their dull lives and petty social ambitions. Concepts like 'quality' and 'niceness' were not in his vocabulary and he sneered at the way the paper espoused comfortable 'middle England'.

But that was nothing compared to his derision for the *Mirror*, with the humbug of its 'concern' and identification with 'the people', which he just thought laughable. Just as bad was the lax attitude on the paper which he described as 'a mink-lined coffin'. 'You could shoot a fucking bullet through the newsroom at ten in the morning and be certain of not hitting anyone,' he told everyone, adding that Mirrormen were champagne socialists who drank red wine at conferences.

There was some truth in his remarks. The *Mirror* was now under the management of Reed International, which had swallowed up IPC and been allowed to spread itself so much that it was a standing joke among its hacks that it was impossible to find anyone after lunch who was sober enough to sign your expenses.

Nonetheless the paper was reputed to have no less than forty-seven features staff, and one features hack who joined in the 1970s had been horrified to be told by an old stager that he had not had anything printed for three years. When the newcomer attempted to commiserate about his plight, the old hack replied: 'No, no, no. You've got it wrong. It's not that they haven't printed what I wrote. The point is that I haven't written anything for them to print.'

In MacKenzie's view there was only one paper worthy of more contempt than the *Mirror*, and that was the *Guardian* which represented all the soggy pinko thinking many of his generation of journalists had fallen for in one way or another. He was proud that he had not fallen for the bullshit and he loudly rejected everything it stood for. More than this he hated it as a product, with its great rambling features, arty pictures and trendy design. He was sincerely convinced that it was the worst newspaper in the world.

But as he arrived as editor the main paper on his mind was the *Star*. He did not admire the paper, which he saw as a straight rip-off of the *Sun*, but unlike Lamb, he saw it as a serious threat which had to be destroyed. The need to beat up the *Star* had been one of the reasons why Murdoch had chosen MacKenzie rather than the more refined and thoughtful Lloyd to edit the paper. Now he armed his new editor with *Sun* bingo, launched within weeks of MacKenzie's appointment, to counter the *Star*'s main selling point. As a result of these measures the *Sun*'s circulation leaped by 500,000 in three months. It was a good start. In complete contrast to Lamb's pomposity MacKenzie introduced himself as 'the bingo editor', explaining to the hacks: 'If sales go down they'll blame me. If sales shoot up I'll never know if it was me or bingo.'

To further help him get the measure of the *Star* MacKenzie poached its features editor, Roy Greenslade, who had begun his Fleet Street career on Lamb's *Sun*. Greenslade was a self-educated working-class hack from Dagenham, the very heart of C2 land, who, as a young man, had embraced revolutionary Maoism. In his early days he had been a militant in the National Union of Journalists Chapel and at one point he even quit his job to study politics at Sussex University as a mature student coming belatedly to the conclusion that the working class, defined in Marxist political terms, no longer existed. By now he had watered down his politics to the point where he could take a senior job on the avowedly Thatcherite *Sun* with few qualms.

With Greenslade's inside knowledge of the *Star*'s strengths and weaknesses both he and MacKenzie agreed it was crucial to destroy the *Star* before it settled down and 'gelled' as a national newspaper, as the *Sun* had done in its first few years under Lamb.

At the start of his editorship MacKenzie dedicated himself to 'driving the *Daily Star* off the streets'. And to do that, he loudly insisted, meant 'fighting fire with fire'. The shell-shocked editorial staff of the *Sun* was about to discover what that meant in practice.

Chapter 6

Mac the Knife

In June 1981 MacKenzie finally got out of his *Express* contract and settled into the editorial chair at the *Sun*. Not that he spent much time sitting in it. The thing that struck the hacks most about him was his astonishing energy. He was instantly nicknamed 'MacFrenzie'. He would always be in the office at 8.30 a.m., or at the very latest 9 a.m., snuffling around, reading the other papers and preparing his day. Traditionally, in an industry geared to night-time production, papers did not really get running until the middle of the morning, but the *Sun*'s earlier print times meant an earlier start – and an even earlier one for the news editor Tom Petrie, who would depart from his home in Hemel Hempstead at 6 a.m. every morning to be at his desk at 7 a.m.

In both men's cases the early rising was also due to their being dedicated workaholics to an extraordinary degree. Petrie, who had been the paper's picture editor and moved across to become news editor during the dying days of the Lamb era, lived and breathed his job just as much as his editor. He was older than MacKenzie and had been one of the last to be called up for national service, where he had met his Gibraltarian wife. Petrie still affected a military bearing and constantly smoked a foul pipe which infuriated MacKenzie, who wanted the whole editorial floor to be a no smoking zone. His boyish military approach was allied to tremendous keenness which suited the organisational side of his job, deploying his team of hacks to get the stories to fill the news pages.

Petrie's total and unswerving commitment to the paper was what MacKenzie was looking for from all the hacks and everyone involved in producing the paper. Both men shared the attitude that working for the *Sun* – or the Currant Bun as MacKenzie called it – was the greatest thing in the world. Petrie would frequently tell the hacks how he would rather be sitting at the newsdesk doing his job than anything else he could think of. (Later legend spread about how MacKenzie, after a big row between them, banned him from the office and ordered him to stay at home as the ultimate punishment.)

Although some of the hacks found Petrie a bore, and remembered him from his earlier days when he had been one of those terrible people who ran everywhere, in general they found he treated them courteously and fairly and could be capable of great kindness, even though he preferred to hide it under his reserved exterior. His saving grace was always his sense of humour, which was welcome after the reign of the sour 'old boy' news editor, Ken Donlan.

Although Petrie enjoyed his job, the reporters also felt sorry for him. The newsdesk at the *Sun* had always struck the hacks as incredibly harassed and now the pressure was drastically stepped up. From the beginning Petrie displayed a dog-like devotion to MacKenzie which characterized their relationship, partly because MacKenzie's depth of commitment to the enterprise exceeded even his. It was already said of MacKenzie that he was the *Sun*'s most dedicated reader and, like Petrie, he lived and breathed the paper twenty-four hours a day, never leaving it alone, even on his regulation days off, when he constantly rang in pestering to know what was going on.

But it was not just the energy MacKenzie showed in putting in frequent twelve-, fourteen- and sixteen-hour days that amazed everyone – it was what he did during them. In another direct contrast to Lamb he was a total 'hands-on' editor, always out on the floor, flying around cajoling, wheedling, wise-cracking, browbeating, exhorting. He was one of those people who moved 20 per cent faster and talked 20 per cent louder than anyone else, constantly on the move, poking his stubby fingers into every aspect of the paper and rapping out a series of instant decisions. And administering bollockings.

Bollockings were nothing new at the paper. When Donlan had been news editor he had been known as a ferocious, though quietly spoken, disciplinarian, with a small alcove known as 'the bollocking bay' where hacks would be taken to be privately and systematically dealt with. The unloved Donlan was now back at *Sun* after an unsuccessful sojourn as editor of the *News of the World*. His new job as managing editor was a considerable move down the pecking order and involved the dreary mechanics of processing the hacks' expenses, a task he carried out with typical stinginess. He once called a reporter to his minuscule cubicle off the newsroom and asked if he had taken up sheep-farming. Producing the expenses form Donlan said: 'Look here, old boy. It says Bar, Bar, Bar.'

As a key member of the Lamb regime, which now had to be rubbished at every available opportunity, MacKenzie curried favour by persecuting Donlan. Walking past his cubicle one day with a group of hacks, MacKenzie peered inside and said in a loud voice: 'I'm thinking of having that fucking door bricked up.' Donlan stared back grimly and said nothing.

But Donlan's bollockings were nothing compared to the frenzy MacKenzie now unleashed. His first real blast was directed at the features department, which he was shaking up with the help of Greenslade. After just a week he called all the features execs into his office and graphically indicated how Lamb's informal get-togethers round the bottle were now a thing of the past.

'What are you lot?' he asked rhetorically before leaning forward and bellowing the answer in their faces: 'I'll tell you what you are. You're fucking middle aged, middle class, overpaid and out of touch. If you don't pull your fucking fingers out, I'll sack the lot of you and bring in some twenty-two-year olds.' Repeating his message about the need to beat up the *Star* he bawled: 'My head's on the fucking block and so are yours. And if I go, your head's going to roll' – his quivering finger fastened on the first of them – 'then yours, and yours, and yours . . .' Each was fingered in turn.

Everybody got a written bollocking immediately. Under Lamb's more easygoing regime the hacks had been accustomed to traditional long lunches in various licensed premises round the Street where they claimed to be 'meeting contacts'. Now each received a storming memo: 'I am disgusted at the length of your lunch hours. Two-hour breaks do not do this newspaper, your country, or yourselves a favour. It is no wonder that Britain is rapidly turning into a Third World nation, if, when we do arrive at work, we do anything but work. I will take severe disciplinary action if I have to raise this subject of long lunch hours again.' MacKenzie himself set an example by going out either for a quick restaurant lunch or for a game of squash, from which he would return bounding with even more energy than before.

Behind the new reign of terror stood Murdoch, glad to see the air of complacency which had overtaken the paper in Lamb's last years being stripped away. Murdoch was no longer referred to as KRM. Now he was the 'Boss' – a phrase MacKenzie used with all the deference of a sarff London gangster describing his omnipotent leader. His respect and praise for the Boss knew no bounds. 'He's as smart as a wagonload of monkeys,' he informed the hacks. 'He achieves more in half an hour than any other human being achieves in a whole day.' In a rare moment of modesty he would add: 'I don't mind telling you – Rupert has forgotten more than I'll ever learn.'

MacKenzie expected the hacks to be as loyal to him as he was to the Boss. Anyone judged lacking, either in general or on a specific occasion, or who had fucked up in any way, would be in for a bollocking. In severe cases he would summon the individual and meet them just outside his office. 'Come in,' he would snap, holding the door open. 'Don't speak. Take your bollocking. Then fuck off – and we'll never talk about it again'. A withering tirade lasting anything between five and thirty minutes would follow. MacKenzie would rage and rant, the veins standing out on his forehead and sometimes pressing his face so close to his victim's they would have to go and wash the spittle off afterwards.

As the bollockings continued bets were taken on when they would start – would it be from the moment MacKenzie stepped out of the lift?; from the fire bucket in the corridor?; as he smashed through the swing doors? People were bollocked in private in his office, bollocked publicly at their desks, bollocked when they were walking across the editorial floor, bollocked even when they were trapped with him in the lift. The bollockings varied in length and ferocity, and when shaking and often tearful hacks fell out of his office there would a standard sympathetic enquiry – had it been a general bollocking (not so bad) or a personal one (could be extremely cruel, distressing and, for some, devastating)? The language he used was always crude in the extreme.

Some buckled, some cried, but most survived, clinging on to the assurance that the subject of the bollocking would never be mentioned again once it was over. Occasionally, but only very occasionally, somebody with enough cheek put one over on him. One showbiz hack, after ten minutes of rant, seized his chance as MacKenzie paused to draw breath. Giving a wink, he grinned and said quickly: 'You're going to give me a bollocking now, aren't you, Kelvin?' MacKenzie, completely disarmed, burst out laughing and dismissed him with a delighted wave of the arm and a dismissive: 'Go on then. Fuck off out of here.'

Petrie also found that humour was the best defence against MacKenzie. On one occasion he spied the editor homing in on the newsdesk and got up sharply from his seat and headed off into the corner, where he started muttering to himself: 'Petrie, you're absolutely fucking useless. Where's that fucking story? Why don't you pull your fucking finger out and get some fucking work done? You're a pratt, Petrie . . .' As he stood kicking the wall with his toe MacKenzie sidled up to him and asked him in a puzzled fashion what the fuck he thought he was up to. 'Oh! Hello, Kelvin!' Petrie replied, barely able to suppress his giggling. 'I saw you coming so I just thought I'd go into the corner and give myself a bollocking to save you the trouble!'

Bollockings as standard management technique began at the start of the day when MacKenzie went through the features pages which had been prepared the day before. MacKenzie was above all a newsman, preoccupied with the news pages and the front page and its all-important splash story. He regarded the features department as an inferior and idle species and most of the pages they produced as lightweight bollocks. He would stand, the proofs of their efforts spread on the desk in front of him, while they nervously lined up for his morning performance.

At first they had been unable to believe the way he had terrorised them in his first week, hoping it was a one-off, over-the-top performance that would never be repeated. Now they were grimly adjusting to it being everyday life. MacKenzie would start a stream of patter, speaking quietly and reasonably, but putting in the needle by continuously adding the general enquiry 'Eh, eh?' in a way which gave them no choice but to nod in agreement. 'Look at you lot, eh?' he would start. 'Useless load of fuckers, aren't you, eh? Right load of wankers, eh, eh?' The features execs would shift uneasily, waiting for this generalised abuse to be directed towards the chosen butt for the day. The favourite was often Mike Terry, the elderly, bespectacled features production editor inherited from Lamb.

MacKenzie would zero in: 'All right, are we today, Mike, eh? Woken up yet, have we, Mike? Brain working? Lights on are they, Mike, eh? Anyone at home, Mike, eh, eh? Now, come on, Mike. Tell me the truth, Mike, eh? Now don't look away, Mike. Because we're not always at home, eh, Mike? Not always in, are we, eh, eh?' The other hacks would snigger cravenly as MacKenzie played them off against each other.

When he had got them laughing he would strike, suddenly raging: 'This is not a laughing matter! It's not fucking funny! This stuff's all fucking crap! You useless c***s. It's crap. Absolute fucking crap!' If any hack timidly enquired the exact nature of the problem, MacKenzie would explode: 'Don't you fucking talk to me, you bastard!' He would jab at the page. 'Look at this fucking mistake here. Look at it, eh? You fucking bastard. Look at it! Fucking word's spelt wrong. Tell me that's right, eh? Tell me that's fucking right! You useless c***.' Then he would fling his

arm out towards the door. 'Get out of my fucking sight. Go on –
fuck off!' The hack would scuttle out, leaving the others still
standing there quaking.

The switch would come again. MacKenzie would be chuckling
gently and smiling, pretending to take them all into his confidence. 'Think he got the message then, eh? I think he got the
message, didn't he? It's all a laugh, innit, eh? Bit of a laugh!' With
that he would clap his hands, give a cheerful yell of: 'Right!
Whaddya got for me today?', lean over the mocked-up pages laid
out on the desk before him, rattling out a set of changes for the
execs to jot down.

Picking a page he would run his eye over it, ringing paragraphs
with his fat green pen. 'That's crap!' he would spit. The pen would
move off across the page again. 'And that's crap!' Another
paragraph, or a whole article, would be ringed. The muttering
would continue as he dotted about. 'Bollocks . . . Fucking useless
. . . Yeah, that's OK . . . Yeah, I like that . . . Naah . . . That's
bollocks.' The criticism would become more detailed: 'Put
something in here about how his father was a bastard to him or
some bollocks like that, will you?' he would say as he studied a
profile of some celebrity or other. The pen would run down the
type. 'Look – this is the best bit here.' A juicy paragraph would be
circled. 'Fucking hell! You've missed it, you c***s. Move it up to
the top, will you, eh?'

Suddenly he would flick half a dozen pages in a flurry of activity
and land on something like the horoscope. An entry would be
stabbed by the pen. 'I don't like that. Tell that c*** who does this
crap to write something else about Pisces.' Another flick might
take him to the 'Dear Deirdre' agony-aunt column. 'What's she
going on about today?' the muttering would continue as he
screwed his eyes to read the column. 'Fuck it,' he would mumble,
raising his voice as he issued another instruction. 'This stuff's
useless. Get something a bit dirty in here, will you? Tell her to put
a dirty letter in here, eh? The readers don't want this crap.'

The scrutiny would continue, from headline down to the
smallest article or detail of punctuation. Nothing, the editorial

execs began to realise, escaped his attention. He was anywhere and everywhere, picking out every weakness, demanding that every word and detail of the layout be polished and worked on until he decided it was perfect. And, just like everybody else, if there was one thing they could not fault, it was his ability. He always knew exactly what he was talking about and if he didn't – like any good newspaperman – he soon found out.

The process would be abruptly wound up for him to turn his attention to his real love, the news pages, with the morning conference to plan the day's coverage. Here again it was a one-man show, starring himself. Feet on desk and tipping precariously back in his chair, he would issue a stream of abusive wit in which he specialised in impersonating other members of staff. The main figure of fun to start with was naturally the departed editor, Sir Albert (Larry) Lamb.

MacKenzie and Petrie would impersonate Lamb's ponderous manner and soft Yorkshire accent as they worked through the news list. 'I 'ave 'ere a story, 'appen a very good story, about an 'ave-a-go 'ero,' Petrie would say in character. 'Oh aye, Mr Petrie,' MacKenzie would reply in a perfect parody. 'And what particular variety of 'ave-a-go 'ero would that be?' (The query was code for the person's colour. White heroes were more likely to make the paper than black ones.) The act would continue, with the others encouraged to join in, until the conference descended into a rerun of the old *Monty Python* 'I were born in t'cardboard box' sketch. 'Luxury! Fooking luxury' everyone would be crying.

But generally the news conferences were less of a pillorying exercise as MacKenzie whipped them through stories and ideas, sparking and energising chains of thought. He would never be still, tipping his seat abruptly forward and shooting upright to bring on a fresh wave of hilarity as he described a story or a suggestion with his most contemptuous remark of: 'I wouldn't wipe my fucking arse with it.' He would then illustrate this in exaggerated fashion by turning round, sticking out his fat backside and miming pulling down his trousers before simulating the sanitary act with the offending piece of paper.

MacKenzie never worried where ideas came from. They could be lifted from the radio or television, overheard in a bus queue or hoicked out of another paper. He was always stealing them himself, meeting old cronies from the *Express* and staying sober while they jawed on, saying, 'Oh yeah, that's all bollocks' to get them to reveal more. Then he would rush off to the toilet to scribble them down on a scrap of paper or the cuff of his shirt. In the morning he would be back in conference announcing, ' 'Ere I've had an idea,' and the stolen material would be trotted out.

But most of all he then had the drive to make the idea work, an absolute determination to push it through that translated it from just general talk or excited chatter into something concrete that would appear in the paper. He would take an idea from anyone. Once a shy and plodding member of staff came up and said: 'I've got this daft idea, Kelvin. You know everyone likes fishing. Well, why don't we do a version of bingo with it? We could attach tags to fish and if they catch 'em they can get a prize, and we can put their picture in the paper.'

MacKenzie was beside himself. His eyes whirling in their sockets, he grabbed the plodder by his arm to steady himself and screeching with an orgasmic yelp: 'Fucking great! What a fucking brilliant scam! You're a fucking genius!' A huge competition was immediately built on the back of the idea, using one fish which, MacKenzie had statistically established, would never get caught and which was tagged for a huge cash prize. Others, tagged for more humble prizes, were more accessible and the whole idea proved to be a great success.

But it was in the afternoon, as the paper built up to its creative climax of going to press, that the real performance would begin. MacKenzie would burst through the door after lunch with his cry of 'Whaddya got for me?' and the heat would be on. He had total control – not just over the front page, but over every page lead going right through the paper. Shrimsley was remembered as a fast and furious corrector of proofs, but MacKenzie was even faster, drawing up layouts, plucking headline after headline out of the air, and all the time driving towards the motto he hammered into them all: 'SHOCK AND AMAZE ON EVERY PAGE.'

All the time he would be playing the yob, the sarff London hard man who didn't give a fuck. His comfy middle-class background had now been buried in the new image of the self-made man risen from the working classes. The whispering disinformation went round – the one O-level, now said to be in woodwork, showed not that he was thick, but how he didn't give a toss about the system; he had been expelled from his posh school, they told each other; he'd been brought up in a council flat; he really came from rough Peckham, not more genteel Camberwell. With this background it was obvious he was the one who understood the readers, who knew what they wanted. Middle-class pretentions were there to be trashed and rubbished.

True to the code of sarff London MacKenzie also wanted to be surrounded by 'made men', who had proved themselves by pulling off some outrageous stunt at the expense of the opposition. One way of becoming a made man was to phone the *Mirror* and ask for the 'stone' where the final versions of pages were assembled for the presses. The trick was to imitate another member of the *Mirror* staff to fool the stone sub into revealing the front-page splash. One features exec became a made man by walking across Fleet Street into the *Express* and stealing some crucial pictures from the library. Hacks refusing to get involved in this sort of behaviour were suspect – falling into the category of those who were not fully with him, and could therefore be presumed to be against him.

Like any other new broom there was plenty he wanted to sweep away. In his previous incarnation as a sub MacKenzie had had vicious rows with some of Lamb's execs. Now he was in a position to get his own back. The first to go was Frank Nicklin, the sports editor. Nicklin had infuriated MacKenzie by repeatedly complaining to Lamb that he was interfering too often with the sports pages. MacKenzie had taken him to one side at a think-in and told him pointedly: 'I'm going to get you one day.' Nicklin had replied at the time: 'You'll have to get up very early in the morning to do that.'

When MacKenzie's appointment was announced Nicklin was

in hospital recovering from a major operation for cancer of the bowel, and had a temporary colostomy. He had not expected to survive the operation, and was still recovering when his wife told him the news. 'That's it,' Nicklin said, realising that MacKenzie would persecute him. 'That's the end of me.'

Nicklin, still far from well, had returned to work in June 1981 on the last day of the first cricket Test between Australia and England, two weeks after MacKenzie had started as editor. He discovered that MacKenzie had already appointed David Shapland, a downtable sports sub on the *News of the World*, as his new 'assistant' and knowing that this was a polite euphemism, suspected that Shapland was being lined up to take over from him. The next day his suspicions were confirmed when MacKenzie began a campaign to destroy him by public humiliation.

England had lost the Test by four wickets, and Ian Botham, as captain, was being blamed. Nicklin had signed Botham as a columnist before he made the English team. He was very proud of having got the paper excellent value for money by signing Botham for the bargain price of £100 per article.

MacKenzie flew into the office after lunch and, already knowing the answer, screamed: 'Who's the c*** who signed that fucking useless c*** Botham?'

Everyone in the crowded newsroom went quiet. Nicklin answered with all the dignity he could muster: 'I'm the "c***" who signed Ian Botham. Do you want to make anything of it?'

MacKenzie sneered back: 'Well, if you signed the c***, you can sack the c***,' and disappeared into his office. (Nicklin ignored the order. Botham then turned out to be the hero of the Test series, being made man of the match for all the remaining games and regaining the Ashes for England. He continued to write for the paper for most of the 1980s.)

A week later Nicklin was called in by Peter Stephens, now editorial director and MacKenzie's titular boss. The two men had a personal friendship cemented by attending Derby County football matches together. Stephens, looking ashamed, told him:

'I'm very sorry about this, Frank. But MacKenzie doesn't like you, and you've got to go.'

Nicklin protested, but Stephens replied that there was nothing he could do. There was an offer of two years' salary, but only if he went that day. 'Take it, Frank,' Stephens advised. 'It's a good offer – the best you're going to get.'

Nicklin was shattered. He had been sports editor for twelve years and the previous week Stephens had told him he could stay until he retired. He went out and rang his wife who, worried about his health, told him: 'Take it with both hands, Frank, and get out. It's not worth staying.' Nicklin left with the money and, as he had expected, was replaced as sports editor by David Shapland. Within a few months Shapland, an archetypal MacKenzie crony, had been further promoted to become deputy editor.

As stories began to circulate in Fleet Street of this wild new editor and his extraordinary management style, MacKenzie appeared to demonstrate it briefly to the public. Soon after he had become editor, ITN reporter Norman Rees visited Bouverie Street to film a lightweight item for *News at Ten* on the escalating bingo war – a good opportunity for television to sneer at the commercial antics of the pop papers. Rees, microphone in hand, stood in amazement as MacKenzie let rip a non-stop rant about how his job as editor was to smash the *Star* and drive it off the streets. When he had finished Rees, appalled, went across to a reporter he knew and told him quietly: 'If that's your editor, God help you!'

Even MacKenzie was worried about the extraordinary ferocity of his outburst. ''Ere, you were watching me. What did I say? Was it a bit over the top?' he enquired anxiously of a hack. The hack, who thought the performance had accurately reflected a bull in a china shop, ducked the question by explaining lamely that he was not an expert on television. The item was broadcast to cringing horror from the paper's management, and the story was soon on the grapevine of how Murdoch had immediately ordered: 'That man is never to appear on television again.' From then on MacKenzie, who had always had a strong aversion to being photographed, withdrew completely from public appearances and refused all requests for interviews, not just from television, but from every paper and magazine. The ban on media appearances shielded MacKenzie from the general public, but not from the tight-knit community of Fleet Street, where hacks on other papers were equally amazed by Murdoch's choice of editor. MacKenzie made regular visits to the Popinjay – the *Express* pub – to keep up contact with his sub-editor cronies and offer an opinion on how they were getting along without him. He would make a typically theatrical entrance and start shadow boxing with his rivals or jerking his neck in a head-butting gesture of greeting. Once this went badly wrong when MacKenzie's old pal Les Diver imitated him and the two men's heads smashed together with an alarming crack. Both clutched their heads in agony until the pain subsided. Everyone thought it a great joke.

But normally MacKenzie would just brag about the *Sun* and the way it had left the tired and old-fashioned *Express* way behind in the mass market stakes. 'What does it feel like to have to produce this load of crap?' he would ask with apparent sympathy and sincerity. 'You know it makes me sick to see what's happened to that paper.' His mood would brighten as he slagged off those present, holding them personally responsible: 'I know what you think. Who gives a toss – fucking *Express*, load of bollocks – not you lot, eh? Useless fuckers!' The *Express* subs would give as good as they got with jibes about Murdoch and Page Three.

But MacKenzie's banter had a serious side to it. The rise and fall of the *Express* was a terrible lesson for the editor of the best selling mass market newspaper. There was no room for the smug complacency which had led the *Express* on to the slippery slope. He returned to Bouverie Street from his *Express* wind-up sessions in a more aggressive frame of mind than ever.

All the time, as he drove his new regime relentlessly through the organisation, MacKenzie was causing stronger and stronger feelings in the office. Some didn't mind the bollockings, thinking they were well deserved in many cases. Everybody agreed the paper had been carrying a good deal of dead wood, and there was scant sympathy for some of those given a hard time. The younger hacks in particular found MacKenzie an energising breath of fresh air after stuffy old Lamb. He led by example and would banter on equal terms with those who could manage it. His intensity was being transmitted into the paper, which began to crackle and spark again. The ones who warmed to him were amused and amazed by his antics and the way he flashed from a harsh bollocking to mock fisticuffs as he played up to his sarff London image.

Once he spotted a group from the *Sun* art desk, where the paper's graphics were produced, walking along Fleet Street as he was travelling in the back of his chauffeur-driven company Daimler. 'Oi – you shower!' he shouted, head jutting through the open window. 'Oi! Fucking wankers! Look at this motor. You'll never have a motor as good as this,' and he waved his arm out of the window, simulating masturbation. ''Ere! Oi! 'Ere! Another thing. Call yourselves artists, eh? You've been down the pub, ain't yah, eh? You're artists all right – fucking *piss-artists*!' He collapsed backwards in gales of laughter.

'Tosser! Fuck off back to the *Express* where you belong!' the art desk chorused back from the pavement, repeating the wanking gesture.

'You cheeky fuckers!' MacKenzie boomed back, ordering the chauffeur to halt. 'Come over here and say that. I'll teach you some respect for your editor. Come on then – over here!'

The artists advanced on the car, surrounded it and began rocking it from side to side. MacKenzie, who had retreated behind the safety of the electric windows, bobbed about inside, laughing uncontrollably, before ordering the horrified chauffeur to drive off. Not very dignified behaviour for a national newspaper editor, the hacks decided when the amazed artists returned to the office to gabble out the story – but good fun.

Others, appalled by his vulgarity and the crudeness of his approach, consoled themselves with the thought that he would not last. They put him down as a glorified night editor, preoccupied with news and lacking the rounded approach to the various parts of the paper they felt an editor needed. Anyhow, they consoled each other in the Top of the Tip, nobody could carry on like him for long. Either he would mellow or he would burn himself out.

Some of the more farsighted recognised MacKenzie as a text book case of the fearful journalistic disease which left victims with no real interests in life outside newspapers. Victims like MacKenzie faced a simple choice – they could end up as workaholics or alcoholics. There was no middle course. At the same time surprising levels of intellectual depth and stamina had been detected in the puzzle which made up MacKenzie's personality. He read voraciously – heavyweight stuff including the *Economist* as well as rival papers – and would praise articles in the unpopulars which explained complicated subjects like the stock exchange in simple language. It was common enough to find people in newspaper offices who could either name every member of the cabinet or all the top ten groups in the pop charts. MacKenzie could do both. He was tremendously well informed and loved any kind of political argument or debate. It was even discovered that his favourite radio programme was *Any Questions*. But whatever the hacks might think, the Boss had sufficient faith in MacKenzie to let him get on with destroying the *Daily Star* whilst he concentrated on new ventures.

Murdoch was now spending most of his time in America expanding the Empire and masterminding the paper from there. News of events in the office were relayed to the Boss by Peter Stephens, MacKenzie's titular boss as editorial director, to whom he had to report everyday. In theory MacKenzie had to check all his activities with Stephens, who appeared to most hacks as a shadowy figure behind the scenes.

Stephens's brief, as he summarised it, was to supervise MacKenzie with a 'light touch' and to 'watch the stew boil and if it got to the top rush out and do something about it'. In practice Stephens was often sidelined by direct communication between the

the Boss and his editor, who were rapidly developing a close relationship. Murdoch later confessed to Charles Wintour, the former editor of the *Evening Standard* and a respected Fleet Street sage, that he had never really understood how MacKenzie worked. 'MacKenzie is what he is. He's out there, screaming and shouting, and he's good. Somehow it works.' The hacks, trying to figure out the exact balance of power between their editor and proprietor, had decided there was a great deal of affection in the relationship. Murdoch seemed to treat MacKenzie rather like a naughty but lovable child, and there was no doubt both had an enormous amount of respect for each other's abilities.

MacKenzie meanwhile was proceeding with his war against the *Star*. Since the Currant Bun had launched its own version of bingo the *Star*'s main weapon had been neutralised, producing an expensive stalemate. Editorial competition focused on the Royals who, in 1981, had become a national obsession with the arrival on the scene of Lady Diana Spencer to inject new glamour into the otherwise stuffy Royals show.

In the old days court correspondents had covered Royal affairs virtually as ordered by the Palace. They would obsequiously attend events like Indian tiger shoots and tours of various parts of the Empire only as invited, filing servile copy which was virtually dictated to them and then printed unaltered, with enormous care taken not to break any form of protocol. Even when they knew a great deal of the inside story in sagas such as the affair of Mrs Simpson and Edward VIII, which led to the abdication, they still did not break ranks.

Things had begun to change in 1976 when Prince Charles came out of the Navy at the age of twenty-eight, announcing that he thought thirty was a good age to marry. Larry Lamb resolved that the *Sun* would be the first to get the story of the engagement and teamed photographer Arthur Edwards with reporter Harry Arnold, the old *Sun*'s former motoring correspondent, to work on the Royals full time. Arnold, a small, dapper hack who took his journalism seriously, agreed with Lamb that he should not become an accredited court correspondent, thus vetoing the Palace PR machine's control over their activities.

Instead Arnold and Edwards treated Charles's search for a mate like any other running story, following him wherever he went, and effectively abolishing his private life in the process. They were joined on the full-time Royals beat by James Whitaker, a florid-faced former *Sun* reporter nicknamed Widow Twankey and reknowned for his booming voice and habit of standing up when using the telephone. Whitaker was now working for the enemy *Star*, where he was billed as 'The Man Who Really Knows', and competition between the two papers resulted in ever greater and more intrusive efforts to find out about the private lives of Charles and his relatives.

After four years of dogged pursuit and careful building of a network of contacts and informants among the Royal flunkeys and servants, the *Sun* team finally got the story they had been waiting for when they were covering Charles's attendance at the Braemar Games at Balmoral in September 1980. Snooping around, Edwards spotted Charles with a girl on a riverbank, only for her to hide behind a tree the moment he brought out his camera. Asking a contact for the name of the suspiciously shy young lady, he was told: 'It's Lady Diana Spencer, and she's following him round like a lamb.'

Arnold wrote the splash under the headline: 'HE'S IN LOVE AGAIN', using a picture Edwards had taken on the off chance two months earlier when the pair had spotted Diana at a polo tournament at Cowdray Park. At the Royal Wedding which followed Arnold provided immense detail based on a combination of tit-bits from his flunkey friends spiced up with what he described as fair 'journalistic enterprise'. He exclusively revealed that armed guards were riding shotgun dressed as footmen on the coach which, he also revealed, was bullet-proof, and the pair surpassed even themselves when the couple came out on to the balcony of Buckingham Palace after the wedding ceremony.

Edwards got the picture of the famous kiss, and Arnold provided the actual words which preceded it. His exclusive story had revealed how the kiss was Diana's idea. 'Kiss me,' she had demanded, but Charles had been reluctant. 'I'm not getting into that caper,' he replied. He then turned aside to ask his mother if it was all right.

Arnold's story came from one of his contacts on the balcony and was initially scorned, but he was vindicated when a lip-reader confirmed it word for word after studying a video of the event. This kind of intrusion was exactly what the Palace was increasingly beginning to complain about, but which Arnold blithely summarised as 'letting daylight in on the magic'. Arnold then made things worse by revealing their honeymoon destination to an agog public with a *Sun* splash of 'CHARLES MAKES DI HIS QUEEN OF THE NILE'.

By now a huge marketing operation was riding on the back of Di, with the papers and women's magazines awash with coverage of her every move and foible. The new 'fairytale princess' had moved the Royals on to become an entire industry, neatly folding into the complementary public obsession with the American soap opera *Dallas*, driven by the same fantasies of wealth and glamour which underpinned the attraction of the Royals show. After the *Sun*'s pioneering success, all the editors started demanding pictures to go with the exciting inside stories their new Royals reporters were filing. The original platoon of Edwards, Arnold and Whitaker was rapidly expanding into an army as the paparazzi pack began to assemble.

Throughout the year the merciless pressure on the Royal couple was kept up. In December, after it had been officially announced that Di was pregnant, the Palace took the un-precedented step of summoning all the Fleet Street editors to a special meeting at the Palace. The Queen's press officer, Michael Shea, told them that she was feeling 'totally beleaguered' and asked them to rein back.

Barry 'The Beast' Askew, whom Murdoch had appointed as his new editor of the *News of the World*, drew gasps by cheekily stating he believed the press had an equal right to cover all Di's activities –whether she was buying wine gums or attending a royal film première. MacKenzie, already putting his personal stamp on affairs, went one further by being the only editor not to attend at all. Instead he sent a note informing the Palace that he had a prior meeting with Murdoch, which he deemed more important. The *Sun* reported the meeting the next day under the headline 'LEAVE OUR DI ALONE SAYS PALACE', which was exactly the opposite of what MacKenzie intended to do.

Many hacks on the Street, who saw the Royals as living a lifestyle which had gone through centuries virtually unaltered, regarded them as fair game. Newspaper proprietors and editors, ensnared in the honours chase, might have been inclined to give them some peace, but not Murdoch and MacKenzie. The Boss regarded the Royals show as a symbol of everything that was wrong with the Poms. They represented the peak of the class system and unearned and unproductive wealth. In their own way they were just as bad as the trade unions – the ultimate closed shop. MacKenzie, who had no strong feelings about them, treated them rather like partridges – dumb creatures to be kept in good health so that they could be shot down whenever he felt like it. They were just people to be used for the sake of the paper, important only because they sold so many copies. The paper's photographers rudely called them 'The Germans' and described taking their pictures as 'whacking the Germans'.

Arnold and Edwards had scored a great personal triumph over Whitaker and the *Star* with the engagement and wedding stories. And they followed up with an opportunity early in the New Year of 1982 when the couple secretly slipped away to a remote Caribbean island in the hope of finding a bit of peace. The rest of the press left them alone, as requested, but Edwards and Arnold, sent after them, found it impossible to get to the beach house where the Royal couple was staying.

Then Arnold had a stroke of luck. He bumped into an American hack just about to leave the island, who had been taking some snatch pictures of the previous celebs using the same beach house. The American obligingly sold him a map of a route through the jungle which ended at a vantage point across a bay. The *Sun* men set off in the early hours of the morning, Arnold clutching torch, map and water bottle, while Edwards struggled along with his camera bag. After crawling through the undergrowth for three hours they arrived at the vantage point just before dawn.

They were just settling when they heard a heavy crashing in the undergrowth behind them. Out stepped the perspiring and red-faced figure of Whitaker of the *Star*, along with his photographer Kenny Lennox, who had followed them all the way from London. As Whitaker emerged, Arnold, quickly recovering his poise, greeted his old foe with the deadpan line, 'One egg or two for breakfast, James?', entreating Whitaker to moderate his loud voice, which had caused hacks to liken him to an army staff sergeant with two deaf daughters.

All were hugely delighted at this modern replay of Stanley and Livingstone, and after another three hours' wait they were richly rewarded when Di emerged on to the beach. But there was also a shock. Instead of the smock or one-piece bathing suit they were expecting, Di, by now five months pregnant, was wearing only a bikini, which clearly revealed the prominent bulge in her tummy. The hacks had a nasty moment when she shaded her eyes with her hand and scanned the horizon, lingering as she looked in their direction. But she did not appear to spot them and both photographers, using their longest telephoto lenses and aided by the bright West Indian light, set their motor drives whirring as they clicked away furiously, egged on by gasping little comments from Arnold and Whitaker, who were still unable to believe their luck.

The race now started to get the first pictures back to London. The *Star* men were convinced that Arnold and Edwards had a plane waiting to fly them to an adjoining island from where they could 'wire' the pictures back to London, using an early version of a fax machine. But the *Sun* team had established that the island's tiny newspaper office had its own machine. Edwards, after giving the *Star* the slip, sent the pictures and called MacKenzie at Bouverie Street. Hearing that the *Star* also had pictures, MacKenzie ordered down the line: 'When you've finished wiring, put an axe through the bloody machine.' Edwards explained that the drastic step was not necessary – the *Star* team had already left to go to the next island.

The *Sun* beat the *Star* to the publication by one edition, with MacKenzie slapping Edwards's pictures on the front page under the headline 'DI-LAND IN THE SUN'. The Palace press office, caught on the hop, reacted with an angry statement that Charles and Di were shocked at the tastelessness of the pictures. But Arnold doubted they had even seen the paper at the time they were supposed to be complaining. He was not sure the photos were tasteless anyway – although Diana was wearing a bikini, she suited pregnancy and looked marvellous as usual. It had been a difficult fifty-fifty decision, which he had been happy to let MacKenzie sort out.

Arnold thought the complaint was more a cover-up for official embarrassment over security. All the Royals watchers' jobs had been made more difficult since Lord Mountbatten had been murdered three years earlier by the Provisional IRA at his holiday home in Eire. Security had been massively tightened, and stunts like this reflected badly on the Royal Protection Squad, even if it was obvious there was no real danger.

The next day, using the row as a pretext, MacKenzie ran the pictures again, this time spelling out the new rules according to the *Sun*. The paper was 'deeply sorry' if it had caused any offence, but, a '*Sun* Says' editorial proclaimed, the pictures had 'brought back a breath of summer into the lives of millions of our readers back in chilly Britain'. The *Sun* was exercising 'a legitimate interest in the Royal family not merely as symbols, but as living, breathing people'.

The incident also provided a graphic indication of where the two papers split. The *Sun*'s counter-attack against the *Star* was beginning to bite, and MacKenzie's aggressive editorial package, and willingness always to go one step further, was working. Lord Matthews immediately called the *Star* off under a grovelling apology entitled 'ENOUGH IS ENOUGH', and ordered it not to sell the pictures on to the clamouring media. The *Sun* on the other hand, sold them round the world. (Later, when Di met the *Sun* photographer Arthur Edwards, she told him he must have made a lot of money out of the pictures. When Edwards replied that he got paid the same wage whatever he was doing, Di looked at him and remarked witheringly: 'Oh, pass the Kleenex.')

MacKenzie was delighted not only at beating the *Star* to the pictures, but at the '3-star ferret' rating the story earned. Even then it was not adjudged as good as the one just beforehand when the delicate negotiations over the ASLEF train drivers' strike were put in grave jeopardy by the *Sun* running a huge feature on the 'favourite fiddles of the filthy train drivers'. In the following gigantic row the paper was blacked on Eastern and Western region trains. The *Sun* set up a special hotline to field a barrage of calls, equally split between dire threats of revenge from drivers and support from the travelling public. This was prime MacKenzie territory – a huge controversy, with the paper right in the middle of it, and its name being splashed about everywhere. Stories like this, which stirred up trouble, would earn one, two or three star ferret ratings according to how big and noisy the argument was. Just as good were 'ferret up the bum' stories, which MacKenzie was always requesting when things were quiet. 'Whose bum can we put a ferret up?', he would go round demanding as the paper hunted for a target.

The Royal pursuit continued undiminished, with the *Mirror* now joining in to follow the *Sun*'s deliberate policy of running a Royals story as the front-page splash every Monday – traditionally a slow day for news as there is usually little to report from Sunday. MacKenzie called Arnold in and ordered him to come up with a steady stream of stories to fill the slot, causing Arnold to blink one Friday as he said: 'Give me a Sunday for Monday splash on the Royals. Don't worry if it's not true – so long as there's not too much of a fuss about it afterwards.'

Arnold went away pondering this. The Royals were a tricky line. Everybody in the business knew that coverage of them was a different matter from 'hard' news and was veering towards showbiz. Stories were known as 'fairytales', and nobody took that side of it seriously. But scrupulous hacks like Arnold did require that there should be some truth on which to construct their 'journalistic enterprise'. Having the editor utter a bald statement like that was something he had never come across before.

But then he had never come across an editor like MacKenzie before.

Chapter 7

Gotcha

It was partly a tribute to MacKenzie's journalistic sixth sense that the *Sun* had a reporter on the Falkland Islands when the Argentinians invaded. The paper had only one foreign reporter (in New York), a 'foreign desk' consisting of one sub chopping up wire service and agency copy, and little inclination or budget to spend on foreign stories anyway. Yet, with Fleet Street wrong-footed by the bizarre start to the war, the only papers that managed to have a man on the spot were the Unpopular trio of the *Daily Telegraph*, the *Financial Times* and the *Sunday Times* plus, to MacKenzie's immense delight, the good old Currant Bun.

The real tribute, however, was not to MacKenzie's prescience, but to the determination of reporter David Graves to get out of the office at all costs. As one of the more experienced hacks, who had been with the paper for eight years, Graves was not enjoying life under the new regime. He had been on duty when the first jumbled reports dropped that a party of Argentinian scrap-metal merchants had arrived on some island called South Georgia and instantly realised that its location in the South Atlantic made it about as far away from 30 Bouverie Street as it was possible to go, worked out the airline schedules, and badgered to be sent.

MacKenzie finally gave him permission in an offhand way. His editor knew no more about the situation than anyone else, but he did see the angle for the *Sun*. 'Tell you what,' he said, blocking out a headline in the air with one hand, 'THE ISLAND IN THE MIDDLE OF NOWHERE THAT WANTS TO STAY BRITISH'. . . . It's

wasting the company's money but . . . Fuck it! Let's have a go!'
Graves delightedly rushed off to Heathrow, toothbrush in hand.

After flying via Madrid, Buenos Aires and Comodoro
Rivadavia in southern Argentina, Graves scrambled on to the
weekly flight to Port Stanley, but missed the monthly boat to
South Georgia. But by now he had been overtaken by events – the
invasion of the Falklands themselves was imminent. So he set up
shop with the three Unpopulars in a reporter's dream. The
Upland Goose Hotel they were staying at was a hundred yards
from Government House; there wasn't another plane for a week;
they had the run of the Cable and Wireless office housing the only
ten telephone lines to the outside world and an override facility on
all other calls. Meanwhile the entire oppostion, which had woken
up too late to the fast-developing story, was hammering to get in.

Now Graves was at dinner in the official residence of the
Governor, Sir Rex Hunt, and finding it very pleasant – similar to a
comfortable evening at a country house in the Lake District. But,
as he sat nursing his brandy in front of the roaring peat fire,
his enjoyment was marred by his preoccupation with the
latest mission from Bouverie Street.

News editor Petrie had been on the phone that afternoon
explaining that Kelvin had come up with a brilliant angle on the
crisis. The desk had dug up some Foreign Office statistics showing
that the Falklands population was made up of three women to
every man – the highest imbalance in the world! Think what that
meant for the forty-two Marines stationed there! They must be
having three or four locals at a go! Great story!

Graves had spent dinner trying to pull the Governor round to
the topic of the soldiers' supposed sex romps and islanders' sex
lives, but it had been hopeless. The conversation that ebbed and
flowed round him had centred on the finer points of diplomacy,
complex speculation about the role of the American State
Department, and the simple matter of whether they would all be
shot or not. Try as he might, he had returned without any material
to feed the Bouverie Street sex obsession.

The next day he was about to set off reluctantly into the cold to interrogate some Marines when he was saved by the sudden declaration of a state of emergency. Filing the news to Petrie, he declared the sex story dead. The Marines were now on full alert and therefore could not be interviewed about it – or even do it, for that matter.

The four hacks confronted the Argentinian forces by hiding under the bed in the chauffeur's cottage in the grounds of Government House, thereby inadvertently putting themselves in the crossfire. The *Telegraph* man had his cheek grazed by a British Marine who mistook him for an Argentian sniper, but the hacks all survived to surrender to Argentinian Special Forces, who spoke perfect English thanks to their American training. To their surprise they were then given press passes and allowed to roam the island. The rub came when they tried to file. The Argentinians refused to let them use the phones, and when two planeloads of Argentinian hacks were flown in to report exclusively on the great victory, the British reporters decided there was nothing more they could do. Persuading the Argentinians to let them catch the next flight, they returned to Comodoro, from where Graves filed reams of copy which MacKenzie liberally spread over the paper while he strutted about the office claiming the glory for having the foresight to send him.

From day one MacKenzie never had a flicker of doubt about the Falklands. Mindless patriotic fervour and flag-waving jingoism had always been the trademark of popular newspapers, and the *Sun*, taking over the mantle of chief John Bull tub-thumper from the *Express*, simply reflected changing circulation patterns. And now, for the first time in a war, the *Sun* could apply all the techniques of modern tabloid journalism.

The paper kicked off by lampooning the Foreign Secretary Lord Carrington as a mouse against Churchill's bulldog along with a splash of 'WE'LL SMASH 'EM!' 'The *Sun* Says' castigated the Foreign Office as a 'safe haven for appeasers since Munich', while Murdoch's newly acquired *Times*, the now feeble-voiced Thunderer, followed the same line by denouncing the Argentinian action as 'naked aggression', without equal since the days of Hitler. Carrington resigned. In America Murdoch's *New York Post* took a more laid-back attitude. Columnist James Brady commented that he was worried about the Domino Theory: 'The Falkland Islands this week, the Sandwich Islands (Hawaii) next, then maybe Coney Island,' he wrote for the benefit of smart New Yorkers.

In Bouverie Street the hacks initially treated the start of the war with the same mixture of astonishment and levity as their counterparts on the rest of the Street. It was a brilliant story, with the Task Force cast as an updated version of gun-boat diplomacy, but it did not look as though it was going to escalate into anything serious. At first some senior execs saw it as similar to Harold Wilson's Cod War. Roy Greenslade, who had been on holiday in Malta when he first read the news, had fallen about laughing. Back at work, he confided his opinion to Wendy Henry, a rising star in the features department, that it was stupid and we should just hand over the islands. But instead of agreeing with him she replied: 'You'll have to watch that. That's a very unpopular view to hold round here.'

Henry had been rapidly rising in influence on the paper under the patronage of MacKenzie. Born in Manchester, she was taken by her mother to Peeblesshire after the collapse of her parents' marriage. At the age of sixteen Henry and her twin sister Sara returned to Manchester to live with their father, Sam, a market trader. The three had a flat near the university, where the twins dabbled in ultra-left politics, and were associated with the Trotskyite International Socialists (IS) group, later to become the Socialist Workers' Party. The twins, who were virtually identical, were both involved in a celebrated incident when a take-away curry was thrown at the screen of a cinema showing *The Green Berets*, the gung-ho, gook-slaughtering John Wayne Vietnam movie.

But by the time she was eighteen Henry had had a baby as a result of a short-lived marriage and resourcefully started making her living working for a news agency in the city, getting her big break in 1976 when by chance she met Geraldine Ellis, the daughter of Ruth Ellis, the last woman to be hanged in Britain. Henry sold the story to the *News of the World*, then edited by Shrimsley and his assistant Nick Lloyd, and made an immediate impression with her tough approach, low-life contacts and endless stream of story ideas.

After three years as an attached freelance at the *News of the World*, she moved to the job of features editor on *Woman* magazine, which was a well-worn stepping-stone to a job on one of the tabloids. At the beginning of 1981 she wrote to the *Sun* asking for a job and Peter Stephens, then caretaker editor while MacKenzie worked out his *Express* contract, hired her to do the lowly job of reading books for serialisation potential. Henry soon became known in the office for her habit of dressing in layers of black fishnet stockings, miniskirts, Lycra boobtubes, legwarmers, boots or high heels and, though not actually dirty, permanently looking as though she needed a good wash, her dark hair, streaked with blonde, invariably a tangled mess. The overall effect was topped off by copious masses of chunky gold jewellery, from earrings at one end to ankle chain at the other.

MacKenzie did not take to her instantly, but once he realised her worth came to rely on her more and more and soon started calling her 'baggage-chops' – by his standards a considerable term of affection. She appealed to him as genuinely working class with a street-fighter mentality, and he loved her market-trader spiel, demonstrated to good effect when she auctioned off the dross of unwanted freebies in the women's department for charity: 'Now then, ladies – smile if you're not wearing any knickers,' she cried, and they did, just as they smiled when they heard her screeching down the phone in her lisping Jewish voice with its northern accent: 'On my life . . .', which signified that she was probably leading someone up the garden path. When the screech intensified to 'On my life and on my *mother's* life . . .' it was certain she was.

MacKenzie promoted Henry to women's editor, telling Greenslade: 'That funny-looking Wendy woman who keeps coming up with all the ideas, we ought to give her a go.' As a

MacKenzie clone, who shared his penchant for foul language, she was now rapidly gaining prominence through her masterminding of the coverage of TV soaps. It was a perfect job for her. Not only was she an avid and genuine fan, but some hacks thought her whole life was lived as if she was starring in a mini-series of her own and were worried by blurring of real life and fictional screen activity in soap stories. Nevertheless, by the time of the Falklands War Henry had risen to become a full member of the editor's inner coterie, pushing Greenslade into a more technical, background role.

As MacKenzie cleared the paper's decks for war a cap was found for Petrie, who was promoted to become 'Commander' Petrie. Petrie, fondly remembering his days of National Service, in turn allocated ranks to all the staff (women hacks were made 'Wrens'). Hacks doing well would find themselves rapidly promoted and a brilliant story could make them colonel overnight. A picture of Winston Churchill was hung on the wall above the newsdesk alongside a map with little flags stuck in to show where all the ships were. Once the 'ops room' had been established, MacKenzie then marched about, back ramrod straight in parody of a sergeant-major, barking out: 'Commander Petrie, you 'orrible little man – what is the situation at the front?' Petrie would jump to attention, salute and bark back: '1100 hours and all calm and correct, Sah!'

As part of its backing for Maggie, the *Sun* grabbed the role of the serviceman's friend. The slogan 'The Paper that Supports Our Boys' was slapped under the masthead and news hackette Muriel Burden was appointed 'Darling of the Fleet'. Burden, a small blonde Geordie with a toothy smile who always addressed Petrie as 'Tommy pet', was in charge of funnelling *Sun* supplies to the lads which varied from love poems to pictures of Page Three girls and video cassettes of the Cup Final. But the *Sun*'s pen-pal service for the troops was abandoned when the *Guardian*, the World's Worst Newspaper, revealed that the lads had started what was known as the '*Sun* Dog Board', to which pictures of the more unfortunate-looking drippy and demented girls were pinned.

But at that time, as the Task Force steamed towards its far-off destination, the trouble was that there was very little to write about. The *Sun* had Tony Snow, a former Press Association reporter, as its man on HMS *Invincible* – an unfortunate choice as he was a committed family man with four children, whom MacKenzie had mistakenly thought was single. The newsdesk was now adjusting to daily harassment by a distraught Mrs Snow, while her husband desperately radioed back from the ship for his blood group, which he was supposed to have on a disc round his neck.

To fill up the news gap, and in tribute to the Lamb/King formula, the paper fell back on its staple preoccupation of knickers which Murdoch had always grumbled about. 'THE SUN SAYS KNICKERS TO ARGENTINA!' informed readers on page 3: 'Britain's secret weapon in the Falklands dispute was revealed last night . . . it's undie-cover warfare.' Thousands of women were 'sporting specially made underwear embroidered across the front with the proud name of the ship on which a husband or boyfriend is serving'. Prince Andrew, out there with the Task Force, had bought several pairs of 'battle briefs'. The Page Three girl, delightful Debbie Boyland, was punningly captioned as 'all shipshape and Bristol fashion' and sporting 'nautical naughties' as she made a 'splashing Deb-ut' in the battle colours of HMS *Invincible*.

The twelve-million-strong army of *Sun* readers was then mobilised by being encouraged to send in for free 'The *Sun* says Good Luck Lads' badges. To bring the battle to their own homes they could buy a computer game for their Sinclair Spectrums called 'Obliterate', in which the player commanded a British submarine torpedoing 'Argie' ships. Then they were urged to hit the Argies in the only place they understood – their pockets – by joining the paper's boycott of Argentinian corned beef. But there was no need for corned-beef fans to go hungry. The *Sun* offered free cans of Fray Bentos non-Argentinian corned beef plus a cash prize of £5 a competition for the best 'Argie Bargie' jokes sent in to the paper. The standard was low.

Meanwhile the question of whether war would break out in

earnest was being entrusted to the shuttle diplomacy of the American Secretary of State. 'Only General Al Haig stood in the way of war last night . . .' MacKenzie mused one night to the splash subs as they stood at the stone waiting to sign away the front page. 'You can't run that!' the sub replied, appalled at such bloodlust but unsure whether her editor was joking or not. MacKenzie appeared puzzled but took the point.

Instead the paper got its first real opportunity to push things along when Graves, now set up in a new base at the Buenos Aires Sheraton along with the rest of the world's media, filed an exclusive that the Argentinians where about to offer a negotiated settlement based on joint sovereignty. Graves angled the story to suggest that peace was now a distinct possibility, as his contacts in the Argentinian forces had told him, along of the lines of 'Hopes for peace were boosted last night . . .' But MacKenzie had turned the story on its head, splashing 'STICK IT UP YOUR JUNTA!' and reporting how the paper's rent-a-quote Tory MPs were promising a fight to the finish. Later editions were beefed up with a statement from a late-night War Cabinet which had also rejected the peace offer. The *Sun*'s promotional department cashed in on 'STICK IT UP YOUR JUNTA!' with 'Are you feeling shirty with the enemy? Want to give those damn Argies a whole lot of Bargie? Why not a "*Sun*-sational" T-shirt carrying the headline at super-low price of only £2?'

Over in South America Graves shuddered when he saw 'STICK IT UP YOUR JUNTA!' But he was soon to get a bigger shock from the spin being put on it by Bouverie Street. His military contacts told him British warships were nearing South Georgia, the island to the east of the Falklands where the 'scrap-metal dealers' had first run up the Argentinian flag. Argentinian troops there were now preparing for a possible British invasion that night. A few hours after he had sent the story Graves was called back by one of the newsdesk minions. 'Great exclusive! Kelvin's very pleased. But we want a blow-by-blow diary of the invasion. Can you do it?'

'Sure,' Graves replied. 'When it happens.' There was a short silence at the other end of the line. 'What do you mean "when"?' the voice demanded incredulously. 'We've just sent away the front page with your story on it. Listen, I'll read it to you: "INVASION! Britain's counter-invasion forces swept ashore on the stolen island of South Georgia yesterday . . ."'

Graves was staggered. He had agonised over including the risky prediction that the invasion was 'imminent' in his report. But Bouverie Street had trumped him by simply announcing it had happened. The huge gamble worked. By the time the *Sun* was in the newsagents in Britain the islands had been reinvaded. Graves was impressed by the bravado of the Bouverie Street war-machine and decided that his editor was leading a charmed life.

But MacKenzie had less luck with his next gamble a couple of days later. Wild rumours from America that British troops, cunningly disguised, had landed on the Falkland Islands themselves were elevated into the splash 'IN WE GO!' The story explained: 'Some commandos are already reported to have landed, waiting for the invasion that could only be hours away.' Substituting 'America's CIA' for the normal 'informed sources', the paper told readers the commandos were 'posing as shepherds'.

Increasingly impatient for action, the *Sun* reworked the 'JUNTA!' headline to 'STICK THIS UP YOUR JUNTA!', illustrated by a picture of a missile bursting out of the sea. The caption read: 'Here it comes, Senors . . .', skirting the awkward fact that the picture was a stock Ministry of Defence press handout showing a Polaris nuclear missile. The article, under Wendy Henry's byline, read: 'The first missile to hit Galtieri's gauchos will come with love from the *Sun*. And just in case he doesn't get the message, the weapon will have painted on the side, "Up yours, Galtieri" and will be signed by Tony Snow, our man aboard HMS *Invincible*. . . .' The copy explained that the paper was 'sponsoring' the missile by paying towards the ship's victory party once the war was over. But it went down badly on the ship, where the servicemen had not been consulted about this munificence. The *Sun*'s thirst for war was angering many of them as they were the ones in the firing line. Copies of the paper were later to be burned in some of the quarters, and disgusted letters were printed in the ship's newsletter. Hacks on the fellow Task Force ship the *Canberra* were so outraged that they jointly sent a message of protest to Bouverie Street, but three days later Snow nonetheless reported that the missile (now a Sidewinder) had hit an Argentinian bomber.

But events in the South Atlantic were at this stage overtaken by a more immediate confrontation at Bouverie Street. The *Sun's* NUJ chapel had finally voted to strike in the latest round of their battle with what they saw as a hard-faced and intransigent management. The money, staffing levels and attention lavished on *The Times* had made their mood uglier and the new militancy chimed with unhappiness about the paper's Falklands coverage among the more left-wing hacks, who were politically more inclined to strike anyway. MacKenzie was furious about the dispute, and the clash of loyalties further soured the tense atmosphere in the office. Graves, out on a limb in Buenos Aires, didn't even know what was happening.

The strike took the form of disrupting production by holding continuous mandatory chapel meetings, and on 3 May Bouverie Street was in chaos as twelve execs, struggling with unfamiliar jobs, put the paper together. Greenslade and David Banks, subbing the sports pages, found them impossible to take seriously and were enjoying themselves, sniggering as they laid down cliché-ridden headlines like 'KICK AND RUSH GLORY BOYS'. Suddenly MacKenzie shouted across the virtually deserted room: 'Christ! We've hit an Argie ship!' He was clutching a wire-service report from Buenos Aires, which simply stated that a warship called the *General Belgrano* had been hit.

Everyone in the room was shocked. The war had suddenly become real. The silence was abruptly broken by Wendy Henry, giving the sort of gut reaction which was her forté. 'Wend' was exultant. 'Gotcha!' she shouted, her ample bosom wobbling, jewellery clanking and ankle chain sliding up and down as she did a heavy little jig. 'Gotcha, Argies!'

'Wendy, you're a bloody genius!' MacKenzie shouted, dashing off to sketch out the splash as the other execs dropped what they were doing and clustered round the backbench. Graves came straight on the line confirming the hit and enterprisingly adding more detail. He had looked up the *General Belgrano* in the copy of *Jane's Fighting Ships* liberated from Government House by an Unpopular hack during the retreat from Port Stanley. *Jane's* gave the ship's full complement as 1,200 men, and it would certainly have been fully crewed. On the back of this Graves filed a story saying that up to 1,200 Argentinians might have been killed. Meanwhile the wire-service reports flooding into Bouverie Street were painting a blacker and blacker picture and soon Commander Petrie had enough hard information to tell MacKenzie: 'Look Kelvin, this is more serious than we thought. They've sunk the bloody thing. A lot of people have died.'

MacKenzie immediately realised the full significance of what they had done. The current splash read 'GOTCHA' above a subhead: 'Our lads sink gunboat and hole cruiser'. The story running reflected the paper's lack of the full facts: 'WALLOP; they torpedoed the 14,000 ton Argentinian cruiser *General Belgrano* and left it a useless wreck.' 'The *Belgrano* and its 1,000 crew needn't worry about the war for some time now.' It ended, 'The ship was not sunk, and it is not clear how many casualties there were.'

Henry, too, felt slightly sick as the stupidity of her unthinking initial reaction sank in. Both she and MacKenzie agreed that both headline and story must be pulled. MacKenzie shouted the order and the compositors started breaking up the plate to replace 'GOTCHA' with the weak 'DID 1200 ARGIES DROWN?' over a new story based on creative journalistic accounting.

But if MacKenzie was shocked by what he had done, Rupert Murdoch, in Bouverie Street to oversee the handling of the strike, was not. Murdoch had been down the corridor in the office of editorial director Peter Stephens, where the two men were immersed in a long discussion about the strike. When a messenger brought in the 'GOTCHA' edition Stephens looked at it, sucked his teeth and told Murdoch he thought the headline was a mistake. Murdoch disagreed. 'I rather like it,' he said.

The pair were still leafing through the paper when MacKenzie burst in, fired up with adrenalin and visibly shaken. 'I've had to change it all because there's a report that there may be 1,200 Argies dead,' he gabbled before rushing back up the corridor. Bringing his discussion with Stephens to an end, Murdoch strolled out on to the editorial floor, where MacKenzie caught up with him. 'I wouldn't have pulled it if I was you,' Murdoch said in a casual way. 'Seemed like a bloody good headline to me.' MacKenzie protested. 'A lot of people have died, Boss,' he said. 'Maybe our own people have been hurt. We don't know yet.' But Murdoch assured him: 'Nah, you'll be all right,' walking off apparently unconcerned.

Murdoch was wrong. 'GOTCHA' was seized on by the country as summing up the crass, mindless bloodlust of the pop papers. But in the following days there was to be much justification of the headline in Bouverie Street as the hacks heatedly debated the row it had caused. The pro-'GOTCHA' lobby argued that the headline brilliantly encapsulated what many *Sun* readers (and others) would have instinctively thought on hearing the first news.

The paper had correctly identified that the readers had been getting fed up with the lack of action. The first wave of enthusiasm for the conflict had been petering out as the risible Argies refused to play their appointed part and cravenly surrender just because the Task Force had turned up. Now they were being taught a lesson – as 'GOTCHA' signified. But, the anti-'GOTCHA' hacks argued, everyone knew a big story breaking in the early evening and then running through the night was a modern newspaper nightmare. As Lamb had understood, because of TV, newspapers were now out of date almost as soon as they went on the presses – and certainly by the next morning when they appeared on the streets. So stories of this sort needed treating with extreme journalistic caution – a quality, they reminded everyone, which both MacKenzie and Henry conspicuously lacked. Furthermore, they added, first reports of big incidents are by their very nature often garbled, sketchy and terribly inaccurate. The mood 'GOTCHA' had captured was that of a fleeting instant – not of the next day when it would be read.

The 'GOTCHA' headline had come as big a shock to many of the hacks as it had to the general public. Most of them had gone straight home from the mandatory meeting and missed the drama in the office. The first they had known about it was the next day when they saw the bald word plastered across the front page as a flat and vindictive statement, without even a triumphant '!' to soften it. That was the sort of trouble people like MacKenzie and Henry got you into, they concluded. They were dangerous.

The paper tried to atone for its mistake the next day by splashing: 'ALIVE! – Hundreds of Argies saved from Atlantic' above a 'special *Sun* report' under Petrie's byline. The story said that more than 400 seamen from the *Belgrano* had already been picked up. 'In the end the toll from the sinking will probably be less than 100,' it stated, in one of the rare examples of the *Sun* underplaying the facts. The final death toll was 368.

In Buenos Aires Graves was amazed and disgusted by 'GOTCHA'. It wasn't MacKenzie who upset him – he thought the headline was typical – but the rest of the staff for not stopping him printing it. It was only three days later that he found out the strike had been on. But by this time Graves had plenty of other worries on his mind. All the hacks covering the war feared they might be arrested or put in jail if the war escalated, and at the back of all their minds was the worst-case scenario of all – the Argentinian junta's terrifying death squads, which had already meted out summary justice by executing or torturing local journalists.

The Argentinians had assured the foreign hacks that they would be safe if they stayed in the hotel reporting the fighting in the Falklands rather than going out on the streets looking for dissidents. But one British reporter had still been badly beaten up and a Thames Television crew kidnapped and dumped in the middle of the countryside with sacks over their heads after mild criticism of the regime. Graves was now wondering what the military authorities would make of 'GOTCHA', coming as it did in the wake of 'STICK IT UP YOUR JUNTA!' and the *Sun*'s personalised Sidewinder missile.

Although the Argentinians had not imposed censorship, Graves knew that they were taping all the calls in and out of the hotel. Other colleagues praised their offices for being enviably circumspect and careful on the line, but he had to keep sitting there rigid with horror as Petrie bawled remarks from Bouverie Street like: 'What these Argies want is a bit of cold steel up 'em, Dave! You sort 'em out, Dave! And that's an order from Kelvin, got it?' In his darkest moments Graves even wondered if he was being set up for his forthcoming execution. 'ARGIES HACK SUN MAN TO DEATH' would make a great MacKenzie splash, he thought morosely. It didn't help that he was working for Murdoch, who owned *The Times*, with the consequent equation in Argentinian minds: Murdoch = *Times* = British government.

Then there was the matter of his copy, which had often been changed beyond recognition when it appeared in the paper. Apart from 'STICK IT UP YOUR JUNTA!' and the premature invasion of the Falklands there had been other incidents. Graves had filed an early exclusive that the Argentinian fleet had sailed, going to great lengths to emphasise that it was heading south to the Falklands, and not on a direct course towards the Task Force. But the story had been promptly turned into a splash of 'THIS IS IT!' above copy which now said the Argies were sailing straight at the Task Force, bent on battle. Now 'GOTCHA' had brought the nightmare spectre of the death squads a step nearer, and anything could happen next.

One evening shortly after 'GOTCHA' Graves was having dinner in a restaurant when an Argentinian admiral approached his table. His heart sank as the imposing uniformed figure asked: 'Mr Graves, may I speak to you?' Graves assented and the admiral went on: 'We have been looking at your reports to London.' This was it, thought Graves – at the very least the boot out of the country, if not torture in one of the junta's dungeons. But then he saw the admiral was smiling gently. 'And these reports of yours, they don't always appear in quite the same way in the paper as you have written them, do they?' The admiral smiled again and walked off. Realising he was obviously sympathetic, Graves relaxed. He had been saved by the military authorities bugging his calls.

Back in Bouverie Street the Argentinian reply to the sinking of the *Belgrano* by reducing HMS *Sheffield* to a smouldering hulk put a new, nasty edge on the patriotism required by staff. MacKenzie drove his reign of terror to new heights by stepping up the harassment of 'lefties' for their lack of whole-hearted enthusiasm for the British cause, and all the hacks now learned to be doubly careful about opening their mouths. You could either be bollocked for not supporting the war effort, or if you made some silly, flippant remark there was a huge danger it would end up in the paper like 'GOTCHA'.

But the escalation of the war had also caused a genuine change of mood among some who had previously been quietly derisive about the paper's juvenile jingoism. Now kids had started dying a strong wave of feeling swept through the office, especially on the subs' desk and the backbench led by the chief sub Roger Wood, that whatever the rights and wrongs of the business it was no longer a time to question things. Instead the paper's job was to get behind the lads to give the 'poor bloody infantry' full support. Senior hacks like Greenslade, who were not so certain, put their heads down and took refuge in reverting to the role of being mere technicians.

There was a different attitude one night when a similar situation arose to the *Belgrano* and the paper was being night edited by David Banks, a popular editorial executive. The newsflash just said, 'British ship hit,' and the desk agonised for precious minutes as the deadline for the edition crept closer and there was no further news. The splash sub and Banks both agreed it would be unspeakably cruel to go with a headline as vague as that which would give a heart attack to everyone with relatives or friends on any of our ships – including Mrs Snow. The edition would just have to be held open until the name of the ship was known. They sat there in an atmosphere of electric tension until more news finally dropped. The ship was the *Atlantic Conveyor*. The edition, now carrying this definitive information as the splash, went late.

After the sinking of the *Sheffield* the other papers split from their previous universal, if muted, support for the war, and the World's Worst and the *Mirror* started editorialising about whether too high a price was being paid. The BBC, maintaining its tradition of impartiality, also cast doubt on the official British versions of the sea battles by quoting Argentinian official sources alongside them. A Tory backbencher then set things up by asking the Prime Minister in the Commons whether the British point of view was being presented in a way likely to 'give support and encouragement to our servicemen and their families'. The Argentinians were being treated almost as equals, Mrs Thatcher replied.

The *Sun* dutifully turned its big gun of leader writer Ronald Spark on the enemy within. 'DARE CALL IT TREASON' 'The *Sun* Says' was headed the next day. The first sentence, heavily underlined, read: 'There are traitors in our midst.' Spark continued: 'The Prime Minister did not speak of treason. The *Sun* does not hesitate to use the word. . . .' He specifically named as traitors firstly the BBC's defence correspondent, Peter Snow, and then the 'pygmy *Guardian*'. But Spark's main vitriol was reserved for the rival *Mirror*. Many of the *Mirror's* editorial staff were Labour Party members, and four senior executives from the paper had been given life peerages in the 1970s. The *Mirror* had been caught between its detestation of Galtieri and its opposition to Thatcher, fully realising, like the *Sun*, that she was so personally identified with the war that her political future rested on its outcome. A *Mirror* leader entitled 'MIGHT ISN'T RIGHT' had warned against mounting hysteria and the cost in lives, concluding: 'The killing has got to stop. . . . If that means Britain and Argentina need to compromise, then compromise they must.'

Spark replied in his leader:

> What is it but treason for this timorous, whining publication [the *Mirror*] to plead day after day for appeasing the Argentinian dictators . . .
>
> We are truly sorry for the *Daily Mirror*'s readers.
>
> They are buying a newspaper which again and again demonstrates it has no faith in its country and no respect for her people.

The first reaction of the *Mirror*'s editor Mike Molloy was to call in the lawyers, who advised that the paper would almost certainly win a libel action. Instead Molloy decided to use Joe Haines, Harold Wilson's former press secretary, who had been the paper's leader writer. Haines took an hour and ten minutes to write the reply, Molloy took out a couple of lines, and it was printed the next day across an entire page under the headline: 'THE HARLOT OF FLEET STREET'.

The *Sun* was a 'coarse and demented newspaper', Haines wrote.

> There have been lying newspapers before. But in the past month it has broken all records.
>
> It has long been a tawdry newspaper. But since the Falklands crisis began it has fallen from the gutter to the sewer . . .
>
> From behind the safety of its typewriters it has called for battle to commence to satisfy its bloodlust. The *Sun* today is to journalism what Dr Joseph Goebbels was to truth. Even *Pravda* would blush to be bracketed with it.
>
> A Labour MP yesterday called for the *Sun* to be prosecuted for criminal libel. There is no point in that. It has the perfect defence: Guilty but insane.

A few days later a motion in the *Sun*'s NUJ chapel condemning MacKenzie for the editorial was roundly defeated. Simon Jenkins wrote in his column in *The Times*, the *Sun*'s new sister paper, that Spark's editorial would have made Senator McCarthy blush, but the paper's leader pages refrained from comment.

Many of the *Sun*'s readers wrote in to praise their paper and the robust stand it was taking against both the Argies and the enemy within. Spark was unrepentant and when asked to attend a disciplinary hearing to expel him for breaching the NUJ's Code of Conduct wrote back:

> As far as I am concerned you can meet at midnight on a raft in the middle of the Thames or at any other time or in any other place. I have not the slightest intention of attending, and no one will have

any authority to represent me. I shall correspond with you no further. I shall ignore any so-called findings. Had I the common touch of, say, a *Guardian* leader writer, my attitude to your committee could be summed up in two words. Get stuffed.
    Yours truly
    Ron Spark

The NUJ committee denounced Spark's leader as 'vituperative, callous and clearly designed to inflame public opinion' and expelled him, but, after an appeal when feelings had died down he was reinstated. Yet the mixed feelings aroused by 'GOTCHA' persisted and MacKenzie defiantly put an ozalid proof of the front page on the wall behind his desk. Many of the subs still thought it was the best headline ever, and went on pointing out that it had only been the timing that had been wrong.

But the reporters, already disenchanted with MacKenzie and the other execs who had worked to get the paper out during the strike, continued to use it as a stick to beat him. It was an example, they confirmed to each other in the Top of the Tip, of how he got into trouble if they weren't around. Some even ventured the opinion that their editor had gone mad and the whole war coverage only accentuated the growing rift between the Lamb reporters and their new editor. They felt that Lamb, for all the DIY sex manuals, tits and his regal aloofness, had been an old-fashioned newspaperman at heart. MacKenzie represented the sloganising power of the despised subs' table. The *Sun*'s coverage, they told each other, had more than amply confirmed the old cliché: 'Truth is the first casualty in war.'

'GOTCHA' and 'STICK IT UP YOUR JUNTA!' – the monster catchy headlines were all that was talked about these days. More and more the hacks felt their words were becoming an adjunct to be bent and moulded to fit a headline that had often been composed in advance. A favourite sign in newspaper offices had used to be 'WHO THE HELL READS THE SECOND PARAGRAPH?' As they now saw it at the *Sun* in the 1980s it was rapidly becoming a question of 'WHO THE HELL READS ANY OF THE PARAGRAPHS AT ALL?'

Graves and Snow, the reporters who had been on the spot, were welcomed back as heroes by MacKenzie, who whisked them off to lunch and explained how worried the office had been about them. Graves, shuddering at the memory of Petrie's crassness on the phone, was just about to complain about how he had been dropped in it, when MacKenzie suddenly went on: 'Yes, we were very worried about you – very worried indeed. We thought the Argies had turned you. Some of that stuff you sent us was very pro-Argie, eh?'

Graves, appreciating that his editor was being serious, took his promised free holiday and accepted a good pay rise, but when a job came up at the *Daily Telegraph* he left thankfully. Anyhow, for *Sun* readers there had been good reason for ending the war. The Pope was visiting Britain, but much more importantly the football World Cup was starting in Spain. The British Airways theme tune, which was the team song, was vying with the music from *Chariots of Fire* to express the spirit of Thatcherism, and hysterical speculation had been mounting that the lads might have to pull out if matches fell so we were up against the filthy Argies.

There was also the awkward fact that the Argentinians were the world champions, and could therefore be expected to reverse the Falklands result on the field. The further random element of the staunch British soccer hooligan taking events into his own hands had enabled the hype to revolve round a dozen potential nightmare situations.

Instead, peace had broken out before the Cup started, the Argentinians blew it, and the *Sun* was able triumphantly to splash 'ARGIES SMASHED' long before things got out of hand. The story started: 'They strutted, they cheated, and afterwards they bleated. That was the arrogant Argentinians last night. They swaggered on as world champions, and crawled off, humiliated by little Belgium. . . .'

The Argies disposed of all round, Lord Matthews's QE2 sailed into Plymouth with the first contingent of heroes and the paper led off its crude celebrations with a front-page picture of a woman baring her breasts, ostensibly for the benefit of the troops on the liner, while Murdoch repaid loyal readers by holding the cover price at 14p when its rivals were putting their prices up to cover increased newsprint costs.

Quite how far MacKenzie would have gone if the war had continued was a subject of intense debate in the office. A pointer had been given when *Private Eye* brought out a spoof *Sun* front page asking: 'IS THE POPE GAY? – 10 TELLTALE SIGNS', and strapping a competition entitled 'KILL AN ARGIE AND WIN A METRO'. When MacKenzie saw it pinned up on the office wall he was lost in admiration. 'Fucking brilliant!' he smiled rapturously. 'Why couldn't we have thought of that, eh?' The hacks found out later that there had been a different reaction to the *Private Eye* spoof on HMS *Invincible*. Many of the sailors on the ship had initially believed that the page was part of a genuine copy of the *Sun*.

Chapter 8

Maggie's Leg-Over

Victory in the Falklands banished any doubts the *Sun* may have entertained about Mrs Thatcher. It was also a relief for the paper itself. There had been a nagging worry that the *Mirror* and the *Star*, which both supported Labour, would gain readers on the back of the unpopularity of Maggie's harsh industrial medicine, which had pushed unemployment over three million. On the eve of the Falklands the Conservatives' opinion-poll rating had fallen to 25 per cent – a drop of twenty points in two years, but afterwards the 1979 election figure of 45 per cent miraculously returned. The Falklands effect had been even more dramatic on Mrs Thatcher's personal rating. Previously it had slumped below the 25 per cent recorded by the party as a whole but during the conflict it soared to an extraordinary 80 per cent.

The effect of the war on the *Sun* was less marked and its circulation remained static, along with those of its two main rivals, the *Mirror* and the *Star*. But MacKenzie still had plenty of reason to join Maggie's victory celebrations. The paper was now selling 4,224,000 copies a day and had increased its lead over the *Mirror* by 900,000 since he had become editor a year earlier. The *Star* was making no impact and could now be safely said to have been nipped in the bud. The combination of bingo and MacKenzie's extraordinary barn-storming style seemed to be working.

Now that Maggie had regained some of her popularity the *Sun's* deification of her knew no bounds, with MacKenzie her most enthusiastic supporter. Like Murdoch, he felt an affinity with her as outside the establishment and would forgive her anything because of her firm convictions and her unshakeable beliefs. Even when he disagreed with her about something he would always say: 'She's wrong – but she's strong.'

As MacKenzie saw it Maggie had saved the country from the soggy centre, the liberals and soft left who read the World's Worst Newspaper and were now emerging with talk of a 'third force'. Despite their small numbers, these people had dominated Britain in the era before Maggie abolished 'consensus' politics.

By now it was clear that the Tory revival owed as much to the self-destruction of the Labour Party, as to Maggie's Falklands success. 'Farmer Jim' Callaghan's resignation after the 1979 defeat had unleashed a bitter struggle between the left and right wings of the party resulting in the election of Michael Foot in November 1980, with Denis Healey, whom Callaghan had favoured, as his deputy.

Soon afterwards, Labour MPs hoping the Foot–Healey leadership combination would prevent the party splitting were disappointed when in March 1981 the 'Gang of Four' of David Owen, Shirley Williams, Roy Jenkins and Bill Rodgers left to form the SDP, tilting Labour's internal balance of power further to the left. The party's internal divisions immediately took another catastrophic turn, appropriately on April Fool's Day, when Tony Benn announced he would stand against Healey for deputy leader in the election at the party's autumn conference. The previous contest had been decided by the votes of Labour MPs alone, but under new party rules this time trade unions and party activists who belonged to an electoral college would vote as well, giving Benn a real chance of winning.

The *Sun* and the other Tory papers promptly erected the nightmare scenario. Labour was ten points ahead of the Tories at that time. Therefore it might win the next general election. And if it did Benn, as deputy, would be ideally placed to take over from the elderly Foot and become Prime Minister. The *Sun* had been against Benn even in the 1970s when it was giving Labour lukewarm support, and urged his sacking as Secretary of State for Industry in 1975. The paper, sneering at him for renouncing his peerage, had used to refer to him as Mr Anthony Wedgwood ('Citizen') Benn and now 'The *Sun* Says' kicked off its coverage of his deputy leadership campaign with 'BENN'S RED ARMY'. 'An end to the sham. A cross on the ballot for a party which has Benn waiting in the wings for its top job is a cross for the bleak and cold regimes of Eastern Europe and for a government on their model,' it said.

As Benn stepped up his campaign a new element was stirred into what was basically the tedious old vendetta between Labour's two traditional wings. Benn was now encouraging single-issue activists like feminists and gays, blacks and anti-nuclear campaigners to pile into dilapidated inner-city Labour Party machines and take over from the right-wing old guard. He himself stomped the country addressing as many fringe pressure groups as he could. He believed he had found a new factor in Labour's complex power brokerage to tip the finely balanced contest in his favour. As his rival Healey was quick to point out, this meant picking up some very weird supporters indeed, including anarchists and the Posadists, who believed socialism would be established with the aid of aliens from outer space.

Benn narrowly lost the deputy leadership contest at the autumn conference, but the margin of less than 1 per cent in the votes put new wind in the sails of the Bennite alliance, which was also gaining ground at the party's grass-roots. The *Sun*, like all the papers except the World's Worst had generally ignored the type of people he was getting on board, unless they did something entertainingly newsworthy, like feminists burning their bras. But now the combination of Benn's 'rainbow alliance' and the elevation of Ken Livingstone to leadership of the Greater London Council brought them increasingly on to the political stage.

Livingstone, bringing together a 'hard left' stance on issues like nuclear disarmament and Northern Ireland with new 'loony' obsessions like radical feminism and gay rights, was a natural *Sun* target and the paper greeted him with the splash of 'RED KEN

CLOWNED KING OF LONDON' when he took over on 8 May 1981. A minute scrutiny of his lifestyle for clues to deviancy disappointingly revealed only that he kept newts and lived extremely modestly.

'Fucking newts!' MacKenzie raged at the team deployed to 'monster' Livingstone. 'All you can find is newts?' They were sent off to try again. But it was still just newts.

Red Ken's private life was relentlessly dull. Instead the *Sun* turned to his political activities and his speeches at endless meetings. There was plenty of mileage for the *Sun* in what he said. 'RED KEN SPEAKS UP FOR THE GAYS', the paper reported; 'THIS DAMN FOOL SAYS BOMBERS AREN'T CRIMINALS' headed a report of a speech saying the Provisional IRA was motivated by political, and not simply criminal, aims. 'NOW THE DAMN FOOL IS TAKING US TO THE PRESS COUNCIL' the paper replied when Livingstone made an official complaint to the Press Council after the *Sun* described him as 'the most odious man in Britain.' (The complaint was rejected.)

Attacks bearing the characteristic head-banging stamp of Ronnie Spark described him variously as a 'little twit', 'the most hated man in Britain', and leader of a 'grubby pack of Marxists' who 'would end up with a punch on the nose' if he 'risked some of his extreme opinions in a pub'.

The Benn and Livingstone show inside the Labour Party and in local government was providing MacKenzie with much better material than the ordinary parliamentary political reporting organised by Walter Terry, the political editor he had inherited from Lamb who already knew he was on MacKenzie's hit list.

MacKenzie bollocked Terry constantly, accusing him of being a member of the parliamentary club and failing to get the sort of human-interest stories the readers wanted. 'Forget all this crap about politicians – who's interested, eh?' MacKenzie would rant at him. 'You only write this bollocks so you can look good with all your fucking mates in Westminster. You are not writing it for the readers – the readers don't give a fuck about politics. The readers, eh, Walter? Know who they are? Pay your fucking wages, eh?

Why don't you get a story for them, eh? One with people they've heard of for a change.'

At one editorial conference, MacKenzie defined his idea of the definitive humdinger political story: 'What I want to know is this. Who's Maggie got her leg over, eh?' Terry, who had already written off MacKenzie as a maniac, decided that the only way to deal with a silly question like this was to tell the truth. 'I presume it's Denis – but it's only a guess,' he replied sarcastically. Then pausing for a second, he added: 'However I do know for certain who Jim Prior has got his leg over.' MacKenzie fell for the sucker punch. Prior was a Tory 'wet' and therefore a sworn enemy of the Prime Minister. Dirt on him would be especially welcome. 'Go on then,' he urged Terry eagerly. 'Who is it then, eh? Tell me!' Terry paused again before confiding conspiratorially: 'Mrs Prior.' 'Don't think you can take the fucking piss out of me, you c***,' MacKenzie hissed back at him. Terry winced. One of the things he most disliked about his editor was his language and his foul sarff London vulgarity. For him the difference between Lamb and MacKenzie was summed up by the way they offered hospitality. Lamb would offer good-quality whisky poured from an immaculate cut-glass decanter while MacKenzie offered lager straight from the can.

Terry resolutely ignored the bollocking and stuck to his parliamentary beat, covering the Westminster angle of the next phase of Labour's disintegration. The Bennites were back on the national stage when Bob Mellish, the ageing right-wing Labour MP for Bermondsey, resigned from the party, tearfully alleging an extremist takeover of his constituency party in the deprived inner-city area of London round the Elephant and Castle. 'The *Sun* Says' marked the event with a soulful leader entitled: 'OLD WARRIOR'. 'Men like Bob Mellish were the heart and soul and the life blood of the old Labour Party. . . . What hope is there for any political body which spurns an old warrior like Bob Mellish and instead embraces an immigrant upstart who is most usually described as "a former activist for gay rights"?' it enquired.

The 'immigrant upstart' was Australian Peter Tatchell, a

Bennite who had come to Britain in 1971 at the age of nineteen to avoid being conscripted for the war in Vietnam. After taking a social science degree in 1978 Tatchell had moved into a council flat in Bermondsey and begun campaigning on the new GLC left-wing agenda, like Ken Livingstone making a strong stand for equal rights for lesbians and gays. In November 1981 he was selected as candidate for Mellish's old seat.

The following month Michael Foot, under pressure from right-wing members of his party, denounced Tatchell in Parliament, during a blundering performance in which he declared that Tatchell was not an endorsed Labour candidate and 'as far as I am concerned, never will be'. Foot's excuse was a mild speech by Tatchell which supported 'extra-parliamentary action' – leftie-speak for the standard tactics of demos and leafleting .

That evening a pack of over 100 journalists crammed into a hurriedly convened press conference at Labour's Bermondsey office. To his surprise the naive Tatchell found the hacks not the slightest bit interested in the 'extra-parliamentary action' issue, but simply pounding away at one question: 'Mr Tatchell, are you or are you not a homosexual?' Tatchell refused to answer directly, hedging by describing himself merely as a supporter of gay rights. His sexuality, he sniffed, was a purely private matter. 'The *Sun* Says' zeroed in on him the next morning under the headline 'SO PATHETIC'. 'Red Pete – otherwise known as extreme left-winger Peter Tatchell, Parliamentary candidate for the constituency of Bermondsey – symbolises everything that is appalling in the Labour Party today.'

In common with all papers on the Street, the *Sun* had been assured by Labour right-wingers that Tatchell was indeed gay and desperately wanted to print the 'news'. But none of the papers had any proof and like them the *Sun* was restricted to describing him by his own euphemism of 'an avid supporter of gay rights', which was nowhere near as definitive. The hunt was on for the great scoop.

The *Sun*'s trawl had an encouraging start with a report of Tatchell appearing at a Communist youth rally held in East Berlin in 1973. He had protested against the persecution of gays in the

133

Eastern bloc, after which the Communists had apparently threatened him, and Keith 'Devious' Deves dutifully reported the nine-year-old news under the headline: 'NIGHT TATCHELL HID WITH GAYS'. Deves, who resembled a ruined Billy Bunter, had a pronounced limp and was renowned for his ability to ferret out quotes on difficult stories. After all, as the hacks enviously told each other, who could resist an orthopaedic foot in the door? The picture desk beefed up Deves's story by producing a shot of Tatchell with his face heavily retouched to give the distinct impression he was using lipstick and mascara.

Pressure from the pack waned when nothing better than this was found, but in November the following year, 1982, Mellish, in addition to leaving the party, finally resigned his seat forcing a by-election. Now it had the scent of a major political upset the *Sun* and the *Mail* led the pack in phoning Tatchell day and night demanding that he 'come out'. Hacks stole his rubbish to sift it for gay clues and trawled gay clubs offering cash for any former lovers who were prepared to kiss and tell. A *Sun* reporter enterprisingly posed as Tatchell's long-lost brother home from Australia, dropping in on his neighbours for a little chat about 'Pete's latest boyfriends'. The baffled neighbours couldn't help. When all these efforts failed the papers resorted to the bottom line of day and night doorstepping and pushing little notes through the door offering him money to talk.

Tatchell's dim-witted answer to the mob outside was to grant an exclusive interview to the *Mail*. Once the 'real story' had been printed, he innocently reasoned, all the other papers would give up and go away. He invited the paper's representatives into his modest flat and found the reporter pleasant enough. But the photographer was much more pushy. 'No good, I'm afraid,' he kept saying. 'Light's all wrong – could you just move a little bit more to your right? Bit more . . . bit more . . . that's it. Now – back up against the wall . . .' Tatchell, eager to oblige, manoeuvred himself into the required postion. He was now standing in front of the standard 1960s poster of the South American revolutionary Che Guevara and the picture duly appeared showing him defiantly posed next to the great Marxist hero.

Tatchell had made his own contribution to this battle of wits by cunningly wearing a tie, but the *Mail* had a simple answer to that. Tatchell's feet were kept out of shot and in the story he was suddenly described as wearing open-toed sandals, which allowed the copy to say he was 'dressed like a hippy'. The hippy angle only showed how out of date the *Mail* was. Tatchell was actually wearing the Dr Marten's boots which were *de rigueur* with the new army of right-ons sweeping through the London Labour Party.

Instead of going away as Tatchell had intended, this first blood drawn by the *Mail* only cheered up the pack, which now descended mob-handed to monster him. They followed him round wherever he went, travelling with him on the tube or when he set off on his bicycle. Potential voters gawped in amazement as multiple hacks hung out of the windows of kerb-crawling cars, firing questions at him as he wobbled along, and his fellow social workers at a homeless advice centre in Waterloo moaned that they couldn't get anything done as the phone was continuously jammed. Worst of all for Tatchell, the coverage had attracted the attention of National Front thugs and his nerves were continuously shredded by being approached by pairs of heavies, never knowing whether they were going to pull out a notebook or a broken bottle.

Labour Party HQ deployed Monica Foot, the ex-wife of *Mirror* campaigning journalist Paul Foot, as Tatchell's press officer to try to stem the tide of PR disasters engulfing him. When she arrived she realised with horror that he was riding a girl's bike with a sissy-looking wicker basket on the handlebars and told him quietly to get rid of it. Tatchell never understood how her job worked and complained that she spent all her time in the pub talking to journalists, which was precisely what she was there for. He wrongly thought she should be immersing herself in what he saw as the important business of composing press releases, couldn't see what she was talking about and refused. Fortunately the hacks missed the picture.

Back at Bouverie Street the failure to stand up the Tatchell gay angle had begun to cause immense friction. The political editor, Walter Terry, was keeping out of it by insisting his beat was solely Parliament and the straight political side of the by-election. When MacKenzie replied with a fantastic bollocking in the middle of the newsroom Terry bravely stood his ground and ostentatiously fanned him with a sheet of paper as if to cool him down.

'If you think I'm so useless why don't you just sack me?' he would always ask when matters reached this pitch, knowing the answer full well in advance. It would cost Murdoch 'an arm and a leg', as MacKenzie had put it, to pay him off. But Terry knew that unless he buckled under the pressure and resigned, sooner or later he would have to be paid off. Both sides were playing a waiting game.

With Terry refusing to step into the breach, the job of proving that Tatchell was gay was now dumped on the news desk. The paper got a tip that Tatchell had taken part in an obscure event called the Gay Olympics in San Francisco in August. Little was known about it, and it had naturally not been covered by sports desk, but one of the most experienced reporters, whose brother worked for the Baltimore *Sun* and therefore had excellent American contacts, established that Tatchell had definitely been to San Francisco that summer for his holidays and that the Gay Olympics had been held there. But unfortunately the story the paper wanted did not stand up. Tatchell had only been in the city after the Olympics had finished. Reporting this to MacKenzie, the hack said he could probably prove Tatchell had met gay activists, but that was all there was.

'You've fucking let me down,' MacKenzie raged at him. The hack said he would recheck everything, but came back with the same reply. There was no truth in it. Tatchell hadn't been at the competition. 'Right,' MacKenzie stormed. 'Well, if you can't do it, I'll find someone who fucking well can.' He rushed off, leaving one of the newsdesk minions to explain the new rules of the game patiently to other startled hacks who were standing around. 'When will you lot get it through your heads that Kelvin's not interested in whether things are true or not,' he told them. 'What you've got to do is give him what he wants.'

The 'story' was passed on to Phil Dampier, an eager-to-please twenty-five-year-old casual from Ferrari's, the news agency MacKenzie had once worked for. According to Tatchell, Dampier promptly infiltrated the Bermondsey Labour Party by using the false name Phil Wilson, which he craftily based on his knowledge of Labour politicians. 'Wilson' first became a trusted member of Tatchell's by-election campaign team and then proceeded to befriend Phil Corr, the leader of the local Labour youth organisation. Corr was then innocently used to construct the required story, and MacKenzie got his desired gay exclusive.

On 25 September the *Sun* triumphantly splashed: 'RED PETE "WENT TO GAY OLYMPICS"'. The story began: 'Left-wing Labour candidate Peter Tatchell has upset his tough Dockland supporters, who say he has been to the Gay Olympics.' The 'supporters' were not identified. After this establishing point, Phil Corr was then quoted as if it had been proved that Tatchell had been to the event. The story continued: "Going to these Olympics is the last straw," Corr said.'

At no point did Dampier's story specifically claim that Tatchell had been to the Gay Olympics and it even ended with a flat denial from him buried in its final paragraph, tucked away on the turn on page 7. If the headline had read, 'RED PETE "WENT TO GAY OLYMPICS" – CLAIM', and if Tatchell's 'supporters' making the claim had been identified, the story would have been more honest. Leaving aside the fact that the *Sun* already had the word of one of its best reporters that the story was not true, it was a classic smear in its construction, containing no evidence to prove the truth of the allegation, yet at the same time leaving all but the most careful readers with the impression that it was a fact.

Tatchell later said he thought the 'GAY OLYMPICS' story was the worst smear in the virulent press campaign which he believed helped contribute to his defeat by 9,300 votes when the by-election took place in February 1983. He was beaten by the Liberal candidate, Simon Hughes, whose majority spawned excited chatter in the World's Worst about a 'third force' to break the mould of British two-party politics. The story also featured prominently in threatening phone calls and written death threats Tatchell was still receiving up to six years later.

He feebly complained to the *Sun*, but the paper robustly defended itself in a letter to his agent which said: 'The single quotation marks in the headline indicate that it was reported information.' The more pertinent question of who precisely had said it was evaded and Tatchell gave up, not even bothering to take his complaint to a Press Council hearing.

On the day after the by-election the *Sun* ran a full-page '*Sun* Says' entitled 'THE TRUTH HURTS – LIES, SMEARS AND PETER TATCHELL'. 'Like the famous horizontal heavyweight Peter Tatchell casts around for excuses and villains to explain away the disaster of Bermondsey. He whines that he was a victim of a campaign of smears and lies. . . . Peter Tatchell was a victim all right. A victim of the truth.' The paper then addressed itself to the main point: '[now] the bell tolls for Mr Foot himself. He is on his way out. The only question is: When? . . . The real power lies today with the triumphant Marxists. Peter Tatchell has lost Bermondsey but his cause is winning inside the Labour Party.'

In the same issue Walter Terry was on the front page reporting Foot's denial of rumours that he was about to resign in the start of a damaging whispering campaign pushed by all the Tory papers, and later revealed to have had an element of truth. The headline read: 'IT'S A RIGHT CARRY-ON – EVEN RED PETE SAYS FOOT MUST STAY AS LEADER', and the story was run with a picture of a duffle-coated Foot hobbling along with a walking stick. 'Foot . . . striding on as Labour leader yesterday,' the caption read.

This campaign of personal vilification of Foot was the main theme of the 1983 general election campaign which began three months later. Murdoch's interest in the political side of the paper became keener as the election loomed. The Boss was now spending more time in New York supervising the rapid growth of the American branch of the Empire which was building up its newspaper and TV holdings. MacKenzie would get regular transatlantic bollockings for not having enough serious coverage in the paper. He would then pass the pressure on to Walter Terry, shouting in a hypocritical reversal of his previous demands that Terry should replace regular parliamentary reporting with the human-interest approach: 'The Boss says the political coverage is crap. It's your fault. You're the one that's fucking it up and I'm getting the blame.'

The election campaign began on 9 May with polling day set for 9 June. Four days later Labour published its manifesto with a strong Bennite emphasis which led Gerald Kaufman, one of the party's leading MPs, to describe it as 'the longest suicide note in history'. MacKenzie buried a brief and dull summary by Terry on an inside page, while the Tory manifesto was given a double-page spread under the headline: 'MAGGIE'S VISION OF GREAT DAYS FOR BRITAIN'.

The Tories' campaign was visually led, in deference to the TV age for which Foot was so ill-equipped, by being based on a round of 'photo-opportunities' aimed at positive coverage on the box. The daily press conferences were even themed with TV in mind by the practitioners of the black arts of marketing, who provided light-blue backdrops for good news 'MAGGIE'S VISION' days, alternated with dark blue for Labour-bashing 'RESOLUTE APPROACH' days.

At a rally at Wembley DJ Kenny Everett brought the Young Tories to delirious flag-waving pitch by proposing, 'Let's kick Michael Foot's stick away,' and the nuclear issue was melted down to 'Let's bomb Russia.' There were caustic comments in the World's Worst about the Wembley show being a straight lift from the American style of conventions which had brought Ronald Reagan to power across the Atlantic but the *Sun*, which had been behind the new personalisation of British politics from the start, headlined its ecstatic report with 'SUPERSTAR MAGGIE IS A WOW AT WEMBLEY'.

In contrast Labour's election campaign largely ignored TV, and Foot was burdened with a series of rallies in Labour heartlands where he mainly preached to the converted, most of which the

Sun did not even bother to cover. But at one rally in Liverpool his wife, Jill Craigie, claimed to have discovered a memo to local freelance photographers from the *Sun* picture desk which read: 'No pictures of Foot unless falling over, shot or talking to Militants.' It continued: 'If Foot talks to any one of these drop a picture,' listing leading members of the city's Militant faction including Derek Hatton. Foot did not oblige but the *Sun* got what it wanted when members of a fox-hunt angry at his opposition to bloodsports unleashed a pack of hounds on him, and provided pictures of him haplessly thrashing about with his stick.

Editorially the *Sun* took the simple line that Foot was scarcely fit for the knackers' yard. Under the headline 'DO YOU SERIOUSLY WANT THIS OLD MAN TO RUN BRITAIN?' the paper commented 'We see a vision of an amiable old buffer, his jacket buttoned too tight, his collar askew, his grey hair falling lankly . . . The party's leftwing wanted Michael Foot as a figurehead, a ventriloquist's dummy who would repeat whatever message was fed into his head. In him they found a willing dupe.'

The *Sun* revealed 'the party's leftwing' just before polling day as a rogues' gallery of grim-faced fanatics, featuring the standard hate figures of Benn, Livingstone and miner's leader Arthur Scargill, coupled with more middle-of-the-road figures like Paul Boateng and Michael Meacher. All were headlined as 'THE LEFTIES WHO WOULD RUN BRITAIN IF LABOUR WON POWER THIS WEEK'. 'Behind Foot', the *Sun* warned its readers, 'are dedicated, ruthless men. Their reign will return this nation back to the days of Feudalism.'

In contrast the Tory Party had lived up to Murdoch's and MacKenzie's expectations. 'GOODBYE TO THE OLD SCHOOL TIE' introduced 'Maggie's new breed of bright, talented, articulate ministers who have risen to the top on their own talents,' with pictures of Kenneth Clarke, Cecil Parkinson, Leon Brittan and Norman Fowler. Norman Tebbit, who got a report to himself, was described as the 'Tory hard man'.

On polling day, 9 June, the *Sun* splashed 'VOTE FOR MAGGIE' as the update of 'VOTE TORY' in 1979, with Mrs Thatcher drawn as Britannia to revive memories of ruling the waves at the time of the

Falklands War. The story hammered home to the paper's twelve million readers: 'More than any leader since Churchill was baying defiance at the Nazis, she has captured the minds and imagination of the nation. . . . Carry on Maggie! – all the way to the GREAT Britain that a great people deserve.'

Maggie swept back with a majority of 152, up from 57 in 1979. The Tories won 42.4 per cent of the vote, which was slightly less than in 1979 but the Labour vote collapsed at 27.6 per cent, the party's worst result since 1935. As in 1979 social group C2, the skilled manual worker households at the core of the *Sun's* readership, had voted strongly for the Conservatives.

More of the apolitical *Sun* readers finally got the message that their paper was pro-Tory. In 1979 about half the readers had thought their paper backed the Labour Party, but during the 1983 campaign BBC research showed that 63 per cent of them now thought their paper supported the Conservatives.

The next day, before all the results were even in, Ronnie Spark and 'The *Sun* Says' were demanding heads with 'WHY MAGGIE MUST GIVE PYM THE PUSH'. 'The Foreign Secretary [Francis Pym] typifies the wets, the people who want it all ways. A comfy seat in the Cabinet, but the right to distance themselves from any unpopular decision. . . . Master Pym, Jim Prior, Waffling Willie Whitelaw contributed nothing to the Tory victory. They were content to cling to the Prime Minister's petticoats. She owes them nothing but the door.' Maggie delivered by sacking Pym three days later and shortly afterwards there was another political parting of the ways, this time in Bouverie Street. Walter Terry finally got his payoff, reported in the *Daily Telegraph* as being 'in the region of £80,000', and left to set up as a freelance.

With Maggie now in supreme control of the country, mainstream national politics moved off the *Sun's* agenda. All that remained was to sweep up Labour's defeated fragments in the town halls, along with isolated trade union militants and left-wing pressure groups, which were all grouped together under the successor to Lamb's phrase 'silly burghers', the brilliantly emotive, all-embracing label of 'loony left'.

The paper's attempt to infiltrate the top loony show of the

Greenham Common women received a setback when the presence of their reporter, feature hackette Jean Ritchie, was leaked to the World's Worst Newspaper and then broadcast on Radio 4. The women had initially attracted public sympathy, but the growing militant lesbian presence at the peace camp soon switched the focus from Cruise missiles to radical feminism. 'The women of Greenham's lament is not for MAN-kind – they are man haters, every one of them,' Ritchie reported after her brief stay.

Although not strictly politics, Greenham only served to put more steam behind the *Sun*'s loony left campaign. Accurate reports that some of the women demanded to be known as 'wimmin', on the grounds that the inclusion of 'men' in 'women' was defamatory, provided ideal loony material which not just the *Sun*, but other publications like *Private Eye* lampooned mercilessly. Even the World's Worst found it hard to maintain any sympathy when the 'wimmin' refused to speak to a male hack from the paper and demanded that a hackette be sent in his place. Peter Preston, the editor, refused.

At a national level the replacement of Foot as Labour Party leader by Neil Kinnock in October 1983 was hailed by the *Sun* as set to take Labour 'further down the road to Marxism and oblivion'. Kinnock was described as 'THE NOWHERE MAN' and dismissed as a windbag with 'the gift for the odd colourful phrase'. A profile was headed 'FUNNYMAN KINNOCK IS JESTER A BORN LOSER' and his followers summarised as 'KINNOCK'S PARTY OF PLONKERS'. He was then put through the mill of the paper's innovation of amateurish psychoanalysis, which concluded under 'CRUSTY KINNOCK ON THE COUCH' that he was 'too touchy to lead'.

In his farewell speech to Labour's conference an embittered Michael Foot rounded on the papers. 'The debasement of journalism is worse in Fleet Street today than at any time I can recall,' he declared. 'I do not say it is all due to the arrival of Mr Murdoch in Britain, although I think he bears his fair share of blame.' Without specifically naming the *Sun*, he then singled out the papers whose editors had been knighted by Mrs Thatcher as 'the ones who have got down lowest in the gutter'.

Foot's suggestions for improving standards included the Labour movement launching its own paper, and asking journalists to adhere to the NUJ's Code of Conduct for fair reporting. Point 3 of the Code warned them to 'avoid the expression of comment and conjecture as established fact, and falsification by distortion, selection or misrepresentation.' Foot's suggestion showed how out of touch he was with journalism as now practised in Bouverie Street. MacKenzie hated the union anyhow and the hacks just fell about with laughter at the thought of referring him to the Code in the middle of episodes like the 'Gay Olympics'.

Phil Dampier, on the other hand, was soon opening a bottle of champagne in Bouverie Street to celebrate his appointment to a staff job. Many older hacks took an instant dislike to him anyhow, and nicknamed him 'Damp Squib' because of his seemingly shy and sycophantic manner, droopy moustache, steel-framed glasses and brass-buttoned blazer which added up to a strong resemblance to a juvenile Alan Whicker. But what made them really grind their teeth was not Dampier's appearance, but his habit of constantly repeating 'Quite extraordinary', in imitation of the sports commentator David Coleman. To their great relief MacKenzie sent him off to be district man in Bristol. (The *Sun*'s regional reporters were evidently a watery bunch. 'Damp Squib' Dampier joined Martyn Sharpe, the *Sun*'s man in the north, who was said to be so slimy by rival hacks that he must live in a pond.)

The older Lamb hacks had already marked the 'Gay Olympics' story as a significant turning point in their relationship with their new editor. They had had a different shock when the paper got a story about a set of quads but was handicapped by only having a picture of two of them. There had been much muttering in the Top of the Tip the next day when it was seen that the problem had been solved by simply reversing the block and joining it up to the original picture, thereby neatly increasing the number of babies to the required four. But it wasn't just this new MacKenzie style which was the point; it was that there were dozens of reporters out there like Dampier, keen as mustard and able to come up with the goods MacKenzie demanded. Most important of all for them, they were all young. And youth was what MacKenzie was concentrating on getting into the paper.

Chapter 9

The Wend and Kel Show

Before MacKenzie arrived coverage of pop music on the *Sun* had been confined to ghetto slots called 'Gossip Column' and 'Pop Shop', which he instantly saw as strongholds of the 'wrinklies', the remnants of Lamb's old Pacesetters features team in their Piranha Pool. He had already decided they were mostly for the chop.

MacKenzie followed the charts, but was not an expert. Straightforward macho rock and roll seemed to be all over. There were so many different cults now, ranging from 'Oi!' to reggae that the old formulae of latching on to the latest supergroup and flogging them to death was useless. The only thing that seemed to work was treating the subject in the same broadcast way as sport or TV, throwing in associated obsessions with the latest nightclubs, films, food, dance and fashion fads and wrapping it all up as 'youth culture'. This approach was mainly the preserve of trendy magazines like the *Face*, but a watered-down version had arrived in Fleet Street in the form of John Blake's 'Ad Lib' column in the *Evening Standard*.

Early in 1982 MacKenzie had lunch with Blake, who had accepted his invitation as a bit of a joke. The *Sun* was derided as the absolute pits by his contacts in the pop world. But as MacKenzie turned on the charm Blake, a tall, thin man with the haggard looks of an ancient Radio 1 DJ, found himself struck by his forthright style. 'Pop's weird these days, John,' MacKenzie kept repeating. 'I can't understand it. It's all so bizarre.' Blake agreed. Bizarre was exactly the right word. It would make a good name for a band, he suggested – in the same vogue as Steve Strange's Visage, a trendy group on the London circuit. It would also make a great name for the *Sun*'s new pop column, MacKenzie pointed out. And Blake would edit it. Money was no problem. He could bring his team. Slightly to his own surprise, Blake accepted.

The column was launched as 'JOHN BLAKE'S BiZARRE' with the 'i' printed lower case to turn the word into a logo. The hyperbole was extraordinary, even by *Sun* standards. Starting with a box on the front page the blurb continued inside, ending on the centre-page spread with an excited report of the column's launch party at the trendy Canteen nightclub. 'The *Sun*'s going totally BiZARRE,' the text read beside a beaming mugshot of Blake. 'He's JOHN BLAKE and when you're with him you can go anywhere. Its a bizarre world and there's only one man who can take you into it – JOHN BLAKE.'

The overkill continued by billing the slot as 'simply the first column ever published in a national newspaper which encompasses every aspect of being young in Britain today. BiZARRE is about Pigbag [an obscure group then in the charts] and hang-gliding, space invaders and pacey paperbacks, the Rolling Stones and zoot suits. BiZARRE will be a must every day for everyone with a zest for life.'

Blake moved in quickly to edge out the 'wrinklies' and replace them with members of his Ad Lib team and new people from the specialist music papers whom he hired to cover the multiple sub-cults. One keen young recruit was Garry Bushell, brought in from the weekly paper *Sounds*, where he had been resident expert on skinhead Oi! music. Bushell's start in journalism had been on *Socialist Worker*, the weekly paper of the Socialist Workers' Party, which he had worked on while a student at North-East London Polytechnic.

But Bushell soon decided that the *Socialist Worker* was dominated by what he called 'middle-class wankers' with no understanding of real working-class people like himself. He thought instead that the authentic voice of working-class youth was the right-wing skinheads, and moved across the political spectrum to become a leading light in Oi! music, helping to produce several Oi! records, with covers illustrated with grotesquely tattooed and snarling boneheads, and 'songs' based on the principle of mindless abuse screamed at insane volume.

Although not a skinhead himself Bushell affected the general air of a snotty lumpen-proletarian yob, loudly declaiming his new right-wing views as he banged on about his own Oi! group, the Gonads. His noisy antics soon came to MacKenzie's attention. Forming the impression that Bushell was a troublemaker he told Roy Greenslade: 'That noisy c*** on Bizarre. I don't like him. Sack him.' But Bushell pleaded that he badly needed to keep his job to pay the mortgage. As a keen Thatcher supporter he had been one of the first council-house buyers. Greenslade relented. The other hacks, who found him totally gross, made sneering jokes about the home bar they heard he was installing, and a visit to a naff camping holiday. But Bushell soon proved he could give as good as he got and became a by-word for sharp and cutting put-downs in which he was soon rivalling his editor.

Other Bizarre recruits were less controversial. Blake struck up a close working relationship with the new breed of young 'paparazzi' freelance photographers earning a lucrative living by hanging around nightclubs and snapping celebs. One of the neatest arrangements was with photographer Dave Hogan, who combined working for the *Sun* with being the resident official photographer at trendy Stringfellows nightclub in the West End. For Hogan it was a big step up from Butlins where he had begun his career taking pictures of glamorous grannies, snotty-nosed kids and winners of knobbly-knees contests. Most of the celebs were falling over each other to get their picture into papers like the *Sun*, so the equation suited everyone. Posing was their profession.

Bizarre never lived up to the initial blurb, but the Second Coming would have been a disappointment after a build-up like that, as the hacks pointed out and Blake was a popular exec in the office. Bizarre gradually drifted back to old-fashioned pop gossip as the 'youth culture' fad melted away in the mid-1980s, backed by

146

mammoth 'BIZARRE SPECIAL' spreads interviewing stars like Sting and Paul McCartney who were among Blake's best contacts.

MacKenzie was pleased by Blake's performance. The section made the paper look bright and young and there was never any shortage of copy. Blake always had some cheerful nonsense up his sleeve to enliven an otherwise dull edition, even if it was provided with help from the growing army of PR agents and hype merchants. Sifting the dross Blake picked up early on Culture Club and their lead singer, Boy George. The group was already on its way up when Bizarre started and Blake sewed them up to run a string of features at the height of Boy George's chart successes between 1982 and 1984. Exclusive interviews extended from Boy George himself to his parents and friends; there were special offers of Culture Club posters from the marketing department and an awful lot of records were sold. Boy George acknowledged the special arrangement by dedicating his record 'Waking Up with the House on Fire', which made number two in the British album charts, to 'John Blake and the big-value *Sun*'.

But there was more to the scene than this kind of mindless pap. Behind the scenes pop was full of horrible things like drug-taking, homosexuality and other deviant behaviour. In the latter part of the decade, after Blake had left the paper to work on the *Mirror*, the *Sun*'s pop coverage was to stray more into this territory. But Blake stuck rigidly to the rules of good, clean young fun. Bizarre had been designed to appeal to younger readers, but from the start MacKenzie had realised there was a danger that if it was too trendy it might put off older ones. Yet as far as he was concerned Blake only strayed off the rails once, when one of the Bizarre team suggested a feature on legalising marijuana.

Blake backed the idea of a cool and sensible look at the pros and cons. Possession had been decriminalised in several US states, everyone knew that the police in places like Brixton turned a blind eye to small amounts for personal use, and there was a music hook. Paul McCartney, now re-themed as a respectable Adult Orientated Rocker, had been busted for possession.

But MacKenzie exploded at the idea. 'You must be fucking

joking!' he screamed, poking Blake in the chest. 'You just don't understand the readers, do you, eh?' MacKenzie rapped out his picture of the *Sun*'s older reader. 'He's the bloke you see in the pub – a right old fascist, wants to send the wogs back, buy his poxy council house, he's afraid of the unions, afraid of the Russians, hates the queers and weirdoes and drug dealers. He doesn't want to hear about that stuff!' he finally yelled, veins bulging. He gave the entire desk a bollocking on its duty to know the 'old fascist' so well they could predict his every thought. 'When you can imagine that bloke saying " 'ere, I tried that marijuana last night – not bad," then we'll write about it. And not before!' Like other MacKenzie rows it blew over quickly and once the limits of the old fascist's toleration of pop culture was taken on board the error was never repeated.

But curiously, although the hacks knew that the 'old fascist' was only one section of the readership, MacKenzie never put forward a picture of the typical reader for the hacks to identify with. Over at the *Mirror* the tabloid sage Keith Waterhouse had explained that the paper had lost its way when it could no longer see the man in a cloth cap as the person it was writing for. He was later to characterise the *Sun* reader as the 'skinhead with a six-pack'.

The question of understanding the readers was central to MacKenzie's power on the editorial floor. When a features hack brought some layouts to him saying, 'Look Kelvin, this is what the readers want', MacKenzie went berserk. He smouldered for a moment and then the blood rushed to his face and his eyes bulged as he exploded: 'You bastard. Don't tell me what the readers want. I'm the fucking editor. I know what they fucking want – not you. Got it? Eh?'

The one lieutenant MacKenzie could trust to get the readers right was Wendy Henry, the features editor who had blurted out 'Gotcha' during the Falklands. Henry was aware that one woman in four over the age of fifteen read the *Sun* every day and she had the gut instinct to trigger what she called the 'Hey Doris!' reaction – 'Hey Doris! Look at this!'

From her time on *Woman* magazine she knew that one of the

best 'Hey Doris!' topics was TV soap operas. Now nearly everybody had colour TV the action had moved from dull old black and white *Coronation Street* to the glitzy Americana of *Dallas* and *Dynasty* which were pulling huge audiences. Cliffhanger episodes, like *Dallas*'s 1982 'Who shot JR?' saga, had become national obsessions attracting more than twenty million viewers.

Henry was personally a genuine and avid fan of all the soaps and could be relied on to generate cheerful nonsense about the new cast of 'bitches', 'superbitches' and 'Mr Nasties' populating the American shows. The endemic confusion of fiction and reality in all soap coverage did not worry MacKenzie. It was only the telly – an important area for the *Sun* but, as he saw it, easy to cover. Stories were mostly based on PR jobs, so if she sometimes added an extra twist it did no harm. 'It's all crap anyway,' he would say. He was therefore quite happy to let Henry organise the features side of the paper, a job requiring a fair amount of the forward planning which was not his strong suit.

Henry would show MacKenzie proofs of the next week's early features, which were made up in advance, and he would quickly glance through them before signing them off and returning to his preoccupation with the news. When the features were duly printed days later he had often forgotten all about them. Genuinely perplexed, he would complain to Henry: 'This is no fucking good! I saw all this somewhere else last week.'

Henry would screech back: 'Of course you've fucking seen it, Kelvin. It was me who showed it to you.' MacKenzie would smile. He admired 'Wend' for the way she stood up to him, as well as matching his strong language word for word. Unlike the rest of the hacks she could get her way with the editor, persuading him to run features even when he was uncertain about their appeal to the readers. 'There, there, puss. You don't know what you want, do you?' she would tease. 'Fuck off, Wend,' MacKenzie would snap back, but she would persist, hamming up her Jewish market trader routine: 'Honest. On my life. No – on my *mother's* life, Kelvin, this is going to be loved.' MacKenzie was unable to resist. 'You're wrong, Wend,' he would say wearily. 'But fuck it. Put it in.' Henry would march back to the features desk exultant. 'I won,' she would mouth, smiling.

At conferences Wendy and Kelvin would banter with each other to the immense amusement of the other execs. It was the Wend and Kel show. If MacKenzie came to a heavy political subject on the list he would turn to Henry and say affectionately: 'This is too serious for you, puss, eh? Wend, eh? It's got long words. And politics. Soci-fucking-ology, eh? Not for you this one eh? Wend, eh?'

But in her own field MacKenzie had to admit that Wend was a wonder and praised the harder edge she had added to features, reflecting what he was doing on the news pages. What he loved about her was her constant fund of ideas. She was always coming up with suggestions. Some would be off the wall, some downright impossible even by his standards, but others would be brilliant and go straight into the paper.

Henry also took much of the credit for the paper's new obsession, '20 Things', which had started with the TV trivia agenda and was rapidly being applied to all subjects, serious or not. The 20 Things formula was an old journalistic trick for disguising lack of in-depth coverage by a list of essentially meaningless 'Hey Doris!' factoids, such as News International's picture library containing 1.5 million pictures. MacKenzie loved it. Anybody could throw it together without knowing anything about the subject, and they both knew it was perfect for readers leafing through the paper in their tea breaks.

And Henry had also helped him declare war on editorial cowardice. She would look disparagingly at limp story efforts written on the back of PR handouts and puffed publicity events and throw them in the bin, lisping at the hack: 'This stuff's all crap. What I want to know is who's fucking who.'

The writers did not mind her impossible demands and the rebukes they got for failing to 'deliver'. Henry rarely gave out the sort of blistering bollockings favoured by MacKenzie. She stood up for her staff, and was a good laugh, always willing to take the rise out of herself. The meetings she conducted with her TV soap writers were informal affairs. During one of these she lolled in her chair, her mini-skirt unconsciously riding halfway up her fleshy thighs.

A TV writer reeled out of the room gasping: 'I don't believe it, you could see her . . . her . . . badger.' The writer was struggling for the correct euphemism to describe a fleeting glance of stray pubic hair protruding from Henry's pants. She had actually meant to say 'beaver' – the term immortalised by Kurt Vonnegut's writing about 'wide-open beavers'. The features hacks immediately nicknamed Henry 'Badger', and 'Badger Watch' and 'Save the Badger' stickers and posters appeared all over Bouverie Street. Henry at first took it as a reference to her ability to 'badger' people relentlessly into delivering the sort of stories she wanted. When the penny dropped, she thought it a great joke.

After a dull period in the soaps marked by a revival of *Coronation Street* and the launch of Channel Four with its equally northern and worthy soap *Brookside*, Henry finally got her chance to do harder-edged stories in 1985. The BBC took a policy decision to launch its new show called *EastEnders* with an extraordinary cast of characters including a resident National Front skinhead, an unmarried mother drifting into prostitution, a heroin addict, a gay couple, a pregnant teenage schoolgirl, and a 'Mr Nasty' publican whose glamorous but drunken wife had endless adulterous affairs.

MacKenzie and Henry, finding this sort of stuff to their liking, took an immediate decision to side with *EastEnders* in the 'soap war' with ITV's Granada, the producers of *Coronation Street*. *The Street*, with its ageing audience, had always been essentially the newspaper property of the *Mirror*. But *EastEnders* was young, southern and rough – just like the *Sun*. There was another attraction about the show. *The Street* was based in Manchester where Granada's PR chief, Norman Frisby, protected the cast from reporters, strictly rationing interviews.

EastEnders, in contrast, set off welcoming all the publicity it could get. But before the show's launch twenty-four-year-old showbiz reporter Kevin O'Sullivan turned up at the *Sun* claiming to have a 'mole' who was willing to sell stories about the cast's private lives. O'Sullivan, who had previously worked for the *People*, was hired on the spot. At last Wendy Henry's demand for details of 'who's fucking who' in the soaps was about to be met.

The first episode went out to huge approval from the *Sun*'s TV critic, Charlie Catchpole. Under the headline 'IT'S GREAT MATE!' Catchpole summed up his feelings in excruciating Cockney slang. 'Would you Adam and Eve it? The Beeb's new soap opera ain't half bad. Know what I mean? . . .' The attraction was simple: 'Albert Square is seething with sex, spite and savagery.' The dull old Beeb, previously castigated for failing to come up with anything new other than snooker, was suddenly getting into the heavy stuff. And so was the *Sun.*

With the exclusive splash 'EASTENDER STAR IS KILLER' the *Sun* broke the news that actor Leslie Grantham, who played the soap's Mr Nasty, landlord Den Watts, in real life had murdered a taxi driver who tried to rob him when he was with the British Army of the Rhine in 1966. After serving his sentence Grantham had been released from Leyhill prison in 1976 and taken up a career as an actor. To protect O'Sullivan's mole the splash claimed that the *Sun* had been contacted by a former inmate at Leyhill who had recognised Grantham on the telly. The story had been in the office for weeks, but MacKenzie had held his nerve and risked the danger of being scooped to run it after the series had launched, when it would have maximum impact.

The *Sun* was also paying its mole for scripts, giving advance information which meant the paper could be cleared for saturation coverage of cliffhanger twists like the episode of 3 October when twenty million people tuned in to find out who had made teenage schoolgirl Michelle Fowler pregnant. The answer could not have been better for the *Sun*. It was none other than 'Dirty Den' Watts, who the *Sun* had revealed was a real-life killer. By this stage MacKenzie had become a genuine fan of the show. 'Did you see that *EastEnders* last night?' he would ask, affecting his version of intellectual art criticism. 'Pure theatre, pure theatre – absolutely magnificent!'

The effect of the *Sun*'s coverage was to get two soap operas running at once – the fictional on-screen lives of the characters, and the *Sun*'s parallel stories of their real lives. The real confusion began when the *Sun* started reporting the actors' real love lives and then weaving together their real and fictional lives into a single plot. 'EASTENDERS STAR IN LOVE AFFAIR' described an affair between Tom Watts, who played the resident wally Lofty, and Anita Dobson, who played Dirty Den's wife Angie Watts. 'FALLEN FOR HER TV SON' (30 November) revealed: 'Two more stars of the smash-hit soap *EastEnders* have fallen for each other.' Gillian Taylforth, who played Kathy Beale, was having an affair in real life with Nick Berry, who played her stepson Simon Wicks on the screen. Adding another baffling twist to the plot the story added: 'Najdet Salih – café owner Ali Osman – has become the real-life lover of Linda Davidson, who plays punk mum Mary Smith.'

Readers soon gained the impression that the entire cast were leaping in and out of bed with each other in an extraordinary number of permutations of their 'real' and 'screen' personalities. And as Henry had correctly calculated it was only by reading the *Sun* that *EastEnders*' twelve million regular viewers could keep track of it all.

The paper ended up running an *EastEnders* splash or spread virtually every day, leading to accusations from the Beeb that it had turned itself into an '*EastEnders* supplement to the *Radio Times*'. Even MacKenzie's wife Jacqui complained that he was 'over-egging the pudding' and the news hacks moaned as they were sucked into the endless hunt for *EastEnders* stories. At first many thought MacKenzie had made a dreadful strategic error but, as both the paper and the show pulled further ahead of their respective rivals, the *Mirror* and *The Street*, they had to admit his instinct had been right all along.

The *Sun* ended its year of saturation *EastEnders* coverage with a readers' poll in which 62 per cent nominated it as their favourite soap. Only 5 per cent said they preferred *Coronation Street*. The ailing *Crossroads* was down to 1 per cent. 'EASTENDERS WE LUV YER!' the paper reported gleefully. MacKenzie had every reason to 'luv' the series just as much as his readers. In February 1985 when the soap was launched, the *Sun* had put on an extra 205,000 copies and by the end of a year which had featured an *EastEnders* story a day for most weeks, it had increased its lead over the *Mirror* by more than 500,000 to end up with 4.2 million – more than a million copies ahead.

But a more important reason for this change had been the drastic change of ownership at the *Mirror*. The paper had now been bought by Robert Maxwell, at last able to fulfil his dream of being a national newspaper proprietor. Compared with the *Sun*'s four million, the *Mirror*'s sales had been stuck at between three and 3.5 million since 1980 and endemic overmanning problems had made Reed International, the paper's corporate owner, eager to get rid of it. After an abortive plan to float the paper Maxwell finally bought the whole group, including the *Sunday Mirror*, the *People* and the *Daily Record* for £113.4 million.

On 14 July 1984, the first day of his ownership, Maxwell comandeered the front page to address the nation under the headline, 'FORWARD WITH BRITAIN!' with a picture of himself and the giant by-line 'By Robert Maxwell, publisher of Mirror Group Newspapers'. His article told readers: 'I am proud to be the proprietor of this group of publications which holds such an important position in the life of the nation.'

The following month Maxwell began his attack with a £1 million bingo prize. But Murdoch, by now a seasoned veteran of the Bingo Wars, was more than ready for his new rival. The *Sun* immediately spiked Maxwell's guns by announcing 'THE BIGGEST BINGO PRIZE IN HISTORY!' – an identical guaranteed payout of £1 million. 'TRUST THE SUN FOLKS, WE'RE GONNA MAKE YOU SUPER RICH' the front page promised – and shortly delivered to David Parsons, a Bristol sign-maker, who became the first person in Britain to win £1 million in any competition, including the football pools. Maxwell played the white man by sending the winners a congratulatory telegram reading: 'We're honestly happy for you.' Maxwell really had little to be happy about. His bingo strategy was in tatters and instead he veered about cutting and raising the cover price, which only succeeded in upsetting the newsagents, whose percentage was affected. The editorial interference signalled by Maxwell's 'FORWARD WITH BRITAIN!' continued with huge coverage of his various good deeds, including his decision to fly emergency supplies to famine victims in Ethiopia and his meetings with sundry Eastern European leaders.

But bingo had brought little cheer to the *Sun* either. The £1 million games caused violent sales fluctuations for the rest of 1984, with each paper gaining or losing up to 200,000 readers and producing an expensive stalemate. Maxwell had some revenge when the *Sun*'s second winner turned out to be a granny from Essex attempting to obtain the £1 million by fraud. The police were called in and the money was never paid.

The hacks hated bingo, and interviewing winners for the required puff stories was regarded as the worst job on the news rota. At *The Times* the appalled hacks had refused to interview winners of 'Portfolio' – a haughty version of bingo based on share prices which they nicknamed 'Dingo' – leaving the hapless newsdesk to do it for them. But the greatest dread of all was that somebody would 'fuck up' and get the numbers wrong. Although few folks realised it, unlike the real game, newspaper bingo had no random element. The papers decided how many people they wanted to win. Winning cards were then printed amid great secrecy and sent to target areas of the country to be activated by the numbers printed in the paper. Millions of duff cards with no chance of winning were then stuffed through the nation's letterboxes. But if the wrong numbers were printed in the paper the winning cards would be rendered useless and an unknown, though potentially huge, number of the duff cards would be all registered as winners.

There had already been two such errors – one at the *Mirror*, when the paper was forced to give away a huge number of toasters variously reported as being between 900 and 35,000. The *Mail* had then put its offices in Carmelite House, just down the road from 30 Bouverie Street, under attack by hundreds of readers who had come to claim their fortune.

At the *Sun* the numbers were the responsibility of Mike Terry, production editor in the features department and the butt of countless MacKenzie bollockings. On Friday, 18 May 1984, Terry made a slip with his pen and passed across a wrong number. The error was even more disastrous as Saturday's numbers marked the end of a week-long game, and therefore decided the winner. Pandemonium broke out early in the morning as hundreds of readers converged on Bouverie Street to claim their £40,000 prize. One couple drove from Carlisle, an unemployed man hired a car to travel from Gateshead, and another reader arrived in a Rolls-Royce, announcing she was now going to pay off her mortgage.

It was a potential PR catastrophe. A panic call was put through to MacKenzie, who came rushing in on his day off and hauled the distraught Terry into his office. He gave him a simple choice – either be sacked or face the public humiliation which was the key to his genius idea to turn the disaster around. Because of his age and his ill-health Terry knew he was unlikely to get another job in the Street. He took the second option.

MacKenzie had Terry photographed wearing a large conical dunce's cap made out of *Sun* promotional stickers. On Monday the picture, with Terry looking forlorn and miserable, glasses slipped down his nose and dunce's cap firmly in place, was run on the front page under the headline: 'I'M THE BINGO BUNGLER'. A strapline boasted, 'THE PAPER THAT SHOWS YOU THE SINNERS', while page 5 followed up with a story entitled 'SIEGE OF THE SUN' showing the hapless crowd of punters milling around in Bouverie Street.

The story explained that many of them were 'downhearted', but stuck to the standard *Sun* line for playing down cock-ups by getting them to admit it was all 'a bit of a giggle', while the promotions department was used to soften the blow by doubling the prize money to £80,000. 'Okay folks,' the paper explained, 'we dropped a clanger with last week's Bingo. But we are going to make it up to you – at the double!'

During the week the paper wrung more mileage out of Terry's public humiliation with features like 'THE WORLD'S GREATEST BUNGLERS', bracketing him with a Nigerian labourer caught trying to cash a forged cheque for £697,000,090.20; and an advertising executive whose Chinese translation of 'Come alive with Pepsi!' had emerged as 'Pepsi brings your ancestors back from the grave!' 'HAVE A LAUGH WITH THE BEST OF LIFE'S BLUNDERERS!' the paper urged cheerily.

Many of the hacks were awestruck by the way MacKenzie had turned the bingo disaster around. Some said it was the perfect example of the editor at his best, showing his gut instinct for how the readers would react, quick wit, steady nerve, ability to see any problem as a challenge and, at the end of the line, sheer barefaced cheek. Others hated it, sympathising with Terry, who to his credit took his punishment and never complained.

But MacKenzie's concentration was not on saving cock-ups, but on the ever-present quest for the great splash – something no other paper would dream of running. His knack of spotting the germ of a 'SUN EXCLUSIVE' buried deep in a workaday news report came to the fore with the saga of *The Crying Boy* picture. It began as a routine agency report of a house fire in Nottingham. The report mentioned that a framed print of *The Crying Boy*, a sentimental mass-market painting sold in chain stores which showed a cherubic child with a giant tear rolling down his cheek, had survived the fire virtually unsinged even though the room where it was hanging was completely gutted. The agency reporter had added a last paragraph speculating about the picture's magical powers of survival.

When one of the senior execs showed MacKenzie the story, pointing out its curiosity value, he jumped at it. *The Crying Boy* was one of the best-selling pictures in the country and just the sort of thing every aspiring C2 had in their house. To the consternation of the newsdesk and hacks convinced that this time he had flipped, he cleared the front page and splashed 'CURSE OF THE CRYING BOY PICTURE' above the story, appealing to readers to phone in with details of any other fires or mishaps which had involved the picture. The next day the paper was deluged with calls. MacKenzie cleared more space to print the strangest and most horrifying tales, and appealed for yet more. 'This one's got legs,' he confidently announced, using his phrase for a story which would 'run and run'.

But the *Sun* magic was also beginning to work in a different way. Worried readers rang in to ask if they should get rid of their copy to stop their houses burning down. 'Sure,' MacKenzie replied. 'Send 'em in – we'll do the job for you.' Bouverie Street was swamped. The hacks were deeply impressed at the service provided by the Post Office as hundreds and then thousands poured into Bouverie Street. The *Crying Boys* were soon stacked twelve feet high in the newsroom, spilling out of cupboards, and entirely filling a little-used interview room. The Inkies joined in the action by starting a side industry of dealing in the most valuable of the frames.

Despite this the pictures clogged the stairways and corridors, adding to the havoc already created by the paper's 'Tiddler for a Toddler' campaign. When the old ½p piece had been phased out the *Sun* had asked the folks to send them in, receiving an extraordinary £1.5 million worth of coins. The highpoint for the hacks had come when Petrie, rounding the corner at a brisk military clip, barged into one of the belljars at the top of the stairs in which the coins were being collected, sending thousands of them showering down the stairwell.

'Bloody hell!' MacKenzie kept saying as he threaded his way through the piles of *Crying Boys*. 'What the fuck are we going to do with this lot?' So far the hacks, who regarded the whole episode as cheerful nonsense, had been unable to work out how much credence MacKenzie attached to the scam. But when Petrie took down Winston Churchill, who had been hanging on the newsroom wall since the Falklands, and replaced him with a particularly tasty *Crying Boy*, whose tear appeared to have been highlighted with some sort of silver paint, they got their answer. MacKenzie, bustling into the newsroom at his normal half-run, stopped dead in his tracks and went white. 'Take that down,' he snapped. 'I don't like it. It's bad luck.' The saga was kept going for six weeks as more horror stories surfaced and thousands more pictures arrived. The story was jacked so high up the list of priorities that Kevin O'Sullivan was temporarily taken off his vital *EastEnders* beat to try to drag a few celebs into the action. The best he could turn up was the BBC newsreader Robert Dougal, who found himself in the paper as: 'Top TV newsreader joins the *Sun's* crusade against the curse of *The Crying Boy*. . . .'

Then came the job of disposing of the pictures. MacKenzie first planned to burn them on the roof of Bouverie Street but the proposal was scotched by the London Fire Brigade, which refused to co-operate and denounced the whole campaign as a cheap publicity stunt which it said was causing it endless trouble. Quite apart from gullible souls believing that the picture was cursed, garbled versions of the story had spread to unsuperstitious people who thought that copies of the picture were made of a dangerous flammable ingredient. The Fire Brigade repeated in vain what it had always known – that it was quite usual for pictures hanging on the wall to survive major fires as they were away from the main heat of the blaze. MacKenzie, it pointed out, had constructed the whole drama out of sheer ignorance.

The *Sun* tried the Thames Valley Fire Brigade, which was more co-operative, and reporter Paul Hooper finally left Bouverie Street with two pantechnicon loads for a site near Reading, where he was photographed setting light to the pyre. MacKenzie splashed the story under 'THE SUN TAKES ON THE CURSE OF THE CRYING BOY', increasing the 'spin' by bylining Hooper as 'Fine Arts Correspondent'.

But the editorial aspect of the circulation war was not just a matter of producing great attention-grabbing front pages. It also involved stealing – or 'lifting' – the opposition's best material and passing it off as original. There was nothing illegal about the practice, which was governed by a series of unwritten rules which involved no paper claiming a lifted story as an exclusive, or pretending a lifted interview had been given directly to it.

Hand in hand with lifting went 'spoiling', another long-accepted practice which Lamb had specialised in. This involved throwing together a garbled and inferior (and free) version of a rival's major exclusive like a series or book serialisation. The 'spoiler' was designed to fool punters glancing at the headlines into believing they were getting the real thing. It was a practice which Robert Maxwell, apparently unaware that the paper he had bought had been doing it for years, was now determined to stamp out.

Still fuming from the way in which the *Sun* had spiked his guns over the £1 million bingo game, Maxwell decided to teach MacKenzie a lesson by taking recourse to the courts. In May 1985 the *Mirror* bought the expensive serialisation rights to a book called *The Killing of the Unicorn*, which told the steamy story of the murder of model Dorothy Stratten, who had been nicknamed the Unicorn and had been the lover of Hugh Hefner, the head of the *Playboy* empire. Maxwell knew MacKenzie would attempt to spoil it.

Five days before the *Mirror's Unicorn* exclusive was due to start on Monday, 10 May, Maxwell's lawyers sent MacKenzie a letter threatening an immediate High Court injunction if he made any attempt to lift it. The next day MacKenzie, spurred by this challenge, announced that the *Sun* would also be carrying 'the full story'. Maxwell's injunction arrived in Bouverie Street at once, putting the *Sun* in the theoretical position of facing a substantial bill for costs and criminal action for contempt of court if it continued with its promised action.

MacKenzie ignored the injunction and published his 'spoiler', pushed together from rehashed old interviews and cuttings. Maxwell's lawyers crawled over the *Sun's* text and concluded that one passage consisting of nineteen words had been directly lifted from the book. Clutching this damning evidence Maxwell triumphantly rushed to the High Court, where he accused the *Sun* of being run by 'thieves and kleptomaniacs'. Magnanimously, he informed the judge that he did not want to see MacKenzie behind bars (contempt carries a potential jail sentence), but he did demand that News International be punished.

The judge, Mr Justice Hirst, was singularly unimpressed. 'The very virulence of this attack', he intoned, 'might suggest that the proverbial adage about people who live in glasshouses is not entirely inapposite.' He could not see how the inclusion of nineteen words from a book of 200 pages amounted to breach of copyright and, rejecting Maxwell's plea, advised the *Sun* and the *Mirror* to call a 'truce'. On the steps outside the court MacKenzie boomed back: 'There will be no truce.' The verdict, he said, was 'a great victory for the *Sun*'.

MacKenzie had played for high stakes during the *Unicorn* affair and had won. 'Spoiling is a legitimate part of tabloid journalism,' he announced triumphantly. As he saw it, the fun of being an editor was all about taking outrageous risks. He knew that Murdoch agreed. So long as the *Sun* did not get caught out.

Chapter 10

Mine Fuhrer

Maxwell's attempt to teach the 'thieves and kleptomaniacs' of the *Sun* a legal lesson over the *Unicorn* saga may have looked ludicrous, but it did have a more serious side to it. The *Mirror* naturally had the most to gain from castigating the *Sun* for stealing stories and constructing second-hand 'spoilers'. Many hacks on the Street thought it was just the pot calling the kettle black. But an earlier *Mirror* leader headed 'LIES, DAMNED LIES AND SUN EXCLUSIVES' had slammed another *Sun* 'lift' which had gone much further than rivalry between the two papers and caused both disgust and alarm in Fleet Street.

In Lamb's period, when the *Sun* could be written off as a tits and bums paper, nobody in journalism took it seriously; its excesses could be explained as having little to do with the rest of the industry. All editors knew that their paper practised journalistic dishonesty of some sort, about which the first rule was not to be caught. But when MacKenzie started flying wildly about, transferring loose journalistic morals across the range from showbiz to deadly serious news stories, it was a different matter. And when he made the cardinal error of being caught at it, the Street began to wake up. The paper was dragging the whole profession down in the eyes of the public, and the dust-up between MacKenzie's *Sun* and the *Star* had given a whole new layer to the bottom of the barrel.

The *Mirror*'s 'LIES' editorial had been written about the *Sun*'s most notorious invention to date – a so-called 'WORLD

EXCLUSIVE' interview with Mrs Marica McKay, the widow of Sergeant Ian McKay, a hero of the Falklands. The 'interview', under the headline 'PRIDE AND HEARTBREAK OF TWO VCs' WIDOWS', was published after the public announcement that Ian McKay and Lieutenant-Colonel H. Jones were posthumously being awarded the Victoria Cross. In fact Mrs McKay had never spoken to the *Sun* – despite the paper using every weapon in its armoury to get her to.

Sergeant McKay's widow was an intelligent and sensible woman who had been deeply affected by her husband's death. She did not want any publicity herself, and had been extremely reluctant to talk to any of the papers. Forced to accept the inevitable, she had consented to a joint proposal by the *Mirror* and Independent Television News to 'protect' her from the pack in return for exclusive interviews. The *Mirror* had accordingly installed her in the Howard Hotel, at the back of the Strand in London's West End, with a vast team of hacks standing guard round the clock.

The *Mirror*'s deal was like a red rag to a bull for MacKenzie. He marshalled his heaviest team to get to Mrs McKay at the hotel, leading to what was euphemistically described at the later Press Council hearing as 'an unpleasant scene' as the two sets of hacks clashed on the premises. Meanwhile 'Commander' Petrie had sent out a 'red alert' mobilisation order to *Sun* hacks all over the country, ordering them to scour their region for anyone they could find. The paper hit gold when a hack interviewed Mrs McKay's mother-in-law, Mrs Freda McKay, and obtained a full report of what her daughter-in-law had told her about the VC award. The resulting screeds of copy were filed to Bouverie Street, other hacks on the mob-handed job got their hands on unscreened parts of an ITN interview and further quotes to throw into the mix were gleaned from older stories in the *Mail* and the *Express*.

The tricky job of assembling this disparate material into one piece to provide a classic spoiler was handed to reporter John Kay. Since his rehabilitation from Friern Barnet mental hospital Kay had been kept in the office where he had matured into the paper's best writer, commanding awed respect from the subs for his speed, accuracy and ability to compose stories in such perfect *Sun*-ese they could just be dropped into the paper without alteration. Kay was also extraordinarily skilled at the black Fleet Street art of sailing as close to the wind as possible when rehashing old material. He knew the line which turned a lift from a classic piece of allowed 'journalistic licence' into a fundamental dishonesty.

However, the *Sun*'s version of the Marica McKay interview crossed that line with a vengeance. It began: 'VC's widow Marica McKay fought back her tears last night and said: "I'm so proud of Ian. His name will remain a legend in the history books forever."' The story continued: 'Hugging her two children at their home in Rotherham, she said: "I'm proud of Ian's Victoria Cross – but I'd exchange all the medals in the world to have him back."'

Mrs McKay had indeed said all of these things at various times, and Kay had never written that she had said them directly to the *Sun*. But what had changed as the story went through the paper's system was that her mother-in-law, to whom remarks had been attributed, had disappeared. And, crucially, there had been a terrible error at the subbing stage. Kay had been extremely careful not to date the quotes. But an inexperienced sub working on the story was not aware what was going on. He had noticed the omission – a serious one on a paper where news was continuously hyped as having happened 'last night' unless it was dated 'recently' which was tabloidese for anything up to five years ago. The sub dutifully wrote in the key words 'last night', nobody noticed this unstitching of Kay's painstaking needlework, and the whole delicate exercise was then put completely over the top by MacKenzie's wild addition of the 'WORLD EXCLUSIVE' tag as a deliberate two fingers to the *Mirror*.

The *Mirror* fired back at the time with a *Sun*-bashing leader entitled 'THE SUN SINKS EVEN LOWER', branding its rival as a 'lying newspaper'. The *Mirror* could prove beyond doubt that Mrs McKay had never spoken to the *Sun* that night. She had been locked up with them in the Howard Hotel. That was as far as the matter looked like going and normally it would have been forgotten as just another Fleet Street lift – the sort of thing that took place all the time.

But the *Observer*'s Pendennis diarist, Peter Hillmore, a leading Unpopular hack in the game of *Sun*-sniping, was disgusted. He determined that the *Sun* should be reported to the Press Council. But the obvious person to make the complaint, Mrs McKay, had returned home with nothing but a deep desire to forget the whole episode and wanted nothing to do with it. So Hillmore asked his secretary to make the complaint in her name, using her private address in Essex. Reluctantly, Mrs McKay then consented to play her part by confirming that she had never spoken to the *Sun*. Nine months later, after grinding through the Press Council bureaucracy, the complaint was upheld, the *Sun* censured, and the *Mirror* printed its 'LIES, DAMN LIES' editorial, using the Council's verdict that the *Sun* had perpetrated 'A DEPLORABLE, INSENSITIVE DECEPTION ON THE PUBLIC' as the subsidiary headline.

Murdoch hit the roof. Although MacKenzie was not personally responsible for the slip which had given the game away, as editor he had to shoulder the blame. This time the stew really had boiled over and MacKenzie's minder, editorial director Peter Stephens, later mildly summarised the ensuing huge row as 'the boat rocking a little'. For whatever excuses could be made for the rest of it, the WORLD EXCLUSIVE tag was impossible to explain away. The hacks had been amazed to see it when everybody knew Mrs McKay was going to be all over the *Mirror* the next morning. But hacks who admired MacKenzie saw it just as his form of naughtiness. He was overseeing the whole thing and he just didn't give a fuck.

The *Sun*'s official moral justification for its action was presented at the Press Council by the paper's managing editor, 'old boy' Ken Donlan. Donlan told the hearing that he was extremely sorry if the paper had caused Mrs McKay any upset. Then he trotted out the *Sun*'s excuse. It was all the *Mirror*'s fault. Naturally the *Sun* would have preferred to do a real interview but, as Donlan explained: 'Our staff were under the strictest instructions not to allow any harassment of Mrs McKay to develop despite the *Daily*

Mirror's continued protection of her.' (Years afterwards a hack went to interview Mrs McKay for a magazine and asked her why she had been so reluctant to make a complaint. She showed him a grudging letter of apology from Donlan and asked if he had still got his job. The hack said he had. Mrs McKay then asked if MacKenzie still had his job. When the hack replied that he had as well, the widow just looked at him. 'There you are then,' she said.)

Underlying the spurious argument for fabrication, apart from his determination to continue with 'spoiling', was MacKenzie's conviction that the *Sun* as the 'the paper which supports our boys' had more right to Falklands heroes than the *Mirror* – the 'timorous, whining' traitor of the war. The same attitude was in evidence when another Falklands hero, Simon Weston, decided to give his story to the treacherous Argie-loving BBC, and ignore the patriotic *Sun*.

In June 1985, Weston, a former Welsh Guards private, was due to appear on a BBC documentary called *Simon's Peace*. The programme, made with extreme care and sensitivity, followed his remarkable recovery from 46 per cent burns he had received when his ship, the *Sir Galahad*, was set on fire during the Falklands War. Weston had had twenty-six skin-graft operations and at one stage had been in such deep depression that he had considered suicide.

Wendy Henry, as the exec in charge of TV coverage, proposed at a morning conference that the paper should interview Weston. MacKenzie liked it – another of Wend's great ideas. But then Henry ran into a snag. Weston turned down the paper's request to talk to him. Henry was not so easily deterred. She instructed one of her features department minions to do exactly what Kay had done when the paper could not get to Marica McKay. The minion duly assembled the story from old interviews, press clippings and a magazine article about the documentary.

It was a straightforward, workmanlike job, recycling old quotes and producing a balanced summary of Weston's life. The article also allowed Henry to indulge her fascination with 'yuck journalism'.

'Yuck' was the latest import from America, where papers like the *National Enquirer* gratuitously printed lurid pictures of physical freaks and the severely injured. Henry had already sickened some of the hacks by waving about pictures of grossly obese women (generically known as 'fat lady pictures'). Now under Henry's supervision the *Sun* gave Weston the 'yuck' treatment by dwelling on his injuries rather than his success in overcoming them.

The article appeared on the day before *Simon's Peace* was to be broadcast. Run under the soft headline of 'FALKLANDS HERO SIMON FIGHTS FOR A NEW LIFE', it put the boot in from the opening sentence: 'He is so hideously scarred people turn their heads from him in horror in the street. . . .' Weston, readers were told, was 'learning to live with a face no one wants to look at'. Lifted quotes filled most of a whole page. 'I look like a panda with these white eyes in the middle of a red face. And people are always shocked by my twisted, gnarled hands,' he said. The article ended by quoting him as saying: 'People have called me a hero, but I'm not. I'm the biggest coward God put breath into.'

The feature was rounded off by being illustrated by misleading 'before and after' pictures showing Weston being cuddled by his mother as though he was a helpless mongoloid child.

The great weakness with Henry's soap-opera approach to copy was pushing stories as far as they could go which was bound to cause trouble one day. But Weston was a small person, without much financial or political clout who had momentarily swept into the *Sun's* orbit. Because he was putting himself on TV, the standard justification ran, he was courting publicity and had no right to complain. But many other hacks did not see it like that. The article caused genuine disgust throughout Fleet Street and was denounced us grossly insensitive and way over the top by some. Weston himself was very upset – it was the exact opposite of the message he was trying to put across.

The Boss came on the phone, furious. Weston had made a distressed complaint about the interview which had been reported in the rival *Mirror*. To save Henry's skin MacKenzie was forced to

167

act, but he just rapped her over the knuckles by suspending her for a month. The admonishment was a humiliation for her, but she was still paid, and was constantly on the phone to MacKenzie and other execs as if she was still at work. The sick joke circulated round her department that if he couldn't stand the heat Weston should have stayed out of the kitchen.

Henry's enthusiasm for physical freaks and gruesome medical pictures was undiminished as prime 'Hey Doris! Look at this!' material. As always when they discussed her, the hacks had mixed opinions about this obsession. Some thought she was simply ghoulish and therefore morbidly addicted to recreating a Victorian freak show. Others thought there were shrewder reasons. Like MacKenzie, her constant drive was to put on more readers, and she had seen in America how certain magazines and papers thrived on a diet of gruesome and macabre horror. Therefore, the hacks claimed, she simply saw it as a way of selling more papers. And she also saw something else just as important –it was the only way left to go. Everything else had been done – or so they thought.

Henry would use the 'appeal to readers' argument when she was trying get this sort of material round MacKenzie, who basically did not like it. 'Aw, go on, puss, give it a try,' she would say. MacKenzie, who knew he could not win an argument on these grounds, would simply fall back on naked power to say: 'No, Wend. Fuck off. I'm not having that. I don't want to even discuss it. And that is it.'

Henry knew when he meant it and, when she got back to her desk, there would be no little smile with an 'I won.' On one occasion there was a particularly bitter row between them after Henry had agreed to buy some pictures and a story. When MacKenzie saw them he blew his top and denounced them as 'absolute crap'. 'We're not paying for this fucking stuff, it's fucking horrible,' he stormed. Henry replied sharply that the pictures had already been paid for, with his approval. That was why they were in their hands. But MacKenzie was adamant. 'I don't care what we said. Just don't give them the fucking money. We're not paying for that crap, and that's it.'

Henry quivered like a jelly as she controlled her anger. 'You know, Kelvin, sometimes I think you're the biggest shit I've ever met,' she lisped. As MacKenzie swaggered off without replying, one of the hacks who had been following the interchange noticed a delighted little smile playing round the corner of his mouth. He was acting as though he had been paid the supreme compliment.

Petrie was delighted when there were bust-ups like this. There was a constant battle between his newsdesk and Henry's and Greenslade's features department for the affections and attention of MacKenzie and the newsdesk disparagingly referred to Henry as the 'Great White Slug'. Petrie, always one for a joke, wound Henry up over her Page Seven fellas, her complement to Page Three.

Henry would get pictures of hunks from model agencies and leaf through them at her desk to pull out suitable candidates. One day as she was doing it, the hacks saw her suddenly reel backwards in horror and give a terrified screech. There, on the desk in front of her, was a picture Petrie had slipped in of himself which he had had taken by Beverley Goodway, the Page Three photographer. It showed him naked except for some tinsel over his private parts whilst characteristically saluting the camera.

It was a matter of professional pride to Petrie that it was his news operation and not Henry's yuck stuff and soap operas which sold the paper. It was the newsdesk under his command which had excelled during the Falklands War and now Petrie and MacKenzie moved to revive the same spirit. The Curranticus Bunticus, as MacKenzie had begun to call his paper, could grab the flag of patriotism and wave it about again and the whole place could build up a fresh head of steam. His opportunity came when what was promptly elevated into the 'Lamb War' broke out with France in January 1984. This time the dispute really was like the Cod War with Iceland. But, although it was essentially silly, it was a brilliant peg for the whole bag of Falklands tricks to be taken out again as the *Sun* got behind the beleaguered Brits.

Larry Lamb's policy of treating events in other parts of the world as of little interest to *Sun* readers had continued under

MacKenzie's editorship. But MacKenzie, as usual, had gone much further and added his own brand of virulent xenophobia. It was extraordinarily old-fashioned, squarely in line with the ignorant national stereotyping acidly commented on decades earlier by George Orwell, which only went to prove that there was nothing new in the *Sun*. As far as the paper was concerned the French, as Britain's old enemy, were still a nation of unshaven beret-wearing peasants riding bicycles, smoking vile cigarettes and carrying strings of onions.

The 'Lamb War' had broken out when French farmers organised a campaign to reduce the EEC quota for the amount of British lamb sold in their country. British lorry drivers – or 'truckers' as the *Sun* called them – were caught up in demonstrations, and their lorries surrounded and then burned. The *Sun* ran the story under the classic headline, 'L'AMBUSH', which was thought up by one of the paper's copytasters, who 'tasted' copy for suitability for the paper. Although MacKenzie was the acknowledged headline wizard, there were plenty of sharp minds in Bouverie Street who could match him from time to time. In line with his open approach he always welcomed suggestions from anyone.

On 14 January 1984 the *Sun* reported under the headline 'MERCI MY SUN' how two 'L'ambush' drivers with the same birthday had saved their lorries from being burned by following their *Sun* horoscope for Capricorn, which told them: 'You will have to fall in with other people's wishes even though they conflict with your own.' As a result they had decided not to get involved with the 'aggro' and peacefully surrendered their lorries. (The stars column hit the rocks temporarily when the paper's astrologer was found to have been recycling predictions. He was sacked by MacKenzie in a letter apocryphally said to have started: 'As you will no doubt have foreseen'. . . .)

The 'L'AMBUSH' report was livened up with an offer of 'HOP OFF YOU FROGS' badges, recycling the 'GOOD LUCK LADS' gimmick from the Falklands. MacKenzie then dragged out another old stunt by asking readers to send in their 'Froggie jokes'. The prize was suitably patriotic. 'Here's a chance to get your own back on the French, folks, and win a super case of fruity *English* wine.'

The folks' jokey offerings were splurged over a double-page spread, with one used as the huge WOB headline: 'WHAT DO YOU CALL FRENCHMEN WHO HAVE AN I.Q. OF 180? – A VILLAGE'. Pulled together under the strap of 'OOH HA! HA! – READERS TELL THEIR FROGGIE JOKES', other gems included 'Why are there so many tree-lined streets in France? – So the German army can march in the shade' and 'What do you call a pretty girl in France? – A tourist.'

More puerile insults followed when MacKenzie, opportunist as always, read a paragraph in *The Times* about a cosmetics-industry survey. He was beside himself with delight to see that it revealed that the French used fewer bars of soap per head than any other European nation. A large pile of toothbrushes, underwear and soap was taken into the embassy and dumped on the entrance desk by a hired Page Three girl. MacKenzie ran the story as a front-page exclusive headed: 'ZEE FRENCH ARE FEEL-THY – OFFICIAL'.

But the real Falklands spirit was reserved for the paper's own invasion of enemy territory through a raid on Calais. The invasion team was hurriedly assembled from a handful of hacks and photographers, two Page Three girls, a town crier – complete with bell – and a butcher carrying some English lamb. The operation had an initial setback when hackette Muriel Burden, the former 'Darling of the Fleet' in the Falklands War, was so sick on the hovercraft that she was instantly turned round on arrival and sent back with the first rolls of film.

The depleted *Sun* party then roamed the streets of Calais in a newspaper version of *Candid Camera*, obtaining pictures and quotes to suit their purpose and visiting a large number of cafés and bars as a vital part of the research. When it was time to file to the office the hack starting to dictate the first paragraphs into the phone was so out of it he simply keeled over in the middle of a sentence. In a feat of journalistic enterprise which was to be the talk of Bouverie Street for weeks, another hack leaped forward, scooped up the receiver before it hit the floor, raised it to his mouth, and seamlessly continued the story without missing a word.

The French riposte to this nonsense came in the suitable form of a group of trainee journalists occupying the British consulate in Burgundy in protest. Two photographers from *Paris Match* then infiltrated Bouverie Street and chased MacKenzie round the office trying, but failing, to get a picture. The French resorted to answering back by running a feature about the cruel British sport of hare-coursing.

Back in Britain the Lamb War was anyhow soon overtaken by the old 'enemy within', Tony Benn, re-emerging on to the national stage. As Chief Loony Benn had fittingly lost his Bristol seat in the general election, but just as MacKenzie was casting round for a new target, he was selected for the safe seat of Chesterfield, where there was to be a by-election on 1 March. The Sun pitched in by accusing him of 'wild-eyed fanaticism' and plugging the updated theme that 'Bogeyman Benn' was now in need of treatment. A week before the election 'The Sun says' set things up by accusing Bennites of supporting the Provisional IRA.

'Anyone who can invest with glamour the skulking, cowardly butchers of the innocent and helpless is worthy more of the psychiatrist's couch than serious analysis,' it declared. To 'prove' the paper's theory MacKenzie ordered features hackette Ros Grose to assemble a 'dossier' on Benn from the clippings library, which was then despatched to Martin Dunn, the paper's sole foreign correspondent, in New York.

Dunn, an immensely smooth operator who MacKenzie called 'the pinstriped chipmunk', then paid a psychiatrist $350 for an opinion based on the dossier. It did not mention Benn's name, but as all the base material had been gleaned from the *Sun*'s increasingly hysterical coverage of his activities, the hired shrink diagnosed from the information that the subject was becoming steadily more unhinged as he got older. The resulting story was scheduled to be run on the day before polling, under the headline of 'BENN ON THE COUCH – A TOP PSYCHIATRIST'S VIEW OF BRITAIN'S LEADING LEFTIE', with

Martin Dunn's byline. But the issue was lost through yet another mechanical problem with Bouverie Street's presses. The delay gave Malcolm Withers, the timid but strongly pro-Labour Father of the *Sun*'s NUJ chapel, time to raise the alarm by phoning the story over to Monica Foot, who was acting as Benn's press officer. The analysis was that Benn was 'a Messiah figure hiding behind the mask of the common man. He is greedy for power and will do anything to get it'.

Foot, as a seasoned veteran of the 'Red Pete' Bermondsey by-election smear, took Withers's news calmly. She thought Benn could easily get an injunction to stop the story being published. The trouble was that would only cause more damage. The real threat was not from the story itself – which Labour supporters would write off as more *Sun* claptrap – but the TV coverage if it was elevated into a row. The early evening TV news bulletin was vital on polling day and if it was dominated by the story of Benn taking legal action to prevent publication of evidence of his supposed 'madness' it would be a PR disaster. She told Withers: 'Thanks, but no thanks.'

The piece duly appeared on polling day and Benn won the by-election, but with a reduced majority, giving the Labour left another axe to grind against the *Sun*. But MacKenzie was basically bored with such a soft target. A more worthy enemy to be engaged on behalf of Maggie had anyhow emerged in Arthur Scargill, the leader of the National Union of Mineworkers, which was now making the last stand of the trade-union-based hard left. MacKenzie pitched into Scargill and the miners' strike with as much zeal as he had shown for the Falklands. But at the same time the strike also plunged him into a head-on confrontation inside 30 Bouverie Street in the form of an alliance between the miners and the militant Inkies.

Round one of the internal war went to the Inkies. In January 1984 Scargill, interpreting the NUM rules strictly, refused to allow a national ballot for strike action and went for the tactic of using flying pickets to bring out the regions one by one. MacKenzie decided to stick the *Sun*'s oar in by printing a ballot form in the paper to allow non-striking miners to cast their vote. The Inkies refused to typeset the form, declaring it was an unwarranted interference in an industrial dispute. After an almighty row, the management agreed to a compromise. The ballot form was still printed in the paper, but attached to it was a statement dissociating the *Sun*'s production chapels from it. Much more importantly, the paper caved in to the printers' demand of a 'right of reply' for Scargill, whose statement was handed to MacKenzie by John Brown, the Imperial Father of the NGA composing room chapel. It was printed without any changes.

The Inkies were over the moon. For the first time in the history of the Street they had forced through a right of reply and they had also achieved a personal victory over MacKenzie. As the militants had hated him since they first ran into him as deputy night editor, this meant a double cause for celebration. The rows with MacKenzie had started in his first week when he gave a group of process workers a fearsome bollocking for insisting on strict observation of demarcation lines. 'You lot are nothing more than fascist, Communist wreckers hellbent on destroying freedom in this industry and in this country,' he raved in a wild mixture of political terminology.

The astounded Inkies, used to Lamb's more accommodating style, demanded an apology if they were not to take industrial action. MacKenzie backed down by churlishly scribbling on a piece of scrap paper, torn out of a shorthand notebook: 'I suppose *some* of the things I said may not apply to *some* members of the process chapels.' The Inkies had let the matter rest at the time, but had been itching to get their own back ever since. (In another incident at the *Express* when production workers demanded £25 for an extra job MacKenzie took five notes out of his pocket, slapped them down on the desk and shouted: 'Now will you do it?')

But it was not MacKenzie, but the *Sun*'s former editor, Larry Lamb, who was next to step out of line in the miners' strike. After a couple of years in the Australian wilderness Lamb had written to Lord Matthews asking for a job and landed the editorship of the *Daily Express*, now more zombie-like than ever. Mackenzie had marked his return with a telegram: 'Congratulations on becoming captain of the *Titanic*.' Lamb's main contribution as editor had been the creation of the '*Express* Millionaire's Club', a bingo competition in which readers could supposedly win £1 million. The gimmick, which had astronomical odds, had done wonders for the *Express*'s flagging circulation, which he had saved from slipping below the *Mail*.

On 9 May, when the miners' strike was under way in earnest, Lamb published a front page that would have made even Lord Beaverbrook blink. Under the headline: 'I AM LEADING MY MEN TO DISASTER' he had Scargill confessing to lying, admitting the strike was purely political, and stating that it could not be won. The 'story' was really a fiction which Lamb pompously felt his Yorkshire pit village background entitled him to compose. It was billed in the paper as: 'The speech that the *Daily Express* believes Arthur Scargill would be making . . . if he cared more about the truth'.

Lord Matthews' jaw dropped when he saw it. The 'story' might have been runnable as an inside feature, but instead Lamb had put it on page one as the splash. Matthews decided Lamb had gone too far and Scargill should be allowed an opportunity to reply. But before Matthews could implement his decision Bill Keys, the head of the SOGAT print union, officially demanded a right of reply on the union's terms, which turned the affair into a point of principle within the paper. Scargill's rebuttal was still printed causing Lamb to offer his resignation, which Matthews refused.

The miners' strike soon degenerated into pitched battles with the huge police presence at the regular picketing of the key Orgreave coke plant near Sheffield. A chance photograph, taken as Scargill was there rallying his troops, showed him with the normal grim expression and fierce determination in his eye. But because of the camera angle his arm also appeared to be raised in a Nazi salute. The overall effect of the 'trick' picture was to make him look remarkably like Hitler.

The picture was sent round all the papers and some, including *The Times*, decided to print it. But MacKenzie also seized on it as a chance to write a great *Sun* headline. Picking up his fat green pen he sketched 'MINE FUHRER' in huge capital letters on the front-page layout and sent it to the printers to be set. The outrage potential of the headline was gratifyingly clear at once. The Inkies refused to touch it, or even to process the picture. After a foul-mouthed re-run of the ballot-form dispute they still refused to budge, and MacKenzie took the dispute to the limit by publishing the issue with a blank front page. Instead of the picture and headline a large message read: 'Members of all the *Sun* production Chapels refused to handle the Arthur Scargill picture and major headline on our lead story. The *Sun* has decided, reluctantly, to print the paper without either.'

This second triumph by the Inkies hugely boosted morale on the miners' picket lines, where the *Sun* was now hated as the most strident mouthpiece of the Thatcher government. Pickets began to shout '*Sun* reader!' at 'scabs' as they crossed their lines. Hatred of the paper was so intense in the miners' heartland of South Yorkshire that the paper's local circulation rep, Ian Jackson (later to become head of circulation at News International) prudently waited until newsagents were empty before making his routine calls.

At Bouverie Street the final showdown with the Inkies over right of reply was to cost both sides a large amount of money. On Friday, 28 September after violence between pickets and police near Silverwood Colliery in South Yorkshire MacKenzie mapped out another front page outrage. 'SCUM OF THE EARTH'. The headline was to be accompanied by a leader which began: 'Miners were rightly once called the salt of the earth. No longer. Too many of them have become the scum of the earth. . . . By scum we mean the mob who perpetrated the vicious ambush of police in South Yorkshire yesterday. This premeditated operation to trap, stone and beat up policemen was the behaviour, not of trade unionists, but of terrorists.' The leader concluded: 'Scargill has totally misjudged the British people. The worse the violence gets, the greater the determination that there will be NO SURRENDER.'

The moment the Inkies saw the copy they stopped work. 'Scum' was the most derogatory word they knew – much worse than 'c***'. The whole 'scum' agenda was something MacKenzie had picked up as part of the sarff London act. Although each group which could be labelled as scum represented a small minority, they added up to a large swathe of the population, including prisoners, criminals, drug-takers, football hooligans, most blacks, homosexuals, militant trade unionists, muggers, students, peace campers, demonstrators, hippies, dossers, tramps, beggars, Social Security scroungers (or bludgers as the Boss called them), squatters, terrorists and especially the IRA, vandals, graffiti artists, prostitutes, gipsies, winos, various foreign groups en masse and all deviants and particularly sex offenders. If individuals fell into two of these categories they would then become 'double scum' – like a homosexual terrorist, or even 'treble scum,' such as a black rapist high on drugs. MacKenzie was certain he could slag off anybody in the scum category as the readers would back him if they complained. Therefore he was delighted when the worst scum individual, Myra Hindley, elevated by the paper into the great bogey-figure, successfully obtained an injunction to stop a *Sun* story. 'EVIL MYRA GAGS THE SUN', he splashed gleefully thereby successfully achieving the 'reverse ferret' of turning her complaint to the *Sun*'s advantage.

The Inkies understood the agenda just as much as him, though they did not include the same groups, and the word put huge feeling into the showdown between the two sides. But when MacKenzie arrived on the composing-room floor to deal with the action they found him much more relaxed than in previous 'right of reply' confrontations. He simply told John Brown, Imperial Father of the NGA composing room Chapel, that he could not get away with interfering in editorial decisions. In reply Brown gave him three choices – remove the word 'scum'; leave the leader unaltered, but print it with a message dissociating the print unions from it; or print a letter from the NGA stating its opinion of it.

MacKenzie flatly refused all three options and walked off. Minutes later, after briefly phoning Murdoch, he came back and ordered the cashiers to close, which meant the printers would not be paid. The Inkies downed tools and that night's paper was lost.

On Sunday afternoon the argument was set to resume as the 'SCUM' leader was rescheduled for Monday's paper, but instead turned into a dispute about payment for the Friday shift which continued into the week, eventually causing the loss of four days' consecutive production.

Soon after this incident the NGA began to notice that MacKenzie's attitude had changed. Instead of being angry about right of reply and the other production disruptions he started marching through the composing room laughing and jeering at them. 'You lot have fucked yourselves. You haven't got much longer, you lot, eh? You're fucking history. You c***s, eh? And – Christ! – will I be glad to see the back of you!'

The Inkies, incorrectly interpreting this as more 'fascist, Communist wreckers' bluster, ignored the import of what he was saying. They had heard the rumour about Murdoch's planned 'dash for freedom' to the new plant known as 'Tower Hamlets' for years which would threaten their power, but few set much credence by it. Ironically, success in the right-of-reply confrontations only served to convince them they were invincible.

The Inkies' successes also made them instant heroes of the political left, which by now had radically changed its attitude to the *Sun*. Just as the fabricated Marica McKay interview had changed the view of the paper in Fleet Street, the paper's actions in the miners' strike, following on from the Falklands War, had changed the political perception of it in the outside world. Now it was cast as the very embodiment of the new hate word of 'Thatcherism.'

The hacks had already noticed the same sort of difference with the readers, especially when doing soft features. Previously it had mostly been a pleasure to ring ordinary people who had popped up in the news. There would be a bit of light-hearted banter about bringing along a Page Three girl, and generally they would be told they were welcome and even that the kettle would be on when they arrived. But now they were detecting a new guarded note in the replies and their requests were being turned down with the standard evasion of 'Not today, thanks.' The 'folks' appeared to be getting the message and reverting to their natural suspicion of the media.

And while MacKenzie had recycled 'thick Paddy' jokes at the expense of the French, now TV comedian Jasper Carrott began turning them on the paper. 'How do you burn a *Sun* reader's ear?' he asked. 'Phone him when he's ironing.' *Spitting Image* introduced *Sun* reporters as new characters, lampooning them as a mass of ignorant pigs, and at a more serious level on 22 November 1985 the *New Statesman* published an article headed 'DAYLIGHT ON THE SUN', based on a diary kept by Peter Court while he worked on the paper's art desk as a graphic designer for a few months.

Court had jotted down remarks made by MacKenzie and his execs on a number of subjects of great interest to *New Statesman* readers – in MacKenzie's view an even harder core than the World's Worst's in their obsession with race, feminism and gay rights. A discussion of rape, according to Court, was blunt. 'I've got a story about someone who's confessed to seventeen rapes,' MacKenzie had said on 13 June. 'Is that a record? If it's a record I want it on the front page.' Eight days later Court overheard MacKenzie discussing another rape story and then excitedly shouting: 'A story of a blind rapist. We've got our front page!' His management style was revealed in his offering a knife to an elderly worker on the art desk and advising him: 'Do us all a favour, you useless c*** – cut your throat.'

The contents of Court's diary also confirmed the political left's worst suspicions on race. 'Well, Botha has said the days of white power are over in South Africa. What he doesn't say is what's going to happen when the darkies come down from the trees,' was one of MacKenzie's choice remarks. 'No, I'm not having pictures of darkies on the front page,' said deputy editor David Shapland, the man who supplanted Frank Nicklin and was deputising for MacKenzie on the night an Asian man won *Sun* Bingo. 'That's the last thing our readers want – pictures of blacks raking it in.'

MacKenzie dismissed Court's diary as more 'crap' from the lefties, maintaining that he was not a racialist. This brought a wry smile from execs who had heard him ask at conference what happened at the end of the film *Gandhi* when it was shown on TV. He had switched channels before the end, he told them, because he was not interested in 'a lot of fucking bollocks about an emaciated coon'.

The nightmare agenda being waved about for the readers had been translated into a feature entitled 'THE MOST DANGEROUS STREETS IN BRITAIN' – a league table of muggings, sex attacks, assaults, burglaries and murders in inner-city areas including Liverpool, Birmingham, the St Paul's district of Bristol, and MacKenzie's old home beat of Peckham in sarff London. The feature was accompanied by a petition form urging the folks to collect signatures and send them to Mrs Thatcher. 'Dear Prime Minister,' the petition read, 'We, the undersigned, urge you to press for life sentences that actually MEAN life and for punishment of violent crime to reflect the true gravity of the offence.'

The preoccupation with 'violent Britain' was often pegged on the growing problem of football hooliganism with various scam stories featuring the antics of the 'SCUM', 'ANIMALS' and 'YOBS' on the terraces. The *Sun* covered the subject so extensively that hacks despatched to the clippings library to assemble a fresh scam were asked by sneering library minions: 'Do you want the real stories or the *Sun* clips?' But it was not just the News International librarians who took their scissors to *Sun* hooligan stories. The police often found scrapbooks of newspaper cuttings during raids on organised hooligan 'firms' attached to teams like West Ham, Millwall and Chelsea.

Roy Greenslade, the features editor and, effectively, MacKenzie's number two, tried to tone down the excesses with varying success. Greenslade was thought by the hacks to be about the only person in the office who could exercise a moderating influence on their editor, but he also had a reputation for playing both sides towards the middle and backing down when it came to the crunch. Once when he attempted to defuse a wildly biased story about social security fraud, MacKenzie rounded on him, his voice dripping with sarcasm: 'Aw, fucking hell, let's hear another couple of words from the Claimants' Union representative.'

Some of the hacks had written Greenslade off as a sycophant, while others interpreted his ability to work well with MacKenzie as due to his skill in tracking his editor's moods and to his readiness to tell jokes against himself. But Greenslade often had a hard time, particularly through MacKenzie's belief in never correcting anything unless he absolutely had to. His attitude was that if something wrong got in the paper it was 'hard fucking luck.' He'd bollock the person who made the mistake, but he never believed in owning up to mistakes in public, saying critics would attack anyway, so why give them ammunition?

Once, after an outrageous article tarring all Irish people with the Provisional IRA brush, a group called the North London Irish Association complained. MacKenzie told Greenslade: 'Take this meeting for me this afternoon, I'm busy. You know about Ireland, just fob them off. Tell them you'll do something for them.' It was an awkward task for Greenslade, as MacKenzie well knew, as he was very sensitive about Ireland because of his love of the country and his Irish wife.

'Aw, come on, Kelvin. I can't defend what you've written. Can't you get someone else?' MacKenzie turned round and glared at him. 'Do it!' he said, adding unhelpfully: 'Just tell them some bollocks about how we'll apologise one day or something and get them to fuck off.' Greenslade had a miserable time dealing with the delegation, which he found to be composed of ordinary people making very decent remarks. Basically, as he admitted afterwards, he had to lie to them.

The paper was also arousing strong resentment from the World's Worst and other Unpopulars for its AIDS coverage. The disease had come on to the news agenda in a big way for the first time in early 1985, bringing out all MacKenzie's instinctive hatred of 'poofters'. A report in the paper in February quoted an anonymous 'psychologist' at an AIDS conference in Washington DC as advocating mass killing of gays. 'All homosexuals should be exterminated to stop the spread of AIDS. It's time we stopped pussyfooting around,' he supposedly said.

MacKenzie responded to hacks expressing mild concern about

the paper's approach to the subject with jeers like 'Come out, have we, eh? One of them, are we, eh?' followed by a shout across the editorial floor: 'Watch out folks! There's a botty burglar about!' MacKenzie found the 'gay plague' an endless fund of great picture-led stories which now folded neatly with Wendy Henry's penchant for 'yuck' journalism.

The Press Council had already censured the paper in 1983 for 'a gross invasion of privacy' in printing a deathbed picture of David Niven, taken with a 'grief detector' telephoto lens. And, although Niven had not died of AIDS, the disease enabled the paper to begin running more of the 'last picture' genre to go with front-page splashes announcing the death of famous AIDS victims like Liberace and Rock Hudson. Hudson had been viciously exploited by the *Sun* and other tabloids which had hyped the AIDS scare by going back over two years to find anyone he had kissed to link them with the disease. Victims of this activity had included Linda Evans, a *Dynasty* star who had kissed him on-screen, and Elizabeth Taylor.

MacKenzie honed the *Sun*'s coverage of the deaths by concentrating on one of the most terrifying aspects of the disease – the way sufferers' bodies wasted away before they died. The paper developed a style of reporting the stories by emphasising terminal body weight. 'ROCK IS DEAD – AIDS VICTIM HUDSON DIES WEIGHING 7 STONE' the splash screamed on 3 October 1985 beside a ghastly picture of the emaciated star. MacKenzie just laughed at the left's outrage at these excesses. He knew these grumbles were about to be overtaken by its new central obsession – the results of the Boss's planned 'dash for freedom'. He and the Boss were about to whisk the whole *Sun* operation out of tired old Fleet Street, to the waiting Thatcherite dream of News International's plant located in the East London backwater of Wapping.

Part Three

Chapter 11

<u>Whopping Exclusive</u>

One of the hacks walking into Bouverie Street on the morning of
Friday, 24 January 1986 was greeted by MacKenzie asking him why
he hadn't come on his bike as usual. The hack, used to being ribbed
about his mode of transport, explained that he had a flat tyre, to
which MacKenzie replied with a diabolical chuckle: 'Well, I wouldn't
bother to repair it if I was you. You won't need a bike where you're
going tomorrow – you'll need a fucking armoured car.' The remark
tripped the office rumour machine into hysterical overdrive.

Everybody had known for months that something big was in the
air. It all centred round what had been known as 'Tower Hamlets'
and was now being called Wapping – the new printing plant
Murdoch had built in the early 1980s in the wastes of London's
old docklands. The Inkies' leaders had smelt a rat about the place
for years, although their complacent rank and file still believed
that Murdoch would never dare to risk an all-out strike by closing
down Bouverie Street.

But it was this very point that had finally determined Murdoch
to move his whole newspaper operation in one fell swoop. In
extraordinary secrecy he had prepared Wapping for his four titles,
the *Sun*, the *News of the World*, *The Times* and the *Sunday Times*,
to be moved there in their entirety. Murdoch's rationale was that
he would never reach agreement with Inkies over Wapping when
they could hold him to ransom by stopping Bouverie Street. The
only answer was to shut the whole place down and start afresh at
Wapping without them.

Several senior members of the *Sun's* management had been roped into the plot and two senior editorial execs had vanished with flimsy cover stories six months earlier. In the new year other heads of departments had suddenly disappeared with what the hacks quickly dubbed 'Wapping cough'. Now, the rumour flew round, it was actually about to happen.

Murdoch had entrusted MacKenzie with the crucial job of driving the hacks into their new hi-tech pen. His strategy was to spring the move from nowhere to give them no time to think or, more crucially, join in solidarity with the Inkies whom he was about to crunch. Throughout the Friday MacKenzie prepared the ground carefully, and notorious troublemakers were despatched on no-hope stories. Not so easily fooled, they, in turn, quickly killed them and scurried back to Bouverie Street for the meeting which had been called for 6 p.m. There was no point in getting the stories anyhow. The Inkies had belatedly woken up to what was going on and had already stopped work. There would be no paper that night.

Over 100 staff crowded into the features room on the fourth floor for MacKenzie's speech. The atmosphere was highly charged and they could sense that the editor was nervous. Unknown to him, he was also being taped for posterity by one of the hacks. MacKenzie started by explaining how Murdoch had negotiated for six years with the print unions over Wapping, but for six years they had said no. One branch secretary on seeing the plant had even said: 'The best thing you can do is blow this place up.'

'In a minute-by-minute industry, when they've got you by the balls, you've got to listen,' MacKenzie continued, his voice rising. 'Well, they haven't got us by the balls any more.' Pausing for effect, he resumed more quietly. 'The situation is simply this . . . the only people that matter any more are the journalists. There can't be papers without journalists and it is with this in mind that we are going to make this momentous step from Bouverie Street down to Wapping.'

Then, emphasising his words by banging his fist into his palm, he said slowly and intensely: 'I personally want every single one of you, including those who are ideologically at the opposite end of the pole from me, I want every single one of you in Wapping.' There was money on the table. 'Despite my protestations,' MacKenzie finished with a wicked smile, 'Mr Murdoch is going to make an extraordinarily generous pay offer.'

How much?, the hacks asked. But MacKenzie, his set speech over, suddenly became evasive. What happened if people refused to go? MacKenzie stumbled for the right words. 'I . . . er . . . think the answer to that is, erm, that those who did not go to Wapping . . . would be considered to be dismissing themselves.' What about redundancies? 'The truth is' MacKenzie replied, 'we will be employing thousands more in the years to come . . . not thousands less.'

The pressure came off as the questioning descended into a babble about health and safety, how the computers worked, what the place was like, and other side issues. MacKenzie, relaxing as he fielded these minor points, chucked in a last sweetener. 'Rupert has bought some of the world's most expensive chairs. They cost $300 each, they go down and round and round at the touch of a button. So every effort has been made.'

With that he left the room and went to phone the Boss, who was waiting tensely for news of how it was going. Back in the features room there was growing uproar as the hacks animatedly struggled to comprehend the full import of what they had been told. Suspicious, they called their editor back.

What about the latest house agreement which guaranteed a four-day working week? MacKenzie saw what they were getting at. 'You are worried that at the end of eight weeks, when the company house agreement is up, we'll introduce the old banging drums – slavemasters – and away we go, seven days a week, eighteen hours a day? Now I put this forward to Rupert and Rupert is dead against it.' The hacks laughed and MacKenzie knew he was winning. 'I am quite happy to assure you that the agreement will be standing another year, right?' He added: 'So there we are, game set and fucking match. I'll drop my trousers. . . . OK?'

The hacks kept up the questioning. 'If I bend over any further I'll be in *Gay News*,' MacKenzie remarked as they raised a final worry. The NUJ had instructed them not to go, so what would happen if they did go and were then thrown out of the union? MacKenzie replied that he'd be astonished if they threw out fully paid-up members and added: 'What the NUJ has done for you could safely fit up a gnat's arse. What you have done for yourselves has been incredible. . . . You think about it.' He left again to bring Murdoch up to date.

The NUJ chapel meeting which followed was dominated more by expressions of loathing for the NGA and the other print unions than by consideration of the hacks' own position. There was still a bitter legacy from the journalists' strike of 1984, which had crumbled after a fortnight of standing on the pavement outside Bouverie Street. MacKenzie, in total Whirling Dervish mode, had worked with a handful of execs to produce a paper of sorts every day, while an inter-union muddle had kept the NGA compositors at their jobs and enabled the paper to hit the streets. Since then hatred for the Inkies had known no bounds among the hacks, who had not been privy to the manoeuvrings behind the scenes.

It was not long before a consensus emerged. They had to go to Wapping, and they would make their own way there without the bloody Inkies. MacKenzie was right – the Inkies were history. At Wapping the hacks would be the masters; they would control the equipment; they would have the power. And anyhow what choice did they each have? You either went along, or you were sacked.

There were angry complaints about playground bully-boy tactics, but that did not alter the fact that not just wages, but pensions and possible redundancy payments were now on the line. And the Bouverie Street wreck was finally finished one way or another whatever happened. Two years earlier a factory inspector had given it a life of no more than eighteen months. If they stayed any longer it might simply just fall in on them. They were fed up with the place and its rat-infested canteen, where there was so much stealing of the cutlery you were charged a 50p deposit if you did not want to eat with your fingers. The resolution to go was passed by 100 votes to 8.

Eventually only five hacks did not join the 'dash for freedom' and joined the more numerous 'refuseniks' from *The Times* and the *Sunday Times*, who in most cases were grinding a separate axe about the decline in their papers' editorial practices since the Murdoch takeover. Even then some of the *Sun*'s refuseniks were objecting not so much to what Murdoch was doing as to the way he was doing it. One of them, Eric 'Scoop' Butler, who had worked on Frank Nicklin's sports desk since the beginning, summed it up as 'industrial gangsterism'. For another, the reason had been burning in his mind ever since the journalists' strike. Having always implicitly believed that the *Sun* was a positive, cheerful paper, he had been appalled to be accosted on the pavement outside Bouverie Street by a vile thug wanting to give the paper a story. The hack had explained that the journalists were on strike and offered to take him round to one of the other papers. 'No, they're no fucking good,' the thug had replied angrily. 'I want this in the *Sun* because it's the slag-off paper, innit.' The hack had never forgotten the remark, and after deep thought had come to the conclusion that it was true.

The final departure from 30 Bouverie Street for the unknown territory of Wapping was an emotional occasion, lightened only by the happy spin-off of ditching the last of the *Crying Boys* which readers had continued to send in since the pantechnicon clear-out and they were still jamming crevices and cupboards all over the office.

Two framed *Crying Boys* were hung in the place of front pages which had decorated the stairwell and had been nicked by photographers as souvenirs of their work. Ignoring the MacKenzie-hyped curse, other hacks grabbed copies, using them as packaging for fragile possessions which they were otherwise expected to carry, refugee-style, in black plastic binbags provided by the management.

After the grot and filth of Bouverie Street, Wapping was a new world. 'It's just like starring in *Lou Grant!*' a gobsmacked features

189

hackette yelped as she walked in. With its blankly glowing computer screens, soothing grey walls and toning blue carpet tiles the new office was very clean, very bland and very modern. In many ways it resembled the dealing rooms shortly to come on-stream in the Big Bang, the City's version of Wapping which ushered in computerised trading and emptied the old Stock Exchange floor overnight.

As Wapping had originally been designed solely as a print factory, the editorial floors had been tacked on top of the press hall to form what was essentially a word factory. The *Sun's* quarters were on the sixth floor, above the *News of the World* on the fifth. For the moment *The Times* and *Sunday Times* hacks were kept in Grays Inn Road, before moving across later into a converted rum warehouse.

From the lift, swing doors led into a large room which was essentially open plan, though broken up by heavy pillars. The ceiling height was low, which some hacks immediately found oppressive, but the brilliant view provided a huge compensation. The all-powerful backbench occupied a row of the $300 aircraft-type seats MacKenzie had promised along one wall. Opposite was a row of three small bunker-like cubicles occupied by MacKenzie and his deputies, with internal windows providing a commanding view of the newsroom. They were instantly dubbed the 'goldfish bowls'.

The hacks' desks were in the middle, with their tops colour-coded by department. The news hacks were disgusted to find they had been allocated shit-brown. All were equipped with the biggest bonus of all – the new technology which gave them what they had always wanted, 'direct input' from their keyboards straight to the pages, cutting out the stage of typesetting. From now on the NGA typesetters with their ancient Linotype machines were redundant. A version of the old compositors' job of assembling the pages from columns of type survived. But this now involved the less skilled job of 'paste-up' – cutting up type produced on photographic paper with a scalpel and sticking it down on the page. The job was done with non-union labour.

Murdoch could have chosen a computer system which eliminated even the 'paste-up' stage and churned out type arranged on pages designed on computer screens by the subs but although this technology was later widely used on other papers it was regarded as full of bugs at the time. Instead he shrewdly chose the American ATEX system, bought off the shelf and popular with hacks as simple and user-friendly. Some were still bemused by the new concepts involved, and one hack at first adamantly refused to move from a particular terminal, insisting that his stories were 'inside it'. Meanwhile there were huge jokes about the fate of the lightweight keyboards as they bounced and clattered across the new desks under ferocious poundings administered by those whose typewriting skills had been honed on old manuals.

The thirteen-acre site of 'Fortress Wapping' had been designed to withstand the expected siege which began immediately. The print unions mounted a permanent and well-organised picket on the entrance, pulling in supporters from other papers and the ranks of the politically committed, and producing some real divisions of loyalty. One of the hacks, knowing that Wendy Henry's twin sister Sara, a production worker at the *Daily Telegraph*, was on the picket, asked how she felt about it – especially as they were sharing the same house at the time. Henry replied: 'We spit at each other over breakfast and then forget about it for the rest of the day.'

Security was handled by Stewart Edwards, a former Rhodesian police superintendent who had once been in charge of 1,500 armed men fighting guerrillas in the African bush. He beefed up the twelve-foot high spiked metal fence surrounding the complex with triple rolls of German-manufactured razor wire. Microwave alarms and remote video cameras scanned the perimeter, which was bathed in the harsh glare of searchlights by night. Each employee was given a colour-coded, numbered pass to show at the only entry point of the electronically controlled gates. Different colours controlled access to different parts of the plant, which was prowled by uniformed guards.

The *Sun* hacks were spared the ritual gatherings on Saturday nights which regularly attracted crowds of 5,000 trying to stop Murdoch's TNT trucks taking out finished copies of the *Sunday Times* and the *News of the World*. On these nights, as *Sunday Times* editor Andrew Neil stressed afterwards, he and others inside were in genuine fear of their lives.

There was also huge anger at the heavy-handed and massive police presence which used the tactics honed in the miners' strike, and the Saturday-night demonstrations regularly sparked brutal and ugly scenes for which both sides were to blame. During the week picketing was much lighter, and *Sun* hacks usually only had to endure verbal abuse, along with the trauma of seeing former colleagues standing miserably outside. There was sympathy for old colleagues like SOGAT copytakers and library staff who had been squeezed out, but the main dividing line was the bussing the management organised to get hacks to work. The 'scab wagons', or 'battle buses' as they were known inside the plant as part of the military flavour of the whole operation, toured London every morning collecting personnel at prearranged locations. They then drove into the plant with curtains drawn across the windows, which were also protected by wire guards. Some timid hacks even crouched in the aisles to avoid being identified, but the prouder ones refused even to contemplate getting into the buses, regarding them as a ritualised form of humiliation which paraded their dishonour in crossing the picket line. Instead they used their own cars or taxis – if they could persuade one to go to the plant as many drivers were on the side of the picket. Some hacks just walked in off public transport. MacKenzie, as he swept by the huddled crowd in the comfort of his blue and grey company Jaguar XJ 4.2 was accompanied by a minder, just in case, but he was never needed.

Anyhow, many of the hacks found it hard enough coming to work past pickets shouting 'Scab! Scab! Scab!' As one said, when they walked into their glistening new environment to be greeted by their editor shouting 'C***! C***! C***!', it was all getting too much. Leader-writer Peter Rose handed in his resignation after a fortnight, declaring he couldn't work in such an atmosphere. (He later changed his mind and was allowed to return by MacKenzie.)

The picket compounded the hacks' isolation. As pioneers in the wastes of docklands they were the first to be cut off from the cosy familiar world of Fleet Street. The Wapping canteen on Floor 4A served excellent comfort food, but there was a major refreshment problem for many, as Murdoch had decreed that the plant be dry. The Wapping house journal, a *Sun*-like tabloid called *The News*, later observed: 'Staff now working at Wapping appear to be more sober in their pursuits than their predecessors in Bouverie Street, whose disappearance from Fleet Street has caused a mini-crisis among the licensing fraternity'. Venturing into one of the grotty local pubs was a hazardous business which carried a serious risk of running into a gang of marauding Inkies.

While hundreds of police kept the pickets at bay at vast expense to the taxpayer, an early visitor was Norman Tebbit. Inviting him into his office after the standard tour, MacKenzie sheepishly offered him the standard Wapping tipple of lemonade, only for the *Sun*'s favourite Tory hard man to reply, to his huge embarrassment: 'You must be fucking joking!'

The isolation also led to a change in the hacks' work patterns which swung the balance on the paper even more towards the subs. Going out on a story was now a major exercise, which started with running the gauntlet of the picket. Hailing a taxi was inadvisable. Many Inkies, as a result of the union's overmanning agreements, had second jobs as taxi drivers and there was a macho East End alliance between the two groups of workers. Most hacks were forced to endure the vagaries of London's miserable public transport system, with twenty minutes' walk to the nearest tube station at Tower Hill.

Only then were they back in the centre of things where most stories originated. On a day-by-day basis their isolation was compounded by being cut off from the grapevine of the Street's watering holes like El Vino's, the Cheshire Cheese, the Punch, the Bell, the Popinjay, the Wine Press, the Printer's Pie, the King and Keys, and the Stab in the Back, as the *Mirror*'s local in Holborn was known.

The attitude of hacks from other papers did not help. Few people on the Street had much sympathy for the Inkies and most agreed that their come-uppance was long overdue. Many of their own employers were now announcing that they would shortly be following Murdoch's lead and the end of the Street was already in sight. But the industry had still been shocked by the naked demonstration of Murdoch's power.

Wapping was also giving another message to hacks in general. Although the *Sun* hacks had been told they would now have the power instead of the Inkies, they had cravenly surrendered it from day one by meekly going to Wapping. It was quite clear from their 1984 strike that their power was limited and that journalists could never stop a paper as long as a handful of editorial execs were prepared to work. But they could at least demand to be bought off, as negotiations between journalists and management at Wapping were proving. Journalism was just about to become a much more lucrative profession.

The move consolidated MacKenzie's power within the office. He was naturally exultant at the crucial part he had played in enabling the Boss to pull the move off so smoothly. The Inkies had been stuffed, and now his team had the new technology, which he revelled in. More importantly, the new open-plan office enabled him to dominate every aspect of the paper infinitely more effectively than in the more warren-like Bouverie Street. He had only to take one step out of his goldfish-bowl bunker to dominate the whole operation.

MacKenzie's activity rate shot up to new heights, and the hacks swore that his decibel level had risen by yet another 20 per cent. The fresh onslaught of bawlings and bollockings could now be heard by everybody. Disillusioned hacks soon found there was nowhere to hide except the toilets. At least, they grumbled to each other, the Bouverie Street flies had not been imported to Wapping. But then a rumour swept round that the new loos might be bugged. Paranoia increased.

Wapping was perfect for the MacKenzie strategy of making the Currant Bun as different from other papers as possible. It was the

194

biggest news for years, and while 30 Bouverie Street summed up all that was wrong with the old England Maggie was steadily demolishing, Wapping was the future. MacKenzie wasn't going to lapse into siege mentality just because the *Sun* was now behind razor wire. Rather, from its new power base he was going to show how the Currant Bun was now going to hammer the opposition it had already physically left behind, and within a month he had done just that by manufacturing a splash which not only left the rest of the Street gasping, but was later to be hyped as the *Sun*'s most talked-about front page of all time – 'FREDDIE STARR ATE MY HAMSTER'.

The original slender base on which the tale was constructed was a three-year-old incident in which Starr, a popular entertainer on the club circuit, had finished his turn at a Manchester nightclub and gone to stay the night with his former girlfriend Lea La Salle and her new boyfriend, Tom McCaffrey. Finding nothing substantial to eat in the house Starr inserted the couple's pet hamster, Supersonic, between two pieces of bread and then bit hard into the sandwich, giving the impression that he was eating the creature itself. It was the kind of zany visual gag he featured in his stage act. Everybody thought it hilarious at the time.

But in February 1986 a rumour started circulating that the hamster had died of fright during the incident. Dick Saxty, a veteran hack in the *Sun*'s Manchester office, picked the story up on the circuit and interviewed La Salle, who confirmed it. Saxty wrote up the story and filed it to Wapping. It was a possible page lead – but a bit off the wall and carrying a strong whiff of showbiz skulduggery. It wouldn't have been surprising if it was killed.

But at Wapping MacKenzie leaped on it and, to universal astonishment, promptly made it the front-page splash. The by-now standard 'editor has gone mad' message flashed round the office as the hacks nudged the story into shape. The key was the headline 'FREDDIE STARR ATE MY HAMSTER', which scored 100 per cent on the Wendy Henry 'Hey Doris! Look at this!' scale, though trumped in the opinion of some people by the classic 'RED JETS BUZZ TOM JONES' or 'WEREWOLF SEIZED IN SOUTHEND'.

MacKenzie added the strap, 'Comic put a live pet in sandwich, says beauty.' The story, now shorn of the allegation that the hamster had died of fright, started: 'Zany comic Freddie Starr put a live hamster in a sandwich and ATE it, model girl Lea La Salle claimed yesterday. "It's something I'll never forget. He put my hamster between two slices of bread and started eating it. He thought it was hilarious," said Lea. "He just fell about laughing."' Her new boyfriend Tom McCaffrey carefully qualified the statement by adding: 'I don't know how much of the hamster he ate.'

After the edition had gone to press Murdoch phoned MacKenzie for his regular check. 'What's on the front page tomorrow?' he asked. 'Well, Boss,' MacKenzie replied apprehensively, 'it's quite a funny story, erm, it's about a comedian, with a good headline, er, "FREDDIE STARR ATE MY HAMSTER".' There was a long silence on the other end of the phone. Silence was a standard Murdoch intimidation technique which MacKenzie knew well. The ploy was designed to break the nerve of the person at the other end and start them babbling. But MacKenzie had become a master of the silent counter-ploy, and it was a standard office joke that hundreds of pounds were regularly eaten up by lengthy silent transatlantic telephone calls as each waited for the other to crack. This time it was Murdoch who broke the silence. 'So there's no news about today, Kelvin?' he drawled slowly.

Greatly relieved, MacKenzie enthusiastically resumed the conversation. 'No Boss, not much, you see . . .' But Murdoch cut him dead. 'Is that the most important story in Britain today?' he demanded to know. MacKenzie, the wind knocked from his sails, resorted to pleading. 'Honest, Boss – it's a great story. You'll love it when you see it.' Murdoch just grunted and cut the line. But MacKenzie proved to be correct – when Murdoch did see it he realized how cleverly irresistible it was and enjoyed it as much as everyone else on the paper.

Freddie Starr was less amused. If his fans got the idea that he was cruel to animals it could do immense damage to his career. All the other papers were now on to the story, and the *Sun* even received the accolade of having its splash featured on Radio 4's

Today programme. Starr's PR agent, Max Clifford, savouring the enormous press interest and publicity potential, told him not to worry – it was just the sort of zany stunt his fans liked. In fact, Clifford reckoned, it could do him a lot of good. 'Just let me handle it,' he said.

Clifford was well known at the *Sun*. He worked closely with *Sun* showbiz hack Kevin O'Sullivan, constructing endless scam stories based on invented celebrity romances and carefully planned 'chance' encounters in the West End clubs. This seedy, but profitable, trade was carried out in Stringfellows or its new rival the Limelight (known in the business as the 'Slimelight' in tribute to Clifford and his fellow operators).

Clifford called O'Sullivan and proposed a follow-up on the story the whole Street was after. Freddie would pose with a hamster exclusively for the *Sun* to show that he was an animal-lover. He told O'Sullivan to get a hamster and meet him at Battersea heliport for the short flight down the Thames to Starr's Maidenhead mansion.

O'Sullivan rushed off with photographer Steve Lewis, picking up a hamster from a pet shop in Islington. As they arrived at the heliport and ran across the tarmac under the whooping rotor blades of Starr's personal helicopter, weighed down with camera bag, briefcase and hamster cage, O'Sullivan could not help thinking the whole trip was like a joke pastiche of Vietnam.

Twelve minutes later the helicopter landed on the lawn of Starr's mansion. Lewis carried his cameras into the house, set them up, and went to get the hamster. But to his horror he found it lying rigid on the floor of the cage. 'Oh no! The fucking thing's died!' O'Sullivan gulped. 'What are we going to do? Kelvin'll kill us if we don't get the picture!' Deadlines were pressing and there was no time to get another one. 'Hang on,' said Lewis, 'I thought I saw it twitch.' He picked it up, placed it gingerly on a table and the team huddled round to give it heart massage with their fingers, while whispering encouragement to the prostrate rodent.

The hamster, which turned out merely to have been catatonic

sprang to life and shot off across the room. Lewis caught it and placed it on Starr's shoulder for the picture. At this point the terrified creature had clearly had enough and shat down the back of Starr's white jacket. 'Don't look now, Freddie,' O'Sullivan prompted, 'but the fucker's done the business all over you.' Starr burst out laughing, providing a superbly spontaneous picture.

Back in the helicopter, O'Sullivan and Lewis set course for Wapping. At the rival *Mirror* hacks had become used to the dreaded sound of Robert Maxwell's approaching personal helicopter, which he parked on the top of the paper's Holborn tower block. But at Wapping the sound of Starr's machine hovering over the pickets caused consternation. MacKenzie dangled out of the news-room window to get a better look and then shouted: 'Fucking hell, action stations everybody! It's a fucking SOGAT airstrike!'

O'Sullivan and Lewis landed in the car park and marched triumphantly into the newsroom where another opposition-crunching splash was put on the layout. The whole hamster saga reduced the newsroom to bedlam, with hacks in hysterics and rushing off proofs on the photocopiers as souvenirs and giving the whole office the boost it needed. The euphoria lingered for weeks. MacKenzie celebrated by putting the 'FREDDIE STARR ATE MY HAMSTER' front page on his office wall, in pride of place next to 'GOTCHA', and the promotions department weighed in as usual with 'FREDDIE STARR' T-shirts.

With stories like 'FREDDIE STARR' whizzing around the circuits of the ATEX system MacKenzie was ready for any challenge. He even turned the pickets into a scam story by enlisting the help of pint-sized Samantha Fox, the *Sun*'s most celebrated Page Three girl. Samantha had provided MacKenzie with the germ of an idea by saying that only way she would cross the picket line was in a tank. The *Sun* obliged by getting hold of an armoured scout car. The resulting staged picture showed her inside the compound, wearing a tin helmet and demure dress standing on the vehicle with arms raised, while razor wire in the background added an authentic military touch. Flanking the machine, although not in the picture, were Commander Petrie and a ragbag of editorial execs in helmets and combat jackets, standing loosely to attention. The hacks delightedly commented that Commander Petrie was at last properly kitted out for his pet phrase, 'Let's run it up the flagpole and see who salutes it.' The picture story dealt the freezing pickets another psychological blow with a public flaunting of their ineffectiveness.

The pickets did however have one bright spot in this unequal media war in the shape of their strike newspaper, the *Wapping Post*. The *Post* was started by Keith Sutton, a former sub on the *Sunday Times* colour magazine, who was in many ways a MacKenzie *manqué*. Sutton, who was MacKenzie's age, had upstaged him in working-class credentials by being brought up in a Nissen hut, and like him made a bright start in pop newspapers, getting to Fleet Street and at one stage briefly working alongside him at the *Express*.

But Sutton had then dropped out to become an activist on the south London squatting scene and his interest in popular newspapers had taken a political and academic turn, when as a mature student he researched his PhD at Royal Holloway College on nineteenth-century newspapers. He was delighted to find that the radicals had used the same technique with headlines like 'Peterloo Massacre', a play on Waterloo used to describe the slaughter of destitute mill-workers by the Manchester Yeomen of the Guard.

Sutton's *Wapping Post* was an inky riot deliberately designed as a parody of the *Sun*, and aping it by devices like printing a policewoman in riot gear as a Page Three girl. But his most notorious story was a reworking of the *Sun*'s psychiatrist gimmick to produce 'MURDOCH ON THE COUCH'. The feature was incredibly rude, with the copy run round a cartoon of a naked Murdoch, complete with tits and privates covered by a copy of the *Sun*.

Sutton's research was a great deal more thorough than the *Sun*'s had been in the preparation of its 'dossiers'. He painstakingly interviewed the office cleaners to dredge up facts about Murdoch's personal life, such as his insisting that the fringes of his Indian carpets be combed into regimented lines every morning and that there must be no marks left behind by the wheels of the Hoover. The cleaners also supplied details of the state of his toilet, and the material was given to a 'Harley Street analyst' who concluded that Murdoch had never overcome struggles with his mother over toilet-training. Sutton gleefully strapped the piece: 'THE DIRTY TRICKS IN LITTLE RUPERT'S POTTY WORLD.' (Sutton was later to go on to be editor of *News on Sunday*, the left's attempt to answer the *Sun* by producing a 'decent paper for the people'. The paper, principally funded by trade unions and loony left councils to the tune of £6.5 million, went bust on issue three.)*

Meanwhile back inside Wapping the Sam Fox armoured car picture-story had appeared just before Clare Short, Labour MP for Birmingham Ladywood, succeeded in bringing her Indecent Displays (Newspapers) Bill into the Commons. Short's Bill was the last flickering vestige of what was now a fifteen-year-old campaign to make pictures of naked or semi-naked women in sexually provocative poses illegal in newspapers. Short argued they should be banned just as they were on public hoardings. She denounced Page Three as 'blatant and crude' and said that like similar pictures it degraded women. She also believed – although she admitted there was no hard evidence – that there was a connection between sex crimes and pictures which treated women as sex objects.

'The *Sun* Says' was outraged at this suggestion by 'killjoy Clare' and got on its highest horse to state that Page Three girls were 'no more provocative than a statue in the park'. 'The charge that they provoke sexual crime is deeply resented by this newspaper, which has crusaded against violent criminals since it was founded,' it thundered, advising MPs to look for another motive from 'Ms Misery'. 'She [Short] has a political animus against the *Sun* because of our break to the land of the free – Wapping.'

The Bill, titteringly described by Tory MP Robert Adley as 'deserving the booby prize', had no chance of becoming law and Norman Tebbit joined a cross-section of political opinion in

* For a full account of this fiasco see *Disaster: The Rise and Fall of News on Sunday* by Peter Chippindale and Chris Horrie (Sphere paperback, £4.99).

saying he saw nothing wrong with the feature. But the *Sun* used it as an excuse to launch a 'SAVE OUR SIZZLERS (SOS)' campaign, led by Sam Fox, who was wheeled out to knock the knockers with a verbal attack on Short which the paper punningly described as 'letting her have it with both barrels'. 'SAM SAYS SAVE PAGE THREE' bumper stickers were dispensed to folks who requested them.

The failure of Short's Bill to carry public opinion showed how events had moved on since Lamb's early days. By now, partly due to MacKenzie's puritanical approach, a full-length shot was unusual and the feature had moved on to a smiling, homely girl-next-door approach. (The 'girl' of most mammarian interest for the hacks had been Tula, who had started life as Barry and had a been a Bluebell girl.) Instead the most popular girls like Sam Fox had moved off Page Three and on to the news and features pages as celebs whose rise to wealth and stardom was now obsessively hyped and tracked for the readers.

Samantha Fox had first posed for Page Three in 1983, a few days after her sixteenth birthday, making her the youngest professional topless model in the country. Her modelling career had been launched by her mother sending her photograph, in a body stocking, to the 'Miss *Sunday People*' beauty competition in 1983. The editor, Nick Lloyd, wanted her to win, but when he did the Lamb trick of consulting the women in the office, they thought her tits were too big and she was placed second.

The ensuing publicity had got her into serious trouble at her Catholic school, and the *Sun* had become interested, leading to the Page Three offer. Her mother, whose career as a dancer on *Ready, Steady, Go* had been cut short by having Sam at an early age, counselled her wisely that she had six years in the topless game before she reached the ripe old age of twenty-two. By then gravity would have taken over.

Sam's main assets, as the *Sun* never tired of pointing out, were made extraordinary by the combination of a height of 5′ 1½″ and a bra size of 36D. But equally important was her down-to-earth north London background, which encouraged the readers to cheer her up the earnings scale. After being voted Page Three Girl of the Year twice, the marketing machine started clicking into place. The readers were informed that she was applying to Lloyds to insure her boobs for £250,000 and that she had signed to be used in a video strip-poker game for the Sinclair Spectrum users, the same target audience as the 'Torpedo an Argie' game during the Falklands.

Then, with many a nudge-nudge and a wink-wink, they were invited to share the world of 'the luckiest lad in the land', her 'real love' Kit Miller, who revealed the delights of having 'her tiny feet in my lap'. Miller, another sharp south Londoner like MacKenzie, was thirty-eight years old and a West End playboy who worked as a TV columnist on the *News of the World*. The hacks regarded him as the ultimate beach-bar lothario, complete with tinted bond highlights in his hair and mandatory ear-ring. They looked on contemptuously as he squeezed himself into trendy jeans to go with his normal white socks and slip-on shoes, and the readers were soon informed that Sam was dumping him because he was too old. Kit defiantly announced in the paper that he was 'not positively gutted'.

All this time Sam had been living at home in Haringey, north London with her mother Carole and her father Patrick, who had switched from being a self-employed builder to becoming her manager. (Kit had slept in the family's spare room when he stayed the night.) But then the *Sun* used her to give proof positive that the new classless 'you are what you earn' society had arrived by sending a ferret up the bum, as MacKenzie called a major wind-up, of no lesser a person than Maggie. Sam, the paper announced, was to move in next to the Prime Minister with the rest of her family.

Mrs Thatcher and Denis had just completed the purchase of their 'retirement home' on a new prestige Barratt development in Dulwich, close to MacKenzie's old school, when the *Sun* splurged 'MAGGIE'S FOXY NEW NEIGHBOUR' across the centre-page spread with the cheery strapline 'Sam's hoping to drop in for tea!' The story was based on a visit to the showhome Sam had made like any other punter and claimed that the Fox family was planning to buy a £425,000 'dream home' two doors down from the Thatchers. Accompanying pictures showed the master bedroom where she would sleep, while Sam informed readers she planned to go topless into the garden. Alongside screeds of detail about the house's luxury features, the article described the estate of twenty-three houses, which bore a remarkable resemblance to Wapping, having the same twelve-foot-high wall, electrically controlled gates and video surveillance system. Only the searchlights were missing.

'Buying the five-bedroomed home should be easy for Sam, who earns £250,000 a year' the paper informed readers. Sam's financial success story was rubbed in shortly afterwards with another huge feature headlining that Sam's earnings of £5,000 a week were '£4,000 up on Maggie'. The feature incidentally gave away the fact that she was paid only £90 for a Page Three studio session. A Downing Street spokesman, surrendering to the new classless market forces, commented grimly: 'This is a commercial development and nobody can choose their neighbours.' The sale, of course, never went through.

But Sam was to get her come-uppance when her next career move brought her up against the traditional British aristocracy in the form of doughty old socialite, the Duchess of Argyll. Sam was cast for a dotty £17 million project to launch a British soap called *Legacy*, in which she was to play a servant girl who was taken advantage of and made pregnant. But when the Duchess, who was also a member of the putative cast, was informed of this she declared in ringing tones: 'It isn't proper for this girl Fox to appear alongside a real-life aristocrat.'

Sam was promptly dumped, and the project anyhow expired shortly afterwards. Instead London Weekend Television, seeing an opportunity for some cheap publicity, hired her as an interviewer for Michael Aspel's lightweight *Six O'Clock Show*. Her first 'story' was interviewing women about their knicker lines showing. Sam, who was still appearing reguarly on Page Three, endeared herself to the readers by maintaining an incorrigible cheerfulness throughout these various adventures, although the hearts of the other reporters at London Weekend went out to her when she pleaded with them to come to the launch of the latest enterprise she had become involved with, a champagne bar called Sam's. They had to come, she explained, because they were her only friends at the moment and she wouldn't know anyone else there.

Eventually Sam made the inevitable attempt to become a pop star. With the full weight of the Bizarre marketing machine behind her, her first single, 'Touch Me (I Want Your Body)', was hyped into the Top Thirty. The follow-up, 'Do Ya Do Ya (Wanna Please Me)', was coming up for release when the publicity operation dropped a faked-up bombshell. On 6 June 1986 the paper splashed with 'SAM FOX: I'M QUITTING PAGE 3' beside a WOB of 'The *Sun* gets the big ones'. Our Sam, the story revealed, was giving up topless modelling as part of her quest to become Britain's answer to Madonna. But her valedictory Page Three exposure only presaged a short retirement. Less than a month later, on 1 July, MacKenzie got another splash with 'SAM'S BACK! (by popular demand)', and there they were again.

After that Sam's singing career continued with considerably more success in America than Britain, although she was soon to be edged out of the top spot in the readers' affections by the new favourites Linda Lusardi and Maria Whittaker. But before the year was out the *Sun* was able to convey the good news that, although they were not moving in next to the Thatchers, the Fox family had at last found their dream home, a pink-washed country cottage in Hertfordshire, which Sam had bought for £300,000 from a second-hand car dealer.

Chapter 12

The Herald of Free Enterprise

In January 1987 the picket at Wapping peaked on the first anniversary of the move. The largest-ever crowd of 13,000 was involved in some of the ugliest violence yet seen, and, out of the 1,000 police on duty, 168 were reported injured, along with scores of demonstrators. But the anniversary proved to be the last emotional gasp of the protest, and the print unions, by now reduced to hanging on for decent payoffs, abandoned it shortly afterwards. Although production had been sporadically disrupted, no issues of Murdoch's papers had ever been completely lost. Brenda Dean, the leader of SOGAT, later admitted she had known Murdoch had won the moment the first TNT lorry drove out of the plant.

This total rout was the last stage in the process of breaking the power of the printers' Fleet Street chapels. It had also exacted a heavy toll in huge personal trauma for many individuals enduring the hardship of a futile year without pay. One picket committed suicide under the strain, a number of marriages were broken, and many were injured in the pitched battles with the police. Their hot-metal craft abolished, all had to retrain for new jobs. Some Imperial Fathers found themselves blacklisted and never worked in the industry again.

There were mixed feelings on the editorial floor once the picket was over. The psychological relief was immense now that there were no more shouts of 'Scab! Scab! Scab!' as the hacks came in to work. But MacKenzie's 'C***! C***! C***!' still awaited them inside. Some of them had seen the pickets as their allies in preventing a crackdown by MacKenzie or the management.

A strange malaise had also begun to grip the office which soon became known as the 'Wapping Factor'. Some of the hacks, although they only realised it afterwards, had begun unconsciously to reject Wapping as a workplace. There was no single cause they could pin down, but much of the reason was thought to be claustrophobia from the low ceilings, now exacerbated by the loss of the only window. One of the delights of the office had been the view, which almost included Tower Bridge, but now they lost that, along with all natural light, as the window was bricked up as part of a giant spiral ramp built for the TNT lorries to queue up to load finished papers.

The Wapping Factor seemed to hit the features department first and a number of experienced female writers began looking around for new jobs. But there were others who were not so sure of their job prospects elsewhere, and yet others who appeared to be barnacles, stuck on the bottom of the good ship Wapping for ever. MacKenzie's pillorying of all these different types stepped up when the pickets had left, as they had all feared. Nobody was actually fired, but some were told to their face they had no future in the place. They were given impossible jobs to do and heaped with huge workloads. Their expenses were slashed, they were personally insulted, told they were useless and subjected to one of MacKenzie's favourite tactics. He would come up to their desks, put his face close to theirs and say: 'You still 'ere, then, eh? Haven't you gone yet, eh?' Nerves started jangling.

The hacks had always known that people who cravenly agreed with MacKenzie only subjected themselves to more abuse. He had seemed to get a particular needle with Stuart Higgins, a minion on the newsdesk who was always eager to please his colleagues. Higgins was a small, plump individual who other hacks joked had dropped out of the rat race to join the mouse race. He was personable enough, but there were divided opinions about his curious habit at parties of dropping on all fours and going round barking like a dog, pretending to bite women's ankles.

MacKenzie used to get intensely irritated by Higgins's habit of just smiling at him however severe the bollocking, and he would be driven to new heights of abuse and denigration. 'You smarmy c***, Higgy, you take it all, don't you, eh?' MacKenzie raged at him one day in front of the desk. 'You just sit there soaking it all up, don't you, eh? Know what you're like, don't you? You're like a sponge. A fucking human sponge.'

Hacks watching this performance saw MacKenzie stop as though a lightbulb had gone on in his head. He scurried off into his office and the hacks heard demonic cackling. Higgy soaked it up so much the readers were about to be invited to join MacKenzie in having a go. It was a public pillorying ranking at least equal with that arranged for Mike Terry, the hapless Bingo Bungler.

The next morning on page 5 a library mugshot of Higgins smiling and holding a telephone appeared next to the strapline: 'Want someone to yell at? Scream at? Fume at? – RING HIGGY THE HUMAN SPONGE, HE'LL SOAK IT UP.' The copy was a public version of a MacKenzie bollocking, shorn of the swear words.

> Are you mad enough to make a life miserable? Is something driving you k-k-k-krazy? Do you feel like a villain looking for a victim?
>   Well . . . GREAT NEWS! You've found him! Presenting the *Sun*'s very own happy, soothing voice of reason . . . HIGGY THE HUMAN SPONGE.
>   He LOVES loudmouths. Can't LIVE without a tongue-lashing. A week without being called a wally – or worse – is a week wasted in his book. So pick up the phone and fume, folks. His Wimpishness is waiting for your calls with a silly-billy grin on his face and honeyed words of love in his heart . . . the fool!

Printed in large type was the number of Higgins's direct line on the newsdesk. Higgins, who still had to do his normal work, was bombarded with calls from inside the paper as well as outside as the hacks joined in by posing as readers and ringing from their extensions. The next day the results were published under the headline 'WE HATE HIGGY!' 'Screaming hordes of *Sun* readers took advantage of Higgy the Human Sponge yesterday. . . . ' A thirteen-year-old schoolboy told him he 'must feel a right pratt sitting there' and a 'well-spoken woman from Essex' said: 'My God. You're so ugly. I've never seen anyone so ugly in my life.'

In all, the paper claimed, hapless Higgins received more than 1,000 calls but, true to form, was still smiling at the end of the day. The most popular caller with the hacks was the one who said he would like to do something to him with 'the rough end of a pineapple.' Higgins did soak it all up, as predicted, but from that time on the divide in the office was even clearer.

MacKenzie's power over the hacks had also been considerably strengthened by the ATEX computer system, which he had mastered immediately. MacKenzie christened the system the 'scamulator' and the terminals 'scamulator machines'. He would rush up to hacks slaving at their terminals, and slyly instruct them to 'give it a bit of that, eh?' while he mimed an exaggerated action of playing the piano with an equally exaggerated nod and a wink. 'Get the old scamulator working, eh?' he would say. If the result was a story which went too far over the top, he would order it to be put back to be 'de-scamulated'.

The various bugs had now been ironed out and the more computer-literate hacks were whizzing round the system, causing noisy disputes as reporters accused each other of hacking into each other's terminals to steal stories and ideas. The cross-over into the *News of the World*, which was linked to the same ATEX system, sparked off more acrimonious accusations from both sides.

MacKenzie's own password, which had to be typed into the machine before his terminal could be accessed, was 'Lions', Millwall football club's nickname. He changed it later to 'Spam' – after the newspaper proprietor in the TV series *Hot Metal*, of which MacKenzie was naturally a fan. He loved the feel the new technology gave the office as much as the machinery itself. With the clattery old typewriters and filthy carbon copies left behind, the hacks now sat in rows in immaculate white shirts and ties, which he approved of just as much as the Boss. As they clicked away at their keyboards, with only the occasional discreet 'beep' indicating the immense new power under their control, the whole editorial floor looked less like a newspaper than one of the new City dealing rooms which were a parallel triumph of Maggie's technological revolution.

As editor he had godlike access to all the terminals and could look in at any of the hacks whenever he felt like it. He would also root about in the N-black (N for 'News') file containing all the copy which had come into the paper from reporters, wire services and agencies and retrieve items which had been rejected by the copytasters, adding them to the list for the day's bollockings. These continued without mercy, but what truly astonished the hacks was that their editor had acquired yet more energy.

His working day had now been extended by installing a carphone in the Jaguar, which he used to bollock Petrie on his way to work. A rumour ran round that when MacKenzie first acquired his new toy he went on shouting into it as he disappeared into the Dartford Tunnel, blithely unaware that he was temporarily out of contact and continuing his diatribe unabated as he surfaced.

MacKenzie's fierce new burst of energy increased the pressure on everyone, especially the newsdesk, which had always struck the hacks as incredibly harassed anyway. The increased pressure also bore down on the subs and the backbench as time and again he came charging up screaming, 'Reverse ferret!' – his code for a sudden decision to scrap the current splash and substitute another, which often meant remaking most of the news pages as stories were shuffled about. The subs, after cravenly submitting to the whirlwind instructions, would start moaning the second he had shot off that it was all quite impossible in the time available. One of them once picked up a dead phone the second his back was turned and said into it: 'Hello. Lunatic asylum? One of your patients has escaped and is loose on the sixth floor at Wapping.'

The remark wasn't entirely a joke. MacKenzie was now so hyper-active that the 'editor had finally gone mad' brigade had gained new recruits, yet his massive enthusiasm and total commitment were enormously infectious, and nobody could complain that he didn't pitch in himself. He might drive them relentlessly, but he punished himself even harder, and they in turn were galvanised into even higher workrates than they had ever thought possible.

MacKenzie had also stamped his personality all over the office through a collection of signs which began outside the swing door with one like a trucker's bumper sticker announcing: 'YOU ARE NOW ENTERING SUN COUNTRY'. Inside, more slogans, professionally made up on laminated cards, spelt out the correct attitude to the paper's task of gathering and dispensing the news. Shortly after the move to Wapping the World's Worst had reported the appearance of a rash of Zen-like maxims such as 'WHOEVER PAINTS THE WORLD MUST PAINT THE SHADOWS AS WELL AS THE BRIGHT LIGHTS'. (An accompanying snide comment remarked that this might refer to a map the paper had just printed, which gave a coastline to Zimbabwe by omitting Mozambique.)

These had now disappeared in favour of the more direct 'NEWS IS ANYTHING THAT MAKES THE READER SAY "GEE WHIZ!"'; 'IF YOU DO IT, DO IT BIG – OTHERWISE DON'T BOTHER, OLD BOY' and 'DO IT TO THEM BEFORE THEY DO IT TO US'. A printed sign dangling over the features desk urged: 'MAKE IT FAST, MAKE IT FIRST AND MAKE IT ACCURATE'. A hack had added in neat felt-tip pen: 'IF ALL ELSE FAILS – MAKE IT UP'. Seven clocks grandly showed the time in different world capitals.

As part of the atmosphere of forced jollity a multi-coloured plastic parrot hung above the newsdesk, which Petrie found preferable to a real one as it could not repeat MacKenzie's foul language or imitate the stentorian noises he himself made with his brass megaphone, given to him by the hacks. Petrie used it to call them up for their assignments, always addressing them by their surnames presaged by 'Mr' or 'Miss'. (All women were 'Miss', whatever their marital status.)

On top of Petrie's terminal was an object called the True Story Alert – a *Spitting Image* puppet of Mrs Thatcher, usually marketed as a squeaky toy for dogs. The rubber Thatcher had found its role when a young showbiz hack who was a byword for dodgy stories rushed up to the desk gabbling details of his latest 'scoop'. When he finished by yelling breathlessly, *'and it's true!'* MacKenzie grabbed the Thatcher, pressed it to make it squeak, and bellowed: 'True story alert, folks! True story alert! We have a true story here.'

Just after New Year the *Sun* got just that, with another brilliant and hurtful scoop at the expense of the Royals, now even more clearly identified as Maggie opponents after reports in the *Sunday Times* that the Queen was upset about the direction in which Mrs Thatcher was taking the country. The splash 'I QUIT' by John Kay on 7 January broke the news that a weeping Prince Edward had decided to leave the Royal Marines only four months after joining, causing huge embarrassment to Prince Philip as the regiment's honorary Captain General. The paper was especially delighted as it was convinced that the Palace had been planning to explain away the resignation as due to a leg injury. Just to rub it in, the *Sun* then exclusively revealed that Edward was going to have to use the money given him by the tax-payers to buy himself out (which he subsequently did at a cost of £10,000).

This further humiliation of the helpless and fuddy-duddy old Royals in casting Prince Edward as a hopeless wimp was another indication of the way the new yobbish affluence which the *Sun* represented was spreading across the country. A spate of fights in small market towns at the New Year – to be repeated on a wider scale the next year in what Douglas Hurd, the Home Secretary, termed 'the shires' – was shifting the violence agenda. The well-heeled yobs of the new phenomenon of 'lager louts' who were making easy pickings in the burgeoning black economy, joined the 'scum' of the emerging deprived 'underclass' on the news agenda.

The new money was also leading to a changed attitude towards Europe. Brits were no longer seeing themselves as poor, deprived relatives of their Continental neighbours. This new bullish attitude formed the basis for a relaunching of the old game of the heroic British animal lover saving suffering dumb creatures from cruel foreign torturers, in this case the greasy Spaniards. The row blew up about a tradition dating back to the Inquisition, when heretics had been taken to the torture rack on donkeyback. The village of Villanueva de la Vera, 150 miles west of Madrid, had ever since marked Shrove Tuesday by having the fattest man in the village ride a donkey through the narrow streets until it dropped from exhaustion. Current legend held that the rest of the villagers then jumped on it and crushed it to death, a fact denied in a statement by the Spanish Ambassador, printed in the *Sun* under the heading 'IT'S A LOAD OF OLD COJONES'. The headline had an asterisk to signal a footnote which explained: 'That's Spanish for b*****ks.'

After the alarm about the ceremony was sounded by the Devon Donkey Sanctuary, the *Sun* and the *Star*, on behalf of outraged British animal lovers, rushed mob-handed to save Blackie, the donkey chosen for that year's ceremony. The *Sun* got in first by handing across £250 in pesetas to the donkey dealer and then parking the beast in a field belonging to a local farmer. It proved an unwise move. The *Star* promptly suborned the farmer, bought Blackie from him, and spirited him away from the *Sun* hacks by hiding him in a hotel room, disregarding the noisy protests of the hotelier. The *Star* reporter called his editor, Lloyd Turner, to report. Everything was fine except for the terrible smell. 'Don't worry,' Turner replied, 'the donkey will get used to it.'

Turner celebrated the paper's victory by splashing 'GOTCHA!', with a picture and a receipt proving ownership. The *Sun*, while also claiming to have bought Blackie, desperately offered the *Star* hacks £6,000 behind the scenes to get him back. The money was loftily rejected.

A noisy and long-running dispute between the two papers culminated in the *Star* winning hands down by bringing Blackie back to England, although there was a nasty punch-up with a *Sun* hack at Dover.

MacKenzie's strategy of slamming the *Star* for cruelty by taking Blackie away from his donkey friends in sunny Spain was rubbished by leading experts including Johnny Morris and David Bellamy. The final disaster was when the *Sun*'s last-ditch plan to have a female donkey waiting for him at Dover backfired badly. Blackie was driven straight past the *Sun* welcoming party of a donkey bimbo, lovely raven-haired Coco (5). The *Star* then rounded off the whole triumphant exercise by revealing that Coco was male. For once, the hacks joked, MacKenzie had been made to look a complete ass. To consolidate its triumph the *Star* delivered Blackie to a donkey sanctuary in Devon where its name was changed by the animal equivalent of deed poll to 'Blackie of the *Daily Star*'.

But the day after Blackie arrived on 5 March the nonsense was stopped in its tracks by the horror of the ferry disaster at Zeebrugge, when the *Herald of Free Enterprise* shipped water through its open bow doors and turned on its side, killing 193 people. It was the first of a series of disasters destined to mark the end of the 1980s.

The story was a huge one for all the papers, but the *Sun* was especially involved as many of the ferry passengers were readers, travelling on £1 day-return tickets bought through a promotions department special offer. MacKenzie's interest in disasters was always directly related to the involvement of British people in general and *Sun* readers in particular. Foreign calamities were only deemed worthy of mention if the death toll was high enough. During the huge floods in Italy the previous year he had been overheard telling the subs: 'We'll run the Italian story if the casualty rate goes over 300. If not we do a piece on the doctor's story that there are 15,000 people in the UK with AIDS. Better still let's do a splash on a drowned Eyetie homosexual!'

Zeebrugge caused great shock in the office, not just because of the tragedy of the deaths, but because of the hole it punched in the whole Thatcherite contention that private enterprise provided better and safer services. But it also gave the *Sun* an opportunity to fight back by demonstrating how effectively its readers could fall in with Maggie's call to the newly affluent to give spontaneously to charity.

Garry Bushell, who had managed to survive MacKenzie's initial displeasure, was seconded from Bizarre to work full-time on the project. Bushell had by now left his Oi! background far behind and had grown a Satanic-looking black beard symbolically marking the end of his skinhead-style days. He suggested raising money by re-recording the Beatles' 'Let It Be' to make a Ferry Aid record copying the successful formula started with Band Aid by Bob Geldof. Paul 'Macca' McCartney waived copyright, and the Bizarre desk dug into its contacts book to recruit a mass of musicians and celebs including old standby Boy George.

Boy George's close relationship with the paper, started by John Blake, had gone through various ups and downs. After helping to hype Boy George to his chart successes Blake had been poached by Maxwell to inject his youth-appeal formula into the *Mirror*. His successor Nick Ferrari, the young high flying son of Dan Ferrari of Ferrari's news agency, had worked under Wendy Henry to change the style of pop coverage in line with her aggressive scandal-mongering approach to the TV soaps.

Ditching Blake's cheerful lightweight pap about George's hairstyles, cuddly toys and faltering diets, Ferrari had moved in to print the inside track of the much more gripping story of George's addiction to heroin. In a classic 'set 'em up and knock 'em down', the *Sun* had cashed in on his fall with 'JUNKIE GEORGE HAS 8 WEEKS TO LIVE', the splash breaking the drugs story on 3 July 1986. The information was supplied by his brother. Other relatives had then been roped in for exclusive after heart-rending exclusive. At the time of Zeebrugge this particular episode in the story had just ended with the highly publicised jailing of the pushers who had been selling him his drugs. He himself was just starting treatment for his addiction, and had a number-one sympathy hit in the charts with 'Everything I Own' which was to be his last burst of glory before he was ditched by the *Sun* and sank back into obscurity.

For Ferry Aid Boy George not only performed free but did sterling work lining up other top acts like Bananarama and Mark Knopfler of Dire Straits. The country's top record producers, Stock, Aitken and Waterman, worked for nothing in donated studios to produce the record with over 100 celebs joining in the last tearful chorus. Enthusiastically plugged in the paper, it went straight to number one, giving the *Sun* huge publicity and grossing £700,000 for the Ferry Aid Trust, which had MacKenzie as one of its trustees.

Comedian Jim Davidson, another old *Sun* favourite and personal sarff London mate of MacKenzie's, hosted a sell-out show for older folks at the London Palladium starring the faithful rude old chestnuts of Bernard Manning and Frankie Howerd. The event was written up in the paper under the headline 'FERRY GOOD SHOW!' and the video direct-marketed at £9.99 to help swell the funds. (The £1 Zeebrugge ticket offer, known as 'drowned for a pound' in the office, was repeated the following year amid great trepidation. To the amazement of many of the hacks it sold even better. They could only presume readers were working on the sensible basis that after the accident the ferries had been made safe.)

Ferry Aid struck a chord not just with the folks, but with the non-editorial staff at the Wapping complex. Bouverie Street money collections had usually been institutionalised union-led affairs to demonstrate solidarity with other workers. Large sums had been donated by Inkies and many hacks during the miners' strike. But in the new world of Wapping these had been replaced by a gamut of fun runs, sponsored diets and stunts of all kinds to raise money for a variety of local hospitals and charity appeals. Petrie, at the age of fifty-one, had even run the London Marathon, albeit slowly. Other keen stalwarts, including reporter John Kay, joined in the regular lunchtime ping-pong games which MacKenzie claimed to approve of because it made them healthy.

In an attempt to stem the grumbling about the new environment Murdoch had personally met with the journalists' chapel and entreated it to join in the new 'spirit of Wapping'. The management's moves to build this through a sense of community were now bearing corporate American-style fruit. MacKenzie was playing his part by attending the Weight Watchers' Club meetings held monthly in the conference room on Level 2. As an obsessive dieter he could also often be heard trumpeting in the canteen as he loudly lauded the latest diet dreamed up by Sally Anne Voak, the paper's slimming editor. He insisted that it should always be available on the menu and would shout at hacks lining up to collect their nosh: 'If it's good enough for the readers, it's good enough for you lot.' The canteen boosted the corporate-fun factor by various 'theme weeks' like Hawaiian week, when the counter staff were equipped with paper garlands, or special US spreads on American Independence Day.

As part of its employee-care programme News International had also created a Human Resources Committee, where all members of staff could meet senior managers to air grievances or make suggestions. For those in more dire need the company had also hired a Personal Counsellor, John Murray, as part of the American practice of 'employee-assistance programmes', calculated by US management experts to save up to £15 for each £1 spent per employee by reducing days lost through absenteeism, stress factors and other illness. Murray, an avuncular figure with a passing resemblance to John Wayne, spent his day prowling the building searching for signs of stress and penned earnest screeds of psychobabble in the house journal on the traumas of being 'being rubbed raw by the rat race'. The hacks, who considered him a complete wally but nevertheless lived in constant dread of his caring hand on their shoulder, likened his style to Patience Strong.

Murray, introducing himself as 'a special friend' and confiding that his greatest sin when young had been pride, invited staff to come and see him voluntarily if they felt 'tense'. Otherwise, he warned more ominously, they could be referred direct by the management. Hacks attempting to evade this fate by throwing themselves on the mercy of a higher, non-corporate authority could join the Christian Fellowship group, headed by a member of The Times's obituaries department.

A bewildering array of sporting activities had sprung up, ranging from a clay-pigeon shooting club to a golf team and a women's netball team called the Wappettes. Meanwhile the staff of the press hall noisily engaged the technicians in regular war-games played with paint guns in a wood near Tunbridge Wells. But the hacks grumbled that there was no sign of the swimming pool they had been personally promised by Murdoch, which was supposed to be part of a multi-gym in a new recreational area. Electric golf buggies, mooted as transport round the vast site, had also never appeared, and a tongue-in-cheek suggestion that the company equip itself with a fleet of Sinclair C5s had fortunately come to nothing.

Ignoring these minor grumbles, the house journal waxed enthusiastic in its vision of the future when further expansion under Phase 3 would add another 600,000 square feet of office space, a fifteen-storey tower, and the shopping plaza which would be a modern version of the company store. To round off the shining vision the journal carried ads for 'Quay 430', a speculative development next door being promoted in bullshit packs as 'Wapping's Covent Garden'. Prices started at £100,000 for a one-bedroomed flat, rising to £450,000 for a converted warehouse. Reading all this, unimpressed hacks just muttered that they felt as if they were being incarcerated in The Village – like Patrick McGoohan in the cult TV series of *The Prisoner*, which was then enjoying a revival.

Having helped compensate for the shock of Zeebrugge by its money-raising activities the *Sun* plunged back into the Continental fray to rerun the Second World War by fighting the Germans again on the beaches. Uproar about the antics of English holiday louts had been taken up in a woodenly jokey manner by the *Sun*'s Teutonic equivalent, the mass circulation *Der Bild*, owned by the right-wing Axel-Springer group. On 11 April the *Sun* fired back at our old foe with the splash 'THE SUN INVADES GERMANY', next to a picture of Churchill giving the V for Victory sign. 'Churchill – He would have been so proud of our brave invasion platoon,' the caption said cheekily.

Under the sub-head 'Wapping task force to teach the Krauts holiday manners', John Kay wrote in his polished *Sun*-ese:

IT'S WAR folks! Your patriotic *Sun* was last night assembling a Wapping task force to invade Germany – and give those lout Krauts a lesson to remember.

> We sprang into action after a blitzkrieg attack on YOU by the vicious, heartless barons of Germany's gutter press.
>
> Their biggest-selling newspaper, *Bild*, branded fun-loving British tourists in Majorca drunken louts; they said our romantic youngsters were OVER-SEXED, and they claimed our wonderful women were FLABBY.
>
> But the last straw was their allegation that British holidaymakers pinch all the sun-beds first thing in the morning.
>
> *How could this great nation stand idle after an attack like that?*
>
> So the *Sun* – which first highlighted the sinister, selfish antics of Germans on holiday in Tenerife – is mobilising a platoon of Page Three girls and *Sun* journalists for Operation Klobber the Krauts. . . . Many are Lamb War veterans who fought in the glorious 1985 campaign when we stormed the beaches of Calais.

The *Sun* 'strategy' was revealed by a map of Germany with broad black arrows resembling the credits for the *Dad's Army* TV show and labelled 'The *Sun*' homing in on various centres, which were annotated in brackets – Hamburg, Lüneburg (it speaks for itself), Hanover (or should it be hangover?) and Münster (or should it be Monster?). The map was labelled: 'Battle plan . . . but readers, please eat this map after inspection, it must not fall into enemy hands.'

But the restaging of the Second World War fell flat after the German 'scumbag' press, as the hacks called it, insisted on being friendly and refused to join in the nonsense. MacKenzie was furious that they would not join in a good dust-up like 'Hop Off You Frogs', thereby giving the story legs, but Maggie's decision to call a general election caused the troops to be withdrawn as the *Sun* wheeled its guns round for the declared objective of boosting its heroine to her third consecutive poll win.

The ground for Labour's defeat had already been laid by the loony left campaign, as the *Sun* had triumphantly emphasised by exclusively splashing a leaked memo to Kinnock from his press secretary, Patricia Hewitt, which stressed how concentration on matters like the gay issue was damaging the party's image. Just before the election a report by the Media Research Group of

Goldsmith's College in South London had analysed ten loony stories and found the *Sun* heading the list by being implicated in nine, with the *Mail* second with seven. The report unravelled the complex and tedious reality behind the stories, some of which had a tiny grain of truth on which vast journalistic edifices were built. Others were simple inventions which once started off had then gone the rounds of both national and local papers, gathering more spin each time they were hoicked out of the clippings file.

The list was a melancholy one for Labour. Hackney had banned the word 'manhole' as sexist and then ordered sewer workers to call them 'access chambers' instead, and supported a nursery school where children were ordered to stop singing 'Baa Baa Black Sheep' because it was racist. A similar story had surfaced in neighbouring Islington when even *Knitting International* magazine joined the fall-out with a spoof article on a 'Campaign Regarding Equal Tonality in Natural Sheep'.

Camden had ordered staff not to call each other 'sunshine' as it was racist: 'YOU'VE BLACKED ME OL' SUNSHINE'. Lambeth had a policy of allowing gay men to go to the top of the housing waiting list; Newham had employed a lifeguard at a swimming pool who had AIDS 'with horrific sores over his body and blood oozing from his hands'; Brent had banned black bin liners as 'racially offensive', substituting green ones, and was also providing free holidays in Cuba for black children only; and Bernie Grant's Haringey was planning to spend £500,000 on providing twenty-four 'super-loos' for travellers and had instructed council workers to demonstrate solidarity by drinking only Nicaraguan coffee – a story headed in the *Sun* 'BARMY BERNIE IS GOING COFFEE-POTTY – STAFF MUST DRINK MARXIST BREW'.

Pegged on the latest scam story that Bernie Grant was personally planning Creole language lessons in the borough's schools 'The *Sun* Says' drummed the national connection into the readers' heads: 'Don't imagine that Bernie's antics will afflict only one suffering part of London. . . . Remember he is a Parliamentary candidate for Labour at the next Election. . . . Labour is now the Official Barmy Party!'

Once the election campaign was formally under way the *Sun* caused one of the few moments of excitement in an otherwise dull campaign with the story of how Denis Healey's wife Edna had gone to a private clinic for a hip operation. The story was an old one, but was dusted off to be splashed two weeks after Labour had attacked Mrs Thatcher, who was suitably unrepentant, for going private for an operation on her little finger. The morning the *Sun* story broke Healey was booked on to TV-am to talk about the Venice summit. Instead he found himself confronted by Anne Diamond waving a copy of the paper about and he was so furious he walked out and was only prevented from getting into a fight by the physical intervention of his assistant.

Anne Diamond was to personally experience the sharp edge of the *Sun* less than a fortnight later when the paper dug up more old 'news' to splash 'TV'S ANNE DIAMOND KILLED MY FATHER' over a seven-year-old story of a road accident from which she had been exonerated of all blame. The story was a prime example of *Sun* muck-raking. There was no reason to run it and the paper even had the gall to finish the story with quotes from her lover, Mike Hollingsworth, an executive with TV South. 'Anne was extremely distressed about this and it took her a long time to get over it. It is too strong to say she killed him. She was involved in an unavoidable accident and has never tried to hide it.'

In general the *Sun* treated the election result as a foregone conclusion, with Spark banging out the now well-worn Maggie adulation. The poofter angle was scamulated with headlines like 'LABOUR PICKS RENT BOY AS SCHOOL BOSS' and 'LABOUR USES GAY JIMI TO WIN OVER YOUNG VOTERS' – a story about Red Wedge, the trendy collection of rock groups campaigning for Labour, revealing the well-known fact that the Communards' lead singer, Jimi Sommerville, was gay.

At one point MP Harvey Proctor threw a spanner into the *Sun*'s election works by confusingly combining the three elements of supporting the South African regime; holding the Tory candidacy for the safe seat of Billericay, Essex; and being a serious 'shirt-lifter' to boot. But the paper soon recovered and enthusiastically joined the other tabloids in running him to earth before welcoming his right-wing successor, Teresa Gorman, soon to achieve minor notoriety by praising Wimbledon ticket touts as a successful example of the enterprise culture.

Taking things one step further as ever, the *Sun* had already applied the jokey formula of 'THE SUN INVADES GERMANY' to send up the loony left issue with a spoof board game called Loonopoly, featuring 'Stupidity Chests' and with rules which ended: 'Just like real-life in the loony boroughs that have banned competitive sports, every player is declared a winner!' The entry under Islington had read: 'Ban heterosexuals from all libraries and bus stops. Advance to Hackney, stopping only to black up at Brent.' 'Use the Meals on Wheels money to buy Armalite rifles and bullets for the IRA. You win a free throw.' 'Make a stand for animal rights – elect a pig to the council. Move back two spaces because nobody notices the difference!'

Huge concentration was applied to the scamulisation of what was basically the same boring old election story. One brainwave was to employ a medium to 'interview' well-known figures from the past to discern their voting preferences. The psychic 'poll' revealed Henry VIII and Boadicea to be Tory, while Labour's only supporter was Stalin. Genghis Khan was a 'don't know', and Keir Hardie plumped for the SDP. Reading the piece, the *Sun's* former political editor, Walter Terry, thought wryly how outclassed he was these days. He might have good contacts but, unlike the *Sun's*, his were still this side of the grave.

Three days before polling the paper pulled out more fictional fun to parody the Kinnocks' successful Presidential-style campaign masterminded by Labour's new media guru, Peter Mandelson. The splash showed a waving Neil Kinnock montaged on to the pavement outside No. 10 under the headline 'LABOUR WINS! A WOT announced a 'Special Nightmare Issue' and a sub-heading read 'wake up folks, this is just a bad dream.' The exercise was a careful and effective piece of 'journalistic' propaganda to counter the effects of a re-themed Kinnock, who rattled Thatcher so badly she took control of the campaign herself. In the last week she went for Labour's jugular with a brutally effective party political broadcast which concentrated on reviving memories of the 1978 Winter of Discontent – the phrase originally coined, with apologies to Shakespeare, by Lamb.

Despite, or possibly because of, confusion over the No. 10 picture, a MORI poll showed 12 per cent of *Sun* readers still grimly hanging on to their belief that the paper supported Labour. Considering its sternly uncompromising views, an even more surprising 7 per cent thought it backed the Alliance. But the all-powerful C2s delivered for the Tories again, with 34 per cent voting equally for both the major parties, according to Gallup. And although Mrs Thatcher got a slightly lower share of the overall vote than in 1983 with 43.3 per cent, Labour only improved marginally to 31.5 per cent – still well down on its 36.9 per cent in 1979.

With the election out of the way and Maggie safely in power for another five years the *Sun* turned to the stock-market mania sweeping the country. The government's drive for 'popular capitalism' had roped in the C2s, primarily through the privatisation of state industries, heavily pitched at small investors and set at prices guaranteeing an immediate profit. Fuelled by computerised dealing and London taking its place as a centre of the new world market, share prices had boomed, with a mushroom growth in trendy second-line stocks like Sock Shop, Tie Rack, Next, Filofax and modern heroic entrepreneurs like John Gunn of British and Commonwealth and Alan Sugar of Amstrad.

The excitement generated by the over-heating market had penetrated Wapping, where some hacks, including John Kay, had piled in and were doing well. In May MacKenzie had enthusiastically endorsed the idea of a *Sun* Share Club for staff with members putting in £40 a month. More importantly the paper was preparing to launch a '*Sun* Money' City page. MacKenzie, with his dislike of specialists, had been opposed to the idea. But Murdoch overruled him when market research alerted the Empire to the fact that one in five *Sun* readers had bought shares for the first time in the past year.

The *Mirror* had started a four-page weekly money special and even the *Star* was haphazardly carrying about thirty popular share prices every day. The *Sun*'s Money Page was launched in a hurry in mid-July, just as the stockmarket peaked. A trailer explained: 'When the *Sun* was launched in 1969, only the toffs and the super-rich had stocks and shares. . . .'

MacKenzie had just been laughed at by his first two choices to run the page. But he had then found a willing taker in Damien McCrystal, who was working on the City Page at the London *Evening Standard*. McCrystal, who had been born in Belfast, but lived a lot of his life in America, was the son of Cal McCrystal, a journalist on the *Sunday Times*, and was enormously enthusiastic. But the appointment was not to prove a success. MacKenzie rowed repeatedly with the unflappable McCrystal, making it obvious he regarded him as a clever dick.

McCrystal identified MacKenzie as being no different from the many small punters now dabbling in the market and excitedly queuing to 'stag' new issues. McCrystal sized up his boss's chances as an investor: his intelligence and wide-ranging knowledge were obvious advantages, and his addiction to risk-taking scams also made him potentially a successful punter. But McCrystal realised he was much too impatient for long-term strategic planning, and was just looking for quick and easy profits. MacKenzie was a penny-share man, he concluded. He was more surprised later when MacKenzie asked him how he would go about raising £500 million. When MacCrystal asked 'What for?' MacKenzie replied: 'A management buy-out, for instance.' The matter went no further but McCrystal himself had worked out that a City valuation of the *Sun*'s worth would put it at something like that figure.

McCrystal first ran into trouble when he picked up the thread of ethical investment and disingenuously told MacKenzie he wanted to run stories to help the Third World and the cause of disinvestment in South Africa. MacKenzie, leaning over his desk and speaking slowly to emphasise each word, replied succinctly: 'Get this through your fucking head. Nobody gives a fuck about the Third World.'

But McCrystal was determined that the *Sun*'s Money Page, which had been the target of a fresh round of Unpopular sneers, should be taken seriously in the City. His contacts were telling him that the chairman of the Stock Exchange, Sir Nicholas Goodison, was under pressure because of various alleged mistakes he had made since the Big Bang. A 'GOODISON MUST GO' campaign would enable the *Sun* to take the credit if he resigned, as seemed likely at the time. But first McCrystal needed MacKenzie's consent.

'I want to run a campaign to get rid of Goodison,' he said. 'Why?' MacKenzie grunted. McCrystal had decided in advance that a full explanation would just bore MacKenzie, who would then dismiss the idea in irritation. Instead he summarised the argument in language the editor could understand: 'Because he's a c***,' he said, and fell silent. 'All right,' MacKenzie replied without a blink. 'If he's a c***, let's fucking have him.'

The campaign was launched and Page Three girls invaded the City pressing 'GOODISON MUST GO' badges on cellphone-waving Yuppies. But MacKenzie was markedly unenthusiastic and the City ignored the *Sun* activity entirely. The campaign soon petered out and Goodison stayed.

The City really hit the front page with the market crash on 'Black Monday' of 19 October. As the Dow Jones index plunged to wipe a quarter off the value of US stocks the immediate question was whether President Reagan would take action with a statement to restore confidence in US economic policy. Shortly after the US market had opened at 2.30 p.m. GMT a flustered MacKenzie rushed over to McCrystal's desk.

'What's Reagan done, eh?' he demanded. 'Has he sorted it out yet, then, eh, eh?' McCrystal read the latest news off the wire. Reagan, true to the spirit of market forces, had issued a statement to the effect that his job was to let the market collapse if it wanted to. MacKenzie, amazed, grabbed the print-out and stared at it in stunned disbelief. 'What a c***! What a stupid fucking c***!' he shouted furiously, screwing up the piece of paper and throwing it away in disgust.

He soon bounced back to McCrystal's desk, searching for a scam front page inspired by the Wall Street crash of 1929. 'You know these people. How bad is it for them, eh?' he asked. 'Will any of them throw themselves out of the fucking window like they did last time, eh?' Then doing a version of his piano-playing 'bit of that' routine and nodding towards the scamulator, he continued, 'Could happen, eh? Must be desperate some of them, eh? Lose the Porsche, eh, eh?'

McCrystal was of the opinion that they would not, but MacKenzie simply ignored him. The next day's front page had a box next to the paper's colour seal reading: 'IT'S THROW YOUR-SELVES OUT OF THE WINDOW TIME FOLKS!', above a massive headline 'CRASH!; and a secondary headline 'WALLOP!' The latter presaged unusual *Sun* fare – a story about a bomb exploding in Iran which normally would have been lucky to make the graveyard page 2. Instead it had been pulled off the wires and jammed on the front page as a vehicle to carry the desired headline.

The spirit of wild excess characterising the share market soon swept into the tabloid newspaper world, where it coincidentally caused another crash which, to MacKenzie's glee, stuffed his deadly rival, the *Star*. The cause was a fresh tabloid plunge downmarket started by *Sunday Sport*, launched by soft-porn king David Sullivan, which used the new technology to launch with a journalistic staff of nine.

Sunday Sport had become a cult hit with the middle classes for off-the-wall headlines like 'WORLD WAR TWO BOMBER FOUND ON MOON' and outrageous topless photos of characters like Tina Small (84″) and Chesty Morgan (74″), who had also starred in a film called *Chesty Morgan's Deadly Weapons*, in which she suffocated her enemies by enfolding them in her gigantic bosom.

Ownership of the *Star* had meanwhile passed to United Newspapers, which had bought the whole Express group. United's chairman, David Stevens, had since been elevated to a life peerage with the same alacrity as Lord Matthews before him. But the *Star* was still selling only 1.2 million copies a day and

Stevens was now alarmed that his rival Lord Rothermere, who owned the *Daily Mail*, might team up with *Sunday Sport* to produce a new downmarket daily which could kill the *Star* off.

Stevens got there first. Trusting in H. L. Mencken's old adage that nobody ever went broke under-estimating the taste of the general public, he negotiated a deal with Sullivan to combine the *Star* and the *Sport*. The *Star* was to be revamped to give what Andrew Cameron, managing director of Express Newspapers, described as 'more zip, pzazz and fun'. *Sunday Sport* would run more news with 'emphasis that this was really a family newspaper'.

Mike Gabbert, *Sunday Sport*'s editorial director, was appointed as new editor of the *Star*, replacing Lloyd Turner and negotiating himself a salary of £120,000 a year. He proclaimed that the new *Star* would not have 'wall-to-wall tits' like *Sunday Sport*, which averaged fourteen sets of nipples an issue. But his first steamy edition then led with story headlines like 'GIRL'S SECRET OATS!'; 'SOD THIS FOR A GAME OF SOLDIERS' and 'HOW DES HE KEEP IT UP' – a short article sharing the 'sexy secrets' of Des O'Connor. The Starbird wore a T-shirt saying 'I GET IT EVERY DAY'.

The *Sport* had been a front runner with 'bonking', the new word for making love which was obsessing the tabloids, and the *Star*'s splash was bonk flavour of the week – a woman called Debbie Cake, also known as 'Lassie' due to noises she made at 'kinky sessions' with soldiers. The headline 'GO LIKE HOT CAKES SAYS BAKER'S EX-WIFE' was run below a starburst of 'HOWLS OF LUST DRIVE NEIGHBOURS BONKERS'. The *Sun* had the story as well, but Gabbert's pebble glasses misted up with pride as he waved around his coffee mug, featuring a pair of tits in 3D, and congratulated his team on getting the first picture of Mrs Cake topless.

But even the *Star* hacks were soon in open revolt and within a week the NUJ chapel passed a resolution stating that it was 'dismayed and disgusted' by the new editorial policies. A senior journalist, announcing that one hack had already left to join the *Sun*, commented: 'It must be the first time anyone has gone there to move upmarket.' Within a month another dozen had walked out in protest against what they called 'sewer journalism', including the chief leader writer, the features editor, the agony aunt and the women's editor. Gabbert furiously denied allegations that he had ordered the agony column to carry letters about a husband 'who tears his wife's knickers off five times before lunch', and hurried instructions came down from above to tone it down.

But it was too late. Within a month Tesco pulled out of its £400,000 a year advertising contract after the paper ran its bad-taste answer to Samantha Fox – a topless picture of a fifteen-year-old schoolgirl with a 40" bust who was featured in a gloating article about 'CLASSROOM CRACKERS'. The supermarket chain, whose 70,000 workforce was half female, said the decision was due to 'disquiet at the [paper's] attitude towards and treatment of women'. Within a fortnight Tesco's example had been followed by Co-operative Retail Services, the Co-operative Wholesale Society and Safeways, losing the paper a total of £1 million in annual advertising revenue. The withdrawals were crippling for the paper, which like the *Sun* depended to a large extent on advertisers of FMCGs – Fast Moving Consumer Goods. Just as alarmingly, sales of the paper itself were plunging.

Stevens got the point. The deal with Sullivan was scrapped and Gabbert was fired. In a desperate rescue operation United allocated £5 million for an advertising campaign and the paper was crammed with prizes, including a trip to the biggest bingo hall in the world in the Florida Everglades. (When the new editor, Brian Hitchen, was interviewed three months later he gave the headline 'HANG 'EM' after the Enniskillen Remembrance Day bombing as an example of how the paper was getting back on the rails with its readers.)

MacKenzie followed the *Star/Sport* débâcle with huge interest and the *Sun* exploited every anti-*Star* opportunity. News International announced it would no longer accept Sullivan's 'adult' girly ads. (MacKenzie objected to the sexy phone services both on principle and because he thought they were a rip-off.) He also thought the *Star* deserved all it had got. The demolition of

227

United's simplistic thinking that you could put an irresponsible idiot like Gabbert at the helm and then just chuck tits and filth about only confirmed what he already knew. Pop papers did not just happen. They were a deadly serious business.

The *Star* disaster put the Currant Bun in a massively commanding position for its triumphant coming of age – the eighteenth anniversary of the first issue published on 17 November 1969. The paper celebrated with a raucous orgy of self-congratulation. 'Every day is a birthday and you get the presents!' the front page yelled at the readers for the whole week. The promotions department urged the folks to join in the fun by attending '*Sun* Readers' Parties' at participating pubs across the country, where coupons printed in the paper could be exchanged for free lager.

Those more in the front line – hacks, printers, advertisers and a medley of business associates – were treated to a free booze-up on a more grand scale at the former Hammersmith Palais de Dance, now refurbished as a garish disco and renamed 'Le Palais'. Topping the bill to transport the revellers back to the paper's 1960s origins were Gerry and the Pacemakers.

MacKenzie basked in the glory of the effusive back-slapping. He was now supremely self-confident. By his standards he was correct in believing the *Sun* to be the greatest paper in the world. Sales proved it. By now he had cranked the paper up into an outrage machine which was the journalistic equivalent of the Sex Pistols, metaphorically gobbing over anyone, or any institution, it chose.

Only a few days before the birthday party his latest victim had been the Church of England Synod, anguishedly wringing its hands over the controversial issue of homosexuality and the clergy. Such was the fear of the tabloids among the clerics that the Synod had even considered closing the debate to the press and the predictions of disaster had been borne out by MacKenzie brutally reducing the outcome of the debate to the splash 'PULPIT POOFS CAN STAY'.

And by now the press hall at Wapping, kept immaculate by

forty-three permanent cleaners, had settled down to deliver smoothly all that had been expected of it. Pagination on the *Sunday Times* was growing almost weekly as new sections were folded in and the paper's American-inspired 'more of everything' formula was confirming its position as market leader. Readers of the Unpopulars were now moaning that it took them most of their supposed day of rest to wade through the mountains of newsprint, no longer even delivered, but which they now had to go and get themselves from the shop.

The *Sun*'s issue of 18 September had set a new speed-production record for Wapping when twelve presses ran off an average of 50,265 copies an hour, delivering 603,180 copies every sixty minutes, with wastage running at only 2 per cent, compared with 5 per cent at the *Mirror*. Overall, the paper's sales for the year had stayed above four million, nearly one million ahead of the *Mirror*. The *Star* had ploughed it. And, most important for the Boss, the *Sun* was now delivering a bottom line demonstrating the immense profitability of the move to Wapping for the Empire.

The November 1986 edition of the house journal had carried a triumphant extract from the annual report of News Corporation, the holding company for the whole Empire, for the year ended 30 June. As chief executive Murdoch had summarised 1986 as 'one of the most constructive and important years in the company's history'. After-tax profits from worldwide operations had increased by 152 per cent to reach £259 million. (The Empire had many branches which contributed to this equation). In the UK, trading profits had increased by 74.2 per cent to reach £83.3 million. The *Sun*'s profits were up by 40 per cent, maintaining its position as the most profitable paper in the Empire.

In a bland summary of the Wapping dispute Murdoch explained to the shareholders: 'In the UK a major change in the methods of production of the two daily papers and two Sunday titles was forced on the Group by a significant industrial dispute. These events constituted a watershed in its history.'

Now, a year later in 1987, News Corporation's pre-tax profits had soared to £367 million, this time an increase of only 42 per cent, but UK profits had significantly out-performed the world figures with profits increasing by 74.7 per cent, to total £145.5 million. At the *Sun* they were up by 38 per cent, despite holding the price of the paper at 18p. Stockbrokers' analysts, poring over the figures, concluded that the paper was now making at least £1 million a week for the Empire.

In the smaller world of Britain the stock-market crash, the first sign of the cracks developing under the surface, had been largely shrugged off by the *Sun*'s share-owning readers and the hapless members of the Sun's Share Club, whose portfolio had been savaged on Black Monday. Both groups treated shares largely as a baffling out-and-out gamble and few had been heavily committed.

There was a cross-over of *Sun* readers among the Yuppie City dealers whom old-fashioned stockbrokers complained were just like barrow boys. But *Sun* folk were largely unaffected by the mass handing-in of Porsche keys giving the first indication that the easy-money days were numbered. More significant for them had been the peaking of general unemployment in the middle of the year. Now they were being happily sucked into the next phase of Maggie's revolution by the tumbling interest rates fuelling the property and consumer boom which was about to dominate 1988.

The *Sun* ended its year of triumph for them on a high note with a special offer by the direct-marketing department of boxer shorts for the lads – 'BE A HIT IN BONKING SHORTS' – and the reliable old standby 'GET YOUR KNICKERS IN A TIN FOR XMAS FOR ONLY £2.75' for the girls. And for all the readers MacKenzie gave a final flourish with an exclusive on next year's news with another two fingers to another hallowed totem of the establishment – the Prime Minister's New Year's Honours List. This was traditionally issued in advance from Downing Street with all the papers agreeing to a strict embargo forbidding them to print any names until 00.01 a.m. on 1 January. But on 30 December MacKenzie simply ignored this to splash exclusively that the George Medal was being awarded to two heroes of Zeebrugge – Andrew Parker, the bank official who had formed a human bridge, and Michael Skippen, the ferry's head waiter who had died rescuing diners.

This time it was Mrs Thatcher's turn to be furious. Her irascible press secretary, Bernard Ingham, describing the *Sun*'s action as 'absolutely disgraceful', shot off an angry letter to MacKenzie. But MacKenzie wasn't interested. The people getting the medals had already been told they were receiving them, the Currant Bun knew, so stuff Ingham. It was another fucking great row, which was fine. Anyhow the paper had a right to the story because of Ferry Aid.

The row completely overshadowed the official publication of the full List, which also contained the name of Sir Robert Armstrong, the Cabinet Secretary, who was now retiring. Armstrong had become famous when he put the government's side in the Australian court case over the publication of *Spycatcher*, the memoirs of the disaffected MI5 man, Peter Wright.

He was now being elevated to a life peerage after his services in being 'economical with the truth'.

Chapter 13

We've All Gone Bonkers!

Now fully of age, and flexing its muscles after its run-in with Maggie over the New Year's Honours List, the *Sun* kicked off 1988 by working over the old favourite of the Royals. Harry Arnold, tipped off by a contact that Fergie was pregnant, checked until he was 98 per cent certain the story was correct. But he was still worried by it. The tip had come while he was in Switzerland covering the Duchess of York on a skiing holiday which had made him doubt the story at first. If Fergie had an accident, losing the unknown baby might be covered up by an anodyne announcement that would explain her short stay in hospital as something like twenty-four-hour flu. His old foe, the Palace press office, would obviously not confirm the story, on the very good grounds that it almost certainly did not know it itself.

In these tricky waters, Arnold decided he had to phone his editor. 'Fergie is pregnant, but we've got a problem,' he told MacKenzie, who barked back down the line: 'What do you mean "we"? File it.' Arnold persisted, demanding to know what would happen if the story did turn out to be wrong. 'Don't worry,' MacKenzie answered, 'just fucking file.'

Arnold was connected to the copytakers and dictated his first sentence, which was all he knew: 'The Duchess of York is pregnant.' Then, ladling on copious dollops of his 'journalistic enterprise', he added reams about how the family was thrilled and a prediction that the baby would be born in July. (In the event he was eight days out.)

The next day, when he received a copy of the paper, Arnold was thrilled to see he had been paid the highest compliment known to any hack. His words had been printed precisely as he had dictated them, without a single change. It was only later, when he was back in London casually chatting with a sub, that he learned what had gone on behind his back. After his copy had dropped, MacKenzie had gone over to the backbench and instructed them: 'Don't change a word of this. Then if he's got it wrong the little fucker won't be able to wriggle out of this one!' Hearing this, Arnold's enthusiasm for the paper dropped by several points. He was not the only one who was beginning to think he had had enough. Roy Greenslade, MacKenzie's number two suffered a bad attack of the Wapping Factor and woke up one morning thinking: 'Christ! I'm forty. I don't want to do this any more.' He left to join the more upmarket end of the Empire on the newsdesk of the *Sunday Times*, where he was treated with a mixture of suspicion and awe as he adapted to the disciplines of Unpopularity.

MacKenzie was perplexed. 'What the fuck's happening?' he would ask his cronies, genuinely mystified as another feature writer resigned. 'Is it me? Do you think I'm getting like that Captain Whateveritis Queeg in the *The Caine Mutiny*?' Petrie was amazed as well. 'I couldn't do what you are doing,' he told Greenslade at his farewell party. 'I could never leave the *Sun*. There's nothing and nowhere on earth like it. It fits with my ideology.'

By this time the only thing keeping many of the older hacks in the building – or conversely out of it as much as possible – was their grim determination to get their redundancy payoff, normally calculated at one month per year of service. By now they were also fired up by a moral justification – the paper was no longer the fundamentally decent, naughty-but-fun outfit they had joined. It wasn't just the increased pressure and the constant driving harassment – they were used to that. But the rules of the game were being changed daily as more and more keen young reporters – called 'my young eagles' by Petrie – were drafted in. The reporters, although in deadly competition with each other for the best stories, had always maintained a bottom line of cameraderie, covering for each other and making sure nobody was dropped too far in it. MacKenzie used to go on about how they and the desk were such a great team, but they did not see it like that. The main reason for banding together was mutual fear and self-protection uniting them against him.

Now even that was changing as MacKenzie used the new younger reporters and set them up against each other. The new 'dog eat dog' attitude would surface when reporters went out mob-handed, or when MacKenzie put a team together to 'monster' some hapless unfortunate. In the old days, as the hacks had spread out to chase different quarry, the junior reporters had always been shepherded by a senior, who would give them a tasty line or juicy quote to file under their own name, proving to the office they had acquitted themselves well in the field.

Now it was all different. On a hectic chase round Kent one of the senior hacks found himself given a frightful bollocking when he filed his story. The desk was screaming they'd got all this bloody stuff already, and why didn't he pull his finger out and do some fucking work for a change. Shaken, he collared his 'young eagle' and discovered that he had followed him and zoomed in to re-interview people as soon as he had left. He had then rushed off to be the first to file. The senior hack, a man of impressive proportions, later pinned the young eagle to the wall and told him his story, but with that sort of carve-up going on, it was now fellow hacks, not the opposition, who were rapidly becoming the real enemy.

MacKenzie was just as pissed off with the old stagers as they were with him, and regularly raved about 'cutting out the dead wood and the red wood'. He belonged to what the hacks termed 'the scrapheap school of journalism', which had no place for the infirm, the slightly faltering and those who had served loyally but were now slowing up. Once they were finished they were finished and they could fuck off. He called them 'the old farts', repeating endlessly that they were useless and past it. He wound one up by cruelly running down his personal appearance, and by sneering:

234

'I'd be ashamed of you if I was your wife.' The hack, who was leaving anyhow, fired back: 'At least she knows who I am.'

Not for nothing, the hacks thought bitterly, did the rumour run round that Murdoch affectionately referred to MacKenzie as 'My Little Hitler'. His version of the Wehrmacht had no room for troopers failing to give the 100 per cent commitment to the enterprise which its tyrannical leader gave. Even the young eagles could not match his twenty-four-hour-a-day total dedication to the job, which continued even when he went on holiday.

MacKenzie had never been known to finish his holiday, always arriving back in the office complaining of boredom before his full fortnight was up. One year he returned from Marbella saying his holiday had been spoiled by taking a day trip to Torremolinos to find out what *Sun* readers did. He thought it was a rotten place and he couldn't understand why anybody went there. As MacKenzie's second week was already paid for there was talk in the features department of offering it to a reader in a give-away. But wiser hacks counselled that the hotel waiters would probably be waiting with baseball bats to take revenge for the bollockings he must have administered when he was there. The idea was dropped.

Anyhow the senior hacks were soon delightedly swopping versions of how the snarling stalemate in the office had been broken. The unhappiness had apparently reached Murdoch's ears, and he had raised it with MacKenzie over lunch. His editor told the Boss he wanted to get rid of about ten people, but couldn't afford it on his budget – most of them had been there so long they would cost '£60k a throw'. Murdoch, the Wapping equation now locking into place and able to afford to be generous, had simply replied: 'What's the problem? Pay 'em off.'

The clear-out was used as a device to pile on more pressure by insisting that the hacks revert to a five-day week, instead of the four days the NUJ chapel had painstakingly negotiated and which MacKenzie had promised as sacrosanct in his pre-Wapping speech. In a memo MacKenzie pointed out that annual salaries had been swollen by a series of pay awards and journalists now averaged £30,000 a year. Five days work a week was therefore reasonable. Those not prepared to accept these revised working terms could apply for redundancy.

The across-the-board offer had shattering consequences. More than forty applications were slapped on MacKenzie's desk in a mad rush – far more than the company possibly wanted or could afford. Those who had missed out in the first dash were confidentially taken to one side by sympathetic execs and warned: Don't apply. There were already too many in and they had no chance. Instead they would have to stay, branded as one of the 'traitors', as MacKenzie was already calling them. He was also realising that if they were all allowed to go it would be a major disaster, completely breaking up the 'great team' he was so proud of and which had taken years to put together.

Eventually MacKenzie personally selected twenty-two whom he allowed to take the offer. Most were the hardy veterans of the Lamb days whom he had failed to drive out in a continuous war of attrition. As well as giving them all the shitty jobs or, worse still, nothing to do at all, MacKenzie's standard weapon had been spiking their copy or withdrawing the powerful drug of the byline to which so many were addicted. According to legend, one hack had already left after not seeing his name on a story for ten years, and another pilloried unfortunate getting the same treatment had been the butt of a particularly callous MacKenzie joke. The news had dropped of a small boy who had been found buried, but still alive, after the Mexican earthquake which had killed and injured thousands. The story said the boy was communicating with his rescuers by knocking once for 'yes' and twice for 'no'.

MacKenzie was highly amused. 'We could use that system here,' he said, and started bawling at an older hack on the other side of the room. ''Ere! You still alive then, eh? Two knocks if you're still alive. Go on! Two fucking knocks.' MacKenzie banged the desk until the hack grudgingly banged his desk in reply, causing MacKenzie and his cronies to break into cruel laughter at the stunt.

(There had been a simultaneous rumour that Larry Lamb had suffered a heart attack over at the *Daily Express*. 'That's bad news,'

MacKenzie told a group of hacks. 'One of you do his obituary. I'll byline it.' The reporters were taken aback. 'Hang on, Kelvin,' said one. 'He's not dead yet. He's had heart attacks before you know, he'll probably pull through.' But MacKenzie was insistent. 'Get it done anyway. Maybe we can use it instead of the Mexican earthquake stuff. Larry's done more for us than a load of spics –you do call Mexicans "spics", don't you?')

The mass farewell party was held in the new office pub, the Sidney Smith across the road. Unlike the homely Top of the Tip, the Sidney Smith was a seedy place with unvarnished wooden floors and a video surveillance camera over the entrance to scrutinise potential customers. The hacks attended with mixed emotions. Although they were getting the big payoffs they had suffered for, those departing were mostly in their forties, or even older. Essentially they had always been company men and they now faced an uncertain future in the choppier seas of freelancing.

Most were facing up to the fact that they were by now too old to get a good job anywhere else. One of the reasons none had left before was because they considered – rightly – that the taint of having worked for the *Sun* ruled out a lot of potential employers. But MacKenzie's relentless war of attrition also had totally destroyed their self-confidence. The years of having it hammered into them day in and day out that they were fucking useless had caused their self-esteem to sink so low that many had actually come to believe it and now considered themselves unemployable. Most, rightly or wrongly, had given the best years of their lives to working for the paper. The party marked the passing of an era.

MacKenzie, who had called them traitors to their face, typically did not attend. A substitute was provided by a Teddy Ruxpin, a child's teddy bear which was the current craze. It had a tape-recorder inside and while the tape played its eyes rolled and its mouth moved. A special tape compiled by deputy editor Patsy Chapman was inserted which proved to be a masterful parody of a MacKenzie diatribe delivered in a high squeaky voice and incorporating the all-time favourite of: 'If that's a story, my prick's a bloater!' The tape went down a storm. But the departing hacks' laughter had a bitter edge. Fortified by their giant cheques and the contents of the Sidney Smith's cellars, many had been looking forward to saying what they had always wanted to say to MacKenzie's face.

They were not surprised he had not turned up – he always bottled out on occasions like this. If there was one thing he would never let anybody have, it was the last word. They all knew that he would never confront anyone outside his sealed powerhouse on the sixth floor. But they were determined not to let him spoil the occasion. A monumental thrash ensued, climaxing in a tremendous fight over a woman, before they staggered home to wake the next morning with epic hangovers as they started the slow process of realigning with the real world.

The Money Page editor, Damien McCrystal, handed in his security pass and followed them out of the metal gates shortly afterwards. After he had been summarily fired McCrystal made a point of seeking out MacKenzie (it was a standard office joke that to find him you just stood in the same place for two minutes, during which time he was certain to whizz past). 'You could have the courtesy to explain why you're sacking me,' McCrystal told him. 'Don't give me that courtesy crap,' MacKenzie fired back. 'I sacked you because you are an unintelligent c***.' Fine, said McCrystal. There was just the small point of his severance pay. He wanted a year's wages. Managing director Ken Donlan, told to sort it out, informed him that in that case they might keep him and make a *Sun* journalist of him yet, but after a brief tussle McCrystal got his way and left Wapping £40,000 richer. He had been with the paper only ten months.

The stock market had anyhow by then taken a back seat to the property boom, which the *Sun* was hyping enthusiastically for the C2s, containing a high proportion of council house buyers. The paper greeted the 1988 Budget with a piece entitled 'YUP! IT'S JUST LIKE A WIN ON THE POOLS', which quoted the opinions of 'a Yuppie estate agent' in Hampstead. The estate agency promptly complained to the Press Council that the quotes had been lifted from a piece in *The Times* and then distorted in a biased and misleading manner. The complaint was upheld.

As house prices soared and the credit boom took off the *Sun* eagerly latched on to the character who came to summarise it all – Loadsamoney, the invention of twenty-six-year-old alternative comedian Harry Enfield. Enfield was on paper a *Sun* enemy – a middle-class leftie with a cushy background and a degree in politics from York University, who now lived in loony Hackney. His inspiration for Loadsamoney came from observing Tottenham Hotspur fans at White Hart Lane, just up the road from his flat and noticing that they jeered at supporters of visiting northern clubs for being so poverty-stricken. He tried out Loadsa', as he was to become abbreviated to, on his normal test audience of Millwall fans in the vile Tunnel Club in Deptford, south London. His flash oik invention, waving his wad of banknotes, was an instant hit.

In the spring, as Loadsa' surfaced on TV to a similarly enthusiastic reception, Enfield was initially indignant at suggestions he had created a monster he could not control. Loadsa' was such a loveable yob he was rapidly coming to celebrate the very culture he had been created to ridicule – the 'you are what you earn' ethic the *Sun* had been tracking since Sam Fox had been hyped as moving in next to the Thatchers in Dulwich. 'I hope that's not the case' he told an Unpopular interviewer. 'I think he's a complete bastard.'

Loadsa' was spotted early on by MacKenzie, playing the Millwall fan. Recognising how he chimed with the aspirations of *Sun* readers, he was immediately hijacked for a *Sun* front-page Lotto and Bingo plug under the headline '£OADSAMONEY' and was pictured, lip curling and waving his wad, with a bubble carrying his catchline: 'Bish Bosh – look at all this dosh.'

Enfield promptly told his solicitors to instruct the *Sun* to print a statement which explained that Loadsa' had nothing to do with the competitions. The *Sun* rounded on him with a feature entitled 'LOADSAMOANIES', in which three 'top comics' gave the lad a talking-to. 'Stan "I hate them Germans" Boardman' told him: 'Your face on the front of the *Sun* is the best advert ever'; 'Jimmy "And There's More" Cricket' chipped in that in his early days it would have been a dream to have appeared all over the front page; and 'Max "I Wanna Tell You a Story" Bygraves' said it could do him no harm at all. A '*Sun* spokesman' advised Enfield: 'Shut your mouff and look at OUR wad. Seriously we believe you ought to buy yourself a decent sense of humour.' Enfield took the point and the solicitors were called off. The paper was plastered with "LOADSA" headlines until MacKenzie got sick of doing them.

Meanwhile the paper was also getting on with its other new staple fare of bonk journalism. Far from dying out with the *Sport/Star* débâcle, the new genre had gained a nastier edge as the popular papers, led by the Sundays, started putting the private lives of celebs and any prominent people in public life on the news agenda. The equation was a brilliant one for them. In general the papers had previously had to pay high prices for this kind of material through purchasing the memoirs of the famous, who of course only revealed what they wanted to reveal.

When the subject had come up of who was fucking who – so beloved by Wendy Henry – MacKenzie had always enquired, using his Lamb impersonation routine: 'And tell me, Miss Henry, who is the fooker and who is the fookee in this particular case?' When it was a homosexual relationship he amended the question to: 'Who is the stooper and who is the stabber?'

Now, with the equation turned round so that it was the fuckee, rather than the fucker, who was spilling the beans it was suddenly an easy game. An endless stream of bimbos, street prostitutes, call girls, masseuses, rent-boys, spurned lovers, axe-grinders, blackmailers and even hairdressers poured into the offices of professional kiss-and-tell merchants. Their stories were priced on a rough and ready scale determined by the quantity and quality of bonks. It was a complicated equation, largely dependent on who was involved, the salaciousness of the details and the current state of the market as they went to competitive auction. The resulting stories were invariably explicit, detailed and devastating for those featured.

The kiss and tells were primarily the province of the Sundays, which traditionally specialised in this field and had the biggest cheque books. The *Sun* was only a mid-ranker. MacKenzie hated paying out anyway and did not see revelations as circulation-builders. When the paper did bid it followed his normal style of first offering the earth and then knocking the sum down to as little as possible. The approach was considered in the office to be honest enough. The informants, spurred on by their agents, were invariably promising the earth on their side and both sides were usually represented by teams of astute lawyers.

In a feature in the World's Worst in mid-1988, Alan Rusbridger had brought appalled readers up to date with a catalogue of the most recent casualties. 'We only had straight sex once or twice. He preferred having oral sex with me. He used to put a blue towel under me and he used to like to shout and scream.' That had seen to the career of John Golding, the former General Secretary of the National Communications Union, he informed them. Patrick Macnee had gone down to a story starting: 'Legendary *Avengers* star Patrick Macnee likes to be brutally beaten by fat hookers while he begs for mercy.' This story had been accompanied by a large picture of Macnee sunbathing in the nude, with his wedding tackle obscured by a magnifying glass drawn in by the art department. 'Our idea to help the short-sighted,' the caption chuckled.

Rusbridger's piece was in answer to Stewart Steven, the editor of the *Mail on Sunday*, who in a correspondence with Lord Rothermere, printed in the *Financial Times*, rolled out the familiar argument that nobody could be expected to feel sympathy for those in the public eye and the 'high and mighty'. What was 'high and mighty,' Rusbridger enquired, when you were getting down to the stag night of an army major (whipped cream and a cherry on top) or the 'news' that Hinge of Hinge and Bracket was a real-life homosexual, with 'sickening' details provided by a rent-boy?

The World's Worst and the other Unpopulars were becoming increasingly worried as the bonk casualty rate mounted. Bill Cash, Tory MP for Stafford, had gained the support of 300 MPs for a Right to Privacy Bill, saying: 'Freedom of the press was supposed to protect the press from the powerful. But now the victims most at risk are the public, not the newspapers. It is the perfect irony of the twentieth century.' But Cash had added a rider by admitting: 'The trouble is that the people who get the most steamed up are those who have been written about. When it's someone else most people don't care.'

Bonk journalism had been enabling Wendy Henry to make hay at the *News of the World*, where Murdoch had appointed her as the first woman editor of a national newspaper in August 1987. Henry's notable scalps had included Frank Bough, then fronting BBC's *Holiday '88*, and earning £200,000 a year. After a ten-month investigation the *News of the World* had splashed the story of how Bough had snorted cocaine at wild sex parties and dressed up in a red camisole, stockings and suspenders to have sex with a prostitute, before going more or less straight from the sessions to appear as presenter of the BBC's *Breakfast Time* show, as the squeaky-clean avuncular man in a sweater. Bough instantly admitted it, but said that neither the BBC nor his co-presenter Selina Scott had known what was going on. He was taken off the screen as Nesta, his wife of thirty years, announced she was standing by him.

The *Sun* enthusiastically followed through by revealing that Bough's Thames-side mansion at Maidenhead was for sale for £500,000, which Bough said was a coincidence, and giving the folks '20 FRANK FACTS ABOUT BOUGH THE COCAINE SNORTER' and 'BOUGH ON THE COUCH'. (In the *Daily Telegraph* Dr Rajendra Persaud, a psychiatrist at the Maudsley Hospital, explained that one of the problems for people like Bough was that suddenly losing the buzz of fame was like a bereavement.)

The *Sun* succeeded in having some nasty goes itself, particularly by printing a story based on letters from his homosexual lover to Mr Martin Bowley QC, who had been chairman of the Bar Committee in 1986 and a Crown Court recorder on the South-East Circuit. Bowley resigned as a judge after the letters were revealed to have been stolen by a man blackmailing his lover, a shopkeeper in

Loughborough, Leics. The blackmailer demanded that Bowley's lover sleep with him once for each letter if he wanted them back. When the lover refused the blackmailer sent them to the *Sun*. Bowley made it clear that he was not resigning as a recorder because he was homosexual, but because of the way details of his private life had been disclosed, which made it difficult to hold other people's respect. He also resigned from the Bar Council but was later re-elected.

The pillorying of Bowley was part of a ceaseless campaign the *Sun* had carried on against individual members of the judiciary. Although it was an avid supporter of law and order, the paper continuously meddled in the dispensing of justice, particularly in emotive cases when the judge had passed a sentence it disapproved of. Traditionally the law held that the process of justice ended with the courts, and the interviewing of jurors by reporters had recently been made illegal, but the *Sun* merely bypassed the court system by appointing its own jury of *Sun* readers.

A device the paper regularly ran called 'You the Jury' invited readers to phone in their verdict on controversial sentences, usually in crimes involving sexual attacks or rapes of women, where individual judges had attracted widespread condemnation from other papers for what were seen by the public as eccentric and male-orientated sentences. Invariably the readers, fired by emotions whipped up by the coverage, joined in enthusiastically and a record 195,000 had rung in two days voting that a judge was wrong to jail a woman who had poured boiling water on the genitals of a youth who had raped her five-year-old daughter. (The Appeal Court later agreed with the readers and the woman was freed.)

The *Sun* had also plunged into the more light-hearted saga of the peccadilloes of Sir Ralph Halpern, the head of Burtons, whose £1 million salary made him one of Britain's highest-paid business-men. Wendy Henry had kicked the story off in the *News of the World* with Fiona Wright, a nineteen-year-old model from Sheffield billed as a 'Selina Scott lookalike', who had revealed that Halpern, hailed as one of the great Thatcherite enterprise success stories, had met her regularly in a London flat set up for the

243

purpose and demanded sex up to five times a night. (Singer Lionel Richie – father of a love child – was to upstage him by being revealed to be a ten-times-a-night man.)

'We had sex non-stop,' Ms Wright explained. 'We did it in front of the fire first, then as we were unpacking the shopping from Marks and Spencer he lifted me up on to the kitchen unit. He got a banana and used it on me before unzipping it and scoffing it down at the crucial moment.'

MacKenzie, not prepared to reveal these fruity details of the 'naughty knight's' antics in the *Sun*, instead wittily alluded to them by adding the logo of 'FYFFE TIMES A NIGHT' on the running story. Another story told how Wright sprayed her cat with perfume used the old 'pussy' double-entendre to explain how she 'perfumed her pussy'. MacKenzie then upstaged Henry when the *Sun* exclusively revealed that in addition to Ms Wright Halpern had a live-in lover at his £2 million town house in Regent's Park. Halpern announced he and his wife Joan, who lived in the country, were getting divorced.

There was more spicy fun for the sixth floor at Wapping when the *News of the World* revealed from the floor below that Fergie's father, Major Ronald Ferguson, was frequenting a 'VIP vice den' in Wigmore Street. The *Sun* gave its readers explicit details supplied by shapely massage girl Barbara Ashley, twenty-five. Ashley summed Major Ronnie up as 'straight all the time – a very caring lover', who had been charged £50 a throw and kept saying he should not really be coming there. But what really interested the *Sun* was the Royal embarrassment angle, mercilessly exploited by concentration on a mild detail, picked out in house style in italics. *'I kissed him passionately as though we were real lovers. It was a full kiss on the mouth. It never occurred to me that he might be kissing me that afternoon, and then kissing the Queen when he had left.'* A Franklin cartoon run with the story showed a topless massage girl at work on his polo steed, with the caption: 'We don't see the major any more, but his horse is still a regular customer.'

When Ferguson was first asked for a quote by the *Sun* he

replied: 'You must be out of your minds. I have nothing to say.' But he was then so amused by the cartoon he foolishly wrote to the paper asking for the original or a copy and using the headed notepaper of the Guards Polo Club at Windsor. A copy of the cartoon was duly despatched, but only after MacKenzie had reproduced his letter as a rag-out on the front page under the splash of 'CHEEKY!' Cartoonist Stan Franklin was quoted as saying: 'It was a very nice surprise to open Major Ferguson's letter. It shows he can see the funny side of what's been happening.' (One reason the hacks suggested for the unfunniness of some of Franklin's cartoons was that MacKenzie himself frequently thought up the idea. Because he thought in words rather than pictures, they often did not work visually.)

But although the Major was judged a good sport, and suffered little but embarrassment after Prince Charles announced he was standing by him, the *Sun* soon scored a bigger hit when it claimed to have caught the captain of England's cricket team, Mike Gatting, leg over bimbo.

Gatting and MacKenzie's names had been joined together earlier in the year after a celebrated incident on the winter tour of Pakistan when Gatting nearly provoked an international incident by rounding on the Pakistani umpire and calling him a 'fucking cheating c***' – an insult made worse by the umpire being a Muslim.

The *Independent*, which Mackenzie hated nearly as much as the World's Worst, printed all three words in full in its sports report. Seeing them, MacKenzie thought it was fucking outrageous. These c***s couldn't be allowed to get away with this sort of thing. Why, his own sons were cricket fanatics and might well read it! Heaping one set of dizzying moral contradictions on another he then personally complained to the Press Council which he had derided so often in the past.

MacKenzie's official complaint said printing 'c***' instead of spelling out 'cunt', as the *Independent* had done, was sufficient for any adult to understand the story. The paper might have a small circulation, but its sports pages were read by a large number of both children and young people. The printing of such socially unacceptable language bestowed a legitimacy 'which could only have a harmful and deleterious effect upon moral standards'.

As usual MacKenzie did not go to the hearing personally to put his case, but former Page Three caption writer and now deputy editor Patsy Chapman was sent to represent him. The *Independent*'s editor, Andreas Whittam-Smith, icily told the hearing that while some national newspapers focused on entertainment, others, including his own, reported news. The *Independent* had a policy of using swear words where they were needed for the understanding of a significant story. The item in question had been the story of the week, and he emphasised that the decision had been considered very carefully. MacKenzie's complaint was rejected.

Gatting himself was entirely unrepentant and soon in the middle of a furious public row after the Test and County Cricket Board demanded that he remove his version of the event from his forthcoming autobiography. As he battled to sort this out on 9 June, two days after the end of the First Test against the West Indies, the *Sun* finished him off with the splash 'GATTING MADE LOVE TO ME'.

'Blonde bar girl Louise Shipman spoke yesterday of her sex romps with England cricket captain Mike Gatting,' the story read. 'Sexy Louise, 20, told how she and Gatting made love on an oak four-poster bed at the England Test team's luxury hotel,' adding that Shipman had found Gatting 'not kinky – just rough'. The rest of the story was based on claims made by a second, unnamed woman, who said she had seen the couple making love in the hotel grounds. 'I could see Louise having her breasts fondled and then I saw Gatting's bare bottom in the air. Another girl was in the grass alongside them with another player. They were having the time of their lives.' She claimed Shipman had told her she had had oral sex with Gatting on the four-poster.

Gatting was instantly hauled up before the Board and gave his account. He said he had merely invited Shipman, whom he had met in a local pub, to a drinks party he had held in his hotel bedroom to celebrate his thirty-first birthday. He denied making love to her. The Board nonetheless accused him of 'behaving irresponsibly during a Test match' and sacked him as captain.

The *Sun* claimed credit with the splash 'GATTING'S SACKED', illustrated by a rag-out of the previous day's front page. Inside more sensational details were served up in a profile of 'brazen barmaid Louise'. Under the headline 'I'M 48 NOT OUT – HE'S LEFT ME TWO SHORT OF A HALF CENTURY IN LOVERS' Shipman was pictured topless above the caption 'Barmaid who knocks men for six . . . blonde Louise reveals the charms that bowled over England's skipper.'

The following day the *Sun* had Gatting's wife, Elaine, stressing her 'complete faith' in her husband's denial of the original allegation, which was buried in the last paragraph of the latest twist – 'GATTING'S GIRL ATE ME ALIVE SAYS CHEF', a story in which chef Dave Massey claimed Shipman 'ate me alive' at a party. He had only rated her as four out of ten, and noted in his diary at the time: 'Went to bed with Louise tonight – no big thrill.' 'She's not all that hot in bed – she goes by volume, not quality,' he explained. 'When we got down to it, she was very attentive but no great shakes.'

But by now *Sun* readers were becoming preoccupied with a subject even more exciting than celebrity sex lives. The consumer-credit boom was really roaring and even Loadsamoney had started playing the *Sun* game. Enfield, having created a popular hero, had quickly given up his original intention of satirising the culture and was now cheerfully admitting he was a champagne socialist. The *Sun* charted his succession of disastrous car and property deals for the benefit of readers hooked into the same greed and credit machine by the government.

New peaks for both the *Sun* and the country's housing show came within a fortnight of each other. On 31 July the house-price bubble burst when new laws abolishing double tax relief on joint mortgages came into effect. Meanwhile at Wapping the house journal, under the heading 'Record Breakers', enthused that sales of the *Sun* in the week ending 13 August had reached a new high of 4,309,000.

In February the *Sun* had averaged a record 4,311,000 sales per day – up 100,000 on the 1988 figure. Many hacks still remembered the excited talk of 'no limits!' when they first moved to Wapping. Freed of the constraints of the militant Inkies and with the speed and capacity of the new presses, a sale of 5 million had been confidently forecast. In the blue-carpeted management corridor of power, which humble hacks entered only at night to steal the teabags, that talk had dried up. The 5 million had not happened, though not for lack of trying. Sages on the paper had concluded that there was a finite limit for the *Sun*'s style of journalism which had really been reached, not under MacKenzie, but under Lamb.

The next light to go out on the *Sun* and Maggie's board was Ronnie Reagan who bowed out as President in January 1989 claiming to have completed the job of destroying what he had once called the Soviet 'evil empire', now that it was embracing Western capitalism under Gorbachev.

The *Sun*'s interest in the intricacies of Kremlinology had been slight though one of the few occasions MacKenzie had been persuaded not to run a headline was on the death of the Soviet leader Yuri Andropov when he came up with 'ANDROPOV POPS OFF'. Now he told hacks he was awaiting the death of the South African anti-apartheid leader, Archbishop Desmond Tutu, to run the headline he wanted more than any other – 'TATA TUTU'.

The threat of Russian military might was now being replaced by the new threat of the financial might of the Japanese, which had been brought home to the newspaper world by a Japanese bank purchasing Bracken House, the *Financial Times*'s offices near St Paul's, for a price way over valuation. Even the *Sun*'s old office at 30 Bouverie Street had been bought by a firm of Japanese developers.

'Mrs Thatcher saw off the Argies. She must now see off the Japs,' Ronnie Spark had demanded in 'The *Sun* Says'. Now the imminent death of Emperor Hirohito, Japan's wartime leader, presented MacKenzie with his chance to put the boot in. Denouncing Hirohito as 'an evil monster' 'The *Sun* Says' blasted: 'HELL'S WAITING FOR THIS TRULY EVIL EMPEROR'.

There are two reasons for sadness as Emperor Hirohito lies on his deathbed.

THE FIRST is that he lived as long as he did.

THE SECOND is that he died unpunished for some of the foulest crimes of this violent century. . . .

At the end, did he suffer any of the pain or sorrow of his multitude of victims?

We shall never know.

But when he goes, he will surely be guaranteed a special place in Hell.

Spark's '*Sun* Says' was published while the Japanese nation was conducting a televised hour-by-hour vigil at the Emperor's deathbed, and it caused immense shock to a nation with no concept of newspapers like the British tabloids. What was described in the restrained language of diplomacy as a 'strong official protest' was delivered by the Japanese embassy in London. In Tokyo the British Ambassador was called in and told that although Japan knew about 'the British freedom of the press' the abusive language of the paper had caused 'distress and regret'. There was even talk of cancelling a planned visit to Britain by the Japanese Prime Minister. The Japanese Cabinet then decided to eject the *Sun*'s correspondent, only to retire in confusion at the baffling ways of Western tabloid newspapers when it discovered the paper actually did not have one.

The leader had been written without consulting Murdoch, whose Empire was locked deeply into the world of international finance which the Japanese were rapidly moving to control. Murdoch naturally wanted to keep on friendly terms with them. This kind of incident was immensely damaging. When MacKenzie dropped the Empire in it like this Murdoch would use one of his most wounding remarks in his regular phone calls. 'You're a political pygmy, Kelvin,' he would tell him.

But the leader Spark had composed in the sanctuary of Wapping was typical of the way that, like MacKenzie, he had been piling it on with nobody left to restrain him. Spark's chosen adjective to describe his leader-writing activity was 'strident', and since Wapping he and the other leader-writers had been delving deep into their phrase-books for more and more mindless verbal abuse. 'The *Sun* Says' had advised striking Spanish air-traffic controllers to 'take up bull-fighting, bird-strangling or donkey-torturing'; during his attempts to change Labour's image Neil Kinnock had been taunted for believing 'the public's memory is as short as a retarded dwarf'; and Sir John Harvey-Jones, the former chairman of ICI, who had criticised the way the print unions had been treated over the move to Wapping, advised: 'Make sure your mouth and your brain are connected.'

Even MacKenzie would confide to the hacks: 'Fuck me, I think old Ronnie's gone a bit over the top this time.' The hacks found Spark personally creepy. He seldom spoke to any of them and his appearance had become bizarre in the extreme. He had taken to wearing a beret and dark glasses, even in the middle of winter, and the hacks now thought he looked like a cross between Giles's granny in the *Express* cartoon and a Mafia bagman. He would come up to London from his home in Rottingdean, near Brighton, where Rudyard Kipling had lived, and sneak across the newsroom, slipping silently into his tiny office, where he and MacKenzie would determine the candidates for the day's verbals. MacKenzie, the hacks noted, would discuss subjects with him, quietly and reasonably, apparently excluding him from the normal bollocking rota.

But by now Spark was being matched by Garry Bushell, who had taken much of the credit for the success of the Ferry Aid money-raising exercise. Bushell's office cred had then shot up when he was given the award of 'The Most Evil Man in Rock' by *Melody Maker* magazine. He had rapidly risen in prominence in the office to fill a gap in MacKenzie's inner coterie, which had been depleted by the two major departures – Wendy Henry and Roy Greenslade.

Bushell, now thirty-one, had found common cause with MacKenzie in the sarff London approach to life, and the two matched each other in the foulness of their language. Bushell, now known as 'The Voice of MacKenzie' was for many the most offensive and loathsome person in the office, as he played up to the image of the macho redneck, reinforcing it by his activities as a boxing fan, which included going one round with world champion Lloyd Honeygan. But he also bolstered his claims to be one of the exciting new right-wing intellectuals by joining MENSA and claiming an IQ of 156.

Bushell's job was now to write a TV column called 'Bushell on the Box', which he composed in the wooden-headed style of a modern-day Alf Garnett. The resulting crude and hysterical right-wing slag-offs had even Ronnie Spark looking to his laurels. But Bushell was a million miles away from Spark's deadly serious intent and sense of gravitas. The more professional hacks and some of the execs were quite worried by his attitude and the copy he provided for the paper. They felt it had a *Sunday Sport* feel and promoted a silly, jokey atmosphere they knew would be extremely dangerous if it was allowed to spread right through the office.

Jokes were already getting out of hand on the screens as juvenile pranks emanating from Bushell's cronies, the features department 'air-heads' as they were known, got into the system – with the consequent risk that they might slip into the actual paper. One hack starting a story: 'Pop star —— revealed today that he . . .' was called away from the terminals and returned to find that the sentence had been completed as '. . . has a prick as big as a hamster.' Bushell was suspected.

Then a story arrived 'global', meaning it came up on everybody's screens. The story was a summary of sexual proclivity involving one of the more active hacks in the field, which had featured a raspberry ripple ice cream: 'A ripple ran round the office yesterday when . . .' This message was read with even greater interest.

MacKenzie had a prurient interest in sexual high jinks round the office as a more localised version of the same tendency he showed in conference. 'They can't hide it from me. I can smell a leg-over a fucking mile off,' he would boast, and to prove his point he once sent a photographer to the airport to snap a hack and hackette returning from what they had believed was a clandestine weekend together. To their immense embarrassment MacKenzie waved the pictures about in the office afterwards, cackling with glee.

The young recruits were the butt of crueller jokes. A showbiz hack in his early twenties, sitting at his terminal on a quiet evening, sensed Mackenzie and Bushell at the other side of the room laughing and pointing at him as the 'message pending' signal started flashing at the top of his screen. He called it up to find: 'You are fired – editor,' and MacKenzie and Bushell burst into even louder howls of laughter. The joke was a poor one. The hack was fired a few weeks later after a row.

Dismissals on the *Sun* were often quick, unpleasant and without particular reason. One day the entire Bizarre desk was told it was fired. Most simply came back the next day and were allowed to carry on as though nothing had happened. But at least one other found himself out of the door without any notice money after being given only a few hours to clear his desk.

MacKenzie's jokes were largely confined to the page proofs he marked up daily. Feature page proofs would come back with crude little stick-man drawings of Bushell (recognisable by his beard) sitting on the toilet and pulling the chain. The mugshot of Bushell which headed his column would be ringed in red pencil: 'Too ugly. Make less ugly.' Like the system jokes, some marks were more double-edged. One features exec found his page returned with the red ring round his byline. Next to it was: 'Wrong – should be —— ', naming a rival hack on another paper.

But this was all a sideshow compared to doing the real business out in the field, where the paper went out for the third round of Royals bashing in the year. Following the Fergie pregnant drama, John Kay had scooped the pack again by revealing that the Royal offspring, first brought to the world's attention by Harry Arnold, was to be named Beatrice – such an unlikely choice that it was rubbished for days before being officially confirmed.

Now Mackenzie thought he had the hat-trick in the battle Royal when the paper got its hands on some family pictures showing the new princess. But this time the *Sun* really hit the royal nerve with a vengeance. One of the most important annual routines in the Queen's life was her Christmas card. Weeks and sometimes months were spent in elaborate photo-sessions to get the right family picture to illustrate it. But on 13 October the *Sun* crashed in on this cosy family totem with the splash 'THE QUEEN BEA'. There, on the front page for the delectation of twelve million *Sun* readers, was the picture the Queen had chosen for that year's card, showing four generations of the Royal Family with the Queen Mother, the Queen and Fergie cradling Princess Beatrice in her arms.

The same day the Queen's lawyers informed the *Sun* that they were considering legal action for breach of copyright. They issued a warning that the picture must not be used again. MacKenzie splashed the story the next day, posing yet again as the readers' cheeky mate. Under the headline 'H.R.H. IS NOT AMUSED – YOU CHEEKY BEAS', the previous day's front page, including the photo, was reproduced in miniature and Phil Dampier reported: 'The magical photo touched the nation with its natural charm and warmth. But the Queen was not amused to see it.'

This time the Queen had really had enough. In massive overkill Scotland Yard's Serious Crimes Squad was called in to investigate how the *Sun* had acquired the photo, while the lawyers started the threatened proceedings for breach of copyright. The Squad soon traced the picture back to a sixth-form schoolgirl from south London who had stolen it while working at a film-processing laboratory in her holidays and then sold it to the paper. (Her case was later referred to the Director of Public Prosecutions, who decided not to bring charges.)

Caught 'bang to rights' and with no defence against a breach of copyright charge MacKenzie had to capitulate. But he still milked the drama for a third splash on 16 November of 'SORRY!', backed by the strapline 'The *Sun* apologises to Queen and pays her £100,000 for that Royal picture'. This time the old ruse of a blank space was printed where the picture should have been.

The story explained that the *Sun* had acknowledged breach of copyright, returned the picture and paid £100,000 to four charities the Queen had nominated. It was a high price for a Royals splash, but by no means terminal and, for the fuss it had created, very good value for money. In the same issue the paper had half as much again on offer in Lotto and Bingo prize money.

But the *Sun* was about to face the consequences of a different legal and financial time-bomb which had been ticking away behind the scenes at Wapping since the heady days of bonk journalism. Now it was to go off – and this time the financial damage would register as more than a blip on the balance sheet of the Empire.

Chapter 14

Elton John Ate My Brother

John Blake, the founder of the *Sun*'s Bizarre section, was a huge fan of Kelvin MacKenzie. He was a great editor, and a great bloke. Of course he had his little prejudices and idiosyncrasies – who didn't? Top of the list as it affected showbiz coverage was the editor's appalled fascination with the topic of homosexuality.

MacKenzie was constantly amazed by the popularity of gay persons in the music business. 'Oh Christ, not another one!' he would say as a group or singer 'came out', genuinely perplexed by successes like Boy George, Freddy Mercury and Frankie Goes to Hollywood. MacKenzie could not understand the popularity of musical poofters. Eventually he made sense of it all by putting it down to some sort of deep conspiracy, through which gays worked together to promote each other's records.

At one editorial conference MacKenzie had even proposed a special feature to bring readers up to date with the current state of play. 'What we need is a fucking table to sort them all out,' he announced. 'We'll have three columns with little symbols, eh? – those who are gay, those who are straight and those who haven't said.' The idea met with approval from some of those present. But like so many which flew about, it somehow got lost in the system and never finally appeared in the paper.

MacKenzie's homophobia extended to the office, where it had now been massively boosted by Garry Bushell continuously banging on about poofters. Any man with an earring was automatically suspect, causing such paranoia among young casuals that they would remove their ring before coming in. Even then they would be in perpetual fear that MacKenzie would notice the telltale hole where their ear had been pierced as he went on with his crude schoolboy wisecracks about 'botty burglars', 'shirt-lifters' and 'bum bandits'. This attitude had percolated down through the whole of the editorial department, provoking great dread of the annual BUPA medical inspection, referred to in giggling terms as the 'thumb up the bum'.

So when, at the height of its power, the paper ran into an alleged story about Elton John, MacKenzie was delighted. It was in the period when MacKenzie was at the peak of what senior execs called his 'roguery'. Wapping was roaring, management execs were crying 'no limit!' on sales and the scamulator was blazing with all its lights on. The Elton yarn looked tailor-made for the Curranticus Bunticus – supposedly sex, drugs and rock and roll, with all the glamour of showbiz and Elton's jet-set lifestyle. But, most of all, it appeared to be a magnificent opportunity for the *Sun* to demonstrate its muscle by dragging a household name through the mud. One side of *Sun* journalism MacKenzie knew the readers really loved was the 'setting 'em up and knocking 'em down' process of creating and destroying popular figures like Boy George. And, like all these stories, the Elton John business could be done with po-faced sanctimony on behalf of the 'outraged' punters.

The alleged story the paper had run into also looked right for earning brownie points with the Boss. Murdoch's contempt for 'poofters' was partly the standard macho Australian attitude, but was intensified by a personal conviction that they were a dangerous mafia which would take over an organisation once let in. Murdoch had come up against the gay network in New York and Hollywood and found that, like the British establishment, it was another club that he was excluded from.

It was well known in the music business that Elton had had an unusually exciting private life. He himself had never pretended he had always been an angel. But, whatever he had done in the past, by 1987 it was history. Elton had then been married for three years, and any story simply revealing that he was gay would be thirteen years old. The singer had admitted to being bisexual in an interview with *Rolling Stone* in 1976, when he declared on the record: 'There's nothing wrong with going to bed with somebody of your own sex.' His bisexuality was common enough knowledge for visiting fans to chant 'Elton John's a poof!' from the terraces of Watford Football Club, which he owned, and for which he would happily fly across the world to see a match.

And there was another element MacKenzie disregarded as he approached the most catastrophic misjudgement of his editorship so far. Elton John was a hugely popular figure with the public. His cuddly appeal stretched right across the age range (including the old fascist). He had stayed in Britain instead of following other rock stars into lucrative tax exile abroad. He had been adjudged ideologically sound enough to be the first big Western star to play in the Soviet Union, even before Mrs Thatcher had put Gorbachev under the political microscope and announced he was someone she could do business with.

The saga that swept the *Sun* into his life began with a tip-off to the paper from a regular informant that a rent-boy known as 'American Barry' operating 'up West' (in the West End) might be sitting on a cracking kiss and tell. The paper left a message for him at the seedy Apollo Club in Soho – a well-known pick-up joint. And when 'American Barry' rang the Bizarre desk, Craig MacKenzie answered the phone.

The fact that his younger brother Craig had a job on the paper was already regarded by the hacks as a major mistake by MacKenzie. Most thought it was pure nepotism and the worst sort of hypocrisy, as he was always banging on about the paper not being able to afford to carry passengers. Many of the hacks thought that Craig was extremely thick, and he was given the nickname of Einstein after claiming to understand the theory of relativity when someone was winding him up about being dim. Otherwise he was known as the 'Bouncing Bog-brush' because of his wiry hair.

Craig had had various jobs on the paper. At that point he was a minion on the Bizarre desk – a post which suited him as he would pick up stories wandering the nightclub circuit. People had been used to seeing him at places like Stringfellows with his tongue stuck down the throat of some Page Three lovely. In the office he was better known for wandering the editorial floor with his distinctive swaggering walk, showing off the family trait of a fat bottom and spawning jokes about the bear in the Hofmeister lager commercial.

Craig was always trying to talk to people and make helpful suggestions, but invariably he was given the brush-off with standard remarks such as: 'Look, Einstein, just go away before you fuck it up,' at which point he would good-naturedly lumber off to pester somebody else.

But, although Craig was not bright, he was not the hopeless dimwit he was parodied as. Many hacks even felt sorry for him, convinced that the ferocious bollockings he got from his brother were mainly due to the family connection. Craig had a soft and cheerful nature. He was constantly clowning, playing practical jokes such as calling up the stone on the intercom system and mimicking Kelvin's booming voice. 'Is that stupid wanker Craig down there?' he would enquire, turning up the volume so the reply blared all over the room: 'No, we haven't seen the stupid fucker all day.' Craig would crack up.

After speaking to 'American Barry' Craig decided he had heard enough to clamber into a black Porsche and go and see him in the flesh. At the rendezvous in the station car park at Twyford, Berkshire, where the rent-boy was living, the snazzy status symbol roared to a stop with a squeal of tyres, suitably impressing 'American Barry', as had been intended. The meeting that followed yielded a string of lurid yarns about Home Counties parties attended by people in the music business, supply of rent-boys, and consumption of massive amounts of cocaine. Various names well known inside showbiz were sprinkled about, but none that would really register with *Sun* readers.

Craig discovered afterwards that his tape of the conversation, which he was relying on, was defective, so he had to go back again. This time as the two spoke another name was introduced into the

258

conversation. And this would mean something to the punters. It was the singer/songwriter born as Reginald Dwight but now known throughout the world by his stage name Elton John. The matter might have gone no further, ending up like hundreds of similar meetings familiar to all hacks which supply interesting but unusable material. The *Sun* was different. It decided to carry on.

'American Barry', now rechristened Graham X by the paper for security reasons, was sent a rail ticket and invited to Wapping to meet the editor. It was an odd meeting. The rent-boy found it hard work braving the pickets with their chants of 'Scab! Scab! Scab!' and MacKenzie was a difficult man to fathom out. 'One minute he was a semi-Australian hard-talking guy, the next he was like a puppy,' he said afterwards. But he liked the way the editor offered him a banana, and was cheered by MacKenzie's promise of some sort of job when it was all over.

The meeting was positive enough for the editor to put another hack, Neil Wallis, into harness with his brother to dig further for dirt. MacKenzie had poached Wallis from the *Star*, where he had been billed as 'The World's No. 1 Reporter'. The hacks at the *Sun* had since translated that into the 'No-one reporter' and since he arrived he had attracted mixed feelings in the newsroom.

Wallis was an affable man with a strong Mancunian accent, and had been nicknamed 'Wolfman' because of his lupine beard and pinched facial features. He had worked on a number of investigations at the *Star* and already earned respect at the *Sun* as a tough operator. But according to Fleet Street legend he was also something of a 'chancer', although the only citation against him at the Press Council was for a story headed, 'THIS CHILD WAS TOLD CHRISTMAS JOY IS EVIL'. The Council had rejected the complaint against him and against the paper he then worked for. But by the time the Elton John saga was over he had collected so many writs that the 'Wallis Collection' had become a stock office joke.

After a fortnight's digging the Elton John team was certain there was something in Graham X's stories about the parties. The problem was that it had no definitive dates. But MacKenzie, typically, was growing impatient with what he saw as the slow progress of the investigation. He pressed for something definite. Scrutinising what evidence it had, the team settled for a spread of dates, including 30 April 1986. It was to prove to be a fatal mistake in much the same way as the disastrous, invented Marica McKay interview – and was to have much the same consequences.

Towards the end of February 1987 MacKenzie suddenly became like a bear with a sore head and prowled the office bollocking the news, sports, features departments and anybody else he could get his hands on. 'For Christ's sake, the paper's getting fucking boring,' he moaned at them. 'Can't you get me something, anything, you useless fuckers?' There hadn't been a decent exclusive for days – not even a decent buy-up.

The only thing on offer was Craig's rent-boy story. One afternoon, on a slow newsday, MacKenzie started interrogating his brother on the editorial floor. Was the story ready to go? he demanded. Craig prevaricated. No, it wasn't, he replied hesitantly. They still needed to check out some points.

MacKenzie stepped up the browbeating, now with an entirely different question. 'Is the story true or isn't it?' he demanded repeatedly. Craig hedged miserably, trying to avoid a direct answer. 'We believe it to be true,' he at last replied, reluctantly. MacKenzie, who by now had lost all patience, demanded yet again: 'Is it true or not – yes or no?' Craig, boxed into a corner, said: 'Well, yes.'

That was enough for MacKenzie. The story was on, and it was the splash. The next job was to put the copy through the lawyers. Their reaction was adamant. Henry Douglas, the legal manager, said that as it stood the story was outrageous. The only evidence was the unsupported affidavit of a homosexual prostitute junkie. 'We'd be ripped to pieces in court,' was his simple verdict.

When MacKenzie, having consulted the legal department, said he was going to ignore it and run the story anyway, Douglas came out on to the editorial floor, demanding that the legal advice be heeded. MacKenzie was then told not to use the story and was given an envelope, which he ripped open. As he read the contents he seemed genuinely surprised. 'Fuck me, they mean it!' he remarked wonderingly to the hacks standing nearby. 'This is the first time they've warned me off with a letter.' But his resolve was unchanged. 'Fuck it. We'll run it anyway.' He walked off to make up the page.

The hacks saw that Craig, who knew better than anyone exactly how far the team's enquiries had got, was obviously deeply worried. He spent the afternoon wandering dispiritedly round the newsroom, trying to clear himself by informing as many hacks as possible that he thought running the story at that stage was 'a helluva risk'. For once there was some sympathy for Einstein. With the computer system everybody could call the story up on their terminals and as they did so eyebrows went up all over the office. Chief sub-editor Roger Wood took a cool look and decided it was interesting, but it was only one man's statement without any corroboration. In his opinion it was research material rather than a finished story.

As the whisper went round, everybody started coming to the same conclusion – it was obviously quite wrong to run the material. Wood gave his final verdict by turning to night editor Roy Pittila and pronouncing: 'I think he's blown it. He's gone right over the top.' Pittila simply turned his hands palm upwards and shrugged his shoulders in reply. After that the main preoccupation of the backbench, the subs and everybody else was to have as little to do with the story as possible.

But now, as MacKenzie finally stood in front of the made-up front page with the headline 'ELTON IN VICE BOYS SCANDAL', flagging 'Star's lust for bondage' on pages 4 and 5, even he seemed to have caught the rest of the office's premonition of disaster. 'Right then,' he said. 'Let's fucking go for it! Elton John! We're all going down the pan!' He held his beaky nose and pulled an imaginary lavatory chain.

The story hit the streets on Wednesday, 25 February, peddling the rent-boy's false and unsupported allegations that he had acted as pimp for Elton, recruiting rent-boys for orgies which had lasted up to four days while the mega-star begged tattooed skinheads and punks to indulge in bondage with him. Bylined Craig MacKenzie and Neil Wallis, the story ended with a classic 'justification' of the filthy allegations by quoting the rent-boy saying: 'I am ashamed of what I did. I am speaking out to show how widespread this sort of thing is and to warn other gullible young kids to steer clear of people like these.'

The fact that the rent-boy had been paid £2,000, and was now on a steady retainer of £250 a week, was not mentioned. And the story was vague on precise detail, except for the specific piece of information of the spread of dates, including the fateful one of 30 April 1986.

The publication of the allegations hit Elton like a hammer blow. His three-year-old marriage was on the rocks and at that precise moment he was in Australia recovering from scary treatment for a growth in his throat. The *Sun*, along with the other tabloids, had already wrongly hyped this into a cancer scare, suggesting that he might lose his voice. When he instantly announced he would sue, Mick Jagger rang him and advised: 'Listen, I've been through this kind of scandal – just leave it for two or three days and it'll be forgotten. In the long run it's not worth fighting because they'll try to rake up so much muck.'

But Elton replied: 'No, I'm going ahead. They can say I'm a fat old sod, they can say I'm an untalented bastard, they can call me a poof, but they mustn't lie about me because then I'm going to fight. And I'm determined to be a winner.'

Elton's lawyer, Frank Presland, served the first writ the next day as Craig and Wallis ploughed on with the second splash, 'ELTON'S KINKY KINKS', bolstered by 'ELTON'S DRUG CAPERS' across pages 4 and 5. A second writ followed with equal alacrity and Presland announced he would be seeking 'enormous' damages. The third day, Friday the 27th, the *Sun* fired back with the defiant splash 'YOU'RE A LIAR ELTON'. MacKenzie was already defiantly strapping the alleged revelations with 'The story they're all suing over'. Presland confirmed this by issuing a third writ.

But writs or no writs, the original story was already self-destructing. Further revelations in the *Sun*, like one which was trailed as 'TOMORROW: Elton's pink tu-tu party', never appeared.

Worse still, the opposition had already scented that the story was, as one of them put it in a crude pun, 'a bummer'. The *Mail*, splashing with 'ELTON IS GOING TO FIGHT', billed the news as 'the biggest showbusiness libel battle since the Liberace case' and Elton ominously told the *Mirror*: '£50 million wouldn't pay for all the harm.'

The *Mirror* led the charge in ripping the story apart. The fateful date of 30 April 1986, mentioned in the initial story, was quickly investigated by former Bizarre editor John Blake. Within two days he triumphantly revealed a different story to *Mirror* readers in a massive front-page splash, 'LIES', sub-headed: 'I was in New York and I can prove it.' Elton had flown home in Concorde that day. He could not possibly have been at the alleged party. The *Mirror* had receipts for limo hire to the airport, and confirmation from British Airways to prove it. But Elton was already having his troubles. The mud thrown by the *Sun* was sticking. Cadbury's, who had bought him to front a major promotion for their Daily Milk, Whole Nut and Fruit and Nut chocolate, scrapped the ads only hours before they were due to be aired.

The ease with which the *Mirror* knocked down the original story was due to a fatal flaw in the *Sun*'s approach to the investigation. Normally Wallis or Craig would have used the ploy of inventing an excuse to quiz Elton's press agent to establish the star's whereabouts on that day. But MacKenzie had forbidden them to approach the enemy camp in any way, in case it alerted the other side to what the *Sun* was up to. No check had been run.

Blake's story increased MacKenzie's deep alarm at the way things were going. The story had also registered in a big way on the Boss's radar, with Murdoch having the additional worry that Elton might boycott his many television outlets. The hacks were soon telling each other about the phone call MacKenzie had received and then loudly talked about in the office. Murdoch, careless of the time as usual, had rung MacKenzie's home in the early hours of the morning.

'Kelvin, are we all right on this Elton John business?' he had asked.

'Yes, Boss,' MacKenzie had replied.

'All right,' said the voice on the other end of the line, and there was a click as the receiver was put down. It was not just the call, but its brevity, which left MacKenzie so twitchingly and uncharacteristically nervous.

By now the *Sun* was heavily on the defensive. The pack, mobhanded, had taken less than twenty-four hours to track down Graham X and his Twyford home was now under heavy siege. The *Sun*'s Thames Valley reporter, John Askill, a huge man known as 'The Jolly Green Giant', was allotted the task of smuggling the rent-boy, his wife and their baby out of the country. He managed it, but only after one of the opposition evaded a cunning *Sun* roadblock made up of four hired taxis, setting off a hair-raising car chase across the Home Counties.

For a month the family was kept holed up at the five-star Melia Don Pepe hotel in Marbella, with no expense spared in mollycoddling them with all the comforts of home. When the rent-boy's wife refused to feed their child on the funny Spanish baby food, a *Sun* hack was instantly flown out with supplies from a proper British supermarket. But the novelty of the luxury lifestyle *Sun* readers were taught to aspire to soon wore off. The family returned home to the bad news that the Vice Squad wanted to talk to Graham X, and the subsequent enquiries culminated in his being charged with living off the immoral earnings of prostitutes.

With the linchpin of the story down and apparently out, the *Sun* now desperately needed fresh evidence to keep up the MacKenzie strategy of hitting Elton until he gave up. This included attempts to get inside the enemy camp, which reached heights of farce when the paper got a tip that Elton, back from Australia, was meeting his mother for lunch in a restaurant in the Home Counties. In a huge operation the paper stuffed the other tables with hacks, to the extent that two were eventually decanted into an overflow restaurant down the road, where they spent their time dejectedly staring at the car park.

Under the fiendish strategy a *Sun* hack and a hackette had been ordered to pose as a newly married couple at the table next to

Elton. The pair were to spend the entire meal gazing silently into each other's eyes in simulated devotion, while earwigging on the conversation at the adjoining table.

The plan met its first setback when the meeting turned out to be between Elton's mother and an agent – Elton himself was not there at all. The team persevered. But the key hack playing the bridegroom, one of the *Sun*'s flashy Porsche owners, then began the normal restaurant habit for which he was an office byword. After reading the menu from right to left and selecting accordingly, he began loudly sending back his courses with a long list of pompous complaints about their various defects.

The climax came when the waiter brought a special cake, which he presented to the happy couple with the compliments of the management. Ostentatiously taking a bite, the hack noisily called the waiter back and pronounced the cake too sweet, ordering it to be returned to the kitchen. By this time both Elton's mother and the agent were so mesmerised they had fallen silent and were staring open-mouthed at the extraordinary theatrical performance next to them. The operation was wrapped, with nil intelligence gained.

The *Sun* appeared, however, to have found a fairy godmother when it was rung by a Scottish conman, homosexual pimp and former rent-boy, who, as he was later to tell Thames Television, had nine convictions for fraud and one for attempted murder. The conman, who operated from Manchester, offered to dig out more rent-boys to support the original Elton allegations by signing affidavits. In a recorded interview with Thames he later explained how the *Sun* had approached the task. 'Basically they wanted to crown the guy. . . . So they [the *Sun*] turned round and says to me, they says, by the way, can you dig up any kind of crap on the guy?'

He then explained the crude *modus operandi*. 'We used to bring people to hotel rooms and they would tell us that they had an affair there with Elton John and you know – I mean it was pure crap.' But it was lucrative crap, with the *Sun* paying £1,750 for each of the promised affidavits (with the rent-boys receiving £500) until it woke up to the fact that they were not worth the paper they were written on. Not only were they all untrue, but some of the signatories were not even rent-boys – and had never even met Elton John. The supply of cheques was cut off.

Mightily affronted, the conman then teamed up to expose all in conjunction with Terry Lovell, a veteran reporter who had also been put on the trail by Maxwell's Sunday *People* as part of a massive Mirror Group operation to rubbish the *Sun*'s stories. Lovell, a legendary figure in the evil world of Sunday muckraking, was known as 'The Prince of Darkness' for the unbridled relish with which he pursued stories of Satanism and the occult. (The 'Prince of Darkness' tag, applied to several reporters, was rightly the copyright of James (Jimmy) Nicholson, a veteran crime reporter famous for his black cloak-like garment which doubled as a coat or jacket depending on the circumstances he found himself in.)

Lovell's brilliant rent-boy contacts had already enabled him to break the 'spanking' story which caused the downfall of the right-wing Tory MP, Harvey Proctor. But, as he told *UK Press Gazette*, he had since become born again. 'I honestly could take no more. The cheating, the lying, the conniving and the utter pointlessness of many of the stories, I was no longer able to justify,' he explained.

Renouncing the error of his ways, Lovell told his employers he could no longer 'do a deal with the Devil' by continuing to work as a Sunday hack and asked for redundancy from his £37,000 a year job. The *People* graciously paid him off and he had now embarked on a new life, working part-time for the *Christian Bookseller Review* and setting up a PR agency called Genesis Media Relations. Lovell and the conman started work together on an exposé book entitled *The Fall and Rise of the Rocket Man*, but by the time it was in workable shape public interest had faded and the manuscript failed to find a publisher.

With the conman now knocked out the *Sun* went worldwide for the massive trawl though Elton's past life which Mick Jagger had predicted. Elton found himself pursued wherever he went, not just by the *Sun*, but by hacks from rival papers following his fight as front-page news. He found many sympathetic to his plight and fans buoyed him up with letters of support, but it was still tough going. He later told *Q* magazine how badly he had been affected by the original stories when he had been in Australia. 'I was mega-depressed. I think they did it to demoralise me and it really worked. I hardly ever went out because I could not stop crying. . . . I'd have breakfast then go back to bed. Eat ice lollies and watch TV all day.' But he had then been further shocked. 'I was really unprepared for how bad it was going to get, I must admit,' he said describing Rupert Murdoch as 'a praying mantis'.

In Los Angeles, where Elton was staying in the hotel suite regularly used by President Reagan, his security man pointed out a piece of Sellotape stuck to the top of the door, explaining it would break when the door was opened to indicate he had gone out. Elton, amazed, at first refused to believe it, but the security man then insisted on having the room swept for listening devices. After the Secret Service had been called in because of the Reagan connection a bug was found stuck on the back of the bar. Elton's paranoia went up another notch.

Back in Wapping there was huge euphoria when a man claiming to be Elton's former gay lover sold the paper three Polaroid pictures for £10,000. The handover, with the money in used notes as demanded, took place in a scene like something from a Le Carré novel outside the gatehouse under the Wapping searchlights after the man refused to enter the complex. The first picture showed Elton in full-frontal nude, the second cuddling another man, and the third the man and Elton in a compromising position.

The hacks who were privileged to be shown the photos in the office declared themselves suitably shocked. But the only story they supported was the original thirteen-year-old admission by Elton that he was bisexual. The man in the picture was a fully consenting adult, and the pictures had been taken at the turn of the decade, long before Elton had married. The actual rent-boy story the *Sun* had printed was not advanced one jot.

267

The paper showed the pictures to Elton and, after he had admitted they were genuine, continued the pillorying exercise by publishing parts of the first two, suitably cropped, on 16 April under the headline 'ELTON PORNO PHOTO SHAME'. The third was omitted. 'The Polaroid photograph is simply too disgusting to print in a family newspaper,' the *Sun* alleged.

But the pictures only added to the central problem which had been dogging the story from the beginning. It was the first real example since MacKenzie became editor of the stitches coming apart with the readers. An enormous postbag of complaints poured into Wapping from grannies downwards, with huge numbers of correspondents saying they would never read the paper again. The postbag was backed up by alarming dips in sales every time an Elton story was printed, and MacKenzie was heard moaning in the office that they had dropped on occasion by as many as 200,000 copies, only to bounce back as soon as Elton disappeared off the front page.

Part of the reason was undoubtedly Elton's popularity and the warm affection in which many readers held him. The *Sun* was appearing more and more like the archetypal bully. But the other serious objection, now being raised within the paper, was that really grinding Elton into the dirt needed allegations which verged on hard-core pornography. That in turn meant the paper skewering itself by putting off readers who found the material too disgusting for a family newspaper and, as the letters angrily or sadly pointed out, did not want their children reading about such things. There were other signs that things were getting out of hand. Elton's manager, John Reid, thumped *Sun* showbiz writer Rick Sky's head against a pillar at a party. It seemed that the saga had got locked into a hysterical spiral which nobody could halt.

The publication of the Polaroids produced a kind of stalemate. As the writs had mounted, more and more evidence had been gathered, principally by the *Sun*'s rivals, which destroyed the original stories. But it was also now obvious that if the case went to court Elton would have to face a long and painful examination of his private life in the witness box.

268

Then the *Sun* made its terminal error. On 28 September 1987, five months after 'PORNO SHAME', the paper splashed 'MYSTERY OF ELTON'S SILENT DOGS' under the byline of 'The Jolly Green Giant', John Askill. The story claimed that Elton had had his 'vicious Rottweiler dogs . . . silenced by a horrific operation' and described them as now 'silent assassins'. Askill had filed the story with a strong disclaimer – as well he might. For when photographer Roger Bamber went the next day to get pictures of the dumb animals, he reported back that they were not Rottweilers, but Alsatians. And, as he could personally testify, there was nothing wrong with their barks. Presland issued writ number seventeen.

On the 6th of November, the *Mirror* gleefully plunged in the last knife with the splash, 'MY SEX LIES OVER ELTON'. The original rent-boy with whom the story had started, American Barry or Graham X, was quoted as saying: 'It's all a pack of lies, I made it all up. I only did it for the money and the *Sun* was easy to con. I've never met Elton John. . . . I've never been to one of his concerts or bought one of his records. In fact, I hate his music.'

Elton's shell of self-pity finally cracked shortly afterwards with the Enniskillen Remembrance Day bombing. He later told *Q* magazine: 'That man whose daughter died beside him under the rubble; he was burning inside but he was so forgiving, so gracious. I thought, Christ, this is what courage is all about – Elton, just shut up and get back to work. After all, once you've been exposed naked on the cover of the *Sun* you ought to be able to face anything.'

However, it was not the shifting statements of the rent-boy, but the dog story which was the killer. It was obviously indefensible, and when Elton's lawyers vaulted it over the other writs to be heard first, the *Sun* was suddenly in a new situation. Instead of putting Elton in the witness box and mercilessly quizzing him about his past predilections, the case would be confined to the dog allegations. Elton would be seen as a hurt and wronged animal-lover. As the facts of the matter were plain, it also appeared certain that the paper would lose. While the case ground its way through the legal labyrinth towards the High Court, the *Sun* gave up the unequal fight and ran no further Elton stories.

The High Court hearing finally went into the lists for Monday, 12 December 1988 – twenty-one months after the first rent-boy story and fifteen months after the dog disaster. The rest of the Street rubbed its hands as it rushed to get the ringside seats for the *Sun*'s come-uppance. But that morning, as the hacks crowded into the court for the start of the hearing before Mr Justice Michael Davies, they all knew the show had been cancelled. Behind the scenes the two sets of lawyers had reached an agreement at the last minute.

Elton had demanded an 'apology which matched the smear' and which gave maximum publicity to the retraction. He did not want it buried in incomprehensible legal jargon on an inside page, but written in language *Sun* readers could understand, which included forgetting the standard euphemism of 'substantial damages'. The story must state that the amount Elton was getting, the fat round sum of £1 million, doubling the benchmark of £500,000 which had been set by Jeffrey Archer in his case against the *Daily Star*.

That morning the *Sun* had come on to the streets bearing the splash 'SORRY ELTON!' in huge typeface over the long and grovelling libel apology Elton had required, which marked another milestone by being the first ever to lead the paper. A *Sun* spokesman was quoted in the story as saying: 'We are delighted that the *Sun* and Elton have become friends again, and are sorry that we were lied to by a teenager living in a world of fantasy.' The article made great play of how much Elton loved his pets, and quoted him as saying: 'This is the best Christmas present I could wish for. Life is too short to bear grudges and I don't bear the *Sun* any malice.'

Although agreements like this were common in the show-business game, Mr Justice Davies was furious at the apology being printed in the paper before the agreed statement had been read in open court. He explained from the bench that he had been told about the settlement the previous evening. But when he tried to stop the story being printed he was informed it was too late. Expressing 'disapproval in the strongest possible terms', the learned judge declared that his court had been manipulated by a 'pre-emptive strike'.

He said of the apology: 'Reading it, one would think that Elton John and the newspaper had formed a mutual admiration society. The Queen's courts are provided for the trial and resolution of disputes, not as the supine adjunct to the publicity machine of pop stars and newspaper proprietors.' The case, he declared, had been used 'to milk the situation in order to obtain maximum publicity for both sides'.

Shortly afterwards MacKenzie, having endured a mega-bollocking from Murdoch, ushered everybody into his office 'for a little celebration'. It was just before Christmas and the hacks all jammed into the tiny space, thinking it was the office party. It was a set-up. Once they were all locked in place MacKenzie started raving at them.

'The next one of you who gets a complaint, never mind a fucking writ, is out. Got that?' he raged as they blanched and quailed backwards. He didn't know why he fucking bothered with them. They were all useless and a fucking disgrace. 'It's got to stop,' he shouted at the top of his voice, face red with rage and veins bulging ominously. 'If I go, I'm going to take you bastards with me!'

The hacks, shaken to the core, filed out silently. There had been no mention of Christmas.

First there had been the Queen Bea, then Elton John, and, rubbing further salt into the wound, days afterwards another trip to the High Court for another 'substantial settlement'. This time the wronged party was Mrs Carmen Proetta, who had been a witness to the shootings of three IRA men by the SAS in Gibraltar. Mrs Proetta had been a crucial interviewee in the controversial Thames Television programme *Death on the Rock*, which had been broadcast in April that year and bitterly attacked by the *Sun* for its suggestion that the shootings had effectively been executions.

The court awarded Mrs Proetta 'substantial' damages for two *Sun* articles which had described her as 'the tart of Gib' and alleged that she hated the British so much she had fabricated her claim to have seen two of the shootings. News International's lawyers told the court the paper now accepted that the allegations were untrue.

The year that had started so well for the *Sun* had come to a sticky and expensive end. The £1 million payout to Elton John was a serious blow financially, with other massive legal costs behind the scenes. For the previous two years the British end of the Empire had enjoyed year-on-year profit increases of 75 per cent, but in the year ending June 1988 this had slumped to a mere 7 per cent – less than half the increase of 16 per cent for the Empire as a whole. The total UK profit had still been £155.4 million, but the momentum of Wapping had been lost.

However, at least the Elton John business, which had been hanging over MacKenzie like a black cloud, was over and although there were inevitably more writs from other stories in the pipeline, they were much less serious. He and the paper, it was hoped, had learned their lesson the hard way. But it was not to be. The worst offence of all, both in the eyes of the public and in terms of financial damage, was just round the corner as the British press faced its sternest test of standards to date.

Chapter 15

You Scum

The Elton John fiasco rattled MacKenzie badly. Old colleagues meeting him for a chat found the subject banned, and could only sympathise with his despondency. 'SORRY ELTON!' had been the most expensive front page in the paper's history – and possibly in history of the world journalism – and as editor MacKenzie had had to personally carry the can. A few libel actions were one thing, and only to be expected with 'SHOCK AND AMAZE ON EVERY PAGE'. But costing the Boss £1 million was something else and on the paper libel was rapidly beginning to look like bingo in reverse, and Elton's jackpot had now given fresh heart to existing litigants.

Behind the scenes the News International legal department was quietly moving to settle some of the cases in the pipeline. There was plenty to do. When Henry Douglas had first started as legal manager in the mid-1970s two-thirds of his cases had come from the *News of the World* and one-third from the *Sun*. But under MacKenzie's wilder and more aggressive editorship the proportions had been reversed. The main trouble had come from the features department. Once, when the paper had received something like ten writs in a week MacKenzie had taken the unprecedented step of sending a memo to all the department heads at their home addresses informing them that the level of legal action against the paper was getting out of hand. In 1987 Douglas had revealed in the Wapping house journal that the two papers were together facing more than fifty writs.

Various other moves were being put in train to close the door to prevent other financial horses bolting. Craig MacKenzie had left the paper and resurfaced at the *Daily Express*, while his brother, who could count himself lucky to be still sitting in the editor's chair, was being as good as his word at the Christmas party. Taped back-ups were now insisted on for all investigative stories and MacKenzie was personally leading a phenomenal drive for accuracy. 'Check, check, check, double-check and then check again' was screamed at the hacks day in and day out. Stories were returned spattered with demands for corroboration, verification, cross-checking, alternative sources and quotes from every single party concerned – even if all they had to say was 'No comment.'

Henry Douglas had retired as legal manager and been succeeded by Tom Crone, his deputy since 1980, who moved to set up additional defences, starting with a series of compulsory legal seminars which all the hacks – subs, feature writers and reporters – had to attend on a rota basis. The seminars, very different from the theory they dimly remembered from their training courses, concentrated very much on the practical side.

A slide show illustrated infamous front pages – including the Jeffrey Archer case – which had cost their publishers a fortune. Crone led them through the stories, pointing out where they had gone wrong, and followed with even more interesting examples showing stories that had got away with it through careful writing. The subs were sternly informed that they were the last line of defence. It was their fault if libels got into the paper, they explained to the reporters in the Sidney Smith that evening, only for the reporters to reply that they'd been told that any libels would be their fault, and they shouldn't expect the subs to save them.

Even more specifically both were given a list of names which 'must immediately ring an alarm bell'. Top of the list was Koo Stark, about whom Crone commented: 'If you see her name in a story, strike it out at once.' There was no reason to take any risks with Stark, he said, the readers were no longer interested in her. MacKenzie's phrase for this was that people were 'officially dead'. Other expensive names included David Steel, Jeffrey Archer and the actor John Thaw, who had had a fierce brush with the paper over an outrageous report about a short separation from his wife, Sheila Hancock.

Inevitably there were still mistakes. As Douglas had pointed out before he retired, you couldn't make an omelette without breaking eggs – and the ensuing bollockings scaled new heights of savagery, with even the seasoned hacks blanching at some of the diatribes that rained down. While the more kindly tried to reassure juniors it was mostly bluster, they could do nothing to alleviate the constant threat of being sacked utilised to instil permanent fear in the recently recruited. An example was one hackette, just into her twenties, who on her own admittance fucked up, in a small way, on a celeb story.

First, she was torn off a frightful strip in front of everybody in the office, with MacKenzie lambasting her under the crude nickname the seniors had given her of 'Fuckwit'. Then she was taken behind closed doors for a second bollocking by one of the features execs, emphasised by the repeated violent kicking of a briefcase across the floor. 'You (kick) are not at a (kick) fucking girls' school now! (kick) Get your fucking act together (kick) or you are out (kick) of that fucking (kick) door!' (huge kick).

The hacks' automatic response was to pull back from the edge and play stories safe, but this then plunged them into a fresh nightmare. If they didn't deliver they got bollocked just the same – this time for the old crime of being useless and letting the editor down. After the great redundancy offer of 1988 MacKenzie had started pulling in younger and younger recruits, but, as one of the senior hacks pointed out, he demanded the impossible equation of twenty-two-year-old reporters with twenty-five years' experience. The result was a constant turnover of youth hired on a temporary basis and fired shortly afterwards after being found wanting.

The new atmosphere of terror did however succeed in its object of cutting down errors on the pages and the facts of stories were now largely under control – as far as they ever could be with the amount of spin the paper put on them. Opinion was another matter, and as the *Sun* had always specialised in dressing up its readers' prejudices and presenting them as fact much of it contained a fatal flaw. C. P. Scott, a former editor of the World's Worst, had famously warned in 1926: 'A newspaper's "primary office" is the gathering of news. At the peril of its soul it must see that the supply is not tainted. Neither in what it gives, nor in what it does not give, nor in its mode of presentation, must the unclouded face of truth suffer wrong. Comment is free but facts are sacred.'

And it was comment MacKenzie was about to apply to the greatest sporting tragedy Britain had ever known – the disaster at the FA Cup semi-final between Nottingham Forest and Liverpool at Sheffield's Hillsborough stadium in April 1989. As Lord Justice Taylor's enquiry was later to state, the deaths of ninety-five Liverpool fans had been a wholly avoidable tragedy, but one which had been long in the making. Taylor's acerbic report threw into sharp relief the way the football authorities had connived with papers like the *Sun* to hype the former working-class game into the realms of television-led fantasy. Multi-million-pound transfer fees for players had soaked up the money desperately needed to update ancient grounds, and had so squeezed smaller clubs that facilities at the grounds had deteriorated into a shabby squalor, summed up for Taylor by 'the all-pervading stench of fried onions' and the sight of men openly urinating against walls because of the inadequate and foul toilet facilities.

The Hillsborough tragedy, as Taylor bluntly concluded, was primarily the fault of the South Yorkshire police in charge of crowd control, with particular blame pinned in his report on the senior officer at the ground, Superintendent David Duckenfield. Games like these semi-finals, held on neutral territory, were always particularly nerve-racking for the authorities as the fans of both sides were off their familiar home ground and in this case, as the match moved towards its 3.00 p.m. start, a potentially lethal crush had developed outside the stadium with 5,000 Liverpool fans struggling to get through the bottleneck of the turnstiles.

To relieve the increasingly lethal pressure Duckenfield had given the order for the gates to be thrown open. But instead of routing the surging fans on to empty terraces, he had allowed them to take the automatic route through a tunnel into one of the pens which was already overcrowded, and from which there was no escape due to the wire cages enclosing the front. As the inevitable push forward began Duckenfield had then frozen in his control box and further compounded his error by treating the fans' desperate attempts to escape by scaling the cage as a pitch invasion. Only when it was too late did he allow the emergency gates to be opened, relieving the pressure.

Few tragedies had been so comprehensively recorded. Every second of the drawn-out horror had unravelled itself, live, in front of a TV audience expecting an exciting afternoon's sports viewing. The mass of sports photographers had taken thousands of pictures, many of which showed such harrowing detail of death and suffering it was an almost impossible editorial decision to decide which could actually be printed.

With such searing and powerful material it was obvious straight away that all the papers would be treading an impossible tightrope with their readers. Somehow they had to strike a balance between adequately portraying the full nightmare of being trapped, yet not use pictures showing such grotesque detail that their readers would be sickened. Seasoned veterans of the Street knew at once that, short of printing no pictures at all, they could not win.

With the fierce competition between them, that decision was anyway out of the question. Any paper taking it would not only be ducking its responsibility to cover the news, but hoisting itself on the petard of the fundamental hypocrisy of the general public. Some people would bay for the blood of the papers printing the most horrific pictures, while at the same time others would pile into the shops to buy the ones with the most shocking images. Words, however, were a different matter and MacKenzie's personal achievement was to use them to turn Hillsborough into an unparalleled journalistic disaster, with huge and continuing financial consequences for his paper.

The story was first the province of the Sundays, for whom it was the biggest since Zeebrugge two years previously. Unprepared, and strapped by earlier edition times than the dailies, they could do little more than react blindly with scant opportunity for any effective analysis. False information disseminated by Superintendent Duckenfield, who lied that the fans had stormed the gates and forced them to be opened, only complicated matters by jumbling up the first impressions.

By the time the Sundays were on the presses the full story was still in its early stages. Dazed parents and relatives, many of whom had just arrived from Liverpool, were still stumbling round Sheffield, inspecting the Polaroid pictures of the dead at the makeshift morgue in a gym next to the stadium, then scouring the city's hospitals in their desperate search for children and loved ones they only knew were missing, and could be safe, mangled or dead.

As the survivors made their way home the city of Liverpool closed ranks in stunned shock and disbelief. The local Liverpool *Echo* had crammed the first garbled reports into its late sports edition and now staff on their day off came into the office unprompted and went to their desks. Some, although they did not yet know it, had lost friends or relatives in the disaster. Vin Kelly, the associate editor running the paper while editor Chris Oakley was on holiday, took a snap decision to produce a special twenty-eight-page issue for sale on Sunday morning. As they started work Alf Green, the news editor, watched both reporters and subs vainly struggling to hold back their emotions as they pieced all the terrible individual stories together. For the first time in his thirty-year career he saw men and women openly weeping as they worked and found themselves overwhelmed by the depth of the tragedy they were recording.

The *Echo*'s special edition went on the presses at 1 a.m., carrying on the front page a close-up picture of a man and a woman in the crush crying in distress and terror behind the wire of the cage. The headline read: 'OUR DAY OF TEARS'. Alf Green thought the page, designed by deputy editor Joe Holmes, the most difficult exercise in taste the paper had ever faced. The picture was horrific, but the *Echo* was correct in its judgement that it captured the agony of the moment without the brutal detail of other pictures which were about to cause a major uproar when they appeared in the nationals. The paper succeeded in running it without complaint, partly – in Green's view – simply because it was the local paper, but also because of the headline, which softened the image. He thought it was right. It was what people were thinking.

The next day, as the city struggled to pull itself together, there was the fresh horror of the invasion by a newspaper pack, mob-handed for its grisly task of prising pictures and tear-jerking stories from parents, relatives and friends of the dead. Not just British, but foreign reporters, photographers and camera crews flooded into both Sheffield and Liverpool. The *Sun* was estimated to have piled eighteen reporters and photographers on to the story.

Shortly after the disaster wild rumours had swept round that photographers on the spot had used their feet to turn over bodies on the pitch so they could get better pictures. Now a spate of stories followed about reporters desperate for quotes posing as social workers and Salvation Army helpers, ringing up Helplines pretending to be relatives or government officials, or trying to get their foot in the door by masquerading as journalists from the local *Echo*. Most of the rumours featured reporters alleged to be from the *Sun*, and, although none could be substantiated, the paper was in no position to complain. Whether they were true or false, it was merely reaping the reward of its public image.

On Monday the *Sun* cleared page after page after page for different pictures and stories, pulled together under a tacky logo labelled: 'Gates of Hell'. The pattern of 'earthquake journalism' set by Larry Lamb had been copied by the rest of the tabloids and further intensified throughout the 1980s. On this occasion the correctness of Lamb's thinking was demonstrated by the Sundays selling an extra 500,000 copies between them, while on the Monday public desire for more detail still seemed insatiable. The *Sun*, like the other dailies, had more time to reflect on which pictures to use. But as the official death list had not been published there was still no way it could tell in most cases whether the individuals pictured being crushed or lying on the pitch were now alive or dead. Like most of its rivals, it printed them regardless.

It was not the *Sun*, but the *Mirror* with its use of colour, so making the pictures even more ghoulish, which brought the wrath of Liverpool down on its head on Monday morning. The *Mirror*, carrying sixteen pages on the story, filled the front page with a grisly picture showing horrible detail of fans who appeared already dead or dying jumbled together on top of each other. The use of colour added to the horror by showing how the victims' faces had turned blue as the oxygen was squeezed from their lungs. In all it was reminiscent of Hieronymus Bosch's vision of hell.

The outpouring of anger at the front page focused in on the local media, and particularly the two local radio stations Radio Merseyside, run by the BBC, and the commercial Radio City. At Radio Merseyside DJ Billy Butler had scrapped his popular morning *Hold Your Plums* show – normally three hours of the cheerful Scouse humour – to concentrate solely on the disaster.

Butler criticised the *Mirror* for cashing in on the disaster by printing the pictures, and as calls agreeing with him jammed the lines, he and producer Wally Scott decided that the *Mirror* should be rung to be asked to defend itself on the air. The call was made by Roger Phillips, who ran the station's *Newsline* programme. The *Mirror* responded promptly by putting on a senior executive, who explained that the paper stood by its decision. He justified showing the full horror of the event as a way of helping to ensure that steps were taken so nothing like it could ever happen in the future, which was why the paper had splashed: 'NEVER AGAIN'. Phillips, like Butler, still thought the pictures had been printed to sell the paper – as did most of the people ringing in. He asked the exec if he would have used that front-page picture if it had been of his own children. The spokesman replied 'I wouldn't then frankly have been in a position to make the decision, but I would have approved the editorial reasons behind it.' The outcry about pictures was not restricted to the *Mirror*, or to the city of Liverpool. At the Press Council the phone started ringing itself off the hook, and practically every paper found itself deluged by a flood of angry callers and complaining letters.

But during the day on Monday a new and more sinister factor began to surface in the story. From the start there had been an understandable knee-jerk reaction of blaming hooligans for the disaster, and it was this preconditioning which had largely accounted for Superintendent Duckenfield's automatic assumption that the unfolding tragedy was a pitch invasion. Even when most of the deaths had already occurred, television commentators had fallen into the same trap by excitedly screaming that fans were tearing down the hoardings. They were – but only to use as makeshift stretchers.

In Liverpool's case memories of the Heysel disaster in Belgium in 1985 had flooded back – another ghastly muddle in which overall blame had rightly been laid on the Liverpool fans. The *Sun* had weighed in at the time by reporting that the fans had fought a pitched battle with the Belgian police before the match had even started, and had looted shops in Brussels city centre, with one group being accused of stealing £150,000 worth of gems.

But, for those interested enough to look beyond the headlines, it had become clear with the benefit of hindsight that the poor state of the ground and the totally inadequate policing had been major contributing factors. It had also emerged beyond doubt that equally bad behaviour by Juventus fans, who mercilessly taunted the Liverpool supporters, had provoked their violent reaction. The forty-one deaths which had followed had been due not to the fighting, but to a badly maintained wall which had collapsed and caused a pile-up in which the fleeing Juventus fans had fallen over each other and been crushed. Again, with hindsight, it was now generally accepted that soccer hooliganism was not solely confined to Britain and that Juventus fans rightly had a nasty reputation for violence which was tinged with the additional element of Italian fascism. At Heysel, one such fan had been clearly identifiable on film waving a gun about, although he had never been found and prosecuted.

Liverpool's more responsible supporters still felt they had been unfairly tarred with a broad hooligan brush, but had recognised they were all guilty by association. And although they had been besmirched by the incident, they were now admitted to be in a different league from organised gangs like the notorious Millwall 'firms' which went to matches deliberately looking for trouble.

One of the city's greatest prides was still that its two clubs Liverpool and Everton, which reflected the old Protestant–Catholic divide, made it a football-mad city in the best traditional sense. Local derbies invariably passed off without incident, and the terraces of Liverpool's famous Kop were still a safe place to stand, even though you might be picked up and carried yards in great surges of the crowd. Diehard supporters still had their own unmarked spots on the steps, which were kept for them by unwritten agreement. The city's matches still remained what the Football Association had been vainly trying to promote elsewhere throughout the 1980s – male-orientated occasions but ones which it was not unusual for three generations of one family to attend together.

But on Tuesday morning the *Sun* started flying the hooligan kite with a vengeance. A '*Sun* Says' headed 'SCAPEGOATS' asked:

> Is it fair to make the police the scapegoats for the Hillsborough disaster?
>
> It happened because thousands of fans, many without tickets, tried to get into the ground just before the kick-off – either by forcing their way in or by blackmailing the police into opening the gates.
>
> So far we have not heard a word of criticism of those fans in Liverpool.

The next day that 'criticism' was to come over loud and clear as MacKenzie demonstrated how his brand of shoot-from-the-hip editorship could be as violent, irresponsible and destructive as any of the hooligans the *Sun* had previously concentrated on so obsessively.

Former Royals reporter Harry Arnold, who had been taken off the beat by MacKenzie and was now a general news reporter, was given the job of weaving an overall story out of the mass of copy that had been filed. Arnold did not like the look of some of it at all.

The hacks and agencies whose names were on it were reliable, but the filthiness of the accusations they were reporting was something else. Arnold loaded his finished story into the system with even more than his usual scrupulous care. In his opinion it now needed handling as delicately as a ticking bomb.

Seeking out MacKenzie, he confided his fears. 'We've got to be really careful with this stuff,' he said. 'These are only allegations that we're reporting, you know.'

'Yeah, yeah,' MacKenzie assured him. 'I know that. It's all right, Harry. Don't worry. I'm going to put in "some fans".'

MacKenzie then did an enormously uncharacteristic thing. He sat for fully half an hour thinking about the front-page layout. The story Arnold had written had been the automatic splash from the moment it came in. But, as he doodled with layouts, for once MacKenzie's flair for instant decision-making seemed to have deserted him. He was obviously torn as he weighed up two alternative headlines. The first was his most vicious slag-off phrase, 'YOU SCUM', bringing into play the vilest word in the *Sun*'s vocabulary and putting all the Liverpool fans on the Scum of the Earth agenda. That was bad enough. But the second, and the one he finally sketched out on the layout pad with his fat green pen, was to prove even more calamitous.

As MacKenzie's layout was seen by more and more people a collective shudder ran through the office. There was an instant gut feeling that it was a terrible mistake. The trouble was that nobody seemed able to do anything about it. By now MacKenzie's dominance was so total there was nobody left in the organisation who could rein him in except Murdoch, who was not there. The whole subs desk and the backbench seemed paralysed, 'looking like rabbits in the headlights', as one hack described them, as they stared at the two huge words in front of them in horrified fascination. The error staring them in the face was too glaring and too terminal to be possible. It obviously wasn't a silly mistake; nor was it a simple oversight, which someone could gingerly point out to their hard-pressed editor, knowing he could admit to it without losing too much face; and it certainly wasn't a typographical error like the ones frequently littering the pages of the World's Worst. Nobody really had any comment on it – they just took one look and went away shaking their heads in wonder at the enormity of it. The subs quickly took refuge in the fact that it was an extremely busy afternoon to keep their heads down and their hands full with other work.

The trouble with Hillsborough was that it had brought MacKenzie's prejudices straight into play. He didn't know much about the facts of the matter but he personally thought it was outrageous that the police should carry the can for all of it. He was convinced he knew what the real situation was. The police obviously couldn't be totally to blame. Football hooligans were scum, and as a Millwall fan he despised Liverpool supporters in particular. The reporters on the story, who could have helped moderate his judgement, were not in the office to be consulted even if he had wanted to consult them. The time he had spent deliberating had been solely about the headline – the details did not concern him.

Roger Wood, who ruled the all-important backbench as chief sub, knew well that the second you hesitated on a story you were lost. That's what happened at the World's Worst, where the bleeding-heart liberals were always agonising about principles and wringing their hands about issues and dithering about being fair and anguishing about seeing the other person's point of view and worrying about upsetting people and saying on the one hand there was this side to it, and on the other hand there was that, and ending up in such a stew they didn't know their fucking arse from their elbow and couldn't make up their minds up about anything. And everybody knew the wishy-washy crap which that produced at the end of the day.

Start thinking like that and suddenly there were a thousand reasons why you shouldn't do something. On the *Sun* – and in tabloids in general – it was as if you had caught someone messing around with your wife. You shouldn't stop to think about it. You just did what you thought was right and went round and punched them in the face.

MacKenzie had no roots in Liverpool or any interest in it. He had hardly ever been there. But although the *Sun*, like him, was not interested in much north of Watford, it had always had a high sale in Liverpool, though not as high as in the midlands, where proportionately it sold the most copies compared with the rival tabloids. In its heyday Liverpool had had a professional and merchant class, but had always lacked a large middle class, and therefore contained a high proportion of the paper's target C2 working-class readers. But, like others, the *Sun* had always had a love-hate relationship with the city.

Liverpool might have been declining, through no fault of its own, since the end of the American sea trade, but the *Sun* shared the country's widespread exasperation with its ruinous hard-left politics and 'first out – last back' attitude to strikes, which appeared to be part of some sort of economic deathwish – especially as it was strapped with being on the wrong side of the north–south divide. Yet at the same time it was still grudgingly admired for its fierce sense of community, its racial tolerance and the steadfast good humour of its inhabitants in the face of their enduring adversity.

The same mixed feelings had been shown by Michael Heseltine when he went there after the Toxteth riots in 1981 to be shocked by the extent of the poverty, unemployment and dreadful housing. Despite its rabidly anti-Tory politics, the city had been singled out by the government for special help, principally expressed by holding the country's first national garden festival there and rebuilding the crumbling Albert Dock into a Thatcherite consumer showpiece to lure visitors and employment.

The same mixed attitudes were in evidence in the grot of the Sidney Smith that evening as the hacks huddled round the tables and discussed the front page that would hit the streets the next morning. Many, on a personal level, agreed with MacKenzie. Liverpool fans, for all they might not be the worst hooligans, deserved no better. They might be a bit better than some of the other scum, that was true, but they were still a loutish load of yobs. You wouldn't want to have them in your house – and there was the fact that they had definitely been out of control. Others, more knowledgeable about the circumstances and less inclined to automatically support the police, disagreed.

But speaking professionally they were unanimous in their verdict – the page was a total disaster. They shook their heads again in disbelief that MacKenzie could even think of running such an angle. It was so wrong, he could never get away with it, they told each other. This time the shit really was going to hit the fan, though there was one other aspect they all agreed on. You had to admire MacKenzie's bottle. He hadn't had 'IF YOU DO IT, DO IT BIG' pasted up on the wall for nothing. Personally, though, many of them would have chosen the second part of the slogan: 'OTHERWISE DON'T BOTHER, OLD BOY'. Watch yourself, they advised each other repeatedly. It's going to be like Elton John again. Make sure you can't be blamed for any part of it. Cover yourself. Some of them were also having a quiet mutter about another thought, and not for the first time. With this sort of stuff flying about, the *Mirror*, which at least appeared to recognise that there was a limit, was beginning to look more and more tempting.

When he had made up the front page, MacKenzie had kept his word to Harry Arnold by including the promised qualification 'some fans'. But for all the difference it made he might as well not have bothered. He had not gone for a clever punning headline or one of his masterstrokes of witty alliteration, but had instead chosen that bald statement which every newspaper prints at its peril: 'THE TRUTH'.

The two words were printed in huge letters on a massive WOB dominating the front-page layout. Underneath, in large lower-case type, were three subheadings:

Some fans picked pockets of victims

Some fans urinated on the brave cops

Some fans beat up PC giving kiss of life

The story started:

> Drunken Liverpool fans viciously attacked rescue workers as they
> tried to revive victims of the Hillsborough soccer disaster, it was
> revealed last night.
>
> Police officers, firemen and ambulance crew were punched,
> kicked and urinated upon by a hooligan element in the crowd.
>
> Some thugs rifled the pockets of injured fans as they were
> stretched out unconscious on the pitch.
>
> Sheffield MP Irvine Patnick revealed that in one shameful
> episode a gang of Liverpool fans noticed that the blouse of a girl
> trampled to death had risen above her breasts.
>
> As a policeman struggled in vain to revive her, the mob
> jeered: 'Throw her up here and we will **** her.'

The story went on: 'One furious policeman who witnessed
Saturday's carnage stormed: "As we struggled in appalling
conditions to save lives, fans standing further up the terrace were
openly urinating on us and the bodies of the dead."'

A 'high-ranking' police officer was quoted as saying: 'The fans
were just acting like animals. My men faced a double hell – the
disaster and the fury of the fans who attacked us.'

At the end of the story the MP, Patnick, was quoted as saying: 'I
have kept quiet about this because I did not want to inflame a
delicate situation. But these are stories told to me by policemen
just after it had happened. . . . one important question that must
be answered is the part alcohol played in this whole tragic
business.'

The *Sun* was not the only paper to carry the story. It had already
been the splash in the last edition of the local Sheffield *Star* the
previous evening and everybody had it. *The Times* and *Today*,
which had now joined the News International stable after being
bought by Murdoch, also splashed on it, along with the *Star*,
which went in hardest after the *Sun* with a front page headed
'DEAD FANS ROBBED BY DRUNK THUGS'. But the *Star* had pulled
back from the edge by tacking on a prominent WOB which
qualified the headline by adding: 'WHAT COPS SAY ABOUT
HILLSBORO'.

The *Sun*'s story was a classic smear, rolling up all the elements used to such great effect early in MacKenzie's editorship with 'RED PETE "WENT TO GAY OLYMPICS" '. All the allegations were non-attributable. They were either made by unnamed policemen or, where attributed to named people like Patnick, were second-hand repeats of things which they only said they had been told, but which they had no direct knowledge of themselves and did not claim to have checked for accuracy.

But for MacKenzie they had two important attributes – they gave the police a chance to fire back and were therefore good news for a paper whole-heartedly supporting the boys in blue. And they precisely fitted his formula by publicising the half-baked ignorant prejudice being voiced all over the country. And there was no lawyer to hold him back. The allegations, if unprovable, were an outrageous libel of all the people involved but they were legally safe as they did not name any names – as Liverpool City Council found out later when it debated suing the paper. The Inkies, who might possibly have been the last stop, especially if he had used 'YOU SCUM', were long gone.

But although Millwall fans and people not close to the story might not know the truth, or even care about it very much, on the Wednesday when the devastating headline hit the streets, most of Liverpool did. Later on the picture which was by now common knowledge was to be confirmed by Lord Justice Taylor. In many ways the events had not been that difficult to reconstruct. Comprehensive analysis based on replaying the television cover-age and examining the mass of press photos showed most of what had taken place. More important were the statements of the fans who had actually been there. Despite its size, Liverpool was still a close-knit community, and the majority of the fans who had been at Hillsborough were part of the even closer community of dedicated followers faithfully attending all the club's games and with great experience of crowd situations. By pooling their knowledge, recollections and the visual material, they had arrived at an analysis of the disaster which had been largely confirmed by excellent reporting in the local press and on local television.

The conclusion was that some fans had been drinking – including some of those who had died. Many had been boisterous in the pubs doing a roaring trade before the match. But this was all par for the course and drinking had had nothing to do with the tragedy, as Lord Justice Taylor was to confirm. As to the specific allegations presented by the *Sun* as 'THE TRUTH', there was no evidence of any kind to support them, and none was ever to be produced. A stark letter in one of the Unpopulars did agree that it was true some fans had urinated and vomited. But, the letter pointed out, that was what people did when the life was being squeezed out of them like toothpaste out of a tube.

The anger which erupted on Merseyside jammed Billy Butler's lines at Radio Merseyside once again. As Butler quickly realised, this time it had a new, harder edge. The callers were not just reacting to the story in a blind, emotional way. They were displaying the righteous anger springing from their certain knowledge that 'THE TRUTH' was a pack of lies. As it had done with the previous outrage over the *Mirror* pictures, the station rang the *Sun* and asked for a spokesman to put the paper's side of the case. They were told they would be rung back. When no call came they rang again, to be given the same promise. But as Butler was soon telling his listeners, the 'caring' *Sun* apparently did not even have the decency to state its position by issuing a 'no comment' – never mind coming on the line to face its critics.

Meanwhile people in Liverpool were turning their anger on copies of the paper itself. Some newsagents put it under the counter; others refused to sell it at all. At nearby Kirkby, the new town continuously featured in the Unpopulars as the prime example of disastrous 1960s planning, people drifting into the run-down shopping precinct started talking to each other and then organised an impromptu meeting. Somebody suggested calling the local Granada TV news, and a crew arrived to film people burning copies of the paper – a protest which was being carried out independently elsewhere. All over the city copies of the paper were being ripped up, trampled and spat upon. People carrying it in the street found it snatched out of their hands and torn to shreds in front of them; the paper entirely disappeared from Ford's plant at Halewood and dozens of landlords banned it from their premises.

The *Echo*, which that day had been named regional daily paper of the year in the *UK Press Gazette* National Awards, came out at lunchtime with the angry front-page lead: 'We challenge the London papers and the Sheffield police: 'PRODUCE YOUR EVIDENCE'. Printed below was an unsolicited statement from the Merseyside Police Federation describing the South Yorkshire Police Federation's allegations as 'despicable' and dissociating itself from them.

Back at Radio Merseyside Butler's advice to the distraught and furious callers who continued to bombard the station was to urge them not to buy the paper. He didn't see any point in trying to complain to scum like the *Sun*. The station's own experience was proving it at that very moment. It had now been on the phone to Wapping many, many times and was still being fobbed off with empty promises that it would be rung back. Butler knew only too well how effective this stone-walling tactic always was. Sooner or later you could be relied on to give up and go away – as his station did in the end when the promised call never materialised.

For years, faced with this sort of situation, Butler had given the same advice to regular complainants who were usually moaning about the price of either beer or petrol. 'Go to another pub – or stop drinking altogether,' he always told them. 'Use another garage or, better still, leave the car behind and get on the bus.' From bitter experience he knew that the advice was seldom heeded.

On a national level the outcry was taken up by Brian Hayes, like Butler a veteran of twenty years of listening to the chronic whinges of *Sun*-style listeners from demographic groups C2, D and E, whom he lambasted on his daily phone-in on LBC radio. Hayes, another media personality who had been personally outraged by the *Sun* story, was currently hosting *Out of Order*, a studio-based TV show which took up the cudgels on behalf of wrongs perpetrated on ordinary people. The programme was given an extra edge in the circumstances by being made in Manchester.

As the focus of the show Hayes had instigated a crude but effective slot using the formula parodied in masterly fashion by *Monty Python*'s classic 'Blackmail' sketch. The slot was preceded by interviews with members of the studio audience, including a Liverpool fan who had escaped but was on crutches. The *Sun* story was universally condemned by the audience but, as Billy Butler was finding in Liverpool, the overall reaction had now moved on from anger to a feeling of sickened sadness at the monstrous slur. Former *Sun* readers joined in by expressing their sadness at what the paper had done, vowing never to read it again.

Hayes then began his 'Blackmail' slot. The camera framed him sitting at a desk, on top of which was a framed photograph of MacKenzie, wearing his customary smirk, a red telephone and a giant egg-timer. Hayes explained that MacKenzie had been asked to come on the programme, but had refused. He was therefore going to start without him. However, the *Sun* editor had been given the number of the red telephone and all he had to do to stop him talking was to ring in. Hayes turned over the egg-timer and the sand started running.

'Life's pretty simple if you're a *Sun* reader,' he began.

> It's all knockabout, exciting stuff featuring a cast of clichés which parade through the pages for your entertainment. You know – the Japanese are fiendish, the French are Frogs, the Germans are Krauts, women are sex-mad housewives, and randy pop stars roam the nightclubs two-timing their girlfriends with anyone they fancy.
>
> Mr MacKenzie, you're living in cartoon land where no one ever gets hurt and nothing lasts for longer than a moment. But the pain you and your paper cause to many people lasts much longer than the moment it takes to read the page. Titillation for a few column inches destroys lives, Mr MacKenzie.
>
> Tell us why you printed the photograph of a distraught London rape victim shortly after the attack. Tell us why you make up interviews. . . . Tell us why you do this, Mr MacKenzie.

291

Of course, you know, accidents do happen. Just last week a hospital consultant wrote to you telling how a child's life had been saved because the mother spotted the symptoms of meningitis in time. She read about them in the *Sun*. So there you see, Kelvin – you can do it if you try.

Why do you have an inferiority complex about ethnic groups? You seem to be frightened of them, so you attack them. You appeal to the lowest common denominator such as the swastika-tattooed, Union-Jack-carrying, brainless wonders and you insult the rest of your readers with trivia about TV and showbiz and, more importantly, lies. . . .

Hayes then briefly outlined two lying *Sun* stories before finishing off, as the sand ran out: 'And this week you danced on the graves of ninety-five football fans under the banner headline "THE TRUTH". The Hillsborough disaster should have brought out the best in your paper, but it seems to me it probably brought out the worst. Mr MacKenzie, your paper lied again and you've had your chance to reply tonight. But you chose not to take it. Maybe some of your millions of readers will think twice before reaching into their pockets for twenty pence to buy the *Sun*.' The studio audience broke into thunderous applause.

But both Butler and Hayes had already been overtaken by events. *Sun* readers in Liverpool had voted spontaneously with their feet and sales of the paper had collapsed. Over at the *Echo* veteran news editor Alf Green was astonished. He had never come across anything like it in his experience of newspapers. The news trade being notoriously secretive about sales, completely accurate figures are always hard to come by, but reliable inside estimates were soon indicating that on the area round Merseyside, including Broad Green, Bootle, Southport, Ormskirk, Birkenhead and the Wirral, *Sun* sales had gone through the floor. From sales before the disaster of 524,000 copies a day, the paper had crashed to 320,000 – a loss of 204,000, or 38.9 per cent. News International themselves admitted to losing 40,000 readers – a drop from 140,000 to 100,000 – within the central area of Merseyside. The *Star*, which had cynically rushed to retrieve itself by splashing with 'LIES' the following day, was also affected, but not as badly. The *Mirror*, which had carried the story but in a much more downbeat way, had risen from 634,000 to 708,000, or an increase of 11.7 per cent.

The enormous strength of feeling had crossed into the trade, where a handful of newsagents in the city did not even want to sell the paper at all. They were soon whipped into line by the distributors reminding them they had an obligation to take the *Sun* along with all the papers – whatever their personal opinion. Newspapers who reacted by putting the paper under the counter received visits from *Sun* reps enforcing their further obligation to display the Wapping product as prominently as its rivals.

But there was nothing anybody could do to force people actually to buy the thing. The heaps of unsold returned copies piling up in the warehouse day after day were showing that the boycott was being kept up. The *Sun* consoled itself with the reminder that there had been occasions like this before, most recently with the slumps coinciding with some of the Elton John allegations. But these dips had always been temporary. Previous experience proved the punters could be relied on to have short memories. A few might have been lost for good during the wild fluctuations of the Bingo Wars, but overall the Currant Bun was proud of the fact that its fans in Liverpool were just as loyal as in the rest of the country. Market research proved that in most cases they had been buying the paper for years precisely to read the kind of outrageous, over-the-top stories of which 'THE TRUTH' was just another example. The *Sun* decided it was just a question of riding out the storm. There was, however, one terrible irony. News International seconded John Murray, the Wapping Personal Counsellor, to help volunteers manning the city's disaster helpline, at a time when some callers were coming through because of fresh distress engendered by the *Sun*'s brutally insensitive story.

But as the weeks went by, the *Sun* began to realise that this time the readers were not dutifully returning to the fold as confidently predicted. Instead sales were continuing to bump along at their new pathetically low level and the full scale of the financial disaster was becoming apparent. Newsagents were slashing their regular orders by as much as 80 per cent. The *Mirror*, which had raised £1 million for the disaster fund by increasing its cover price, was piling into Liverpool to seize the opportunity it had been given and rapidly gaining more ground.

Slowly the whole trade began to wake up to the fact that the *Sun*'s sales graph was tracking that of food products which had been tampered with or had objects inserted in them in attempts at blackmail. The food companies had made desperate efforts to win back customers by putting new seals on jars and placing reassuring ladies in supermarkets. But they had been finding that once consumers had been scared off most had permanently switched to other brands and were proving impossible to win back. Now precisely the same sales message was coming out of Merseyside about the *Sun*. A huge number of its readers had personally discovered their Currant Bun contained razor blades. They had reacted, and were continuing to react, accordingly.

Part Four

Chapter 16

The Bonfire of the Tabloids

On 11 October 1988 the playwright Alan Bennett rose in St James's Church, Piccadilly, to speak at the memorial service for Russell Harty, the television chat-show host who had died earlier that year. In the congregation were a number of leading figures from the worlds of television and the arts, including Sir Ian Trethowan, the former BBC director-general, Melvyn Bragg, David Frost, Frank Muir and Lord Snowdon.

Ned Sherrin, Sue Lawley and John Birt, the BBC's new deputy director, had all given readings. Now Bennett, as Harty's oldest friend, was to give the chief oration on this sad and emotional occasion. Bennett paid his tribute, as was his duty, but also took the extraordinary step of using the oration as a platform for an angry 'recrimination' against the 'gutter press', indirectly blaming Rupert Murdoch's *News of the World* for his old friend's death.

Bennett explained to the congregation that Harty had never made a secret of his homosexuality, seeing it as neither an affliction nor a crusade. 'But with the gutter press systematically trawling public life for sexual indiscretions, he knew he was in a delicate position,' he said. 'So when in March last year the *News of the World* set him up, then broke to an unstartled public the "shocking news", Russell thought his career was over.'

The story Bennett was referring to had been run on 1 March 1987, only five days after the original Elton John story had been splashed in the *Sun*. It was based on a statement by 'handsome six-footer' Dean Cradock, a twenty-year-old rent-boy working for the Ecstasy escort agency, which ran magazine ads offering 'especially selected stunners' for 'home/hotel visits'.

The story was headlined 'SMACK HAPPY HARTY, MY £60-A-NIGHT LOVER' with the strap 'EXPOSED: The secret sordid life of chat show king who mixes with the mightiest in the land.' The revelations were painfully dull by bonk journalism standards. Cradock merely stated he had met Harty at a flat in Lexham Gardens, Earls Court, where 'he asked me to massage him, and smacked me'. Harty paid him £60. But the *News of the World* stretched the thin material to a double-page spread by gratuitously adding five pictures showing Harty in the company of Mrs Thatcher, Princess Di, Michael Parkinson, Terry Wogan, Kate Bush, Cliff Richard and the BBC newsreader Jan Leeming.

Bennett then explained that, certain that offers of work were bound to dwindle, Harty had decided to try to save his career by working harder than he had ever worked before, accepting every offer that came his way. He had always been very busy, making documentaries and writing a column as well as hosting his chat-shows.

Ironically he had not lost any work, but he had been right in his first instinct that he was finished. 'The gutter press had finished him, because they had panicked him into working so hard that by the time he was stricken with hepatitis, he was an exhausted man.'

Bennett went on to explain how the *News of the World* story had started a flurry of press activity in Giggleswick, near Skipton, Yorkshire, where Harty lived. 'Reporters intermittently visited his home village for more than a year, bribing local children for information about his life, forcing their way into the school – even trying to bribe the local vicar.'

The activity by the pack had placed Harty's home under virtual siege. Reporters sat on his doorstep, searched through his dustbins, harassed neighbours, chased his car and forced their way into the public school in the village, where he had once been a master. The attempted bribe to the vicar was in the devious form of the offer of a large 'anonymous' contribution to the restoration fund for the church roof. But the reporters were disappointed. The villagers closed ranks and displayed a fierce loyalty to his privacy, appalled by what was happening.

More than a year later, in the early hours of 4 May 1988, Harty was rushed to St James Hospital, Leeds. The *Sun* had chosen the same day to run a feature on 'The life and times of Russell Harty' under the headline: 'I'D RATHER BE IN BED WITH A GOOD BOOK THAN A GOOD LOVER.' The article was the latest instalment in the paper's obsession with his private life. 'Over the past 18 months,' the paper claimed, 'Russell has been linked with teenage rent boys and was reported to have been sharing his home with a teenage boy.'

The Fleet Street pack converged on the gates of St James, the biggest hospital in Europe and at that time probably the most famous because of a Yorkshire Television fly-on-the-wall series about 'Jimmy's' – as it was affectionately nicknamed.

Professor Monty Losowsky, the liver specialist treating Harty, tried to deal with the situation by calling a press conference and giving a full medical briefing. He told the hacks that his patient was suffering from acute liver failure caused by hepatitis-B and firmly denied rumours that Harty had AIDS. He was in a critical condition.

Now Bennett described the scenes at Jimmy's as he continued his oration. 'As he fought for his life, one newspaper took a flat opposite, and a camera with a long lens was trained on the window of his ward. The nurses would point it out when you visited. A reporter posing as a junior doctor smuggled himself into the ward, and demanded to see his notes. Every lunchtime, journalists took the hospital porters across the road to the pub, to bribe them into taking photographs of him.'

Another ploy had been sending a huge spray of flowers, concealing the number of a paper's Manchester newsdesk and some money, to another patient in the intensive care unit. They were found by a nurse and never reached the patient, who was anyhow in no condition to receive flowers. The hospital, gallantly struggling to maintain good relations with the press, refused to reveal the identity of the paper responsible.

Bennett commented: 'One saw, in the tireless and unremitting efforts of the team at St James, the best of which we are capable, and in the equally tireless and rather better rewarded efforts of journalists, the worst. The final touch came when Russell was actually on his death-bed. The woman who had written the original story in the *News of the World* could not be restrained from telling the story of her investigative triumph.'

As the full sordidness of the story he was recounting sank in, Bennett concluded: 'Some of you may think that these kind of recriminations are out of place at a memorial service, and certain it is that Russell would not have approved.'

Referring to Harty's regular contribution to the *Sunday Times* of a column called 'Notebook', Bennett finished up by saying: 'Had he lived, he would have gone on going to Mr Murdoch's parties, and doing his column for a Murdoch newspaper. The world is like that. Or, at least, England is like that.'

Bennett did not mention how the hounding had continued after Harty's death on 8 June, five weeks after he had been admitted to the hospital. The *Sun* had sharpened up its vilification, safe in the knowledge that as he was dead Harty could not bring a libel action. It used as its vehicle the 'exclusive' memories of former Detective Chief Superintendent Drummond Gordon Marvin of Scotland Yard's Serious Crimes Squad. Marvin, known as 'Lee Marvin', and described as a 'top cop crimebuster', had just retired.

The article said that Harty's friends had claimed he had contracted his illness while filming a TV series in Europe, but that hepatitis-B could only be contracted 'in the same way as AIDS'. The original allegation that Harty had 'smacked' Cradock, the rent-boy, was expanded into his having 'beaten and sodomised' him, adding the fact that 'older men like Harty' were known as ' "chickenhawks" – who prey on vulnerable lads sucked into the cesspool of corruption and disease'.

The *Sun*'s normal style was simply to ignore criticism from the likes of Bennett. But this time it decided to hit back with A '*Sun Says*' leader on behalf of its sister paper:

It is absurd for his close friend, playwright Alan Bennett, to accuse the 'gutter press' of hounding Harty to an early grave.

And it is nauseating for showbiz stars at Harty's memorial service to cheer Bennett's claim.

Stress did not kill Russell Harty.

The truth is he died from a sexually transmitted disease.

The Press didn't give it to him. He caught it through his own choice.

By paying young rent boys to satisfy him, he broke the law.

Some, like ageing bachelor Mr Bennett, can see no harm in that.

He has no family.

But what if it had been YOUR SON whom Harty bedded?

As the *Sun* leader had identified, more than any other bonk journalism story the vilification of Harty by the *Sun* and the *News of the World* united important figures, principally in the media, in their attempts to find a way of stemming the flow of bonk journalism.

The *Sun* had also been responsible for another incident now being held up as one of the grossest invasions of privacy, which had also aroused widespread public odium. The *Sun*'s actions came after an attack on a vicar and his family in their home in Ealing, West London, in a case which was to become known as 'the vicarage rape'.

Three men, high on drugs and drink, broke into the vicarage in what started as a robbery and escalated into a brutal attack on the three inhabitants of the house. The vicar, who was fifty-three, was beaten repeatedly over the head with his own cricket bat, sustaining serious injuries including a fractured skull. The fiancé of the vicar's daughter received similar treatment. The daughter herself, a devout Christian and also a virgin, was then taken to another room by two of the men where they brutally attacked her sexually. She was subjected to multiple rape and buggery and forced to have oral sex.

The attack happened on a Friday and attracted huge publicity in the media next day. On the Sunday the vicar was still in hospital, but the rape victim and her sister came out of the vicarage to go to church with a small group of other people. The massed ranks of photographers and TV film crews openly took pictures of them all, with no attempt made to stop them. The purpose of the pictures was to cover the photographers for future events which might arise. The group picture also served another purpose, in that minor characters in the drama could be cut out of it and printed separately on their own.

It had always been tacitly agreed by all the papers that they did not identify rape victims, though there was no law against it. In this case nobody had been charged – which would have meant that legally a picture of the victim could not be printed. At that stage the massive police hunt had only got as far as centring on one of the attackers, who had been dubbed 'Spiderman' because he had a spider tattooed on his hand.

One of the many photographers among the pack was Roger Bamber, who had been with the *Sun* since the beginning, and had once won Photographer of the Year in the national press awards. After Bamber had taken a roll of film he biked it back to Wapping and stayed on the scene. He then found himself being pestered by the picture desk, demanding to know which of the two women was the rape victim, and which was her sister. Bamber co-operated, presuming that the careful enquiries were to ensure that there was no question of a picture of the victim being printed by mistake.

But when he returned to the office he found that the reason for the ultra-careful checking was exactly the opposite. MacKenzie was putting the picture of the victim on the front page. There had already been a great rumpus in the office about the decision. MacKenzie had been walking past the picture desk when he had seen the photograph, picked it up, and said he had got his front page. When objections were raised, he simply asked: 'Why not?'

It was a point that had never arisen before as far as the objectors were concerned. They all knew of the unwritten agreement by all the papers, and took it for granted it would be followed. But, as MacKenzie kept demanding them to tell him a reason why not, all they could say was that it was a matter of ethics. Legally, they had to admit, there was nothing to stop him. 'Right,' he said. 'It's going on the front page then.'

Bamber found the picture editor of the day very unhappy about what was happening. He protested as well. When he had been taking the pictures it had never occurred to him that there was any possibility of their being used. But Bamber could get no further than successfully having his credit removed.

MacKenzie had one answer to the identification point. The paper would not specifically name the victim or her father, the vicar. But it had already printed the following details about him on the Saturday, the day after the robbery: 'He has been a figure of controversy for ten years for his thoughts on sex and the Queen and repeatedly hit the headlines with a trendy new version of the National Anthem . . . which whipped up a storm of protest four years ago, and the book AND SO TO BED, giving advice about pre-marital sex.'

The picture of the rape victim was run on the front page on Monday as MacKenzie had decreed. There was a thin black line superimposed across her eyes but this was merely token. She was clearly recognisable. At the same time another tabloid, though not carrying the picture, printed names to the extent that if the two papers were put together, and then combined with the picture of the vicarage which several of them had run, it was simplicity itself for anyone interested to identify who she was, what she looked like and where she lived.

After the familiar grind through the Press Council bureaucracy the printing of the picture had been duly condemned. But as MacKenzie had correctly said, no other action could be taken against the paper. Once again he had gone further than anybody else. And got away with it.

The incident had been typical of the problem facing those demanding action to curb these excesses. The majority of invasion-of-privacy and bonk journalism stories could only be objected to on the grounds of standards, decency and ethics. Ironically for the complainants, most 'kiss and tells' were shining examples of high-class journalism apart from their subject matter and had been impeccably compiled to the highest standards of proof. Very few had been denied outright, or proceeded against at law, although some victims had quibbled about minor details.

The most notorious example of this had been the unfortunate 'Fyffe times a night' Sir Ralph Halpern. The *Mirror*, looking to bash Murdoch publications, had taken up cudgels on his behalf and given him a double-page spread to 'open his heart' (with an attentive lawyer beside him). The *Mirror* move came after the *News of the World* returned to the Halpern fray after a gap of several months to publish a new statement by his ex-bimbo Fiona Wright that Halpern had goosed Mrs Thatcher's bottom at a Downing Street party. The story quoted Wright as saying: 'Ralph told me he found Mrs T very sexy. He thought she had an attractive bottom.'

The next day the *Mirror* splashed Sir Ralph's reply under 'EVIL LIES', quoting him as saying that the story was 'an evil and disgusting invention'. He did, however, at the same time smirkingly refuse to deny the 'five times a night' allegation which had previously brought him to the attention of the general public as 'the bonking boss of Burton's.'

Robert Maxwell's paper then laid into News International with a leader punningly entitled 'THE BOTTOM OF THE BARREL', which many hacks found hard to take seriously.

> Never in the sleazy history of his newspapers has Rupert Murdoch published anything as revolting as yesterday's *News of the World*. . . . The allegation – of Mrs Thatcher giggling as Halpern pinched her bottom – bears all the hallmarks of the inventions for which the Murdoch press has become notorious.
>
> *The Times* and the *Sunday Times* tells up-market lies and the *Sun* and the *News of the World* trawl the gutter for their fantasies. . . .
>
> The *Daily Mirror* has little time for the Prime Minister's policies and even less for Sir Ralph's morals. But nothing she has ever said or done remotely deserves this kind of insulting tale.
>
> Politically Mr Murdoch has been the loyal parrot on Mrs Thatcher's shoulder. Yesterday she must have thought he was more like a carrion crow.

Those pushing for privacy laws had, however, been given recent encouragement by a jury implicitly backing the *Sun's* £1 million settlement with Elton John by awarding punitive £600,000 damages to Sonia Sutcliffe, the wife of the Yorkshire Ripper, against an aghast *Private Eye*. Editor Ian Hislop had announced that the satirical magazine would have to close saying: 'If that's justice, I'm a banana.' (The award was reduced to £60,000 on appeal.)

The massive jury settlements had indicated how outrage was moving from the Unpopulars to a much wider cross-section of the public, and MPs, receiving more and more letters of protest, had begun to realise that the issue was becoming one they needed to heed. Now the public outcry about Hillsborough roped in the entire public. Finally, the government had to act.

Hillsborough could not have come at a more unfortunate time for the papers. Two Private Member's Bills had churned through the machinery of the Commons and were coming on to the floor of the House. The first, the Right of Reply Bill, sponsored by Tony Worthington, Labour MP for Clydebank and Milngavie, went before the House as scheduled on Friday, 21 April – five days after Hillsborough.

Worthington already accepted his bill was doomed. Although theoretically attractive, the question of effective right of reply conjured up visions of entire newspapers composed of long, boring wrangles and nit-picking details. Nobody could explain how it could work in practice, it did not have government backing, and Tory backbenchers had anyhow run the Bill into the sand of parliamentary procedure by the tactic of prolonged discussion which had prevented its report stage being completed.

The morning the Bill was due in the Commons, the government pre-empted it. The Home Office hurriedly announced that a special committee was to be set up to conduct a wide review of the press and deal with all the concerns raised by invasion of privacy. The review was to be completed within a year. Home Office Minister Timothy Renton specifically cited the techniques used by the tabloids in their pursuit of bonk journalism exposés –

the 'doorstepping' of members of the public, intrusions into private lives, clandestine photography, persistent trick questions and harassment of ordinary and innocent people at times of great distress. He said editors and proprietors were now 'on probation'.

The only Tory supporter for the Bill, Jonathan Aitken, MP for Thanet West and great-nephew of Lord Beaverbrook, replied that 'the thoroughly evil clique of lower tabloid editors' were as suitable for probation as Jack the Ripper or the Boston Strangler. There was even a warning for the proprietors from Norman Tebbit during the debate on the Bill, which was still held despite the announcement about the committee. 'Newspaper proprietors must be beginning to think that, however many friends there are of a free press in this House,' Tebbit said, 'sooner or later we will be rolled over by the forces of those who say we are prepared to dilute the freedoms of the press in order to deal with a perceived wrong.'

David Mellor, who took over from Renton shortly afterwards, astonished observers used to mealy-mouthed Home Office prevarication by saying in a television interview: 'The tabloids are now drinking in the Last Chance Saloon.' (This remark caused huge merriment at dry Wapping. Since the Tebbit 'you must be fucking joking' incident, executives had been allowed to keep booze in special executive fridges which were locked.)

Mellor explained how his thinking had been changed by the way in which the tabloids had dealt with Hillsborough: 'I couldn't believe it when I arrived in my office on the Monday morning and saw some of the pictures, particularly in the *Mirror* – people who were in extreme distress or who were perhaps dying. I think it's intrusive, I think it's morbid, I think it's disgusting to think that the public are interested in seeing death as close up as that. The problem is that there are people who are interested. So it isn't only damaging to the press. It's damaging to society when there are no standards.'

Mellor dismissed the *Mirror*'s 'NEVER AGAIN' argument. 'I think that's a rationalisation of sensationalism driven by the circulation war, and throwing out of the window standards acceptable in a civilised society. I think it is in the public interest that there should be a free press in Britain. But what is of interest to the public is not always in the public interest. The fact that some people are morbid and curious about death and are morbidly preoccupied with other people's private lives is not a justification for it. . . . People have become almost in despair over some of the standards that prevail.'

The second Private Member's Bill, now made redundant, was the Right to Privacy Bill started off by Bill Cash, which had attracted much wider support among MPs. The Bill had been sponsored by John Browne, Conservative MP for Winchester, who had proved to be a particularly unfortunate champion of the privacy cause. Browne was already under heavy fire from the Unpopular investigative team of David Leigh and Paul Lashmar at the *Observer*, and after being condemned by a parliamentary committee for concealing business interests from the MPs' register, eventually agreed not to stand at the next election.

The Right to Privacy Bill sought to protect information, including the privacy of the home and personal communications, relationships, behaviour, health and financial affairs, throwing up yet again the earnest and academic debate about press freedom and the public interest. At a seminar on media freedom at the London School of Economics other Unpopular editors agreed with Andrew Neil, editor of the *Sunday Times*, when he blamed 'the excesses of the tabloids' for the bad odour the press was held in. Max Hastings, editor of the *Daily Telegraph*, said the problem they were facing now was how to raise press standards 'to a point where the British public believes press freedom and integrity is something worth talking about'. The keynote speaker, Dr David Owen of the SDP, said he did not believe the law could clean up the press – the proprietors had to do it themselves.

The Unpopulars' argument, as always, was that restrictions on press freedom would prevent them from printing stories and conducting enquiries which exposed genuine wrongs, although stories of this type had largely dried up of late. There was great tub-thumping about the government's hypocrisy in being opposed to curbs on the press, yet using the Official Secrets Act and injunctions against papers to stop them publishing things like extracts from Peter Wright's *Spycatcher* book. Ken Morgan, the director of the Press Council, added that he was worried that 'irresponsible or offensive behaviour' was building support for legislation. The *Sun* had headed the league of complaints considered by the Council in 1987 with fifteen upheld, one partly upheld and six rejected followed by seven upheld and fifteen rejected in 1988. The *Sun*, however, fiercely defended the right to press freedom in a '*Sun* Says' leader, which Murdoch, who had become an American citizen in 1985 took a big part in writing. It declared:

The Establishment does not like the *Sun*. Never has.

We are so popular they fear our success, since they do not understand the ordinary working man and woman.

The *Sun* has never much worried about the views of the Establishment. Until now.

Now we are concerned.

Because there is a growing band of people in positions of influence and privilege who want OUR newspaper to suit THEIR convenience. They wish to conceal from the readers' eye anything they find annoying or embarrassing to themselves.

Living lies and hypocrisy on high can have no place in our society.

If a star who profits enormously from being idolised takes drugs we shall say so. Such an act is a breach of public trust.

If a TV performer who sets himself up as a paragon of domestic decencies is a lying sham, we shall say so.

When politicians supposedly serving the public are on the private make, we shall tell our readers. . . .

Our readers want us to be questioning, courageous and free. The 'privacy' lobby would prefer tame, timid newspapers that are as much the house magazine of the Establishment as Pravda is the parrot voice of the Kremlin.

For the Sun's part we shall fight to stay exactly as we are.

It is not just our struggle.

It is the struggle of all those concerned for freedom in Britain.

But privacy, and the setting up of the special government committee, was only one of the problems being heaped on the paper and its readers as the Thatcher dream began to implode. Soon after the paper's eighteenth anniversary in 1987, market research had indicated that *Sun* readers were getting older, a problem which affects all newspapers as their readers grow up alongside them. The promotions department under Graham King, responsible for the paper's original slam-bang commercials, had rejuvenated the competitions side by supplementing bingo with Lotto. In this variation the players choose the numbers, rather than having them chosen for them, and research had already shown it to have higher youth appeal. The move had been such a success the first game had gone into the *Guinness Book of Records* after it attracted 4,305,162 registered entrants – a 100 per cent entry rate on sales, which compared with the norm of 2.5 per cent. (The least successful competition ever on the paper had been for twenty firkins of beer, which attracted a mere thirteen entries.)

On the editorial side various moves had been tried to increase the youth appeal, and following the Great Redundancy Offer of 1988 younger and younger hacks were being employed, all earning between £25,000 and £30,000 a year and mostly in their mid-twenties. Although Petrie continued banging on about his 'young eagles', the older hacks still left on the paper called them 'MacKenzie Rottweilers' in tribute to the way they were sent out to 'monster' their victims, or, as MacKenzie told them, 'piss all over them.'

The nation's shopping malls were emptying as credit victims retired hurt to nurse their mortgages and before the 1989 Budget a furious '*Sun* Says' screamed on their behalf, 'GIVE US OUR DOUGH LAWSON!' castigating the Chancellor as Maggie's latest enemy within. The paper sympathised with its readers by running a bitter piece on the Money Page entitled 'Five Things to Do with a Dead Estate Agent'.

The *Sun* had also thrown itself whole-heartedly behind the latest attempt to deal with the damage – the Red Nose Day organised by Comic Relief in March. Acres of space were devoted to 'fun' events and the paper added its own coarse spin to the proceedings with stories like car owners placing two red noses on their radiator grilles to simulate a pair of tits. The paper's underlying theme was a whining plea for charity to begin at home now that things were getting harder. It reported approvingly on the way the country had turned itself into a giant version of a university Rag Week with thousands of juvenile stunts, like sitting in baths of cold baked beans and porridge all day. Other commentators had acidly made the point that it would have been more productive to cut out the middleman and simply send the beans or porridge to starving people in the first place.

The paper tried to make up for its readers' vanished funds by obsessively concentrating on the mega-sums being raked in by young superstars like Madonna and Michael 'Wacko' Jackson, who were being handed up to £3 million a time to make ads for giant corporations like Coca-Cola. This renewed concentration on youth, which was part of the repositioning for younger readers, also marked the beginning of a return to the days of standard showbiz hype after the abrupt halt to bonk journalism, which at one stage had even speculated that raunchy man-eating Madonna might be a lesbian.

Dave Hogan, the *Sun*'s favourite freelance paparazzi, was beginning to enjoy life again. Bonk journalism had complicated relations with the celebs on whom he depended for a living, because, although he had not specialised in the hunt for compromising pictures, he had inevitably been tarred with the same brush as more aggressive colleagues doing the real stuff. After regarding him as a leper the PR agents were co-operating again and offering photo-opportunities, relaxed in the knowledge that they would now get good clean, wholesome publicity.

Hogan had seen the sign of the change in the times when all the tabloids turned down a picture story about a squeaky-clean female teenybopper idol who had been rushed to hospital after a drugs overdose. Before Elton John they would have paid thousands for the pictures. Now they wouldn't touch them with a barge pole.

The new soft agenda was also perfect for exploiting the growing concern about the environment and the *Sun* duly acquired a 'Mr Green' in the person of Patrick Hennessy, an Old Etonian and a keen young Oxford graduate. Instructing him in his new post MacKenzie ended up by bawling over his shoulder as he shot off down the newsroom: 'And by the way – not too many fucking whales!'

The Mr Green decision had been made on the back of the Green Party's startling two-million vote in the Euro-elections, which had elevated their media profile from the normal sneering about brown rice, sandals and Neil from the *Young Ones*. The arrival of the Greens in force had aroused deep suspicions in Garry Bushell's gigantic 156-IQ brain. 'We ought to watch these people,' he told a group of hacks darkly. 'If they ever get into power they'll turn from green to red quicker than a frog in a blender.'

The success of the Greens, heralding the changed priorities of the coming decade, was another factor overshadowing what should have been the triumph of Maggie's tenth anniversary. But the Tory publicity machine had already decided that the milestone should be celebrated in a muted fashion, after Thatcher had raised public alarm by saying she would go 'on and on and on'. The *Sun* toed the line on 3 May by dutifully splashing 'THAT'S GRAND SON' above a picture of a grinning Thatcher holding her grandson, brought from Dallas by Mark and his American wife Diane, to provide a suitable photo-opportunity.

'Tough-talking Premier Margaret Thatcher cradled her baby grandson in her arms for the first time yesterday . . . and her heart melted,' gushed John Kay on the centre spread, 'Posing with two-month-old Michael on the steps of No. 10, Mrs Thatcher cooed: "Isn't he beautiful! Isn't he good! Isn't he peaceful!"'

Michael, blond, blue-eyed, and dressed in a blue and white sailor suit, slept throughout the photo-call, which Denis astutely avoided by going on a brief business trip of an undisclosed nature. Inside another kiddie pic bashed the Royals yet again with a telephoto shot of 'Royal rascal Prince William', with the headline WILLIE THE GROPER and subhead of 'Prince pinches teacher's bum.'

The day before the anniversary 'The *Sun* Says', under the crosshead of 'She's the best', had summarised Maggie's ten years as 'a decade which has seen a sea change in our fortunes'.

'Most of us have never before enjoyed such a high standard of living,' the paper stated. And, the paper showed its loyalty to Maggie was undiminished even though she was getting more unpopular. 'An opinion poll shows disenchantment with Mrs Thatcher,' the leader said. 'The voters want to bite the hand that feeds them. There is a clamour for a new leader. . . . We would put up with the Hunchback of Notre Dame at No. 10 if he could do the job half as well as her.'

On the same page as 'The *Sun* Says' an 'alternative view' was provided by Jimmy Reid, the former Communist shop steward who had led the work-in at Upper Clyde Shipbuilders at the start of the 1970s. Reid was now writing a weekly column for the paper, which he defended in an interview with the World's Worst by saying that the important thing was to communicate with the people, whatever their views. His favourite biblical quotation, he said, was 'spew out the lukewarm'. * Under the heading 'THATCHER LOUTS RULE OK?' Reid slammed Thatcher for having 'a philosophy uncluttered by sophisticated thoughts such as human kindness and care for others'.

Garry Bushell's Bushell on the Box column muddled the official line by slagging off at a TV show called *The Thatcher Years*, which had sought to put Mrs Thatcher in the dock, as 'slightly less riveting than the Grantham small claims court'. 'Why knacker the trial by narrowing the case to just economic arguments?' Bushell asked disingenuously, apparently unaware that 'The *Sun* Says' had done just that. Anyhow, as he pointed out, the prosecution in the programme had been nobbled by having 'that smug mug, Peter Jay' as 'prosecutor' – to the delight of the 'defence counsel' Norman Tebbit. 'Personally I'd like the idea of putting politicians on trial a lot better if we could reintroduce

* 'I know thy works, that thou art neither cold nor hot: I would thou wert cold or hot. So then because thou art lukewarm, and neither cold nor hot, I will spue thee out of my mouth' (Revelation, 3: 15, King James Version).

hanging,' Bushell ended up. (Earlier in the same week, to the hacks' great delight, Bushell had been slagged off in the 'Monday Moan' slot by his wife Carol, who had written complaining about her husband's 'ridiculous review' of the London Marathon. 'Garry is only jealous because he can't even run a bath,' she said, asking for the £5 Moan money to be donated to Great Ormond Street children's hospital.)

Rupert Murdoch and Anna dutifully made a special trip across the pond in Concorde for Thatcher's anniversary. They were personal guests at the celebratory dinner laid on at Chequers for her most important friends. As they raised their glasses, the Boss and she both had plenty to thank each other for during the past ten years. Between them they had seen off the trade union movement, risen to new heights of prosperity, and furthered the cause of the Americanisation of Britain. The world for both of them was a free place where enterprise ruled supreme.

But the toast they drank was as much to the future as the past. Ronnie might have gone in America, but their own special relationship was not yet over. Rather it was now moving into the realms of the extra-terrestrial as Murdoch staked the entire future of the Empire on an operation based in the unlikely setting of an industrial estate towards the end of the tube line in Osterley, West London.

Chapter 17

The Empire Strikes Back

Sky television was Rupert Murdoch's most spectacular gamble to date. It had started broadcasting via the Astra satellite in February 1989, three months before Maggie's tenth anniverary, with start-up costs estimated at £320 million, and the weekly loss had soon stabilised at £2 million as the station struggled to find an audience.

Sky was the logical development of Murdoch's underlying commercial strategy of tracking the members of the post-war baby boom. The *Sun* had cashed in during the 1970s by spicing up their naughty twenties. In the 1980s it had hyped their dreams of avarice and success when they were in their thirties. Now, the rationale ran, the chosen generation was into or approaching its forties, and becoming dull and boring – worried about the environment, the size of its mortgages and credit repayments, and the cost of its children's education and their subsequent job prospects. Sky had been carefully targeted at forty-year-old C and D males who had bought their houses and were now heavily into home entertainment, supplemented by visits to the off-licence and take-aways, which were all they could afford. The new service had been conceived in the boom years of the mid-1980s when the credit supply which the Cs and Ds were expected to use to buy their dishes was flowing freely. In the chillier financial climate of 1989 sales were spluttering badly as interest rates went sky high.

The overall Sky concept had received another major setback when Murdoch failed to get the Disney channel, which had been dubbed the 'dish driver' by the industry in recognition of its key role in the programming. Research had identified that the latest development in patterns of television watching was for families to split up inside their houses by going to different rooms to watch different channels.

The role of the Disney channel had been to enable Sky to be promoted as a group family activity. The substitute of the MTV pop music channel was proving adequate in its role of hooking in the kids with a vacuous televisual version of the John Blake Bizarre approach, but it was still a sideshow.

Murdoch had structured Sky's content on a deliberately non-provocative basis. The existing TV companies, as part of their axe-grinding about the new threat to the 'quality television' they provided, had taken out press ads to say that the new channels would be full of low-budget porn, with features like amateur housewife strippers. But the most daring thing they got from Sky Movies was the old classic *Emmanuelle*, after which the channel withdrew from the porn stakes.

But the real key to defusing criticism was Sky News, the twenty-four-hour news channel carried at ruinous expense to curry favour with the middle classes. The channel was attracting only a small audience as expected, for research showed that most punters were buying their dishes to watch films and sport. But by providing a straightforward, balanced and workmanlike service totally at variance with MacKenzie's 'SHOCK AND AMAZE ON EVERY PAGE' *Sun* formula, it was a symbol of bland respectability which the chattering classes found hard to fault. Mrs Thatcher was an early interviewee and Norman Tebbit, who had retired from the Tory Party chairmanship to spend more time with his wife, disabled in the Brighton bombing, got a job. Tebbit started work hosting a discussion show alongside Austin Mitchell, Labour MP for Grimsby, who was promptly stripped of his post in the shadow Cabinet by an angry Labour Party. Frank Bough, whose career in mainline television had been wrecked by Murdoch's newspapers, was brought in to host a chat-show, as was former *News of the World* editor, Derek Jameson.

But Murdoch's ownership of Sky TV was still politically sensitive because of the way it skirted strict Department of Trade regulations on cross-ownership of newspapers and television. According to the rules no national newspaper proprietor was allowed to own more than 30 per cent of a British television station, but the government had taken a very soft line on Sky. Murdoch had been permitted to define it as a European station on the grounds that, although it was produced in Britain, it broadcast via the European Astra satellite on European frequencies.

Partly due to the advent of Sky there had been a change of strategy at News International. The company had decided to drop its previous stance of either reacting defensively to criticism or trying to ignore it, moving instead to a more aggressive PR stragegy in which it was coming out to meet its critics. The change had been flagged by the appointment of Jane Reed as head of corporate affairs in March 1988. Reed, a dumpy woman and author of a book called *Kitchen Sink or Swim*, had been a successful women's magazine editor and as features editor on Eddie Shah's original *Today* had been one of the few execs to survive the shake-up after Murdoch bought it.

In 1989 the Broadcasting Bill was before Parliament, giving MPs the chance to tighten up cross-ownership rules. News International lobbied hard behind the scenes, pointing out that Sky's studios could beam programmes up to the satellite from anywhere in Europe. If Sky was defined as a British station, threatening Murdoch's ownership, the Osterley studios (which were scheduled to transfer to Wapping in Phase 3) could be closed and the station moved to somewhere in Europe, losing 2,000 British jobs.

The argument showed how little power national governments had in reality over international operators like Murdoch. But Sky was still politically vulnerable to comparisons with the *Sun* and, as 1989 marked the paper's twentieth anniversary, in the current climate there was an obvious peg for pundits and MPs to trot out the argument that the paper had led a twenty-year charge downmarket which Sky was about to mirror in the world of television.

The sort of sneering jibes News International had anticipated from the Unpopulars had come in the first week of Sky's operations when the *Observer*'s television critic, John Naughton, commented on the advent of what he called 'tabloid TV' by revealing that the technical expert from the BBC's *Blue Peter* had calculated that sending the signals from Osterley via the satellite to a house in London involved a journey of 71,546 kilometres, 'which could make Murdochvision the longest garbage-run in history'.

In August Murdoch fought back with a speech at the Edinburgh International Television Festival when he said: 'Much of what passes for quality on British television really is no more than a reflection of the values of a narrow elite. What I have in mind is best illustrated by many of the up-market costume soap operas which the British system produces, in which strangulated English accents dominate dramas which are played out in rigid, class-structured settings.'

Having got the first punch in at Edinburgh Jane Reed prepared for the counter-attack on the *Sun*. The main danger was identified as *Hard News*, a new series started on Channel Four by an independent production company. The show's opening graphics indicated its approach with ordinary people frustrated and trapped by stylised newspaper headlines and columns which nightmarishly came to life to strangle them. The programme had instantly made a name for itself by ripping into all the papers, especially the *Sun*. MacKenzie and News International hated it.

One of the first programmes had attempted to recreate a famous incident three years previously when John Sweeney, an ambitious young left-wing freelance writer, had doorstepped MacKenzie at his house on behalf of *Tatler*. The enterprising Sweeney had obtained a commission from the society magazine to give the *Sun*'s editor a taste of his own medicine. He duly arrived chez MacKenzie at 6.40 a.m. on a bright June morning. Sweeney described MacKenzie's house as 'an ugly rhomboid tetrahedron of brown slate and whitewashed brick . . . part of a newish housing estate whiffing strongly of polish for fake brass knockers, estate agents' hype and cheap money'.

Sweeney, accompanied by a photographer, had engaged MacKenzie in conversation from behind the bedroom curtains, but had soon been reduced to the bottom line of shouting through the letter-box to ask MacKenzie what he called 'the John Mortimer question'. 'Do you believe in God?' He had received no reply.

Unknown to Sweeney his activity had sent MacKenzie into a panic, and he had immediately phoned the office, where Petrie, early bird as always, was already at his desk. Petrie, expecting the normal early-morning bollocking, had at first thought it was a joke when his editor gabbled that he was being doorstepped by *Tatler*. Then, when MacKenzie persuaded him it was serious, he nearly fell off his chair laughing at the incongruity of the publication that had hemmed his editor into this corner.

MacKenzie then started pleading for advice and demanding to know what he should do. 'Try a reverse ferret,' Petrie replied, barely able to conceal his mirth as he rattled off a series of anti-monstering instructions. But the inexperienced MacKenzie botched the job, and the chauffeur was reduced to nudging Sweeney out of the way with the bumper as he reversed the Jaguar down the drive to the front door. Sweeney informed *Tatler* readers that MacKenzie's sudden scuttling emergence from his house and leap into his Jaguar had been like a scene from the nature programme *Badger Watch*. 'As it left Kelvin indulged us with a big raffish smile, acknowledging our cheek. But before the car took him entirely out of view Kelvin's expression changed: as his limousine headed for central London he looked like a man who has just had his face rubbed in doggy-poo. The man who has ordered more paparazzi stake-outs of pregnant Princesses and bereaved relatives than most of us have had toad-in-the-hole, did not, it seemed, appreciate the piquancy of our dawn door-stepping.'

MacKenzie had attempted to make light of the incident in the office by telling the hacks: ''Ere, you'll never believe this. Some fat c*** was sitting outside my house last night. What an arsehole!' But more of the real story had soon gone round the office and there was much sniggering in the Sidney Smith that evening. *Tatler*!

The repetition for *Hard News* had not proved so successful. But the item had only confirmed the News International opinion that this was the programme that needed to be spiked. The initiative was taken by MacKenzie, who rang an astonished Paul Woolwich, *Hard News*'s editor, to offer an interview with the paper. He *News*'s editor, to offer an interview with the paper. He explained affably that it was not really his idea, but Murdoch's. Rupert felt they should be a little more accountable and explain themselves a little better. 'Anybody would think, the way we're treated, we run the country,' he moaned. 'What we want to do is show people we're not the great monsters we're made out to be.'

MacKenzie would not be doing the show himself, he told Woolwich. It was OK for a smoothies like David Montgomery, the softly spoken editor of *Today*. But MacKenzie said, it was not his job to go in front of the cameras – he was too busy editing the *Sun*. He added in an unusually modest fashion that anyhow he was not very good at that sort of thing. He wouldn't even be watching the programme when it was broadcast, he added, but instead would 'probably go down the pub'.

But, he told Woolwich, News International did have a representative for them in the shape of Martin Dunn, the former New York correspondent and architect of the 'BENN ON THE COUCH' scam, who was now his deputy editor. Not only was Dunn a senior member of the team, he had been sent on a television training course, MacKenzie explained, adding that Dunn was 'young and articulate.' (MacKenzie's nicknames for him behind the scenes were 'the Patsy Kensit of journalism – better looks, less talent' and 'the handsome Munchkin'.)

Woolwich, very excited by his programme being the first to get a *Sun* representative, accepted MacKenzie's offer with alacrity and started organising the programme. It was an experience he said afterwards he never wished to repeat. Woolwich had dealt with News International before when he had made a documentary about Wapping for *Panorama* shortly after the move. After weeks of negotiation he had succeeded in being the first programme to be allowed to take a television crew inside the complex. But the facility had been granted very much on the company's terms. Woolwich had had to wait for weeks on permanent standby before he had finally been rung and told to go to the plant immediately. It had been very hush-hush, and he had been told he could film for only twenty minutes. Inside the plant he had met MacKenzie, who had warned him not to film him under any circumstances and told him in a disgusted fashion: 'I don't know why Rupert fucking allowed you fuckers in here.'

This time round, despite the fact that MacKenzie had made the initial approach, Woolwich found nothing seemed to have changed. News International was still intensely suspicious. After the now familiar weeks of negotiation he had finally had an extraordinary lunch in Covent Gardent at which he spent an hour and a half stating every aspect of the programme's position and content that he could think of. As he did so Woolwich was painfully aware of how ridiculous it felt. He had worked for the BBC for thirteen years, mostly as a *Panorama* producer, and had never given this depth of advance briefing and co-operation to anyone anywhere else in the whole world, not even to two British Prime Ministers, numerous Cabinet ministers and Ronald Reagan. When he had finally sat back, exhausted, Dunn had replied: 'Mr Woolwich, you are either a very good salesman or a very honest man.'

Knowing that *Hard News* needed Dunn more than the *Sun* needed *Hard News*, Jane Reed and the company had bargained hard to gain control over the show's format. The first part was to be a filmed report of a complaint about the paper, which Dunn would see in advance. He would then be interviewed by the programme's presenter Ray Snoddy, who was also the newspaper industry expert for the *Financial Times*. The interview was to be taped on the morning the programme was broadcast and not cut, to ensure that Dunn's replies would not be distorted.

Woolwich was so nervous on the day that he had prepared an alternative item in case Dunn did not turn up. The director had also stationed a cameraman near the exit ready to film him if he decided to make a run for it. Ray Snoddy was just as nervous when Dunn walked into the studio just off Regent Street, took one look at the cramped, hot conditions and pronounced: 'This really is the cheap end of television.' He was calm, collected and, as *Hard News* discovered later, extremely well prepared after an exhaustive coaching by Brian MacArthur, the first editor of *Today* and now the resident media pundit of the *Sunday Times*.

Although the *Hard News* studio was spattered with blow-ups of disastrous front pages including 'THE TRUTH' and 'SORRY ELTON', none of these subjects had been put on the agenda. Instead, in line with its central thrust, *Hard News* had chosen as its main subject the vilification of an ordinary little person – in this case Jonathan Hunt, a five-year-old disabled boy. The show started with a film report of the case in which Jonathan's mother, Mrs Josephine Hunt, explained how her son had suffered from both septicaemia and meningitis, and now had no sense of fear or danger. As a result he was constantly having accidents. In an attempt to get publicity for the effects of the disease on children she had talked to Tony Bassett, a freelance journalist, who had written what he described in a statement read out on the programme as a 'lovable rascal' story.

The programme then showed what had actually been printed when the story appeared exclusively in the *Sun*. Under the headline 'THE WORST BRAT IN BRITAIN' the story read (Mrs Hunt's version of events is printed in square brackets): 'Terror tot Jonathan Hunt was last night dubbed Britain's naughtiest kid after WRECKING his parents' home [untrue – not wrecked], CUTTING off his ear [lobe severed by falling on edge of coffee table], KILLING the cat by putting it in the washing machine [post-mortem said died of feline leukaemia] . . . and PAINTING the dog Jessie with blue emulsion paint [brush fell off top of freezer]. . . . Child expert Dr Alan Franklin said he was the worst-behaved boy he had ever come across.' Dr Franklin, medical adviser to the Hyperactive Society, was then interviewed to explain how he had only been questioned over the phone by a *Sun* reporter. He did not know

Jonathan, had not examined him, and would never have made the comment attributed to him if he had known that the child was brain-damaged.

'THE WORST BRAT IN BRITAIN' story had been illustrated by a picture of Jonathan bunching his fists and with his face screwed up to make him look like a little hooligan. But the *Hard News* film revealed that the picture had been a set-up, obtained by getting Jonathan to sing a song he had been taught at school which involved pulling various faces, of which this was one. Mrs Hunt then described the story as 'a hatchet job on my little boy's already sad little life'. She told viewers how afterwards in her home village of Sawston, Cambridgeshire she had been spat at and called a bitch.

She had also received several sickening letters and phone calls. One letter, in crudely printed capitals, read: I CAN TELL YOU WHAT TO DO WITH THE LITTLE BASTARD, BELT HIS ARSE OFF while a telephone caller had issued a death threat to Jonathan for killing the cat. Mrs Hunt explained that when she got in touch with the paper, the *Sun* had offered an apology in the form of another article. But this had only made more untrue allegations. She had finally had a letter of complaint published, but only in the Monday Moan grumble slot. A tiny addendum had said: 'EDITOR'S NOTE: We are sorry for any distress the articles caused.' MacKenzie had answered her renewed complaints by making an offer on paper of £750, but only on condition she signed away her legal rights to sue – which she explained she could not afford anyhow – or to go to the Press Council. Finally, when Mrs Hunt refused this, she claimed she had been threatened by the *Sun*'s lawyers if she continued going on about the matter.

The film then cut to the studio and Martin Dunn, the Patsy Kensit of journalism, sitting opposite Snoddy at a round table. Dunn was wearing an expensive blue suit, a crisp white shirt and a pale blue and white tie, and exhibiting a rehearsed look of wounded innocence. Smoothly and firmly, he insisted that the *Sun* had 'bent over backwards' to help Mrs Hunt get the publicity she had wanted. Since then they had made her the offer of

322

money and told her they would not be using the freelance Bassett again. But, Dunn said sadly, somehow there seemed to be no way of satisfying her. Using his spaniel eyes to their maximum effect, he softly emphasised: 'Mr Snoddy, we are not heartless people.'

Changing the subject, Snoddy quickly ran Dunn round the loop of the *Sun's* abuse of foreigners, pointing out that we had to do business with these people. Dunn replied that we were all entitled to our opinion, and defended the paper as 'using the language of the working man and woman of this country'. Dunn rounded off by telling Snoddy that he did not think the *Sun* was about to clean itself up. He did admit there was 'going to be a certain evolution in newspapers', which he did not elaborate on. Snoddy afterwards gave his opinion that Dunn had done 'a good job' defending his paper. He had wanted to make the questioning much tougher, but had known that if he did so he would have defeated his own object by appearing to be a bully.

Next into the firing line came the hated BBC, openly in cahoots with the World's Worst, which had decided to scrutinise the *Sun* in a programme to coincide with its twentieth anniversary, as News International had thought would happen. Unfortunately the 25 minute documentary being made by BBC2's Public Eye ran into a fatal contradiction from the start. Media correspondent Nick Higham wanted to make a straightforward nuts and bolts film about the paper, but the BBC was in the throes of its current affairs revolution following the arrival of John Birt from London Weekend Television. Another faction in the programme therefore argued for the Birtian analytical approach, which involved making a film about an issue – in this case the invasion of privacy – rather than about the *Sun* itself. The result was an uncomfortable compromise which never got to grips with its subject and satisfied nobody.

BBC2 found News International as hard to deal with as Paul Woolwich and *Hard News* had done. Jane Reed refused permission to film the hacks at work in the newsroom, or to attend an editorial conference, or to go out with a reporter. MacKenzie refused to appear as usual, and access was restricted to one interview with Dunn, wheeled out again as the *Sun*'s public face, and the shooting of some wallpaper film in the office without talking to anyone. Even this was regarded as astonishing by the hacks. After Woolwich's brief *Panorama* foray three years previously, only Sky had since been allowed into this sacred inner sanctum of British tabloid journalism.

Dunn's interview passed off amicably enough. Nick Higham and producer Fiona Macbeth found the Patsy Kensit of journalism very bright, very pretty and very adept at avoiding questions. While they were chatting before the cameras rolled Dunn also volunteered the information that he was very proud of the *Sun*, and never felt ashamed to put it on his parents' coffee table.

The filming was being done first thing in the morning, and as the hacks came in for work and started quietly logging on at their terminals, Fiona Macbeth felt the whole experience becoming more and more bizarre. She found Wapping a weird environment anyway, and now she sensed fear dominating the atmosphere of this strange, windowless room. There was none of the relaxed bonhomie of a normal office starting its day, despite the forced jollity of Petrie's parrots and the squeaky Thatcher True-Story Alert. Instead Macbeth noticed a terrible stress and tension in the air which she had never found in a newspaper office before. What struck her most of all was that it was not at all creative, as it should have been.

There was also MacKenzie. When the crew started shooting the allowed wallpaper footage he emerged from his office and started hovering at their elbow, keeping up a steady patter of remarks. He was blunt, though friendly enough, but what struck Macbeth was the way he strutted and stomped around the place just like a little Roman emperor. She began to have an extraordinary feeling this whole odd place was simply not for real. Higham later decided that it was like a bizarre toytown, and both were glad to wrap the shoot and get out back into the open air beyond the security gates.

The programme then moved on to a joint exercise with the World's Worst to produce a one-off tabloid version of the *Guardian*, cleansed of offensive elements and called the *Fun*. The programme showed the *Fun* being put together, with various World's Worst editors dithering about what was offensive and was not, and finally deciding they could not use the word 'Kraut' in a headline.

The *Fun* splashed with LOCKERBIE BOMB SHOCK and was spattered with *Sun*-type headlines such as FERGIE IN JET DRAMA; MERCY DASH TO AID LIVER MUM; and LOVE TRIANGLE THAT ENDED IN DJ's DEATH. The Page Three problem was skirted by head and shoulder shots of 'top models in a million' under the heading ITS FUNTASTIC! and Alan Watkins contributed a column entitled 'Let's hear it for the chattering classes'. There was a weak dig at News International's publications in the weather slot: 'Today will be generally fine, with little or no sun. Outbreaks of truth spreading across the country later.'

A limited run of the *Fun* was distributed on a hard-core C2 Reading housing estate, where it met with a generally unenthusiastic response. Higham tried to thrust a copy into the hands of one reluctant punter with the words 'Take it, it's a collector's item.' The punter contemptuously replied: 'Well, you collect it then.' MacKenzie thought the *Fun* was pathetic. Fiona Macbeth heard afterwards that when there was a special showing of the programme at Wapping the editorial execs found it hilarious and all fell about laughing.

Now that the exercise to go out and meet the TV critics had been brought to a successful conclusion, issue no. 6,230 rolled smoothly off the presses on 17 November with the intriguing splash 'MUM LEAVES SON'S £20,000 TO QUEEN'S DOG'. Inside, the paper headed page 2 with 'STRAIGHT SEX CANNOT GIVE YOU AIDS – OFFICIAL', in which Labour peer Lord Kilbracken was wildly misquoted to back '*Sun* Doctor' Vernon Coleman's claim that the AIDS scare was 'the biggest hoax of the century'. 'The *Sun* Says' advised: 'Forget the idea that ordinary heterosexual people can contract AIDS. They can't . . . anything else is just homosexual propaganda.'*

---

* Kilbracken, furious, was given a right of reply to clear himself of the association five days later, and the matter eventually ended up at the Press Council, where the paper was censured 'as falling below acceptable standards'. Printing the adjudication, an historic 'The *Sun* Says' editorial added: 'The *Sun* was wrong to state that it was impossible to catch AIDS from heterosexual sex. We apologise.'

The only mention of the paper's anniversary was buried in the regular 'Happy Birthday to' spot below the horoscope on page 28. After 'TV chat-show host Jonathan Ross, 29, model Jilly Johnson, 36, comic Peter Cook, 52, actress Fenella Fielding, 55, *Sun* reader Angie Booty of Bow, E. London, 31,' a line of tiny type added: 'and the *Sun*, first printed 20 years ago today'. The paper's horoscope for Scorpio was a typically positive, if slightly illiterate: 'Make up your mind that the next few days are going to be exciting, enlivening and fun and they will.'

But they were not to be for *Hard News* editor Paul Woolwich. During its interface with the programme the *Sun* had found out that Woolwich had left his wife for Michal Levine, the programme's dishy reporter. Back in Wapping, the second the programme had been broadcast MacKenzie called in the Rottweilers. 'Do it,' he ordered. The consequent 'monstering' job involved the normal sordid scenes of photographers hanging about in people's gardens, doorstepping and intrusive phone calls and the consequent appearance of a page lead story headlined 'TV BOSS LEAVES WIFE FOR A STAR REPORTER'. The story described Woolwich as 'the self-appointed upholder of media morals'.

Woolwich bore his punishment stoically, even though he thought bitterly that 'top telly boss' was hardly an apt description for someone editing a minority programme for 1.5 million viewers. That was more appropriate for the producer of the police series *The Bill*, which was the competition on the other commercial channel and which he knew would have been the choice of those *Sun* readers who had not succumbed to the Murdoch propaganda and bought their dishes to tune in to Sky.

But there was another aspect to the story which mortified Woolwich even more. It was run under a joint byline, the first of which was Shan Lancaster, the hackette who had done the monstering business on the ground. But it was the second byline which really made him reflect bitterly on the ironies of the world. It was that of John Kay, who, confined to the office as usual, had interviewed people on the phone to put the story together. That was a bit rich, Woolwich thought. Here he was, plastered all over the *Sun* when all he'd done was leave his wife, yet the story had been written by a man who had killed his.

MacKenzie, unabashed, had been on the phone again shortly before this, outlining how the involvement with *Hard News* had inspired the *Sun* to start a column called 'Hard Views' to expose the iniquities of television. 'I'm going to clean up TV if it kills me,' MacKenzie told Woolwich. (The column was dropped after a few weeks.) Woolwich asked if the *Sun* had had any response to the programme. MacKenzie replied that there had been one letter from a viewer, who had said he had never been so disgusted and he thought Martin Dunn was a 'slimy and deceitful little turd'. Chuckling, MacKenzie explained that he had written back words to the effect that 'You only saw Martin Dunn for ten minutes. I have known him for ten years, and I can assure you that he is a slimy, deceitful *and obnoxious* little turd.'

Chapter 18

Kelvin Comes Out

MacKenzie sneered at the television 'coming out' of the *Sun* and the mincing appearances of the 'Patsy Kensit of journalism', mercilessly winding Dunn up in the office afterwards about how he had looked a complete pratt. Like most journalists, MacKenzie saw corporate relations and PR as bullshit. For him there were only two things that mattered – the readers, translated into sales figures and letters and phone calls to the paper, and the Boss.

Murdoch kept MacKenzie on his toes by making his calls at all times of day and night. They always followed the same format. 'Hello, Kelvin, how's it going? What's your splash?' MacKenzie would explain. A long intimidating pause would follow before there was a comment from the other end. If MacKenzie had done something 'naughty' he would sit worrying, waiting to see if he was to be bollocked or whether the matter would be ignored. Afterwards he would emerge, sighing with relief and saying: 'Thank Christ! He didn't mention it.'

The hacks had always noticed how strongly influenced MacKenzie was by the Boss's day-by-day comments on his performance. Sometimes he would come charging out of his office with a broad grin, clap his hands, rub them together and announce: 'Rupert loves the paper!' If the verdict had been the highest praise Murdoch was capable of giving – 'You're doing a good job' – it would give a tremendous lift to the office all day.

But it was not always like that. To keep his total control Murdoch ruled by silence. His strategy was to make every one of his editors feel that his phone call, from whichever part of the Empire he was currently inhabiting, was the most important event of their day or the week. Sometimes he would not call for days, and the silence would be terrible for all of them. They would sit fretting, waiting for the phone to ring. Was his attention simply concentrated elsewhere, or were they in purdah? They never knew. If the silence went on long enough the editors would get into a sweat and their nerve would snap. The one getting the treatment would then go behind Murdoch's back and ring the others. 'Has he called you? Yes? Oh fuck! I must be in it!'

Then when the call did come, it could be bitingly critical. Murdoch had three cards in his hand – circulation, budget and the content of the paper. He was always bound to get them on one of them. The worst times were when things on the paper were quiet, and the voice at the other end would endlessly nag and carp as it picked holes and found fault. MacKenzie often found this pressure hard to take, and when the niggling turned to a harsh bollocking he would get frustrated and angry.

But sometimes it would be the most terrifying statement of all: 'You're losing your touch, Kelvin. [Pause] Your paper is pathetic. [Pause] You're losing your touch, Kelvin.' Then the phone would go down. After a call like this, life in the office would be hell for everyone.

MacKenzie had his own way of pretending to shrug it all off by joking to his senior execs: 'The Boss is right behind me on this one, eh? Right fucking behind me . . .' while he graphically mimed being stabbed in the back. But now he had plenty of reason to fear the 'losing your touch' horror coming on one of the long, partly silent transatlantic conversations.

One problem on the paper, fortunately was not his doing, but the Boss's. Murdoch had made a major error when he moved to Wapping by deciding there was no evidence the readers would prefer colour in the paper. At the *Mirror* Robert Maxwell, often described by sages as more of a printer than a publisher, had taken the opposite view. The *Mirror* now had colour, giving good crisp pages which were popular with the readers and formed the basis of an aggressive sales drive. In comparison, whatever genius MacKenzie applied to the layout, the *Sun* looked tatty, dirty and out of date. Murdoch had now seen his mistake and ordered German MAN-Roland colour presses at a cost of DM 1 billion – the biggest-ever contract in the world printing industry. But it would be some time before they came on stream.

It was not MacKenzie's fault either that the readers were having a hard time now that the Loadsamoney dream the paper had peddled so assiduously had crashed. MacKenzie had tried to console them by revealing that Harry Enfield, Loadsa' himself, was now broke – 'BISH BOSH I'VE SPENT ALL ME DOSH . . . I'm a champagne socialist and I'm skint, says Loads . . . despite earning an incredible £500,000 last year!' But the paper was still stuffed with ads from moneylenders and remortgage companies offering seductive-looking loans at astronomical rates of interest. MacKenzie did not like them, though he could do nothing to stop them. Things were no better for the *Sun* Share Club members. The portfolio was still well down, and one investment had been so disastrous the paper had instead turned it into an exposé of a swindle.

As 'The *Sun* Says' had pointed out on Maggie's anniversary, the voters were now biting the hand that had fed them. Pushing the Thatcher line was becoming more unpopular each day. And now papers were filling up with even more environmental coverage, which was also becoming the bane of MacKenzie's life in a different way. *Today*, now completely restructured, had become the new star in the News International firmament on the back of acres of green consumerism. The paper had been awarded the accolade of Newspaper of the Year by Granada TV's *What the Papers Say*, and was getting all the attention, even though it was still costing a fortune.

MacKenzie constantly told the hacks he personally thought all this 'green' stuff was crap. The scare about the hole in the ozone layer was a load of bollocks drummed up by the bearded old hippies and bleeding-heart liberals who read the World's Worst. Anyhow, he informed them, if by any chance there was a hole the mysterious 'they' would solve the problem one way or another. The hacks were amazed. Like Mrs Thatcher, MacKenzie seemed incapable of adapting to the changing climate of the coming 1990s. But they did have to smile at the Kelvinism with which he dismissed it – 'It's all a load of fucking hot air.'

MacKenzie soon decided that the paper's Mr Green experiment was hopeless. Hennessy had only had the odd short story and slab on the graveyard page 2 to show for his efforts. MacKenzie called him in and informed him: 'The readers aren't interested in this green stuff. What they're interested in is money. So you're moving to the Money Page.' The hacks joked there was at least one consistent element – they were both the same colour.

Money was also a new problem on the *Sun* in yet another way. Huge resentment was building up in the office about the devastating effect of the bill for Sky. The *Sun* was now being mercilessly milked as News International's cash cow and its £1 million-plus a week profits were being soaked up by Sky's losses of £2 million a week. Budgets were being slashed, facilities withdrawn and even hacks' expenses minutely scrutinised to squeeze every ounce of profitability out of the paper. The hacks were also grumbling about how the paper had been pulled into the corporate Sky-plugging effort. Sky stories had superseded bingo winners as the most hated reporting jobs as the hacks were ordered out to do crap features such as puffing strapping young disc installers. The paper had even splashed one day with a scam court story headed 'TV LICENCE SENSATION' about a person acquitted on a charge of not having a TV licence because he claimed he only watched Sky. Murdoch obviously thought that was the most important story in Britain that day.

The hacks started noticing how MacKenzie seemed depressed. In dark moments he confided to some of them with deep sighs that he did not think he would last long as editor. Outside Wapping his few friends were concerned that after nearly ten years of constant pressure he was simply worn out. They reminded him that Larry Lamb had suffered a heart bypass operation. It just wasn't worth it, they told him. It was only a fucking newspaper, after all.

For MacKenzie was already having trouble with his health. By now he was forty-three and getting increasingly bald and tubby to match his fat bum, despite the Weight Watchers activity. More seriously he had developed *petit mal*, a mild form of epilepsy, which gave him black-outs. One occurred when he was at lunch with Eve Pollard, editor of the *Sunday Mirror*. Pollard faithfully promised to keep it quiet, but she need not have bothered. MacKenzie roared back into the office afterwards shouting: 'Guess what, eh? I passed out – I nearly fucking died! Where's my fucking obit.? You c***s should have it ready. I could fucking go at any time! So get it written, you bastards – now!' MacKenzie put a bottle of champagne on offer for the best one and when the results came bollocked the writers of craven, toadying versions. He awarded the prize to the one starting: 'Here lies Kelvin MacKenzie, and lies, and lies, and lies . . .', which he thought was hilarious.

But his biggest problem of all was the government warning that the tabloids were now 'drinking in the Last Chance Saloon'. MacKenzie now needed the Boss's full backing all the way. He and his old partner in outrage, Wendy Henry, with their shows run on 'SHOCK AND AMAZE ON EVERY PAGE' and 'HEY DORIS! LOOK AT THIS!' were the two editors most responsible for the current turn of events and Wendy Henry had already parted company with Murdoch as a result of the new pressures.

Henry had been a successful editor of the *News of the World* in a way. Under her fierce edge it had fulfilled its historical obligation to lead the pack in crucifying people with bonk journalism. But she had finally gone too far in her personal crusade to return the paper to the Victorian values of the freak show. A senior exec at the *Sun*, startled by some of the material she had been running, had shown it to MacKenzie, remarking: 'Wend seems a bit over the top these days.'

'Yeah. Silly bitch. I wouldn't stand for that,' MacKenzie had replied off-handedly. In December 1988 after she had been in the chair for fifteen months, Murdoch asked her to change the paper's direction. She screeched loudly that she had put on

400,000 sales. Wasn't that what she was there for? 'Sales aren't everything, Wendy,' Murdoch told her, but Henry resigned rather than give in.

Henry had not stayed in the wilderness for long. Three months later she had been hired by Robert Maxwell to edit the *People* at the comparatively low salary of £75,000. The other newspaper editors had agreed she was hardly in a position to dictate terms.

MacKenzie's salary, it was reliably said, was closer to the magic six figures of £100,000 a year. But, as he openly admitted to the hacks, he was hopeless with money. As well as being a wild and reckless share gambler, he bought a docklands flat for over £200,000 close to the peak of the market. Then he tried to fulfil his ambition of being a newspaper proprietor by starting a free sheet near his home in north Kent, with his wife Jacqui as editor. But the paper missed the market and the venture did not prosper, forcing him to sell the flat at a thumping loss to meet his commitments.

But it was not just the money that made his affinity with the readers more theoretical than real. Ever since the 'lived in a council house/one O-level' disinformation exercise which had been swallowed by the Unpopulars, MacKenzie had lived his life shut off from the rest of the community. Since Wapping this isolation had increased. For more than three years he had been starting his day by walking the half dozen steps out of his house, past the wishing well in the front garden (illuminated with fairy lights at night) and into the chauffeur-driven Jag. He was then wafted to Wapping in the plush leather interior and spent all day and half the evening in the sealed windowless room behind the razor wire and security gates. Then he walked into the lift, and went outside to the Jaguar to be driven straight home, where his workaholic day had been extended by the installation of a fax machine. Pages were now sent down to him all evening, enabling him to bollock the backbench late into the night. Next morning the process would start all over again.

As far as anyone in the office was aware MacKenzie had no other life whatsoever. Most days he ate in the canteen and apart from the odd lunch with one of his editor cronies he appeared to be on the job twenty-four hours a day, seven days a week. The new standard office joke was that, having got the Dartford Tunnel point, the only time there was now any peace was the five minutes he was temporarily out of contact on the carphone as he was driven through.

His faithful secretary, Rosann Alvez, a beautiful Guyanese, had always arranged his life for him by paying his bills and picking his clothes for him on brief shopping trips. The biggest failure had been an attempt to make him look trendy with a coat from Paul Smith in Covent Garden which on his shortish body had resembled a bell tent and had soon been abandoned. But even Alvez had now left, another victim of the changes in the office due to Wapping.

Yet although MacKenzie's personal isolation put him a million miles away from the readers' lives, the hacks still had to admit he retained an instinctive flair for seeing the world through their eyes. But the question that was endlessly debated in the Sidney Smith was whether he really meant it when he constantly repeated that they were the salt of the earth. The cynics were adamant that this was just a front, and said that the readers were only important to MacKenzie because they supported the commercial equation by buying the paper. He was a cynic just like them, they claimed. His attitude was that you just pissed all over them and they loved it. They must be a lot of stupid punters, othewise why would they buy the sort of rubbish which was served up in the *Sun*?

Nobody was sure what the real answer was and the question was the biggest ambiguity in the whole organisation. But then, as the hacks always said, that was the thing with Kelvin. You never knew where you were with him. One moment he was a smoothie with perfect Queen's English; the next doing his coarse sarff London gangster simulation. One moment he was a bollocking tyrant; the next a quiet muser with his own home-spun philosophy. Switch, switch, switch, it went. Maybe it was the same with the readers. None of them would ever know.

Although he never met them MacKenzie still maintained a cheerful and anarchic relationship with readers who wrote to the paper or rang to complain. There had been a famous incident back in Bouverie Street when a woman reader rang in and MacKenzie, incapable of passing a ringing phone without answering it, picked it up and started listening to her long moan. Getting bored, he cut in and demanded: 'Who are you? Right, what's the name of your newsagent? Right. Well, from now on you are banned from buying the *Sun.*'

The next day there had been a sequel when a mischievous hack persuaded a friend to ring in pretending to be the woman's husband. Getting through to MacKenzie, the impostor asked if he was banned as well, or was it all right if he bought the paper and he read bits of it to his wife? Permission was grudgingly granted.

MacKenzie felt the paper could afford to lose a few complaining people as they were just a drop in the ocean. He would pick up their letters and say: 'What a wank. What a complete fucking wank,' spitting the words out and holding the letter at arm's length between finger and thumb as though it were made of some particularly repellent substance. Sometimes complainants would get a stinging slag-off reply. On other occasions page after page of complaint about an item, finishing politely, 'Can I have a right of reply?', would merit his simplest answer of all:

Dear X

No.

Yours in sport
   Kelvin MacKenzie
   Editor

The attitude was very different to the old days of Larry Lamb, where readers' letters had been treated with great reverence, as they still were on the *Mirror,* where there was a standing rule that they had to be replied to within forty-eight hours. But by now Lamb was another who had parted company with the *Sun.* He had resurfaced to say he would no longer have it in the house, moaning in interviews that he regretted starting Page Three and had even lost his faith in Mrs Thatcher after seeing what her tenure of office had done to the country. In moments of deep reflection, he said he had created a Frankenstein's monster.

But as part of the News International corporate strategy a buffer had since been installed between MacKenzie and the readers. Amid much sneering from the Unpopulars the *Sun* had announced that it was to be the first paper to appoint an ombudsman to investigate readers' complaints. The appointment was accompanied by a statement from Murdoch: 'The rest of the press in Britain will be watching this project closely. Newspapers and journalists today have heavy responsibilities to preserve the freedom we all enjoy by living up to the best traditions of British journalism.'

The new ombudsman was Ken Donlan, the former managing editor, who promptly astonished detractors by ruling that a *Sun* story about actor Leslie Crowther being treated for alcoholism at a special clinic was an intrusion on privacy. Donlan stated that the *Sun* should not have bought the story, though he did add realistically that as it had been for sale a rival paper would have printed it sooner or later anyway.

Donlan was now wheeled in to adjudicate on the biggest single problem facing the *Sun* in its relations with the readers – the disastrous Hillsborough 'THE TRUTH' story. He did his best to wriggle round the subject by saying the paper had 'a duty to publish the facts about supporters' misbehaviour, no matter how hurtful or unpalatable at the time'. He then pointed out irrelevantly that 'similar material had appeared in other papers'. But finally he grudgingly admitted that none of this justified the headline 'THE TRUTH' because 'allegations can never be printed as facts'. (This was precisely the point Harry Arnold had made to MacKenzie when he warned him how sensitive the story was.) However, Donlan did not see fit to apologise on behalf of the paper.

After Donlan's rebuke came the Press Council's report on the same subject. The Council had received hundreds of telephone calls and 349 written complaints, including a petition from Liverpool signed by 7,000 people. The complaints named thirty-five newspapers, including all the nationals except the *Morning Star*. The report concluded that the publication of pictures showing a section of the crowd in 'distress, pain and fear' was justified and 'served serious public interest'. There was, however, criticism for a small number of pictures which had showed individuals in 'terror and torture'.

The *Sun* was the only paper singled out for criticism over a front-page report. The Council described 'THE TRUTH' as an 'insensitive, provocative and unwarranted' headline, while the article itself was described as 'unbalanced and its general effect misleading'. Its publication was condemned.

The Council's report was widely attacked for being feeble. Joe Ashton MP, the chairman of the all-party House of Commons Football Committee, and ironically a columnist for the *Daily Star*, commented: 'It really is a very short, pathetic report. If this is the best the Press Council can do when its is supposed to be acting in the public interest it is time it packed up.'

But for News International the Press Council was a sideshow compared to the verdict which had been handed out by the people of Liverpool. As a result of 'THE TRUTH' the paper was now belatedly facing up to the fact that it had suffered the biggest-ever sales disaster in the entire history of British newspapers. There was now no question that large numbers of people in Liverpool had switched the paper off for good.

There had been a faint recovery from the low sales point of 320,000 on Merseyside, but give or take a few thousand, the paper had lost 200,000 readers. This represented an annual loss in revenue of £10 million – more than had ever been lost in any whole year with the exception of 1979, after the launch of the *Star* in Manchester. On that occasion Murdoch sacrificed an entire year's profits by cutting the cover price by 15 per cent, introducing bingo, launching a massive TV advertising campaign and, not least, by changing editors to retrieve the situation.

In Liverpool the *Star* had been trying to make amends for its splash of 'DEAD FANS ROBBED BY DRUNK THUGS' by running competitions with prizes including season tickets to Liverpool's ground and the house featured in the TV comedy series *Bread*. But News International had appeared either too indifferent or too proud to do anything. When Bob Gill, the secretary of the Liverpool Supporters' Club, had challenged it to match the *Mirror* and pay £1 million into the Disaster Fund there had been no response.

News International waited for the Press Council report in July before taking the unprecedented step of releasing a statement from Murdoch as chief executive of the company. 'At a time of great emotion and great tragedy, our coverage that day was uncaring and deeply offensive to relatives of the victims,' it said. 'More thought on our part would have saved more anguish, which we deeply regret.'

Even more momentously, MacKenzie, a gun in his back from Empire HQ, was told that he personally had to face the critics. He was to go public for the first time since his disastrous bingo interview with Norman Rees of ITN eight years previously. But this was not to be a front-page job like the treatment he had meted out to Mike Terry, the Bingo Bungler and Stuart Higgins, the Human Sponge.

Instead the vehicle chosen by the News International corporate machine was Radio 4's *World This Weekend*. The programme's deputy editor, Rod Liddle, had put in a standard request for an interview to Wapping. He had no hope of it being granted. But to his astonishment he was told MacKenzie was consenting to an interview, to be conducted live from a radio car outside his house.

John Harrison, the presenter, led into the interview by talking to people in Liverpool, including Frances Clarke, the mother of actress Margi Clarke, who had been involved in the spontaneous demonstration in Kirkby and now said MacKenzie should apply for a job on *Jackanory*, because some of the stories his paper was telling were so unbelievable.

Harrison ran through the paper's coverage on the Monday after Hillsborough for the benefit of listeners before cutting to MacKenzie. He asked him if accepted that the pictures had been intrusion of the worst possible kind.

MacKenzie replied in his best middle-class accent, speaking slowly: 'I think, er, with hindsight I would say that most of the newspaper coverage of Hillsborough was a mistake. Including ours.'

Harrison then asked: 'And in the immediate aftermath you offered again on page one what you called "THE TRUTH" – that was the headline. You reported Liverpool fans stealing from the pockets of injured fans. Now the Press Council condemns this as one-sided, misleading, insensitive. Do you accept that?'

MacKenzie's voice came across wearily, as though his patience was being strained: 'Er, yes I do,' he replied. 'Erm, I think we should divide this question into two parts. Firstly, we did not make the allegations. The allegations were made by a member of parliament, a named and senior Police Federation official, and we simply reported them, as did other newspapers including the *Daily Telegraph.*'

Harrison asked: 'Did you not consider that reporting these allegations might offend?'

MacKenzie, sounding mournful, said: 'Erm, I must say that, er, it was my decision and my decision alone to do that front page in that way and I made a rather serious error.'

Asked if the *Sun* would be taking a different attitude to disasters in future, MacKenzie replied: 'Yes we will.' Then he paused, as though he was hoping Harrison would quickly move to another question. When he did not, MacKenzie went on: 'Yes we will. We have taken on board not only what has been said in this report by the Press Council but far more importantly, the er, the er moves in Liverpool and the beliefs of the Liverpool people who were, prior to erm, er, the way we covered Hillsborough, er, one of our most important areas of readership. They didn't like it. We don't like it.'

Harrison, broadening out the discussion, asked: 'The *Sun's* track record is one of causing offence on a number of stories, and I just wonder if you take the view that it's all about selling papers, whatever the offence?'

'No, not at all,' MacKenzie said. 'I don't accept the earlier part of your question that we have caused offence. . . . We certainly caused offence on this occasion which is the reason why I am talking to you today in this manner.'

MacKenzie's 'apology' had caused palpable shock in the studio. Harrison said afterwards you could have heard a pin drop.

Linda McDermott, a feature writer on the Liverpool *Echo* who was also being interviewed, was the first to recover. 'I am absolutely staggered by Mr MacKenzie's apology,' she said. 'It's a pity he didn't choose to do that nearer the time. He did more than offend the people of Merseyside who were directly affected by this tragedy. He absolutely devastated them. The reaction here was one of absolute outrage and fury, which he will no doubt be aware of, and to retract his words now, several months after the damage was done, well – it is a bit late.'

Harrison professionally sprang to MacKenzie's defence: 'It may be late. But he's made it and made it publicly. Is that not in the circumstances sufficient?' he asked.

McDermott was adamant. 'The damage was already done. Those reports went all round the world and people in Canada, America and Australia echoed those reports in their newspapers there. . . . A terrific amount of damage was done and no amount of apologies, really, will take away from that ever.'

Harrison then returned to MacKenzie with the key question: 'Mr MacKenzie, given the scale of the protests at the time, did you consider resigning?'

MacKenzie (who sounded distant because he had gone off-mike) answered simply: 'No, I didn't.' There was a pause.

Harrison prompted: 'You did not. Were you not urged to consider resigning?'

MacKenzie (still distant) said: 'No, I wasn't.'

Harrison said afterwards he thought MacKenzie had been brave to do the interview. But, as an experienced interviewer, he had also formed the opinion that MacKenzie had been made to do it, and he had detected the duress he was under, which had come across in the way his answers had seemed as though they were being forced out of him.

Those close to MacKenzie knew even better how traumatic the experience had been. It was quite the worst thing that he could be made to do. Under the sarff London code it was the ultimate humbling experience – the dreadful ignominy colloquially called eating shit. And when they listened to the broadcast they could hear what Harrison had also detected. Eating shit was nearly choking him.

According to his own theory of successful editorship, MacKenzie should have been fired for losing so many readers because of 'THE TRUTH'. But, as he had told Radio 4 listeners, Murdoch had not asked him to resign. The official corporate line now emerged via Jane Reed. In Liverpool there was a layer of people waiting to have a go at the *Sun* because News International had made people in the area redundant some years earlier. Hillsborough had been their excuse to have a go, and the city anyhow had a 'bubbling anger' which was 'displaced' on the *Sun*. Now MacKenzie had apologised, that was the end of the matter as far as the company was concerned.

But for MacKenzie it was now even more crucial that he and his drinking partner in the Last Chance Saloon, Wendy Henry, did not fuck up on this scale again. Yet in the middle of November, on two consecutive days, they both did. MacKenzie came first, on Saturday, 18 November, the day after the paper's twentieth anniversary, with the *Sun's* report of a death which devastated the fast-disappearing world of British 'quality' journalism.

The man who died was David Blundy, 44, one of the best and best-loved of the journalists of the 1970s and 1980s. Blundy was covering the bloody deadlock of the civil war in El Salvador for the *Sunday Correspondent*, doing the week's story, which he must have already known was destined for a mediocre slot on an inside foreign page. The war had dragged on so long it was no longer front-page news. But he had still gone out into the action one last time, when other journalists would have been content to file from the comfort of their hotel room, to put a final definitive top on his copy. He was hit by a random bullet from a sniper, rushed to hospital, and died almost immediately.

Blundy had previously worked for the *Sunday Times*, both as a foreign correspondent and member of the campaigning and investigative Insight team in the great days before Murdoch bought the paper. He had been one of the many who left in a mixture of disgust and regret at the changes introduced by the Dirty Digger. His older editor, Harry Evans, who had been sacked by Murdoch around the same time, was later to say of him at his memorial service: 'He was one of those reporters who give what we call the freedom of the press its moral energy. That moral energy is renewed whenever journalism enables people to make free, informed choices. It is destroyed when it does not. . . .

'The whole of ethics is based on the presumption of free will and the freedom to make choices. David would mock the assertion that this is what he did, that he legitimised and honoured his profession. But he was in the front line of truth – not so much because he exposed himself to danger as that he never ceased to expose himself to doubt.

'That is a risk that some of us go to great lengths to avoid. There is comfort in certainty. In journalism it is simpler to sound off than it is to find out.'

Evans continued: 'It is a testament to the integrity of David's endeavour that he hung his long frame over his portable for so long at such ungodly hours, scowling gloomily at his notebook. "Do you find a problem," he said, "in getting the words in the right order?"

'Writing may be hard to everyone, but it's easier to dazzle, shock and entertain than it is to get the words in the right order when you have set yourself in the rough urgent compressions of journalism to grapple with truth – and get it read. Is my story accurate? Is it clear? Is it fair? Is it boring? David naturally doubted whether he met the tests he set himself. But he did, in deceptively simple prose. Some words he wrote for the *Sunday Times* from El Salvador in 1981 bear re-reading today:

'Lolita Guardado was awoken at about 4 a.m. by a strange noise. There was the usual sound of persistent drizzle pouring from the roof of closely packed palm leaves and through the

342

walls of mud and sticks. But outside across the Sumpul river she
could hear men shouting. Groups of peasants gathered anxiously
in the grey dawn to watch as Honduran soldiers formed a line on
the far bank and ran to and fro carrying stones from the river bed.
Only later in the day, after her family, friends and neighbours had
been slaughtered, did she fully understand why they were there.'

'Philip Larkin, in 'Church Going', wrote: "someone will
forever be surprising a hunger in himself to be more serious." May
we find that hunger in ourselves and in our dedication when we
remember him with affection and gratitude.'

Blundy's pointless and unexpected death caused such shock to
many seasoned journalists that they burst into tears at their desks,
and there were many sad wakes for him later. The next day all the
newspapers carried fulsome obituaries, illustrated by small head
and shoulder shots, except for the *Sun*. Instead MacKenzie
printed the wire-service picture of his dead body on the morgue
slab, which had been sent to all the other papers. The 'story',
under the headline 'BRITISH NEWS ACE KILLED', was composed of
three short paragraphs.

The Press Council was so appalled that one of its representatives
took the unheard-of step of ringing MacKenzie before an official
complaint had been lodged in writing. MacKenzie brushed the
call off by replying: 'None of our ten million readers has
complained.' (A complaint was later filed by Shamira Osman, the
mother of Blundy's two-year-old daughter Charlotte. For the
Sun Martin Dunn claimed that the picture was justified as 'in the
public interest as it brought home the horrors of war'. The
judgement said in rebuttal: 'The picture told readers nothing
about Mr Blundy, the tragedy of his death, the risk he ran as a
journalist, or the nature of the conflict he was covering. It was
simply a very sad picture which intruded into his death. . . . Its
publication was insensitive and an error of judgement.' The
complaint was upheld.)

The day after MacKenzie published the Blundy morgue
picture, it was Wendy Henry's turn to fuck up. The readers of
Sunday's *People* were treated to two front-page pictures of Charles

and Diana's seven-year-old son in his school uniform, urinating. The cackling headline of 'THE ROYAL WEE', embroidered with a tacky Crown logo on the WOB, was run above a subhead of 'WILLIE'S SLY PEE IN THE PARK'. The story started:

> Young tearaway Prince Wills couldn't wait when he was caught short at playtime.
> He headed straight for the nearest bush, unzipped his shorts and brazenly took a leak.
> Seven-year-old Wills was just one minute into his morning break in a park opposite his posh school when the call of nature came. . . .

The story twittered gloatingly on: 'And unlike other pupils, who would be severely scolded for relieving themselves in public, the future King of England was let off scot free. Until now, that is. Once mum Diana gets to hear about his liberal use of the Royal Wee, he's in deep trouble.'

Prince Charles, exasperated at this latest gross intrusion into his family's privacy, blew up. Maxwell fired Henry the next day.

But, as Maxwell later revealed to Hugo Young of the World's Worst, he had not fired Henry for 'THE ROYAL WEE', as most people had supposed. The real reason had been an extremely nasty inside-page picture of Sammy Davis Jr, who had just undergone a major operation for cancer of the throat. (He died not long afterwards.)

Maxwell explained that Henry had signed her cards earlier in July, around the time of the Press Council adjudication on 'THE TRUTH', when the *People* ran sickening pictures of the Sioux City air crash in America when 109 people had died and another 186 miraculously escaped. Under the headline 'KILLING FIELDS' the picture showed partly dismembered bodies and badly injured passengers in a prize example of 'yuck' journalism. The strap read: 'Horror on Flight 232 . . . the pictures television could not show'.

Maxwell was appalled. He called Henry in and told her: 'I can't take this paper any more at home. Do that once more and you're dead.' In the second-fastest report in its history the Press Council had taken just twenty-one days to come out with an adjudication describing the 'KILLING FIELDS' pictures as 'horrific, distressing and offensive in the extreme'. It ruled that their publication 'was not justified by any public interest and was an error of judgement'.

Henry had vigorously defended herself at the Council by saying that if airlines realised they might get harsh coverage when their planes fell out of the sky it might make them more vigilant. But she did admit to the Council that she had been surprised by the volume of criticism. More than 100 of her readers had sent letters of complaint direct to the paper, while forty wrote direct to the Council itself.

Maxwell explained the fresh incident which led him to fire her: 'Publishing pictures of Sammy Davis's raw, racked, cancerous throat is what she really got sacked for, and nothing else. She just believed in shocking people. I don't.' He added that the dismissal had met with 'universal approval both inside the house and outside'.

Maxwell had preened himself for spotting the way the public mood had changed, and the timing of this demonstration of his new insight could not have been better. The day after he fired Henry the twenty editors of the national papers solemnly gathered in the World Trade Centre near Wapping to sign their Code of Conduct, the paper promise they had concocted binding them to clean up their act. The four-hour meeting was chaired by Andreas Whittam-Smith, the editor of the *Independent*, whom Wendy Henry called 'goody two-shoes'. Whittam-Smith was also MacKenzie's enemy, not just for editing an Unpopular and getting the Code organised, but also for the 'c***' incident when MacKenzie had lost his hypocritical complaint to the Press Council.

The Editors' Code started with a lofty preamble stating: 'We, the editors of Britain's national newspapers, declare our determination to defend the democratic right of the people to a press free from government interference.'

It then detailed five points: privacy would be respected; a right of reply would be granted 'when reasonably called for'; mistakes would be corrected with 'appropriate prominence'; journalists would obtain information by 'straightforward means' and not pay criminals or their families for stories; and irrelevant references to race would be 'avoided'.

Commentators rubbished the Code as a smug and self-serving attempt to fend off criticism. Larry Lamb said he thought it was a cynical and superficial exercise to try and avoid legislation which he thought was inevitable and ought to come. Paul Johnson wondered aloud in his column in the *Spectator* who would decide the meaning of the vague phrases like 'reasonably called for', 'appropriate prominence' and 'avoided'. He predicted endless muddle.

MacKenzie attended the meeting and signed the worthy document, but unlike most of the other editors did not parade it on the front page of the next morning along with a pompous and solemn leader. Instead he indicated his opinion of it by bunging it down one column on an inside page.

A MORI opinion poll shortly afterwards confirmed just how little confidence readers now had in their papers, with 96 per cent thinking that people ought to have an automatic right of reply; 84 per cent that the papers had no right to invade the privacy of the Royals; and 73 per cent believing it wrong to report purely private matters such as adultery.

As he signed the Code MacKenzie knew that the heady days of Rottweiler journalism were over. No more 'SHOCK AND AMAZE ON EVERY PAGE' just for the hell of it; no more sending ferrets up bums just for the God-awful row that would blow up afterwards; no more lighting up all the lights on the scamulator. From now on the tap-dancing would have to be a lot lighter, and a lot niftier. The Code bollocks, like Petrie's fucking newsdesk parrot, would be sitting on his shoulder. The whole 1980s triumphalism was over anyhow. The *Sun* was going to have to be a very different paper in the future. He would be walking a very delicate tightrope indeed.

But Murdoch had stood by him so far. He might own other TV stations as well as Sky but, MacKenzie knew, the Boss was still a newspaperman at heart. He had recently indicated to a TV interviewer that if it came to the crunch on cross-ownership he would sell his TV stations, even Sky, to keep his papers. And of all the eighty-four papers he owned around the world, the *Sun* – MacKenzie's good old Currant Bun, the Curranticus Bunticus – was still his favourite. And he, Kelvin MacKenzie, was still his favourite editor. That was what counted.

But there was one more score to be settled. After the radio shit-eating exercise and with the smarmy TV appearances of the Patsy Kensit of journalism, MacKenzie had a needle with the pratts from the World's Worst and the other Unpopulars. He would call them in to Wapping and tell them a thing or two.

He informed Jane Reed what he was intending to do. Reed was very unsure. So was the Boss. He thought it was a doubtful exercise. But MacKenzie was adamant. The Unpopulars were still sniping away, just as they had been since he was first appointed on 19 April 1981. During the intervening years hundreds of requests for interview had piled up at both Bouverie Street and Wapping. He'd refused them all, in most cases by simply not bothering to reply. Now he rejected suggestions that he would be putting his head in the lion's mouth. Rather the Unpopular merchants would be entering the lion's cage by coming to Wapping for the meeting. Once he had them in, he'd have them. The Boss always said these people couldn't cut the mustard, anyhow. MacKenzie was given unenthusiastic consent.

The result was a surprise phone call from Jane Reed to the media correspondents of the Unpopulars whom he had personally selected. 'Would you be interested in coming to lunch with Kelvin MacKenzie?' she crooned. Without exception, they accepted. *

The specialists MacKenzie had chosen were the media editors of the *Daily Telegraph*, the *Independent*, the *Financial Times* and the world's worst *Guardian*. *The Times*, as part of the Empire, sent the

* A request by the authors to attend was rejected by Ms Reed. 'Kelvin', she told us, 'is not holding a press conference as such, but meeting a few specialists he has chosen. It is all on the record, and he will answer any questions, but access is restricted.'

media correspondent's deputy, who remained totally silent throughout the proceedings. When the hacks arrived at Wapping for the meeting, already billed as 'historic', their excitement had already been heightened by a false rumour that Murdoch had tried to call the whole thing off at the last minute. That alarm now subsided, Reed led them into the oak-panelled *Times* boardroom, where the dining table was set with plates embossed in gold with *The Times*'s lion-and-unicorn masthead.

The hacks, agog with anticipation, were introduced to Martin Dunn and Tom Petrie. Reed made apologies on behalf of MacKenzie, who was carefully stage-managing his entrance. After a quarter of an hour he bounced cheerily into the room, smiling and charm itself. He wasn't really interested in meeting them, he joked – he'd only come to see the boardroom. He'd never been inside it before.

Then he abruptly switched to explain the serious side to the meeting: 'There's growing hostility towards us from journalists and in Parliament, that's undeniable. The criticism needs to be answered in some way. . . . These days we've got to think about what our non-readers think of us. We don't want them to dominate our thinking, but in the whole picture they have a role to play.'

Eating stopped there. In the non-stop torrent of wisecracks, cruel remarks, sharp observations and jokey abuse which followed, the hacks were too busy defending themselves and scribbling down the details of the outrageous performance even to lift a fork.

MacKenzie had looked up their CVs, and they were all 'crap'. Only Ray Snoddy of the *Financial Times* received any respect, for having worked his way up through local papers. The hacks laughed uneasily and shifted in their seats. This might be what they believed was termed a 'wind-up'.

MacKenzie put Maggie Brown of the *Independent* into the frame first. He castigated her for her shorthand, pronounced her useless, and said she wouldn't stand a chance of getting a job on the *Sun*. She didn't have 'enough intellectual ability'. 'You don't look old enough for the job you do – how old are you?' he demanded. When Brown replied 'Thirty-nine,' MacKenzie broke into loud guffaws: 'Well – the prune juice must be working then!' he chortled.

Brown was having very mixed feelings. The conversation was confirming all she had thought – MacKenzie was amusing, alarming, funny, quick, enormously entertaining and hugely self-confident here in his own world. But there was a cruel edge, and she was already feeling slightly soiled by the experience. She reminded herself that MacKenzie was, after all, the editor of a highly successful newspaper. The lunch was still one of the highlights of her year, and she determined to make the best of it.

But MacKenzie, having used her to warm up, had already dumped her in order to home in on his main target, the media editor of the World's Worst, Georgina Henry. Henry had been observing how MacKenzie had been eyeing them all up as he talked away. She realized he was one of those people who seemed to be able to see right through you and know all about you.

MacKenzie sneered as he jockeyed her into the firing line. 'I suppose you're going to give me all that feminist crap about Page Three being sexist,' he said. The MacKenzie magic was working. The other hacks could not resist joining in the laughter, even though they were becoming aware that they were being expertly played off against each other.

It was time to broaden the attack. 'Most Fleet Street editors couldn't edit a bus ticket,' he smilingly informed them. He ran them through the Currant Bun thesis. It was only the *Sun* that understood ordinary people. Lots of black and Asian people read it and all this racism and sexism stuff was 'hogwash', part of the orchestrated 'wall of criticism', all rubbish, and mostly inspired by jealousy.

'The critics attack popular papers because they can't understand that what we do so touches the nerve of the nation. The *Sun* arouses hatred because we represent a power outside of the establishment. In a sense nobody likes it. I am baffled at the criticism. I love the paper, love the readers, really enjoy producing the paper.' Ray Snoddy, his shorthand tested to the limit as he tried to keep pace with the stream of glib remarks, was thinking that MacKenzie was like a guided missile without a control system. He should do a one-man show. It would be a great West End replacement for Jeffrey Archer's newspaper play, *Exclusive*, which had just flopped. Snoddy had his pen ready as one of the hacks dared to ask the big question – 'What about the Elton John fiasco?'

'We were totally duped,' MacKenzie replied instantly. 'Elton John was a big error. When you're as big as the *Sun*, when you drop a clanger it's a big one – that's the danger. When we do it we feel disgrace. We are a great newspaper, and I apologise for our errors. But our strengths outmatch our errors.' It happened to all papers from time to time, to the *Sun* less than most. In future he was going to 'double, double, double-check facts'.

'When we get things wrong people are fired and there are terrible rows.' He added, 'The idea that we are just marching on regardless of what people say is just rubbish.'

Settled and confident, MacKenzie effortlessly upped the stakes by turning a question about journalistic ethics into a cheap joke. 'Ethics?' he replied, laughing. 'As far as I'm concerned that's that place to the east of London where people wear white socks.'

Petrie, who the media hacks thought seemed frozen to the spot, winced. He was coping with the lunch by putting forward the image of the tough, silent newsman and obviously thought Kelvin was sailing very close to the wind at this point. But Dunn, who the media hacks had noticed was much more relaxed, smirked at the wisecrack. The Patsy Kensit of journalism knew better. Kelvin was tapdancing beautifully.

Georgina Henry of the World's Worst was becoming irritated. This was a very clever exercise indeed. She realised they were not going to be able to pin MacKenzie down, as any of them would have in a one-to-one interview.

Jane Thynne of the *Daily Telegraph* was also torn by conflicting emotions. She too was finding it impossible not to like or be impressed by this extraordinary man. The lunch, which none of them was actually eating, was turning out to be quite the most fascinating and astonishing meeting of its type she'd ever attended. MacKenzie was displaying enormous charisma and the sort of charm that always won people over.

Nonetheless she had a job to do. Managing to break into the stream of remarks, she challenged MacKenzie on his official boast that the *Sun* covered the same stories as the Unpopulars, only more briefly. Thynne had carried out some careful research beforehand to prepare her ground, and she now explained that she had established that the *Sun* had yet to cover a single exchange of fire in the civil war in the Lebanon.

The second she had finished speaking MacKenzie pounced with a glib riposte. An Arab getting shot in the Lebanon wasn't news – it was an everyday event. 'Now if there's a day when someone doesn't get shot in the Lebanon,' he chortled, tipping back on his chair, 'that's a story, and we'll be happy to print it.'

The only slip-up in the virtuoso performance came when one of the hacks, wearying of the clever jokey remarks, asked why they were there if MacKenzie wasn't going to be serious. MacKenzie started replying, 'This is just a PR job, and you've all fallen for it . . .' when he pulled himself up. 'No – don't print that or I'll get a good kicking from. . . .' He faltered again.

'Murdoch?' one of the hacks volunteered for him. MacKenzie quickly changed the subject. Jane Reed, who had been urging him on with her eyes not to blow it, visibly relaxed. Kelvin was doing just fine. And, thank God, he also knew when not to over-egg the pudding. After jocularly speculating that he would be omitted from the list of alumni at his old school of Alleyns, suddenly, with no prior warning, he rose from his seat. 'That's your lot,' he told them all. 'I've got work to do.' He started bustling out of the room.

A last question was fired from the table. What did Kelvin think his lasting contribution to journalism would be?

MacKenzie, halfway across the room, stopped abruptly in his tracks. He wheeled round and paused for a second, arrogantly surveying them. Hands thrust deep into the trouser pockets of his double-breasted suit, he grinned mockingly. Dunn and Petrie flanked him like a pair of minders. There was a pause. Then he suddenly doubled up and burst into peals of raucous laugher. 'We'll have to wait for the Honours List,' he roared. 'Maybe there'll be a surprise move – Lord Kelv of Wapping!'

He was still laughing as he vanished out of the door. The hacks, suddenly slumping as the room emptied of his presence, looked at each other in disbelief as his blaring faded away down the corridor.

A minute later, the Unpopulars already dismissed from his mind, MacKenzie burst back on to the editorial floor – the windowless Wapping powerhouse where he ruled supreme.

'All right you useless load of c***s!' he bellowed, tearing off his jacket, clapping his hands, and rubbing them vigorously together. 'Whaddya got for me today then, eh?'

Postscript

By June 1990, when the committee set up by the government to enquire into privacy and the press finally produced its report – two months late – much had already changed in the world in general and that of the tabloid papers in particular.

The sudden removal of the Berlin Wall and the collapse of Communism across Europe had been accompanied by an 'end of the 1980s' industry in the British media, retrospectively painting the decade as one of greed and excess and predicting a more restrained and responsible society in the 1990s.

And as the tabloids continued their drinking in David Mellor's 'Last Chance Saloon' Wendy Henry surfaced in February on Sky News to denounce the Editors' Code as 'silly and hypocritical'. It was now a case of 'Spot a story and win a Metro' she complained, pointing out that the Sunday tabloids alone had lost more than one million readers in the ensuing thirteen weeks. The Editors' Code had already meant no more sneaky pictures of the famous caught off guard, no more prying into the private lives of the rich and powerful, no more kiss and tells.

Henry went on: 'The rules have certainly changed. . . . In future concentrate on the soft targets, the little people. Have you got that, boys? It's back to the massage parlours and the ladies of the night. Get stuck into choirmasters who get stuck into choirmistresses and vicars in stockings and suspenders.'

Forced, like all the others, to cut back on editorial outrage the *Sun* retreated to the stand-by of competitions by introducing 'Spot the Balls' with a £5 million first prize supposedly on offer. Devised in enormous secrecy, the competition was launched in March with a massive TV advertising campaign. The *Mirror* immediately ran a knocking campaign pointing out that the odds against winning the jackpot – which was promised to be paid in instalments of £250,000 a year – were more than 2,000,000,000 to 1. (At the same time a *Sun* article put the odds of an alien invasion at 50-1 – 40 million times more likely than winning the prize.)

But the main problem was that readers had to pay 25p a week to enter the contest, rather than getting their card for free like bingo. The payment system also caused great confusion within the news trade. The competition was abandoned after a few weeks with predictably no £5 million winner.

The gloom caused by this fiasco was exacerbated on the editorial floor at Wapping by Robert Maxwell's appointment of MacKenzie's former lieutenant, Roy Greenslade, to edit the *Mirror*. Greenslade, whom MacKenzie had thought had been safely parked on the *Sunday Times*, was, he confided to the hacks, 'a man to be reckoned with'.

Greenslade knew the *Sun*'s strengths and weaknesses only too well and immediately proved the prediction by poaching the key figure of the *Sun*'s chief sub-editor, Roger Wood, along with other important hacks including Harry Arnold, the former Royals reporter, who was made the *Mirror*'s chief reporter. The poaching operation was in many ways as significant as Lamb's raids on the *Mirror* in the early 1970s and produced a further plummeting in morale at Wapping.

Inevitable speculation followed that he would be replaced, just as Lamb had been. Rumours emanating from the sister-paper *Today* settled on 18 April 1990 as the expected date of departure. On the day the *Sun* office buzzed with anticipation but when nothing had happened by 3.30 p.m., John Kay broke the tension by yelling: 'They're waiting for the stock market to close so there isn't another crash!' Shortly afterwards MacKenzie, well aware of the rumours, announced that the only way he would be leaving was in a wooden box.

Conditions for the *Sun* were only worsened by the results of the government committee, which had been headed by David Calcutt QC, the Master of Magdalen College, Oxford. The committee had taken ten days of oral evidence from thirty organisations and individuals, including Murdoch and MacKenzie, who made an impressive appearance to say there was no need for legislative machinery, since the tabloids had largely reformed themselves.

These days, he said, there was nothing in the *Sun* he couldn't show his maiden aunt. The change had been demonstrated by the number of Press Council complaints against the paper, which had fallen off dramatically. Laying thirty issues of the paper on the table, MacKenzie defied the committee to find anything in them to object to.

The committee's 124 page report, highlighting the *Sun's* Elton John story amongst others, was published to mixed reactions. It said that in general freedom of expression should override protection of privacy. Where protection was given it should be in the form of narrow remedies to curb specific abuses, rather than sweeping measures which might restrict access to information.

It continued, 'The past two decades have seen changes in the character of the tabloid market, with a degree of competition not present since the pre-war circulation battles. This may have led some tabloid editors to feel "let off the leash" and to become more intrusive in pursuit of competitive advantage.'

The committee findings were accepted in principle by the Home Secretary, David Waddington, who said the industry was now being given 'positively the last chance'. 'I hope it will not come to statutory legislation,' he said. 'But it is up to the industry – proprietors, editors and journalists – to realise that hope, for no one else can.'

Chief recommendations of the Calcutt report were abolishing the existing Press Council and creating criminal offences for physical invasion of privacy. Extending drinking hours in the Last Chance Saloon, the report gave the industry another twelve months to replace the abolished Press Council by a new Press

355

Complaints Commission. If it failed to do this it would be taken as a clear sign that voluntary self-regulation could not work and the government should then set up a statutory tribunal.

The new Commission should have twelve members, instead of the thirty-six of the old Press Council, and should draw up a new code of practice on press behaviour, with a twenty-four-hour telephone hotline for complaints. In addition, unlike the old Council, those complaining would no longer have to waive their rights to proceed through the courts.

MacKenzie refused to comment on the findings but News International wheeled out the more suave and telegenic David Montgomery, the editor of *Today*, who welcomed this specific proposal by saying: 'OK. We've been badly behaved and now we need a new instrument to discipline us.'

But Montgomery described the other major proposal, the creation of criminal offences for intrusion, as 'draconian and very sinister'. The proposed offences were: entering private property without permission to obtain personal information for publication; planting a surveillance device on private property to secure personal information for publication; and taking a photograph or recording a voice on private property without consent with a view to publication that intends the individual to be identifiable.

The committee gave the newspapers a defence of exposing a crime or 'seriously anti-social conduct', but this was widely commented on as setting up a bonanza for lawyers, with widespread suggestions in the Unpopulars that it would seriously interfere with legitimate investigative journalism.

But there were more serious worries within the Empire as Murdoch struggled to get Sky off the ground and cope with various problems at Wapping. The *Sun*'s much vaunted colour presses, which were to have been on-stream in time for the World Cup, were postponed once again after an immense power surge when they were switched on blew out an electricity sub-station. The performance of the *Mirror* under Roy Greenslade had been improving. Both papers were losing readers, but the *Sun* was losing them faster.

The Wapping product's sales graph had been a melancholy story. From its peak of 4.30 million in August 1988 it had slowly declined to 4.21 million at the end of that year and then 4.01 million by the end of 1989. The unofficial figures for Merseyside showed this loss as almost entirely due to the Hillsborough 'THE TRUTH' story and Liverpudlians were still not returning to the fold.

As the decline continued, it became clear that the paper was losing popularity in parallel with Mrs Thatcher, who was doing even worse, crashing to the lowest rating of any Prime Minister ever on the back of bringing in the hated poll tax.

Throughout the long hot summer of 1990 technicians toiled in the giant print hall bedding down the new colour presses which were the key to reversing the dramatic slide in circulation which started with Hillsborough. But problem followed problem as the deadline of the World Cup loomed and a heroic last-minute scramble finally produced some smudgy colour pictures the day after the final. By that time the paper had already charged off with the new Gazza obsession which was to dominate the news, feature and sports pages for months.

After this shaky start the presses rapidly settled down and MacKenzie found himself shorn of the excuse of lack of colour when he was pleading with the Boss about declining sales. He was firmly instructed to get circulation back over 4 million. Editorially this led to a new outburst of colour-led nonsense and lightweight features, with MacKenzie obliged to pussy-foot on the news pages because of the new climate signalled by the Editors Code 'bollocks'. He managed to stay out of serious trouble with the notable exception of a terrible Royals blunder. In August the paper ran pictures of Prince Charles by the side of a pool in Majorca with his arm round Lady Romsey, an old friend. The headline PRINCE HUGS HIS OLD FLAME was accompanied by a nudge-nudge, wink-wink caption which read: 'Royal snuggle . . . Charles, wearing white bathing trunks, cuddles gorgeous Penny at the remote villa.' The story, labelled EXCLUSIVE, was run under the byline of the Sun's uxoricide specialist, John Kay.

The reality behind the pictures was that Lady Romsey had just broken the news to Prince Charles that her four-year-old daughter, Leonora, had been diagnosed as having cancer. The Prince was comforting her when a paparrazzo shot the pictures with a huge 'grief-detector' telephoto lens from more than half a mile away.

When the real story emerged after the pictures had been printed the Sun went into reverse, running a front page piece headed THE SUN APOLOGISES TO CHARLES AND LADY ROMSEY. The paper admitted the words of the story accompanying the original pictures 'had contained innuendos which were false', but printed them again just the same.

More interestingly the *Sun*'s subsequent explanation to the Press Council demolished MacKenzie's assertion at the (now famous) media correspondents' lunch that the paper would henceforth 'double, double, double-check' its facts.

John Kay explained how he bought the photographs from a Spanish freelance. The anodyne caption that came with them made no mention of Leonora's illness and, he said, the article was therefore 'done in our usual fun way'.

'There was no way of telling from the pictures that Lady Romsey was upset because she was wearing dark glasses,' Kay said, continuing: 'On the day of publication, the sad story behind the embrace emerged and details of Leonora's illness came out. We immediately took steps to inform our readers of the true circumstances.' The paper was duly censored by the Press Council, which ruled: 'The taking of the pictures and their use by the paper was a gross invasion of privacy; it was reckless and irresponsible.'

But the goof had been forgotten by the time of the paper's 21st birthday, celebrated in riotous fashion with wall to wall retrospective Page Three girls. The host of supportive birthday messages from various celebs included one from Margaret Thatcher. She wrote 'Your 21st anniversary offers tremendous encouragement to a Prime Minister eleven and a half years into office. The *Sun* has become a great British institution. If it can come up fresh and bubbling and vital every day for 21 years, then so can I. And I shall do so.'

Thatcher, wrong to the end, was gone within weeks. The paper did its best to keep her in power, hitting Michael Heseltine well below the belt with a classic smear story, run under the headline THE ADULTERER, THE BUNGLER AND THE JOKER. The article consisted of guilt by association based on some superficial character assassination of 'Tarzan's' leadership campaign organisers. The smear revived excited talk of a deep political conspiracy between No. 10 and the *Sun*, with unproved suggestions that Thatcher's team had planted the story. But in the end it merely proved the strict limits on the direct political influence wielded by a paper like the *Sun* over the short term. The paper which, according to some, had done so much to keep Thatcher in power could not save its greatest fan in her hour of need.

As the archetype C2 Thatcherite convert Garry 'The Gal' Bushell was given space to sum up their feelings. Bushell addressed his task in typical bone-headed fashion:

> 'So the back-stabbers have won,' he whined, 'The tin pot Judases and two-bob traitors of the Tory party turned on the woman who had kept them in power for 11 years. What a gutless rabble. What a bunch of spineless saps . . . I speak as a Labour voter who voted Tory ONLY because of Maggie . . .'

Bushell then burnt his boats with Maggie's eventual successor by describing John Major as 'the tight-wad Chancellor' who gave less away than 'a maiden aunt at a vicar's tea party'. The official valediction notice was a 'Sun Says' run down the side of a Franklin cartoon showing Thatcher (complete with handbag) on a plinth next to Nelson, Wellington, Churchill and Monty.

With suitably epoch-making hyperbole the paper lamented: 'When the history of the 1980s is written, the name Margaret Thatcher will appear on every page . . .' and it listed her main qualities as honesty, principle, vision, stubborn courage and 'sheer guts'. But the article was strangely melancholic and seemed to betray a realisation that things were changing for the *Sun* as well:

'We hope her torch of freedom is taken up by someone who proves worthy of it. But things will never be quite the same again. Margaret Hilda Thatcher has richly earned her place amongst the greats of history.

'And she deserves to be remembered with gratitude, respect and affection in the hearts of the nation.'

On page 7 Stuart 'Higgy the Human Sponge' Higgins – the paper's internal cowardice expert now elevated to news editor – joined in with a story headed GUTLESS TRAITORS. Disregarding the sour slagging off Bushell had given Major, the paper then dutifully swung its weight behind Maggie's chosen successor, predicting MAJOR BY A MILE above a front page 'Sun Says' headed 'Why Major is the Man for No. 10'.

The dumping of Maggie was soon overtaken in the news stakes by the looming prospect of the Gulf War. The *Sun* had reported the original invasion of Kuwait in August under the classic headline PETROL TO GO UP 20P. In fingering the price of petrol as the key issue MacKenzie had, with massive irony, lined itself up with the loony brigade of Benn, Livingstone and CND – whilst the rest of the press and body politic plied the official line that the emerging conflict was 'not about oil'.

As the actual coalition lined up for war over Christmas 1990 MacKenzie was much more subdued and steady than in the run up to the Falklands war. Some of the right-wing thinkers MacKenzie admired agreed, saying that, unlike the Falklands, the conflict had nothing to do with Britain and it was not worth risking British lives to support one Arab regime against another. And, after all, MacKenzie had told the media correspondents that one Arab shooting another was not news – it was an everyday event.

But the deployment of British troops amid genuine fears of horrendous chemical casualties simplified matters and the *Sun* readjusted to swing itself, Falklands style, behind 'Our Boys and Girls' in the Gulf. The hacks were soon sick of hearing MacKenzie singing the 'Earwig Song' – ''Ere we go! 'Ere we go! 'Ere we go!' as George Bush's deadline approached.

The *Sun* used its new colour facility to good advantage producing a front page poster with the legend SUPPORT OUR BOYS AND PUT THIS FLAG IN YOUR WINDOW over a union jack with the face of a British 'desert rat' squaddie at the centre. Readers were grateful for this simple act of goodwill, even if there were greater doubts – and much more confusion – about this war than there had been about the more straightforward Falklands. Significantly the paper's 'thought' for the day was not a Falklands style STICK IT UP 'EM but a wish that the soldiers would COME HOME SOON.

Once the bombing began there were periodic diatribes against the World's Worst newspaper for its craven attitude and whining pleas for peace, but not everyone thought like MacKenzie. The *Guardian*'s coverage of the war was one of the factors which helped it to gain the coveted accolade of Newspaper of the Year.

MacKenzie and leader writer Ronnie Spark cranked up the 'traitors' line which had gained the paper so much useful notoriety during the Falklands. But the second time around it had far less impact, partly because it was expected. The main outrage was caused by 10 FACTS TO DAMN SADDAM, a *Sun* splash which accused the Iraqis of deliberately plotting the death of the dozens of women and children who died when an air-raid shelter in a Baghdad suburb was precision bombed. Robert Fisk in the *Independent* rubbished this idea, originally put about by the American high command, by pointing out most of the casualties were the wives and children of top ranking Ba'ath Party officials.

But Spark was unrepentant, telling *UK Press Gazette* 'truth is sacred. But a newspaper that tells only part of the truth is a million times preferable to one that tells the truth to harm its country.'

The war's real winner, in media terms, was television. The 'electronic media', as it was now being ponderously called, demonstrated its domination of raw news gathering – part of the original thinking behind Murdoch's moulding of the *Sun* – was now absolute. The American Cable News Network carried the bombing of Baghdad live, providing a gripping sideshow of reporters desperately pulling on gas masks and leaping into bunkers with the live wail of sirens in the background. More than ever all the papers had to fit in behind the TV pictures, personalising the conflict around the televisual figure of 'Stormin' Norman' and filling in with endless head-counts of weaponry and speculation about strategy.

But the Gulf War number-crunching was nothing compared to the statistical battle going on inside Murdoch's Empire as it lurched into a massive debt crisis on a scale larger than some Third World countries. And this too was largely the result of TV developments.

Over December and January Murdoch had had to fight tooth and nail to keep the Empire afloat as News International's and News Corporation's share price slithered, and it was only after weeks of brinkmanship at the negotiating table that the debts were successfully renegotiated.

Meanwhile Murdoch was wrestling to stem the alarming drain of cash from Sky Television, by now merged with the rival BSB squarial people to form BSkyB, and costing some £8 million a week.

In desperation Murdoch brought from Australia a rival for Kelvin MacKenzie in management style in the shape of Sam 'The Animal' Chisholm, who had started life as a floor wax salesman in New Zealand. But even the ruthless Chisholm found himself daunted by the task, especially after Murdoch refused to implement his major cost-cutting decision of closing down Sky News.

Sky had always been known in the *Sun* office as 'Pie in the Sky' and the paper's main role had been advertising it wall to wall on the news and features pages. This had been toned down after vociferous protests to various authorities by BSB before it was merged and the paper's main role was seen as generating cash to underwrite the fearsome cost of the venture.

Sun expenses were slashed to the bone, the gloomy de-unionised staff were locked into their new personal contracts and told bluntly there would be no more pay rises, and first the car phones, and then the cars themselves, were taken away. But by then most of the hacks were grateful just to have a job. As the various 80s roadshows crashed and advertising went into recession there were massive job cuts throughout the media industry and all but the very best freelancers found themselves frozen out completely.

It is hard to date the precise end of Thatcherism, but as good a date as any is 14 March 1991, the day the Birmingham Six were freed and it was announced the poll tax would be scrapped. The issue of the Birmingham pub bombings had always obsessed the *Sun* and throughout the sixteen-year saga the paper had backed the West Midlands police and the judiciary in continuously insisting the Six were guilty. The paper's way of increasing the spin on this unwarranted conclusion was the illogical but effective one of interviewing the unfortunate relatives of the dead whenever the subject came into the news.

It has also vilified campaigners for the men's release, homing in on Chris Mullin, by this time a Loony Left Labour MP. Mullin, as a left-wing journalist, had courageously investigated the original convictions and harnessed the resources of Granada Television to put the case back on the public agenda. At the abortive Appeal Court hearing three years earlier every day he had defiantly carried into court a *Sun* front page headed LOONY MP BACKS BOMB GANG. (Even his admirers did however have to admit that his appearance, and Michael Foot style of dress, did give some visual substance to the 'Loony' tag).

The *Sun*, particularly spiteful in defeat, gave the men's release the front page splash of £500,000 PAY DAY. John Kay and David Kemp speculated in their story that the men might become millionaires, giving them the aura of pools winners and implying that all you had to do to be rich these days was blow up a few innocent Brummies. On the inside pages the bewildered relatives of the victims were hauled out yet again under the headline WE HAVE BEEN LEFT WITH NOTHING, with the sub-head: 'Victims' fury as Six are freed'. But the freeing of the Six was at least a cloak for burying the scrapping of the poll tax, the arrogant measure which had brought Thatcher down and seriously threatened Tory rule for the first time in a decade. Whilst the other papers split their front pages to give the two stories equal prominence, the *Sun* relegated the poll tax news to a short and inaccurate report on the graveyard Page 2.

But with the opinion polls showing that even the scrapping of the poll tax had failed to get the Tories off the hook, the figures emanating from the circulation department of the *Sun* confirmed an equally gloomy picture.

Figures for the second half of 1990 showed a decline in sales to 3.85m – a loss of quarter of a million on the figure for the same period in the year before. Added to the quarter million drop after Hillsborough, the paper had lost half a million sales in less than two years.

More importantly the *Sun* was losing market share to the *Mirror* – a much more important factor for advertising revenue and a situation which could not be blamed on the recession or new competition in the form of German owned women's magazines like *Bella* which had pulled away a lot of women readers. These factors hit the *Mirror* just as hard.

By December 1990 the combined sale of the *Mirror* and its Scottish version, the *Daily Record* (with approximately 650,000 readers) was 3.86m – 10,000 more than the *Sun*. There was much grumbling at Wapping about the way the *Mirror* presented its figures but nothing could disguise one basic fact: the *Mirror* was treading water whilst the *Sun* was sinking fast.

Figures for the first months of 1991 confirmed the trend. In a declining market the *Mirror* had been losing readers too, but much more slowly. It was just like the last days of the Lamb regime when the joke was that the *Mirror-Record* was poised to 'undertake' the *Sun*. By March the *Sun* was down to 3.75m which – projected forward – indicated a possible loss of up to half a million readers for the year.

The decline was starting to take on the same sort of momentum as the soaraway rise in circulation under Lamb in the 70s. The conclusion being drawn was that readers no longer regarded the papers as newspapers, but as entertainment, and as such lagged way behind TV in spending priorities. And with the abolition of the TV listings duopoly the tabloids lost a powerful selling point.

A vast, but unknown, number of punters had previously bought tabloids simply because they were the cheapest thing on the rack which told you what was on telly. The success of the *Sun* in the 1980s was largely based on Wendy Henry's formula of turning the paper, as the BBC once complained, into an 'Eastenders Supplement' to the *Radio Times*.

Now the listing were all over the place. The new downmarket *Radio Times* and *TV Times* gave you an entire week for one purchase and the Germans had weighed in to eventually dominate the market with a loss-leading 10p listings magazine massively advertised on TV. At the same time all these new mags reversed the editorial equation previously exploited by the *Sun* by turning themselves into comics. Stuffed with celeb interviews, pop gossip and prize competitions they turned the tables and ended up like '*Sun* supplements' to the TV listings.

The *Sun* fought back with a return to Lamb-style activity such as 'pussy week' and spent £5 million on the appropriate tacky 70s-style TV adverts. But this rearguard action was quixotic. The *Sun* – and all the tabloids – looked increasingly like victims of the society they had helped to create; dominated by TV, with fleeting obsessions replacing consumer loyalty.

Above all there was a new concern that they had contributed to poor standards of literacy and a mass loss of critical faculties. By being so visually led they had killed the goose which laid the golden egg. The supply of new readers with at least the inclination to read the words instead of just looking at the pictures and headlines, comic-style, was apparently drying up.

It was beginning to look as though the heyday of not just the original Comic itself, but of all the other comics, had been and gone.

Chronology

1979 and before

1964   IPC relaunches the *Daily Herald* as the broadsheet *Sun*

1968   Murdoch buys the *News of the World*

1969   Murdoch buys the *Sun* and relaunches it as a tabloid edited by Lamb. Sales reach one million within 100 days

1970   *Sun* backs Labour in general election. Conservatives win. Heath replaces Wilson as Prime Minister

1971   *Sun* sales top 2.50 million

1972   Shrimsley replaces Lamb as editor. Lamb becomes editorial director of the *Sun* and *News of the World*

1974   *Sun* refuses to back Labour in the year's two general elections. Labour wins both

1975   Lamb returns to edit the *Sun*

1978   *Sun* overtakes *Mirror* with sales at more than four million. Express Group launches *Star* as regional paper. Lamb coins 'Winter of Discontent' phrase

1979   Sales drop 300,000 to 3.70 million in wake of successful *Star* launch. *Sun* tells readers to vote Tory in general election. Thatcher, elected Prime Minister, thanks Lamb for his help

1980

January	Lamb knighted
August	Unemployment passes two million
October	Thatcher 'not for turning' speech at Tory conference
November	Ronald Reagan elected US president

1981

February	Murdoch buys *Times* and *Sunday Times*
March	Tough monetarist budget. Public spending and tax cuts
	Formal launch of SDP
April	Unemployment passes 2.5 million. Brixton riots
	MacKenzie replaces Lamb as editor of *Sun*
June	*Sun* cuts price to match *Star* and starts bingo
July	Charles and Diana's Wedding

1982

January	Unemployment tops three million
February	*Sun* prints 'DI-LAND' pictures of pregnant Diana
March	Murdoch sacks *Times* editor Harry Evans
April	Argentina captures the Falkland Islands
May	*Sun* 'GOTCHA' headline on sinking of *Belgrano*
June	Falklands recaptured
November	Fabricated Marica McKay Falklands hero interview
December	*Sun* sales 4.18 million, almost one million ahead of *Mirror*

1983

January	Inflation drops to 5.4 per cent, lowest for thirteen years
February	Sam Fox, 16, makes *Sun* Page Three debut. Peter Tatchell loses Bermondsey by-election
June	Tory landslide in general election
October	Neil Kinnock elected Labour Party leader

1984

January	'Hop Off You Frogs' badges promoted by the *Sun*
March	Miners' strike starts
May	'MINE FUHRER' headline dispute at the *Sun*
July	Robert Maxwell buys Mirror Group
August	*Sun* and *Mirror* compete with £1 million bingo

1985

February	FT All-Share Index goes over 1,000 for first time. *EastEnders* launched by BBC
March	Miners return to work after defeat of strike
May	Bradford football fire, English soccer riots and the Heysel soccer disaster
June	Simon Weston story 'lifted'. Wendy Henry suspended
July	Live Aid raises £50 million
September	*Sun* starts the 'Curse of the *Crying Boy*' panic
October	'Dirty Den' *EastEnders* cliffhanger breaks viewing records
December	Maxwell 'survival plan' for Mirror Group: 1,600 jobs to go

1986

January	The *Sun* moves to Wapping
February	Sam Fox debut as pop star
March	West London Vicarage Rape case. 'FREDDIE STARR ATE MY HAMSTER' splash
September	*Sunday Sport* launched
October	'Big Bang' in the City

1987

February	Wapping picket ends. 'ELTON JOHN IN VICE BOYS SCANDAL' splash starts series of libels against Elton John
March	*Herald of Free Enterprise* sinks. Ferry Aid launched. *Sun* and *Star* both claim to have saved Blackie the Donkey
April	'SUN INVADES GERMANY!' splash
May	*Sun* Share Club starts
June	General election: Tories returned with reduced majority Ferry Aid gala at Palladium. Murdoch buys *Today*
July	Jeffrey Archer wins £500,000 libel damages from the *Star*
September	*Star/Sunday Sport* 'merger' announced. *Sun* launches *Sun* Money City page. Elton John 'silent dogs' story
October	'Black Monday' stock market crash
November	Rent-boy in Elton John story confesses to the *Mirror* that he lied
December	*Sun* breaks New Year Honours embargo

1988

January	Judge Martin Bowley QC resigns after his homosexuality is revealed by the *Sun*
February	The *Sun* launches Lotto with 4.1 million entries in first three months
March	*Today* wins Newspaper of the Year award
April	Great redundancy offer: twenty-two *Sun* hacks leave the paper. 'Loadsamoney' becomes *Sun* national hero
May	MacKenzie takes the *Independent* to the Press Council. Major Ferguson massage parlour saga
June	Russell Harty dies. Mike Gatting barmaid affair
August	House market begins to collapse. *Sun* sales peak at 4.309 million
October	'QUEEN BEA' pictures published. Thatcher's 'Green' Tory conference speech
November	*Sun* pays £100,000 to HM Queen over 'QUEEN BEA'
December	£1 million libel settlement with Elton John

1989

January	Bush replaces Reagan as US President. Ken Donlan appointed *Sun* Ombudsman
February	Sky TV launched
April	Hillsborough disaster and *Sun*'s 'THE TRUTH' splash. Government announces Calcutt Committee
May	Tenth anniversary of Thatcher's election as Prime Minister
June	Euro elections. Green fever peaks
July	MacKenzie admits on BBC radio that 'THE TRUTH' headline was his mistake
August	Murdoch attacks Sky's critics at Edinburgh TV festival
September	Martin Dunn appears on *Hard News*
October	Calcutt Committee convenes. Murdoch gives Sky five years to come into profit. Nigel Lawson resigns as Chancellor of the Exchequer

| November | Twentieth anniversary of the Murdoch *Sun*. Editors' Code agreed. Maxwell sacks Wendy Henry as editor of the *People*. David Blundy killed in El Salvador |

1990

February	Roy Greenslade appointed editor of the *Mirror*
March	*Sun* £5 million 'Spot the Balls' competition flops
April	Intense rumours MacKenzie is to go
May	*Sun* sales fall to 3.87 million, lowest since 1980
	Combined sales of the *Mirror* and *Daily Record* overtake the *Sun*
June	Calcutt Committee report published

Appendix

Sun

(July–December) Sales (millions)

1969	0.65	[estimated IPC broadsheet sales at time of relaunch as tabloid]
1970	1.51	
1971	2.08	
1972	2.63	
1973	2.93	
1974	3.30	
1975	3.44	
1976	3.64	
1977	3.72	
1978	3.95	[4 million exceeded in June]
1979	3.71	[*Daily Star* launched (November 1978)]
1980	3.74	
1981	4.14	[*Sun* bingo introduced (June 1981)]
1982	4.18	
1983	4.14	
1984	4.08	
1985	4.13	
1986	4.05	
1987	4.05	
1988	4.22	
1989	4.02	
1990	3.85	
1991	3.75	[average for month of march only]

Mirror

Year	Sales	
1969	4.92	
1970	4.70	
1971	4.38	
1972	4.29	
1973	4.26	
1974	4.19	
1975	4.02	
1976	3.84	
1977	3.84	
1978	3.83	
1979	3.65	
1980	3.63	
1981	3.46	
1982	3.21	
1983	3.27	
1984	3.50	[£1 million *Mirror* bingo introduced (August 1984)]
1985	3.03	
1986	3.14	
1987	3.13	
1988	3.16	
1989	3.09	
1990	3.05	

Source: Audit Bureau of Circulation. Average daily sales over a six-month period ending 31 December of each year unless otherwise stated.

Bibliography

Tom Baistow, *Fourth-Rate Estate: An Anatomy of Fleet Street*.
Comedia Publishing Group, London, 1985.

Robert Blake, *The Conservative Party from Peel to Thatcher*.
Fontana, London, 1985.

Peter Chippindale and Chris Horrie, *Disaster: The Rise and Fall of News on Sunday*. Sphere, London, 1988.

Graham Cleverley, *The Fleet Street Disaster: British National Newspapers as a Case Study in Mismanagement*. Constable, London, 1976.

Simon Garfield, *Expensive Habits: The Dark Side of the Music Industry*. Faber & Faber, London, 1986.

Roslyn Grose, *The Sun-sation: The Inside Story of Britain's Bestselling Daily Newspaper*. Angus & Robertson, London, 1989.

Robert Harris, *Gotcha! – The Media, the Government and the Falklands Crisis*. Faber & Faber, London, 1983.

Denis Healey, *The Time of My Life*. Michael Joseph, London, 1989.

Mark Hollingsworth, *The Press and Political Dissent*. Pluto Press, London, 1986.

Derek Jameson, *Touched by Angels*. Penguin, London, 1988.

Simon Jenkins, *Newspapers: The Power and the Money*. Faber & Faber, London, 1979.

Larry Lamb, *Sunrise*. Macmillan Papermac, London, 1989.

Michael Leapman, *Barefaced Cheek: Rupert Murdoch*. Coronet, London, 1984.

Linda Melvern, *The End of the Street*. Methuen, London, 1986.

Robert Munster, *Rupert Murdoch: A Paper Prince*. Viking (Penguin Books Australia), Sydney, 1985.

373

Henry Porter, *Lies, Damned Lies And Some Exclusives*. Coronet Books, London, 1985.

The Press Council, *The Press and the People*. Annual reports of the Press Council, London, in series 1970–88.

Simon Regan, *Rupert Murdoch: A Business Biography*. Angus & Robertson, London, 1976.

Sunday Times Insight Team, *The Falklands War: The Full Story*. Sphere, London, 1982.

Peter Tatchell, *The Battle for Bermondsey*. Heretic Books, London, 1983.

Simon Weston, *Walking Tall*. Bloomsbury, London, 1989.

Charles Wintour, *The Rise and Fall of Fleet Street*. Hutchinson, London, 1989.

Index

TERRY KIRBY

The Trials of the Baroness

'I know who I am and I am quite happy to leave it at that. . . The one thing money can't buy is breeding, don't you agree?'
BARONESS SUSAN DE STEMPEL

The extraordinary but true story behind the dramatic trials of the Baroness de Stempel reveals a complex web of murder, fraud, intrigue, and eccentricity among the upper classes.

At their centre was the enigmatic figure of the Baroness herself – the debutante who was cleared of murdering her former husband but pleaded guilty of conspiring, with the Baron de Stempel and two of her children, to defraud her aunt, Lady Illingworth, of all her money and possessions before allowing her to die in poverty.

The case, which cast a cloud of dishonour over the distinguished family of William Wilberforce, and a harsh spotlight on the fading aristocracy of England, left behind many mysteries. Most importantly, who did take an iron bar and batter to death Simon Dale, the first husband of the Baroness?

Alfred Hitchcock and the
Making of *Psycho*

'This time you're going too far,' warned one of Hitchcock's associates about *Psycho*, the film now indelibly stamped upon the American sub-conscious. Charted here from grisly conception to dramatic aftermath is the course of one of the true landmarks in the history of horror.

'Joyously entertaining'
GERALD KAUFMAN, *Sunday Telegraph*

'Rebello takes us right through the project, from the original murderer – Ed Gein of Wisconsin, who made Norman Bates look like David Attenborough – to Robert Bloch's overloaded novel, to Hitch's five scrupulous weeks of storybashing. . . A heartening account of a shockeroo being distilled into pure cinema'
Independent

'Rebello's book combines a gossipy retrospective with a serious work of criticism, presenting an articu-late guide to Hitchcock's idiosyncratic approach to film-making and the collaborative efforts that under-pinned it. The author has conducted interviews with all those involved in the making of *Psycho* – its casting, scripting, shooting, art design, lighting, editing, selling – in the course of which we inch closer to the bizarre, unpredictable quality of its director'
ANTHONY QUINN, *Sunday Times*

LINDY CHAMBERLAIN

Through My Eyes

'This is the story of a little girl who lived and breathed, and loved, and was loved. She was part of me. She grew within my body and when she died, part of me died, and nothing will alter that fact. This is her story, and mine'

'In 1982 thirty-two-year-old Lindy Chamberlain was convicted of murdering her nine-week-old baby at a campsite near Ayers Rock. Her insistence that little Azaria had been carried off by a wild dog or dingo was ultimately dismissed as rubbish and the heavily pregnant woman was sentenced to life imprisonment. Two and a half years on, and incontrovertible proof came to light that Chamberlain's story was in fact correct. . . In *Through My Eyes*, Lindy Chamberlain puts the record straight'
Literary Review

'Compulsively fascinating. Lindy Chamberlain has not forgiven or forgotten anything'
Evening Standard

'*Through my Eyes* makes you want to put forensic scientists through a series of detailed and painful tests'
MARK LAWSON, *Independent on Sunday*

HUGH JOHNSON

The Story of Wine

In *The Story of Wine* the world's leading wine writer traces Man's love affair with the grape across 8,000 years of history. The colourful chronicle brings in monks and emperors, Christianity and Islam, trade and war. Wine is there from the very start of civilization, part of religion and ritual.

In this epic story, all the great wines we enjoy today have their roots. Hugh Johnson traces in fascinating detail the rise of claret and champagne, the emergence of New World stars and the decline of once-great names.

This is the first book ever to win all the prizes for wine writing. Critics were enthralled:

'Monumental in every sense: *a tour de force*'
EDMUND PENNING-ROWSELL, *Financial Times*

'Were teetotallers to read it, they would surely turn into wine drinkers to a man'
JOSEPH BERKMAN, *Daily Mail*

'One can say without hesitation that this is the world's greatest book about wine'
Le Nouvel Observateur

'Hugh Johnson should have a Nobel Prize for this book'
Magazine Littéraire

'Only a writer of Johnson's talent could pull off such a synthesis: quite fascinating'
TIM ATKIN, *Guardian*

PAUL MATHIEU

The Druid's Lodge Confederacy

The Druid's Lodge Confederates were a syndicate of five inspired gamblers – a stud owner, a Royal vet, a Master of Foxhounds and two City financiers – who decided that racing could, and would, pay handsomely. In almost total secrecy, from isolated, purpose-built stables near Stonehenge, the 'Hermits of Salisbury Plain' prepared a string of horses to secure some of the most fabulous betting coups ever landed on the Turf.

'Reads like an enthralling whodunnit. If you are a bookmaker don't buy this book – it will give you sleepless nights. If you are a punter, it is a must, and a hugely entertaining one'
The Racegoer

'An immense amount of research has gone into this cracking book. I almost felt like shedding a tear for the old enemy [the bookie] once I'd finished. It's a wonderful read. Buy a copy'
The Sporting Life

'Quite the best racing book to come my way this year. . . Mathieu has put flesh on the bones of old rumour and half-truth to produce the real story of the greatest 'sting' in racing history. . . *The Druid's Lodge Confederacy* deserves to become a bestseller'
CHRISTOPHER POOLE, *Evening Standard*

MARK AARONS & JOHN LOFTUS

Ratlines

In 1944, inside the Vatican, a secret cabal of right-wing priests established a network for smuggling Nazis out of Europe. In the name of intelligence, the group allowed fugitive war criminals to escape from justice and gave Soviet Intelligence their greatest Cold War triumph – for many Nazis were later recruited as agents and 'freedom fighters' by the intelligence agencies of Australia, Great Britain, Canada, Italy, West Germany and the US.

Ratlines is a shocking litany of disaster, duplicity and betrayal which reveals a Vatican deeply compromised by its nefariousness and thoroughly infiltrated and manipulated by communists *and* fascists.

A Selected List of Non-Fiction Titles Available from Mandarin

While every effort is made to keep prices low, it is sometimes necessary to increase prices at short notice. Mandarin Paperbacks reserves the right to show new retail prices on covers which may differ from those previously advertised in the text or elsewhere.

The prices shown below were correct at the time of going to press.

☐ 7493 0961 X	**Stick it up Your Punter**	Chippendale & Horrib	£4.99
☐ 7493 0988 1	**Desert Island Discussions**	Sue Lawley	£4.99
☐ 7493 0938 5	**The Courage to Heal**	Ellen Bass and Laura Davis	£7.99
☐ 7493 0637 8	**The Hollywood Story**	Joel Finler	£9.99
☐ 7493 1032 4	**How to Meet Interesting Men**	Gizelle Howard	£5.99
☐ 7493 0586 X	**The New Small Garden**	C. E. Lucas-Phillips	£5.99
☐ 7493 1172 X	**You'll Never Eat Lunch in This Town Again**	Julia Phillips	£5.99

All these books are available at your bookshop or newsagent, or can be ordered direct from the publisher. Just tick the titles you want and fill in the form below.

Mandarin Paperbacks, Cash Sales Department, PO Box 11, Falmouth, Cornwall TR10 9EN.

Please send cheque or postal order, no currency, for purchase price quoted and allow the following for postage and packing:

UK including BFPO £1.00 for the first book, 50p for the second and 30p for each additional book ordered to a maximum charge of £3.00.

Overseas including Eire £2 for the first book, £1.00 for the second and 50p for each additional book thereafter.

NAME (Block letters) ....

ADDRESS...

....

☐ I enclose my remittance for ....

☐ I wish to pay by Access/Visa Card Number

☐☐☐☐☐☐☐☐☐☐☐☐☐☐☐☐

Expiry Date ☐☐☐☐